SECOND EDITION

# *The* HEART *of a* CHAPLAIN

**EXPLORING ESSENTIALS FOR MINISTRY**

EDITED BY

DR. JIM BROWNING AND DR. JIM SPIVEY

*The Heart of a Chaplain, 2nd Edition*

Published in conjunction with Iron Stream Media
100 Missionary Ridge
Birmingham, AL 35242
IronStreamMedia.com

*Copyright © 2022 and 2025 by Dr. Jim Browning and Dr. Jim Spivey*

No part of this publication may be reproduced, stored in a retrieval system, or transmitted in any form or by any means—electronic, mechanical, photocopying, recording, or otherwise—without the prior written permission of the publisher.

Iron Stream Media serves its authors as they express their views, which may not express the views of the publisher. While all the stories in this book are true, some of the details and names have been changed or deleted to protect the storyteller's identity.

Library of Congress Control Number: 2024926983

All Scripture quotations are taken from the NEW AMERICAN STANDARD BIBLE®, Copyright © 1960, 1971, 1977, 1995 by The Lockman Foundation. Used by permission. All rights reserved. www.lockman.org

Scripture quotation taken from The Message, copyright © 1993, 2002, 2018 by Eugene H. Peterson. Used by permission of NavPress. All rights reserved. Represented by Tyndale House Publishers.

Cover design by twoline || Studio

ISBN: 978-1-56309-783-6 (paperback)
ISBN: 978-1-56309-784-3 (e-book)

1 2 3 4 5—29 28 27 26 25

In honor of Dr. Gerald E. Marsh,
Chaplain, Major General, USAF, Retired,
who invested his life educating students
for chaplain ministry and mentoring chaplains

In memory of Dr. Bobby Smith,
Founding Director, Baptist Chaplaincy Relations,
trailblazer, endorser, and staunch supporter
of chaplains and their families

# CONTENTS

CONTRIBUTORS . . . . . . . . . . . . . . . . . . . . . . . . . . . . . . . xv
FOREWORD . . . . . . . . . . . . . . . . . . . . . . . . . . . . . . . . . . xxi
PREFACE . . . . . . . . . . . . . . . . . . . . . . . . . . . . . . . . . . . xxiii
ACKNOWLEDGMENTS . . . . . . . . . . . . . . . . . . . . . . . . . xxvi

**SECTION ONE—WHAT IS A CHAPLAIN?** . . . . . . . . . . . . . . 1

1. "SO YOU WANT TO BE A CHAPLAIN?" . . . . . . . . . . . . . . 3
    What Is a Chaplain? . . . . . . . . . . . . . . . . . . . . . . . . . . . . 4
    Why Be a Chaplain? . . . . . . . . . . . . . . . . . . . . . . . . . . . . 8
    The Growing Demand . . . . . . . . . . . . . . . . . . . . . . . . . . . 9

2. SPIRITUAL FORMATION AND THE CALL . . . . . . . . . . . . 12
    Essential Questions . . . . . . . . . . . . . . . . . . . . . . . . . . . . 13
    A Case Study . . . . . . . . . . . . . . . . . . . . . . . . . . . . . . . . 14
    Working Out Our Identity . . . . . . . . . . . . . . . . . . . . . . . 19
    A Chaplain's Call . . . . . . . . . . . . . . . . . . . . . . . . . . . . . 24

3. PROFESSIONAL COMPETENCIES . . . . . . . . . . . . . . . . . . 25
    What Are Competencies? . . . . . . . . . . . . . . . . . . . . . . . . 26
    Identifying and Managing Anxiety . . . . . . . . . . . . . . . . . . 27
    Learning Competence . . . . . . . . . . . . . . . . . . . . . . . . . . 28

  Do I Have What It Takes? .................................30
  Who Should Not Become a Chaplain? ......................31
  MEMORABLE MOMENT—"CHANGE HIS
  CIRCUMSTANCES" ....................................34

**SECTION TWO—WHAT ARE THE FOUNDATIONS
    OF CHAPLAIN MINISTRY?. . . . . . . . . . . 37**

**4. SPIRITUAL FOUNDATION**. ...............................39

**5. CONSTITUTIONAL FOUNDATION**. .......................43
  Is Chaplain Ministry Constitutional? .......................45
  Providing Free Exercise ...................................46
  Preventing Establishment. .................................47

**6. HISTORICAL FOUNDATION**. .............................49
  Previous Patterns .........................................49
  Modern Military .........................................52
  Modern Health Care .....................................54
  Modern Workplace ......................................57
  Modern Correctional .....................................58

**7. THE GLOBAL NATURE OF CHAPLAINCY**. ................61

**SECTION THREE—HOW IS CHAPLAIN MINISTRY
    UNIQUE?. . . . . . . . . . . . . . . . . . . 71**

**8. ROLES, RESPONSIBILITIES, AND TASKS**. ..................73
  Alignment of Roles and Responsibilities. ...................76
  Mission, Roles, and Duties of Chaplains ...................82

**9. INSTITUTIONAL LIFE** ....................................89
  Institutional Setting. ......................................89

  Institutional Duality . . . . . . . . . . . . . . . . . . . . . . . . . . . . . . . . . .91

  Role Conflict . . . . . . . . . . . . . . . . . . . . . . . . . . . . . . . . . . . . . . . . .92

  Accountability . . . . . . . . . . . . . . . . . . . . . . . . . . . . . . . . . . . . . . . .97

  Advocacy—Two-Way . . . . . . . . . . . . . . . . . . . . . . . . . . . . . . . . . . .98

  Ministry to All . . . . . . . . . . . . . . . . . . . . . . . . . . . . . . . . . . . . . . . .98

  Insider Ministry . . . . . . . . . . . . . . . . . . . . . . . . . . . . . . . . . . . . . . .99

10. THE MARGINAL AND LIMINAL NATURE
  OF CHAPLAINCY . . . . . . . . . . . . . . . . . . . . . . . . . . . . . . . . . . . 102

11. SPECIAL ISSUES AND CHALLENGES . . . . . . . . . . . . . . . . . . . . 108

  Legal . . . . . . . . . . . . . . . . . . . . . . . . . . . . . . . . . . . . . . . . . . . . . . 109

  Social Issues . . . . . . . . . . . . . . . . . . . . . . . . . . . . . . . . . . . . . . . . 119

  Personal Boundaries and Ethics . . . . . . . . . . . . . . . . . . . . . . . . . 123

  Understanding Perspectives: An Important Journey . . . . . . . . . . 128

  Professional . . . . . . . . . . . . . . . . . . . . . . . . . . . . . . . . . . . . . . . . 133

  Stamina for the Long Haul . . . . . . . . . . . . . . . . . . . . . . . . . . . . . 135

  MEMORABLE MOMENT—"A UNIQUE PRIVILEGE" . . . . . 141

12. FREQUENTLY ASKED QUESTIONS . . . . . . . . . . . . . . . . . . . . . 142

  1. Can I Volunteer as a Chaplain? . . . . . . . . . . . . . . . . . . . . . . . 142

  2. Why Did You Leave the Ministry? . . . . . . . . . . . . . . . . . . . . . 143

  3. Who Pays the Chaplain for Services? . . . . . . . . . . . . . . . . . . . 144

  4. Does Government Payment Violate Church and State
    Separation? . . . . . . . . . . . . . . . . . . . . . . . . . . . . . . . . . . . . . . 145

  5. Can You Evangelize and Preach the Gospel? . . . . . . . . . . . . . . 146

  6. Can Chaplains Pray in Jesus' Name? . . . . . . . . . . . . . . . . . . . 147

  7. Are You Required to Perform Rites & Rituals for Other
    Faith Groups? . . . . . . . . . . . . . . . . . . . . . . . . . . . . . . . . . . . . 148

8. Do You Compromise by Working with Non-Christian Groups? .................................................. 149
9. Are You Legally Bound to Report Sexual Abuse? ............ 150
10. How To Mitigate Family Tension Regarding DNRs ......... 151
11. Explain the Coexistence of God and Suffering. ............ 152
12. Can You Bear Arms for Self-Protection? ................... 154
13. Must You Obey Orders in Violation of Your Religious Beliefs? 155
14. What Does a Chaplain Do After "Retirement"? ............ 156
MEMORABLE MOMENT—"THE CHAPLAIN IN ME" .... 158

13. CALLED TOGETHER INTO MINISTRY .................. 160

## SECTION FOUR—WHAT ARE THE QUALIFICATIONS FOR PROFESSIONAL CHAPLAINS? ........ 167

14. THE PROFESSIONAL CHAPLAIN ....................... 169
    Preparation and Qualification .............................. 170
    Credentials and Endorsement .............................. 176
    The Guild—Entry and Sustainment. ........................ 180
    Mentoring .............................................. 182

15. THE CHAPLAIN AS A MORAL GUIDE ................... 184
    Tools .................................................. 186
    MEMORABLE MOMENT—"INVESTING MY LIFE INTO OTHERS" ......................................... 193

## SECTION FIVE—CHAPLAINCY TYPES .............. 197

16. HEALTHCARE CHAPLAINCY. .......................... 199
    Hospital Chaplaincy ..................................... 207
    Long-Term Care Chaplaincy .............................. 214

Dementia Chaplaincy . . . . . . . . . . . . . . . . . . . . . . . . . . . . . . . . . .217
Hospice Chaplaincy. . . . . . . . . . . . . . . . . . . . . . . . . . . . . . . . . . . .221
Veterans Administration (VA) Chaplaincy . . . . . . . . . . . . . . . . . . .226
MEMORABLE MOMENT—"BEN" . . . . . . . . . . . . . . . . . . . . . . .232

17. MILITARY CHAPLAINCY . . . . . . . . . . . . . . . . . . . . . . . . . . . . . .235
The Role of Religion in the United States Armed Forces . . . . . . . .247
Army Chaplaincy. . . . . . . . . . . . . . . . . . . . . . . . . . . . . . . . . . . . .262
Navy, Marine Corps, and Coast Guard Chaplaincy . . . . . . . . . . . .268
Air Force, Space Force, and Civil Air Patrol Chaplaincy. . . . . . . . .277
MEMORABLE MOMENT—"A LIGHT
AMID THE DARKNESS". . . . . . . . . . . . . . . . . . . . . . . . . . . . . .283

18. CORRECTIONAL CHAPLAINCY. . . . . . . . . . . . . . . . . . . . . . . .286
Federal Bureau of Prisons Chaplaincy . . . . . . . . . . . . . . . . . . . . . .293
Jails and State Prisons Chaplaincy . . . . . . . . . . . . . . . . . . . . . . . . .299
Juvenile Chaplaincy. . . . . . . . . . . . . . . . . . . . . . . . . . . . . . . . . . .304
MEMORABLE MOMENT—"THE LEAST OF THESE" . . . .310

19. CORPORATE/WORKPLACE CHAPLAINCY. . . . . . . . . . . . . . .312
Contracted Service (Marketplace) Chaplaincy . . . . . . . . . . . . . . . .322
MEMORABLE MOMENT—"LIFE SUPPORT" . . . . . . . . . . .324

20. PUBLIC SAFETY CHAPLAINCY . . . . . . . . . . . . . . . . . . . . . . . .328
Firefighters and EMS Personnel Chaplaincy. . . . . . . . . . . . . . . . . .332
Law Enforcement, District Attorney, and Victim Advocates
Chaplaincy. . . . . . . . . . . . . . . . . . . . . . . . . . . . . . . . . . . . . . . . .336
Disaster Relief Chaplaincy. . . . . . . . . . . . . . . . . . . . . . . . . . . . . .338
MEMORABLE MOMENT—"IT'S ALL ABOUT
RELATIONSHIPS" . . . . . . . . . . . . . . . . . . . . . . . . . . . . . . . . . .340

21. COMMUNITY/LIFESTYLE CHAPLAINCY . . . . . . . . . . . . . . . . . 343
    Transportation Industry Chaplaincy. . . . . . . . . . . . . . . . . . . . . . . 345
    Biker Chaplaincy . . . . . . . . . . . . . . . . . . . . . . . . . . . . . . . . . . . . . . . . 348
    Sports Chaplaincy . . . . . . . . . . . . . . . . . . . . . . . . . . . . . . . . . . . . . . 351
    Independent School Education Chaplaincy . . . . . . . . . . . . . . . . . 354
    Higher Education Chaplaincy . . . . . . . . . . . . . . . . . . . . . . . . . . . . 357
    Neighborhood Chaplaincy. . . . . . . . . . . . . . . . . . . . . . . . . . . . . . . 360
    MEMORABLE MOMENT—"HALLELUJAH" . . . . . . . . . . . . . 364

APPENDIX ONE: A Mentoring Tool—Toward Competency as a
Professional Chaplain. . . . . . . . . . . . . . . . . . . . . . . . . . . . . . . . . . . . . . . 366

APPENDIX TWO: Case Studies . . . . . . . . . . . . . . . . . . . . . . . . . . . . . 379

RESOURCES . . . . . . . . . . . . . . . . . . . . . . . . . . . . . . . . . . . . . . . . . . . . 394

WORKS CITED. . . . . . . . . . . . . . . . . . . . . . . . . . . . . . . . . . . . . . . . . . 403

BIBLIOGRAPHY . . . . . . . . . . . . . . . . . . . . . . . . . . . . . . . . . . . . . . . . 414

# CONTRIBUTORS

Dr. Lindell Anderson, CH (COL) USA (Ret.); DMin, Vanderbilt University School of Divinity; served fifty-three years as military and hospital chaplain; currently serves as ACPE Certified Educator, Emeritus.

Ch. Steve Ballinger, AA, CC Golden Springs School of Theology; nineteen years in Law Enforcement / Fire Service / Disaster / District Attorney's Office / School District Chaplaincy; current Founder/President of Living Shield Ministries.

Michael Berry, Vice President of External Affairs, Director of Military Affairs and Senior Counsel for First Liberty Institute. Mr. Berry served as an Adjunct Professor of Law at the United States Naval Academy. Mr. Berry serves in the Marine Corps Reserve.

Reverend, Ch. Ben Boland, Bsc (Hon), University of New England; MDiv, Sydney Missionary Bible College; Grad Dip (Aging and Pastoral), Charles Sturt University; has served as an older person's chaplain for over fifteen years. Has coauthored three books (*Jesus Loves Me, Joy to the World, Priceless People*). He also lectures, researches, and writes about gospel ministry in later life.

Mr. Jason Brown, MBA, Texas Tech; thirty-eight years of sales and marketing experience; in his twentieth year with Marketplace Chaplains now serving as Chief Executive Officer and President.

Dr. Jim Browning, Ch, Col, USAF (Ret.); DMin, Southwestern Baptist Theological Seminary; served twenty-nine years in military chaplaincy; currently serving as the Director of the Marsh Institute for Chaplains.

Ch. Jeffrey Claes, MACM, Dallas Baptist University; eighteen years as a Business/Recreation chaplain; current Pastor, Rushing Wind Fellowship and Chaplain, Harley-Davidson Owners Association.

Ch. Brian Clingenpeel, MDiv, Southwestern Baptist Theological Seminary; serving twenty-five years as Fire/EMS chaplain; current Chaplain/Community Outreach Coordinator at Roanoke County Fire & Rescue.

Rev. Dr. Gary W. Clore, Captain, Chaplain Corps, U.S. Navy (Ret.); thirty-one years in military chaplaincy, currently serving as Director of Endorsement of the Global Methodist Church.

Ch. Judy Collins, MDiv, Southwestern Baptist Theological Seminary; serving thirty-five years as healthcare chaplain; retired as the Manager of Pastoral Care for Texas Health Kaufman.

Mr. Scott Collins, Accredited in Public Relations; MDiv, Southwestern Baptist Theological Seminary; spouse of a hospital chaplain; currently serving as Senior Vice President of Communications, Buckner International.

Ch. Todd Combee, CH (COL), USA (Ret.); MDiv; Director/Endorser, Baptist Chaplaincy Relations Texas Baptists; served forty years as a pastor and thirty-four years as Reserve and National Guard US Army Chaplain.

Ch. Charles Cornelisse, Ch, Col, USAF (Ret.); MDiv, Calvin Theological Seminary; served twenty-eight years primarily as military chaplain; MarketPlace Chaplains (Ret.).

Ch. James Denley, Captain, US Navy (Ret.); MDiv, Princeton Theological Seminary; served thirty years as a military chaplain; current Military and Veterans Affairs Chaplaincy Endorser, General Council of the Assemblies of God.

Ch. Karen Diefendorf, CH (LTC) USA (Ret.); STM, Yale University; served twenty-four years as military chaplain and six as a corporate chaplain; former Director Chaplaincy Services for Tyson Foods.

Dr. Tara Dixon, Ch, Maj USAF; PhD, Union Institute & University Interdenominational Theological Center, ITC, Turner Theological Seminary; currently serving as a Deputy Wing Chaplain, Scott AFB, IL, and as a Professor, Dickerson-Greene Theological Seminary, and Director of Chaplaincy, Turner Theological Seminary.

Dr. Vance Drum, Ch., DMin, Abilene Christian University; Former Director of Chaplaincy Operations, Texas Dept. of Criminal Justice; forty years in correctional chaplaincy; current Peer Ministry Consultant, Prison Seminaries Foundation.

Ch. Mary Flin, MAT, Fuller Theological Seminary; forty-three years in Christian education and leadership; twelve years in urban ministry and leadership training in community and correctional facilities, currently Director and Dean of the Seminary of Urban Leadership in Topeka, Kansas.

Dr. Ron Fraser, MDiv, DMin; BCPPC BCCTR; served fifteen years in chaplaincy and counseling; current President and CEO of TFC Global and the International Christian Trucking Association, providing chaplaincy to the trucking industry.

Rev. Dr. Janet Fuller, DMin, Yale Divinity School, Wesley Theological Seminary; forty years as Higher Education Chaplain; (Ret.), writing about chaplaincy and theologies of grief.

Dr. Scott Gardner, Ch, Col, USAF (Ret.); DMin, Reformed Theological Seminary; served thirty-three years as military chaplain; currently serving as Online Instructor for Liberty University.

Ch. Mark Grace, MDiv, Southwestern Baptist Theological Seminary; served thirty-seven years as healthcare chaplain; recently retired as Chief Mission & Ministry Officer, Baylor Scott & White Healthcare.

Ch. Jay Johns, CH (COL) USA (Ret.); ThM, Gordon-Conwell Theological Seminary; served twenty-seven years as military chaplain; currently serving as a leadership consultant at one of the fastest-growing, privately held companies in the US.

Dr. Mark Louis Johnson Sr., Ch.; DMin/PhD Residency, New Orleans Baptist Theological Seminary; twenty-one years in sports chaplaincy; currently Assistant Professor of Evangelism.

Dr. Dennis Leedom, PhD, Psychology, George Mason University; served ten years as a hospice chaplain, currently Chaplain II, Baylor Scott & White Healthcare.

Ch. David Little, JD, University of Texas School of Law; MDiv and candidate for DMin, Logsdon Seminary; practiced law for over twenty-nine years, currently at D. E. Little Law Firm, PLLC; served as a chaplain at Baylor Scott & White Health System and St. David's Healthcare in central Texas.

Ch. R. Steve Lowe, Founder/President Pacific Youth Correctional Ministries, Senior Protestant Chaplain for the Orange County Probation Juvenile Justice Center (CA); three master's degrees from Pepperdine University, Biola University / Talbot School of Theology, and California State University San Bernardino.

Rev. Ch. David Mann, MDiv, BCC; Southeastern Baptist Theological Seminary; served twenty-nine years as healthcare chaplain; current Director of Chaplaincy, Ventana by Buckner.

Rev. Dr. Jan McCormack, APC/BCC, AAPC/PCE, ACPE/National Faculty Certified Educator; DMin, Denver Seminary; served almost twenty-one years in military chaplaincy; served as Chair and Associate Professor of Chaplaincy and Pastoral Counseling Programs; Director, Denver Seminary CPE Center; Denver Seminary, Littleton, CO.

Ch. Dick Millspaugh, MDiv, Union Theological Seminary, New York City; served thirty-five years as hospital chaplain; retired as Chief of Chaplain Service, San Diego VA.

Ch. Hector Perez, Certified CISD Specialist; served ten years as a chaplain in the workplace; current Executive Director of Operations at Marketplace Chaplains, Southern California.

Ch. Lorraine Potter, Ch, Maj Gen, USAF (Ret.); Doctor of Humane Letter, Keuka College; served thirty-five years as military chaplain; first woman chaplain and Chief of Chaplains USAF; currently provides worship services in a retirement community.

Ch. Joe Pryor, MDiv, Southeastern Baptist Theological Seminary; served thirty years as correctional chaplain, assistant warden, warden, and senior director for reentry services; former Chief Chaplain, Federal Bureau of Prisons; currently serving as president and CEO, Crossroads Prison Ministries.

Dr. Steven Richardson, Ch, Col, USAF; DMin, Gordon-Conwell Theological Seminary; serving twenty-three years as military chaplain.

Ch. Maytal Saltiel, MDiv, Harvard Divinity School; ten years as a university chaplain; currently Associate University Chaplain at Yale University; President of the Association for Chaplaincy and Spiritual Life in Higher Education (ACSLHE).

Rev. Dr. Joanne Sanders, DMin, Seattle University; twenty years as Higher Education Chaplain; retired recently as Senior Associate Dean for Religious Life at Stanford University, CA.

Ch. Ken Schlenker, MDiv, Talbot School of Theology; served thirty years as First Responder & District Attorney Chaplaincy; current Founder & President CAREForce.us; RKM Crisis Team dba CAREForce; Professor.

Dr. Bobby Smith, DMin, Southwestern Baptist Theological Seminary; twenty years as Denominational Endorser; past Director of Baptist Chaplaincy Relations.

Dr. Jim Spivey, CH (BG) USA (Ret.), DPhil, Oxford University; retired Senior Fellow of B. H. Carroll Theological Seminary; served fifteen years in military chaplaincy; Pastor, Gambrell Street Baptist Church and Associate Director, Cofounder of Marsh Institute for Chaplains.

Dr. Robert Vickers, CH (COL) USA (Ret.); DMin, Lexington Theological Seminary, EDD, Vanderbilt University; served twenty-eight years in military chaplaincy; retired as a denominational endorser.

Rev. R. Michael Warner, Ch, Lt Col, USAF (Ret.); MDiv, Southern Baptist Theological Seminary; served twenty-nine years as military chaplain; current Director Clergy Care Services, Indianapolis, IN.

Dr. Eric Whitmore, Ch, (Maj) USAF (Ret.); DMin, Logsdon Seminary; served fourteen years as military chaplain; served ten years as Associate Endorser, Baptist Chaplaincy Relations; adjunct seminary professor.

Dr. William Whitmore, PhD, University of Gloucestershire; School Minister, Religion and History Department Faculty, Mercersburg Academy, an independent college-preparatory school in south-central Pennsylvania.

Dr. Gene Wilkes, PhD, B. H. Carroll Theological Seminary; serving fifteen years as City, Police and Fire Departments chaplain; past president and current Dean, B. H. Carroll Theological Seminary at East Texas Baptist University.

# FOREWORD

## Dr. Gene Wilkes

For the first edition of *The Heart of a Chaplain*, I wrote this on the eve of the twentieth anniversary of the terrorist attack on September 11, 2001. We all remember where we were on that day and the impact it has had on the American psyche.

When I remember the stories of that day, I recall first-responder, hospital, and military chaplains who bravely stepped into the chaos and death and continued to impact lives for the weeks, months, and years that followed. Chaplains were at Ground Zero in New York City, the Pentagon in Washington, DC, and in homes, hospitals, and military installations across the nation, bringing hope and help to those directly touched by that day's terror. Some who have written in this volume walked boldly into the fear and loss of that day to serve as a chaplain. Their stories and insights from their experience and knowledge will deepen your appreciation for those who answer the call to be chaplains.

When Dr. Jim Spivey, a founding Senior Fellow of B. H. Carroll Theological Seminary, came to me with the vision for a center for chaplain studies as part of our seminary, I did not realize the depth and breadth of that vision. I was enthusiastic about adding additional pathways to equip men and women called to serve in ministry. However, I was unprepared to realize the expansion of chaplaincy, both in numbers and in its many forms in the last few decades. My personal experience as a volunteer police and fire department chaplain widened my perspective and influence to the needs of first responders and those they helped day in and day out when I was a local church pastor. Through my interaction with Drs. Jim Spivey and Jim Browning, I have come to see the significance of chaplains in every arena of life.

In many ways, chaplains are the new pastors. Local church pastors are essential to the mission of God through the church, but chaplains often are invited where pastors are no longer welcomed or cannot go. Chaplains find their way onto the battlefield, into border crises, prison cells, hospital rooms, classrooms, and boardrooms—all arenas of influence to which pastors do not always have equal access. Chaplains carry hope, healing, and health into these diverse and various venues to represent the mystery and holiness of God to all people, no matter their faith or lack of faith in God. Chaplains comfort and confront the brokenness of humanity when they are called upon to serve. They do this in the storms of battle, the calm of a human's last breath, or a baby's first cry. In this volume are the voices of those ministering as chaplains. Read carefully, and you will sense their call, identity, passion, and motivation—the heart of a chaplain.

I am grateful to the Senior Fellows for their vision for a chaplain studies center to educate and train chaplains and Drs. Jim Browning and Jim Spivey for working to bring that vision into reality. *The Heart of a Chaplain: Exploring Essentials for Ministry* is a tangible expression of this vision. The information presented here comes from studied students and seasoned practitioners in the field. You will not find wish lists or theories of what may be but accumulated centuries of experience, study, and application in real life.

My prayer is that this volume will be the first of several resources that encourages and trains those who are called to chaplaincy and that more and more men and women will answer the call to this vital service to the spiritual needs of all people.

# PREFACE

## Dr. Jim Browning

Chaplaincy is the fastest-growing ministry in the United States, if not globally. Chaplains minister to persons of all faiths in various nonreligious settings. The growing global demand for effective chaplains requires a more refined and collaborative way to equip, support, and advocate for chaplains in diverse settings. *The Heart of a Chaplain: Exploring Essentials for Ministry, Second Edition,* acknowledges the rich legacy and ministry of chaplains across the globe. While this book remains primarily focused on the United States, we recognize the incredible ministry of chaplains worldwide. We offer our insights to chaplains from other nations and welcome a collaborative interchange. We can learn so much from one another.

Acceptance of *The Heart of a Chaplain* as a primer for seminaries, clinical pastoral education classes, denominations, organizations, and institutions affirms the generous contributions of many experienced chaplains. Responding to feedback and reviews of the first edition, we have added reflection questions, case studies, and several additional chapters, including a brief survey on the global nature of chaplaincy.

*The Heart of a Chaplain* contains five sections. Section One defines what a chaplain is. Our definition highlights the sacred and stresses the importance of God's call and spiritual formation. Understanding and developing a chaplain's foundational competencies starts an individual on a lifelong learning journey.

Section Two explores the spiritual, constitutional, and historical foundations of chaplaincy. It also explores the global nature of chaplaincy.

Section Three focuses on various subjects that are significant to being a chaplain. After defining a chaplain's roles, responsibilities, and tasks, we delve into many issues critical to most chaplains' success. We conclude this section with some keen insights from a chaplain's spouse.

Section Four details the value of endorsement, professional chaplain standards, and continuing education.

Section Five gives an extensive overview of the six chaplaincy types: healthcare, military, correctional, corporate/workplace, public safety, and community/lifestyle. By no means do we cover every conceivable functional area of chaplaincy. However, we offer examples to expose readers to the diversity of chaplain ministries.

At the end of chapters, reflection questions will help the readers to pause and think about what they just read. Instructors will find these questions as an added resource.

The appendixes offer an assessment tool for the individual and a trusted mentor to complete. The case studies will provide real-life examples for the reader and student to think through these often complex scenarios.

Finally, the resources section highlights many professional organizations that support chaplains and their ministries. This section also lists the endorsing organizations and agents identified by the Armed Forces Chaplains Board. Our bibliography gives an extensive categorized listing of chaplain-related resources.

This edition reflects the collaborative nature of chaplains. The mission of The Marsh Institute for Chaplains is to collaborate, equip, support, and advocate for chaplains in diverse and global settings. Through partnerships, our vision is to enhance the competency and effectiveness of chaplains. By partnering with chaplains, educational institutions, professional organizations, and religious faith groups, the Marsh Institute (1) collaborates with domestic and international partners to enhance the effectiveness of chaplains, (2) equips by developing and supporting curricular materials designed explicitly for chaplains, (3) supports by researching and promoting solutions to issues related to chaplain ministry, and (4) advocates publicly for chaplain ministry. This second edition is our continual effort to invest in the lives and ministries of those discovering and following God's call in ministry as a chaplain.

As editors, we acknowledge the work of others who have brought a greater understanding and appreciation of the who and what of chaplains.

This volume does not replace the pivotal works of others but joins in the discussion. Use the bibliography to find some exceptional books from both a broad and specific perspective. Also, explore books published outside your own country. In doing so, you will discover both the uniqueness and the commonality of chaplaincy across the globe.

As you read the second edition of *The Heart of a Chaplain*, we hope you will experience the calling, passion, commitment, and dedication of those who contributed to this resource. We are grateful for our diverse group of contributors who shared their experiences, insights, wisdom, and stories. Through this resource, we collaborate to equip, advocate, and support the next generation of chaplains.

Chaplains are making a difference in people's lives and institutions. May this second edition book stimulate your imagination for ministry and nurture your heart as a chaplain.

# ACKNOWLEDGMENTS

## Dr. Jim Browning

The transformation of an idea to reality often takes the support of many. *The Heart of a Chaplain: Exploring Essentials for Ministry* is no exception. The concept of this book began with God's relationship with us. His love. His passion. His mission. His heart.

The first edition began with the visionary support of the B. H. Carroll Theological Seminary's leadership. The second edition continued with the support of seasoned chaplains who freely contributed their wisdom and experience and the financial support of those who believe in chaplains. We are grateful for their spirit of giving.

The first edition's outline matured with the affirmation and input from forty-three highly seasoned professional chaplains. A diverse group of thirty-seven chaplains with 914 years of experience shared their insights. Together, they transformed *The Heart of a Chaplain* idea into a superb resource for those investigating or preparing for a chaplain's ministry. The second edition added material highlighting the contribution of forty-four professionals. Take a moment to review the contributors listed at the beginning of this book. This book is their labor of love for chaplaincy's legacy and the future.

Writing and editing the manuscript is only half the effort. Without the professional involvement of John Herring and Iron Stream Media, this book would have languished. We appreciate the entire team at Iron Stream Media. Their support has been spectacular.

We would be amiss not to mention the spouses of chaplains who have loved and supported all along the way. Their encouragement buoyed many a chaplain who struggled to stay afloat amidst constant demands and pressures.

Finally, we thank you, the reader, for investing your time and interest in entering this journey. As you explore the essentials for ministry, we pray your ministry will genuinely reflect the heart of God.

# SECTION ONE

## WHAT IS A CHAPLAIN?

CHAPTER ONE

# "SO YOU WANT TO BE A CHAPLAIN?"

### Dr. Jim Browning

I turned a corner on my assigned hospital floor and saw Bob, a part-time hospital chaplain and full-time seminary student, walking with a patient. The patient walked slowly and painfully with her right hand gripping the wall rail. Her left hand punctuated her story. Bob walked to her left, nodding his head and listening. He was not in a hurry and showed his concern and care for her. I had no idea what she was telling him as they were well beyond my hearing range. It didn't matter. The image of Bob walking alongside this woman transformed my approach to chaplain ministry. This image would become central to my understanding and definition of chaplaincy.

I was early in my two years of Clinical Pastoral Education (CPE) experience and struggled to develop an effective ministry model. My first approach to pastoral care was to brighten the spirits of patients and families, as the hospital can be a rather depressing place. This method did not meet the approval of my CPE supervisors, so my second approach was investigative. Like a detective, I sought information about patients and their condition, intending to include a prayer at the end of my visits. My supervisors disapproved of this approach and quickly told me. We both were frustrated, and they wondered out loud if I would survive this educational experience.

Then it happened.

As I watched Bob listen intensely and share this moment with a patient, I learned a crucial lesson in understanding what a chaplain is and my ministry model. As a result, my understanding of chaplain ministry evolved through three self-described stages: my "clown ministry" (to cheer people up), my "detective ministry" (to learn crucial facts about their condition), and eventually my "sojourner ministry."

I discovered an effective chaplain's ministry was to "sojourn" with others, to walk alongside, understand their story, and discover a deeper understanding of God and our response to Him. This new approach became a powerful and effective ministry model for me as an active-duty military chaplain in my nearly twenty-nine-year ministry. I had the privilege of walking alongside our military members and their families in many joyous and challenging times. This approach to ministry continues to inform how I engage individuals. With a willingness to sojourn with people while carefully listening to their stories, I am no longer surprised when it leads to an intersection with God, often for both of us.

## WHAT IS A CHAPLAIN?

In the simplest of terms, a chaplain is a "visible reminder of the Holy." Chaplains' acknowledgment of the Holy within their own lives and ministry to others is essential. Otherwise, one is simply a counselor or a life coach. Representing the sacred is neither a badge one wears nor a job. Serving as a chaplain is a response to a call, a passion, and a profession.

Professor John Swinton, Chair in Divinity and Religious Studies at the University of Aberdeen, UK, stated, "Chaplains are always and inevitably people of the heart." The heart is the dimension that focuses on one's desire to relate, love, and be in communion with that which is beyond. Chaplains can assist people in living out their humanity in organizations that too often can be cold, clinical, and deeply materialistic in their goals and values. Within any institution or system, chaplains bring others back to the issues of the heart.[1]

Chaplains are unique in that they care for the *souls of others* and listen to matters of the heart. They often work in very technical worlds, be it the hospital, military, industry, transportation, and so on. While others primarily focus on missions with complicated tasks and objectives, chaplains sojourn

---

[1] Andrew Parker, Nick J. Watson, and John B. White, *Sports Chaplaincy: Trends, Issues and Debates* (London: Routledge, 2016), xvii–xviii.

with their people and families. Being seen as a trustworthy and confidential agent, people readily seek out a chaplain to share their stories, off-load some of their pain, and find a new perspective on how to cope with an overwhelming issue. Chaplains earn this opportunity by walking with others where they work and live. And when invited, chaplains must listen—actively listen—to what is and is not being said. John Swinton wrote that chaplains work passionately to comprehend the meaning of what people are going through and draw on spiritual and religious traditions to enable others to find a level of healing. He stated,

> Most of what chaplains do relates to the listening to and the telling of stories. Stories reveal a form of knowledge that is not only grasped with the mind but also with the heart. Stories demand interpretation, intuition, imagination, all gifts which are fundamental to chaplaincy when people are practicing well. As in their day to day encounters with human pain, suffering and joy, chaplains struggle to understand the human spirit and to translate that into understandable forms of spiritual practice which can enhance the healing process."[2]

What is a chaplain? For this book's purpose, stated in a more comprehensive and foundational way, *chaplains fulfill a **sacred calling** to accompany and provide professional support and spiritual nurture for everyone in their distinctive secular communities, which authorize and hold them accountable.*

A chaplain's spiritual/faith perspective, personality, experiences, skills, and education inform the form and style of ministry and spiritual care. A chaplain is a minister (pastor, rabbi, imam, etc.) to some and a chaplain to all. A chaplain may be a single volunteer among a loosely associated group of people or a paid team member providing ministry to a particular, highly regulated organization. Additionally, chaplains represent their faith groups and seek to provide (or provide for) persons' spiritual or pastoral care. Chaplains

---

[2] John Swinton, "A Question of Identity: What Does It Mean for Chaplains to Become Healthcare Professionals?," *Scottish Journal of Healthcare Chaplaincy* 6, no. 2 (2003): 6–7, https://www.researchgate.net/publication/255577564_A_question_of_identity_What_does_it_mean_for_chaplains_to_become_healthcare_professionals.

are sojourners with others in their spiritual journey, providing a ministry of purpose and a calming presence in the middle of chaos.

Authors Naomi Paget and Janet McCormack note similarities and distinctions between clergy and chaplains. Both clergy and chaplains lead worship, teach, provide spiritual or pastoral care, counsel, and perform religious rites. Clergy's positions and authority come from religious congregations or ecclesiastical bodies. Chaplains' positions and authority come from the secular institutions that employ them and the ecclesiastical bodies that endorse them. Clergy operate primarily from a place of worship, whereas chaplains minister primarily in the marketplace.[3]

Chaplains should be accessible, engaged, trustworthy, humble, and relational. They should be compassionate, confidential, curious, creative, and credible. They should be listeners, counselors, and collaborators. They serve as advisors, honest brokers, leaders, confidants, and friends. Chaplains are hopeful and optimistic. They walk with those who often work in challenging and dangerous environments. They seek their welfare and care about their morale and outlook. Chaplains see the blind spots of leadership and advocate for those with muted voices.

Chaplains go where others cannot readily go because of training constraints, safety concerns, or institutional restrictions. Chaplains deliver free exercise of religion to those whose jobs take them far away from their usual places of worship. Chaplains meet others where they are and prioritize others' beliefs before their own. They minister to those who believe in a God different from their own or have no theistic belief. Chaplains express genuine care for the souls of all individuals within their purview, regardless of how different they may look, act, think, or believe. They work in a secular environment, remain true to their theological convictions in a pluralistic environment, and deal with the tension of competing demands and ideologies. Depending upon the type of chaplaincy, chaplains care and advocate for both the individual and the institution.

Respect and dignity are central to chaplain ministry. Chaplain Steven Schaick puts it succinctly.

---

[3] Naomi K. Paget and Janet R. McCormack, *The Work of the Chaplain*, 1st ed. (Valley Forge, PA: Judson Press, 2006), iv.

> The price of admission into the USAF Chaplain Corps is to believe that every man and woman is precious and that every human has with him or her the very likeness of our Creator. And if that truth does not emulate from your soul, then I ask you to consider another profession.[4]

Chaplains navigate the seams within an institution. They are part of the mission but never at the forefront. They are fluent in the languages of the institution and the heart. Chaplains are a bridge between the institution's culture and the needs of the individual. Chaplains also advise leaders of the organization, institution, corporation, or company. Chaplains are a voice on issues of moral and ethical behavior. Chaplains are a critical part of a leadership team, providing a source of faith, hope, safety, and clarity, especially during uncertain times. They are a calming, reassuring presence in tragedy and times of uncertainty. Chaplains' perspectives can be valuable to leaders as they respond to crises. Chaplains scan for issues or problems and bring them to the leaders' attention. Most leaders value what chaplains bring to the individual and the institution and welcome them as part of the crisis action response team. A senior military commander described it this way:

> The image of a chaplain ministering to battle-wounded troops is a comfort for me, a calm in the midst of chaos, a thoughtful example of faith and fellowship, a focus through the leadership chaos where uncertainty and volatility can become a heavy burden over time. When I was a young squadron commander, a master sergeant committed suicide in my unit. The Air Force places great emphasis on commander involvement and leadership to prevent suicide. I blamed myself for the tragedy. Despite my strong faith, I took my eye off the living in a moment of chaos to focus on how I could have prevented the past. My unit Chaplain saw I was hurting, asked if he could help, prayed with me, and helped me regain focus on leading the unit as we grieved a loss.[5]

---

[4] Chaplain Major General Steven Schaick, 19th Chief of Chaplains, Department of the US Air Force, made this observation the center point of his 2020 training video for USAF Chaplain Corps personnel.
[5] This Air Force general shared his thoughts in an email.

Institutions or chaplain organizations typically select a symbol to distinguish individuals as chaplains. In military service, for instance, Christian chaplains wear a Latin cross, rabbis wear a tablet, and imams wear a crescent.[6] The logo of the Marsh Institute for Chaplains, a hurricane lamp with radiating light, symbolizes chaplains carrying messages of encouragement, hope, and support amid the storm. Chaplains do not seek the shelter of safety but go into harm's way to accompany those battling danger, confusion, heartache, loneliness, isolation, trauma, tragedy, upheaval, uncertainty, helplessness, hopelessness, and loss. In doing so, chaplains genuinely make a difference.

## WHY BE A CHAPLAIN?

Why would anyone want to be and do the work of a chaplain? Why would any organization want chaplains as part of its team? Why serve the needs of others? What is powerful enough to motivate one to walk the halls of a hospital, cells of a prison, battlefields of war, offices of a corporation, streets with police, shelters for the abused, communities of the elderly, or any place where chaplains serve? Why reach out to the outcast, the misunderstood, and the ignored? The answers to these questions are as complex and diverse as the individuals and the institutions they serve.

An acquaintance once told me, "If you can do anything other than vocational ministry, then do it. However, if God has called you into a vocational ministry, then you will not want to do anything else." This belief in a divine call into a vocational ministry provides a foundational motivation to persevere through the preparation for and delivery of chaplaincy. Yet, one should explore this issue further and consider other reasons for becoming a chaplain. Simply saying "God called me to this ministry" may gloss over other factors needing personal discovery. Some seek ministry as an appeasement to God or others. Some become chaplains to escape from difficult ministry situations. Others seek perceived power or access to an institution. Some seek financial stability. With every encounter, a chaplain needs to ask whose needs are being met—the chaplain or others?

Consider these questions:

---

[6] Military chaplains' insignia has evolved. Initially, the Army used a shepherd's hook for all chaplains. Eventually, however, the military adopted different symbols for different faith groups.

- How does your relationship with God determine your sense of identity?
- Do you believe God has called you to vocational ministry?
- Do you understand this calling in a broad or a narrow sense?
- Is the call to a specific institution or style of ministry?
- What are the educational and certifying requirements?
- What are the institutional requirements?
- Does it require physical standards?
- Are you seeking to please someone else by going into chaplaincy?
- Who may be upset with your decision to become a chaplain?
- Who would be happy with your decision?
- Do you have a caring heart for others, a passion for making a difference, and a determination to get involved?

Serving as a chaplain may mean long hours, constant demands, and working within a secular institution or with a specialized group of people. Serving as a chaplain may mean supporting leaders who do not understand or value the chaplain's work. Chaplains should understand and articulate the value of their work as essential to the institution's mission. A chaplain's ministry, however challenging it may be, is equally rewarding.

## THE GROWING DEMAND

Chaplaincy is the fastest-growing ministry in the United States. Already commonplace in military, healthcare, correctional, legislative, corporate, and first responder (police/fire/EMT) settings, chaplaincy is expanding to other fields: disaster relief, sports, recreation, national parks, cruise ships, civic organizations, retirement communities, and special interest groups.

Traditionally, seminaries focused on preparing ministers for denominational service in local churches, with little thought given to chaplaincy. Typically, chaplains moved from a pastorate to a chaplain ministry. Then they trained in clinical programs or specialized schools that retooled them for cross-cultural ministry. Seminarians today expect a different approach. Many already sense a call to chaplaincy and are eager to sharpen their chaplain skills while in school.

Additionally, attitudes are changing toward those interested in chaplaincy. Church pastors and members typically viewed those entering chaplaincy as leaving the "real ministry." Most, however, understand chaplaincy is a specialized ministry and is equally relevant.

Because of these changing attitudes toward chaplaincy, theological schools offer more chaplain-focused programs. Wendy Cadge et al. noted that, in 2020, approximately seventy of 270 Association of Theological Schools (ATS) member schools, candidates, and affiliates had some specialized chaplaincy program.[7] Three years later, Wendy Cadge et al. recorded that this number had increased to 107 theological schools with chaplaincy or spiritual care degrees.[8]

The growth in chaplaincy has also led to an increase in clinical training. The Association of Clinical Pastoral Education (ACPE) was the standard for many years and used the hospital setting as its classroom. Today, other organizations offer clinical training, with many using a hybrid delivery model and a community-based ministry location as the focus of the clinical training. A noteworthy example is the Clinical Pastoral Education International (CPEI). The Distance Education Accrediting Commission (DEAC), recognized by the US Department of Education and the Council for Higher Education Accreditation (CHEA), accredited CPEI in 2024. CPEI's institutional outcomes address the benefit to the chaplain student:

- Provide educational programs that enable self-motivated, independent learners to acquire core competencies.
- Prepare students to function as competent pastoral caregivers and supervisors/instructors in the marketplace and qualify for credentialing.

---

[7] Wendy Cadge et al., "Training Chaplains and Spiritual Caregivers: The Emergence and Growth of Chaplaincy Programs in Theological Education," *Pastoral Psychology* 69 (2020): 187–208. https://doi.org/10.1007/s11089-020-00906-5, accessed 30 August 2021. Cadge, a sociology professor, draws these conclusions from a survey of twenty-one schools offering educational programs for chaplains.

[8] Wendy Cadge, Grace Tien, and Trace Haythorn, "What Are Chaplains Learning? Perspectives on the Supply Side," https://chaplaincyinnovation.org/resources/working-papers/supply-side, accessed 24 August 2024.

- Assess student learning and institutional effectiveness to improve student and educator performance.
- Provide professional development opportunities to enhance lifelong learning.
- Conduct fiscally responsible planning that balances the institution's commitment to academic excellence.[9]

While fewer Americans identify with specific religious affiliations, interest in spirituality remains strong.[10] Perhaps this trend is part of the impetus for significant growth in chaplaincy in the United States and abroad. Your path to becoming a chaplain may be as a volunteer with basic preparation and limited skill sets. Or it may be a long, arduous adventure with years of education, training, and credentialing. Whatever path you take, your journey should begin with your response to a sacred calling followed by thorough preparation, guidance, and continual learning. Chaplain opportunities abound for those willing to meet the challenge. We will continue to need chaplains eager to walk alongside others, seeking to understand their stories and discovering together what God desires for all our lives.

## REFLECTION QUESTIONS

1. Is a recognition or representation of the Holy in the life and ministry of a chaplain important? Why or why not?
2. In the simplest of terms, this chapter defines a chaplain as "a visible reminder of the Holy." Is this definition adequate? How does this definition shape or influence the ministry of a chaplain?
3. Which elements are most important to you in the more comprehensive definition of chaplains used in this resource? Why?
4. Some organizations are substituting the title "Spiritual Care Provider" for "Chaplain." Do you believe "chaplain" is outdated and should be changed? Why or why not?

---

[9] CPEI Mission and Vision, https://cpei.edu/mission-and-vision/, accessed 24 August 2024.
[10] David Masci and Michael Lipka, *Americans May Be Getting Less Religious, But Feelings of Spirituality Are On the Rise* (Washington, DC: Pew Research Center, 2016). https://www.pewresearch.org/fact-tank/2016/01/21/americans-spirituality/, accessed 30 August 2021.

CHAPTER TWO

# SPIRITUAL FORMATION AND THE CALL

## Dr. Jim Spivey

Have you ever questioned your calling to ministry? Have you ever felt vulnerable, alone, and defeated to the point of giving up because everything in your life was falling apart?

I have—more than once. I was a thirty-five-year-old husband and father, pastor, Army reservist, and doctoral student in England when it hit me—the first time. I was "passed over" for promotion to major. My doctoral supervisor told me to pack my bags and go home. Our church seemed to be on the verge of a split. And the money to support my family was running out. When I asked the Lord why all this was happening, He asked me a simple question, "Who are you?"

I quickly answered, "A husband, father, pastor, captain, and doctoral student. And all of that—my whole identity—is under attack."

He then asked me, "Who am I?"

I responded, "You are the Lord God."

He probed further, "But who am I to you?" Long pause.

Then I said, "You are my Father."

So—again He asked me the same question, "Who are you?"

This time it stripped away all the masks I had been hiding behind. The light bulb began to flicker. I was beginning to understand: my identity was not husband, father, pastor, captain, or doctoral student. Those were roles—important ones, but not essential.

I blurted, "I am your child." You probably can guess what He said next. It went something like this.

"If I am your Father who made you for a purpose and who loves you with an everlasting love, don't you trust me to know what is best for you? Even if it means never wearing an Army uniform again, not getting that degree, and being fired as pastor?"

What else could I do but surrender—just as I had done many years earlier (to Christ) and later in life (to His call to ministry)?

Of course, the lesson should have been obvious enough for me to understand from the beginning. Identity is fundamental—it is who I am. And there is a big difference between my identity and all the rest of life's stuff—my calling(s), the roles I fulfill, and the image I sustain. The good news is, I was promoted, I got the degree, the church did fine, and God provided amply for my family. I wish I could say I learned my lesson well enough that I never again experienced an "identity crisis." The bad news is, I am a slow learner. More than once, the Lord again has asked me that simple but hard question, "Who are you?"

## ESSENTIAL QUESTIONS

Whether we are seasoned chaplains or are just beginning to inquire about this ministry, the world of chaplaincy challenges each of us to revisit basic issues concerning our spiritual identity and growth, as well as how we should respond to the call to ministry. Chaplains serve in situations that challenge us to rethink traditional views about ministry. We face issues parish ministers typically do not encounter and deal with questions they rarely ask. How can we share our faith in pluralistic settings where we are obligated to serve people of all, or no, religions? How do we cope in stressful institutional settings where our roles as ministers and administrators seem to conflict? How can we collaborate with chaplains whose religious beliefs contradict our own? What if our supervisors expect us to do things against our conscience? In other words, how can we minister in secular settings with personal integrity and religious fidelity?

The chaplain's world is not for the fainthearted with unclear or weak convictions. It pulls us in contradictory directions and pushes us to the very boundaries of our theological frameworks. Before becoming chaplains, it is imperative to be well-grounded in our faith and committed to our confessional beliefs. We should know what and why we believe before trying to be "all things to all persons." Otherwise, we risk losing our moorings. Yet, we should remain flexible and avoid the kind of dogmatism that incapacitates and prevents us from doing ministry in places parish pastors rarely go.

Not everyone can do the work of a chaplain. It is a unique vocation. We are "called out" from among like-minded denominational ministers to do something quite different and special. But that calling also puts us in stressful situations that may raise doubts about our calling and may even challenge our identity as denominational ministers. Such "crises of faith" or "identity conflicts" cannot be resolved simply by knowing confessional statements, applying theological principles, or using management tools for conflict resolution. As important as these approaches may be, we also need to plumb the depths of spiritual formation and answer more fundamental questions that lie at the heart of those issues.

First, we should answer the question, "Who am I?" This is not just an abstract, philosophical question—what am I as a human being? It is not just a general, theological question—what am I in God's scheme of creation and history? As important as those questions are, this one is more personal and existential—who am I at the core of my being—my own personal identity? Why am I living in this time and place in history—and how does my "identity" drive my purpose in life? When we answer the "identity" question, we begin to understand how to cope with stressful situations in any kind of ministry. Our answer also begs three more questions that help us put ministry into perspective: (1) what is my call (and do I have more than one), (2) what is my role (and do I have more than one), and (3) what is my image?

## A CASE STUDY

How might Abraham have answered the "identity" question? Initially, he was identified by his lineage and family: a Semite and Hebrew, son of Terah, husband of Sarai, brother of Nahor and Haran, and uncle of Lot.[11] But when God called him to become a great nation, his name Abram, "exalted father," assumed new meaning. Then he thought his identity was to be a patriarch whose call was to bless all people. To his credit, he trusted God and "called upon the name of

---

[11] Gen 11:10–32

the Lord."[12] But when his patriarchal identity was threatened by Pharaoh's pursuit of Sarai, Abram resorted to deception instead of fully relying on the Lord.[13]

Though God caused him to thrive and Abram continued to follow God, he still had a blind spot concerning his identity. When God renamed him Abraham, "father of many nations,"[14] he became even more convinced that his core identity was patriarchal. This became obvious when King Abimelech also pursued Sarah, and again Abraham lied to protect his family.[15] Afterward, Abraham experienced an "identity crisis" when God tested him by commanding him to sacrifice his son Isaac. Surely, Abraham thought such an unthinkable act would devastate his family and, at his advanced age, destroy any hope of fulfilling his identity as patriarch and his call to bless all people. But he was redeemed by his willingness to obey, relinquish his false identity, and trust God completely.[16]

I think two patterns in this story apply to anyone in ministry. The first illustrates how God strengthens us through the progression of our faith: from His call, in our failures, through crises, to redemption. The second pattern shows how we act and interrelate at four levels of being: (1) identity, (2) call, (3) role, and (4) image.

## Progression of Faith

At first Abraham responded in faith, but he misunderstood his true identity and call. Though he trusted God enough to follow Him, he put too much confidence in his perceived identity as patriarch. This self-reliance weakened his trust in God and caused him to lie to Pharaoh. Yet God remained faithful to His word, promised Abraham a son,[17] and sealed it all with the covenant of circumcision.[18] This symbolized God's personal and reciprocal promise by which He gave Himself to Abraham and his descendants. In return, by circumcising

---

[12] Gen 12:1–8
[13] Gen 12:10–20
[14] Gen 17:1–5
[15] Gen 20
[16] Gen 22:1–18; Heb 11:17–19
[17] Gen 15:4
[18] Gen 17:1–14

himself, Abraham gave himself to God. This act marked Abraham's true identity. At the core of his being, he was not a patriarch but God's own possession. That he did not fully grasp this fact is revealed in how he dealt self-reliantly and deceptively with Abimelech. So, God put him to the test. By ordering him to sacrifice Isaac, God was asking the question, "Who are you?" Finally, Abraham understood. His identity was not to be a great father, a father of many nations, or even a blessing to all people. It was simply to be God's—period.

The same was true of Sarah, who also experienced similar crises of identity involving failure and redemption. She was fully complicit with Abram in deceiving pharaoh. Then, not fully trusting the Lord to provide Abram a son, she conspired to provide one through her maid, Hagar. But her "identity" was not to be the stepmother of a great nation. God made this clear when He established His covenant with Abraham. No longer was his wife to be called Sarai, the "princess"; instead, she would be known as Sarah, the "noble queen." Apparently, she did not understand the reason for this change until she overheard God reaffirming to Abraham that she would give birth to Isaac in her old age. Sarah not only laughed in disbelief at this revelation but also lied to the Lord about having done so. So, to her surprise, when Isaac was born, her apparent "identity" as matriarch of a great nation seemed secure. Imagine her great sense of terror and the threat to that identity years later when Abraham left their tent one day to sacrifice Isaac as a burnt offering to the Lord! When God spared Isaac by providing the ram sacrifice, He redeemed not just Abraham's true identity but also that of the whole family. Sarah was more than a "noble queen," and Isaac was not just "one who laughs"—more profoundly, they were God's own possession.

To some degree, all great biblical leaders followed this pattern. Jacob coveted the identity of tribal chief and stole Esau's inheritance and Isaac's blessing. His wife Rachel also started off on the wrong foot. After years of marriage to the man who had received the Lord's promise at Bethel, she continued to cling to her father's idols and even stole them when fleeing Laban's house. So, at Peniel, when God changed Jacob's name to Israel ("God prevails"), He redeemed both of their identities. Jacob and Rachel were more than parents of a great nation; they, too, were the Lord's own possession. Consider Joseph. He started as a spoiled favorite son, but God made him savior of Egypt and his people, Israel. Moses was an Egyptian prince, but God made him Israel's deliverer, prophet, and judge. David was a shepherd, but God made him king of an everlasting covenant. Peter was a fisherman, but God made him a fisher of men. James, son of Zebedee, aspired to be Jesus' prime minister, but God made him a martyr for Christ. Mary Magdalene was a demon-possessed woman, but God used her to help fund Jesus' Galilean ministry and made her the first messenger of Christ's resurrection. Saul was a Pharisee and zealous persecutor of Christians, but God made him apostle to the Gentiles.

All their false identities were unmasked by failures precisely at their points of perceived strength. God challenged them to face who they really were in relationship with Him, tested them in the crucible of crisis, and then redeemed them to become more than they had ever imagined.

In our faith-walk, we all face similar challenges that lead to a "crisis of faith." This is an inevitable part of our progressive journey of faith. First, we respond optimistically to God's call. Then we stumble and fail because we forget our true identity and rely on self, not God. When God tests us, the ensuing crisis of faith presents an opportunity for us to grow. His grace enables us to trust Him more, our faith is strengthened, and we are reminded that our total reliance and real identity are in Him.

**The Progression of Faith**

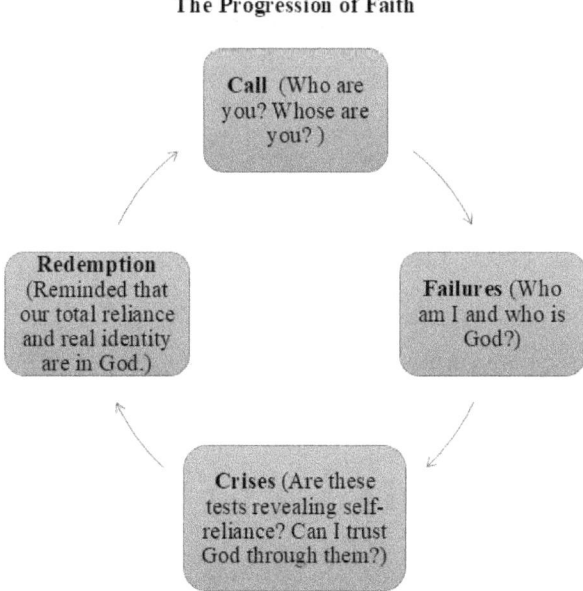

## Levels of Being

To deal with identity crises and role conflicts effectively, it also is helpful to understand how we interrelate at different levels of being: (1) identity, (2) call, (3) role, and (4) image. Our "identity" answers the question, "Who am I?" This is the essence of our being-ness—who we are when all façades are stripped away. It is the starting point for knowing why we exist and defining our purpose in life.

Our "call" (or calling) is a primary pathway of life. As we seek to fulfill our purpose, this is where we live and function. Where do we habitually walk, and with whom do we regularly interact to give life meaning? A call is more substantial and broader than a professional vocation or job. And most of us have more than one call.

A "role" is some aspect of our being we exert to fulfill our call. We take on roles in several ways: primary relationships, key positions, or functions we perform. For every calling in life, we fulfill at least one role, but usually more than just one.

Our "image" is how others see us and is the basis for our reputation. When we walk with integrity, all four levels of being are in alignment: our image squares with the roles we fulfill in the legitimate pathways of life that accomplish the purpose for which God made us to exist.

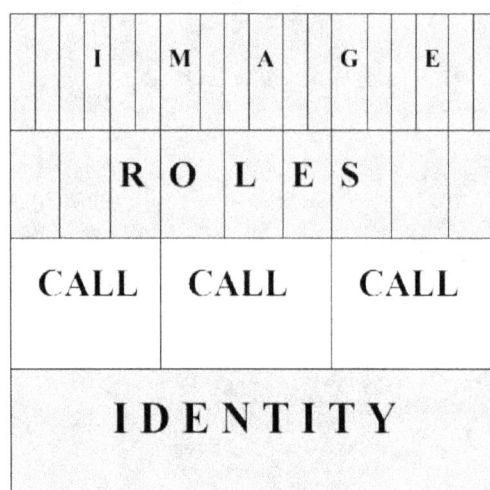

Abraham's story illustrates these points. His identity was to be God's possession in covenant relationship. His call was not to go to Canaan or even to follow God to a specified place. No, following God was already an inherent part of his identity. Instead, his call, as an extension of his identity, was to bless people wherever God led him. He walked several primary pathways, or callings. Among them were his domestic calling among family, his social calling among kings and tribal chiefs, and his religious calling to obey and worship God. His domestic roles were son, father, husband, brother, and uncle. His social roles were shepherd, landowner, businessman, and soldier. His religious roles were patriarch and priest, as he interacted with Melchizedek and built altars to God. What was his image? His names were "great father" and "father of many nations." In God's sight, he was blessed and righteous. To humans, he was a prosperous, wealthy, and godly man of prayer and devotion, and a mighty ally in battle.

## The Crisis of Faith and Identity Conflict

Most great biblical leaders experienced an identity conflict during a personal crisis of faith. At some point, they became confused about their identity, call, role, and image. They mistook a role for their identity. When that role was undermined by crisis, they failed to come to terms with their real identity and resorted to role-playing in order to save face and protect their reputation. And they failed.

Then God caused them to go through a "wilderness" experience—a crisis of faith—during which they lost self-confidence. In those dark days, they learned that their identity was not defined by some role—a human relationship, key position, or function they performed. God used the wilderness as a redemptive tool to awaken them concerning who and whose they really were. They were not great father or favored son, not prince or king, not shepherd or fisherman. Instead, they were simply His. They underwent profound transformations of identity that shaped the rest of their lives and affected how they responded to God's call, fulfilled their roles, and how they perceived their image.

## WORKING OUT OUR IDENTITY

Of all people, chaplains need clearly to delineate these things in their own lives. Identity is foundational. It is the essence of our being in relationship with God, and everything else flows from it. Our "call to chaplaincy" is not our only calling in life. Each calling is a broader pathway which encompasses several roles, just one of which is to serve as a chaplain. In this role, we fulfill our calling in our relationships with others, through positions we fill, and by functions we perform. All these expressions build our reputations as chaplains. That image is important. We should take reasonable care to protect it and to maintain a positive image. More than just our personal reputations are at stake. We should take seriously how others perceive us as God's representatives.

But we should not become obsessed with desire for success or fear of failure. No, external measurements of performance in ministry should not drive our internal being and purpose. Instead, quite the opposite, our image and reputation should be energized by our identity in God. It should be the same for all the callings we walk and all the roles we fulfill.

All four aspects of our being are important and ought to square with each other. This is a matter of personal integrity: we should do and say what we are—we should be what we say and do. But for that to happen, we need to come to terms with our identity.

Unfortunately, many ministers never do this most fundamental thing. Others lose sight of it along the way. They confuse their roles with their identity, and the resultant identity conflicts inevitably lead to crises of faith. It is especially important for chaplains to understand this point: as strange it seems, at the most fundamental level of identity, we are not chaplains or even ministers. Those are roles we fulfill.

This principle applies not only to chaplains but to everyone in every pathway of life. In the community, we are not first church members, citizens, taxpayers, employers, or workers. At home, we are not first mothers or dads, brothers or sisters, sons or daughters. Those are roles associated with callings derived from our identity. That identity is defined by our relationship with whom or what is most important to us, and this gives us purpose for being.

For Christians, identity is rooted in God, however we express this personally: "child of God," "Christ-follower," or "believer" are a few examples. This does not discount the importance of corporate identity, confessional standards, or denominational solidarity. But seeing ourselves as Catholic, Baptist, or Lutheran is no substitute for our core identity in God Himself.

This personal identity with the divine is similar in other theistic traditions. Jews emphasize being part of a covenant community, and religious adherents to Judaism also affirm that Jehovah can and does relate to them personally and holds them individually accountable.

While there are many sects of Islam, all Muslims identify with one global socio-religious movement. At the same time, a primary tenet of Islam is also personal accountability to Allah. So, the core identities of most theistic chaplains are rooted, to some degree, in their relationship with God, and obedience to Him is the basis for their call to ministry. Regardless of one's religious tradition, that identity should be singular; otherwise, we are divided in mind and unstable in all our ways. That identity is foundational not only to a chaplain's call to ministry but also to the roles we fulfill and to the image we maintain as ministers.

## The Call to Ministry

Our call to ministry is subjective. Its meaning varies between faith traditions and from person to person. Technically, it means a professional "vocation" (Lat. *vocatio*)—or "calling" (Lat. *vocatus*)—whereby God "calls" (Lat. *vocare*) clergy to do the work of a minister. But in a broader and more profoundly biblical sense, God calls all believers, clergy and laity alike, to serve Him in various roles wherever they go in their primary pathways of life. God calls some to serve as plumbers and others as teachers or nurses.

Our professional "call to ministry" is not the primary pathway itself but a role we fulfill along the way. Some do this as pastors, others as chaplains; some full-time, others bi-vocationally. So, what are those primary pathways where chaplains are "called" to serve? There are at least three. One is the "hearth-call" to serve family. Another is the "community call" to collaborate alongside like-minded people to serve others. It takes many forms, such as a local congregation, civic group, or affinity group related to a special interest.

Finally, the "marketplace call" is to a workplace where skills are employed to earn a living. Most believers clearly delineate between their community and marketplace calls. Though they may serve voluntarily in their community (local church), their professional vocation is in the secular world. For chaplains, however, the line may be blurred. Their professional vocation is as religious ministers in the secular world. But in their community (local church), they may serve either as vocational ministers or as voluntary members in a nonvocational capacity.

In each calling or pathway, chaplains fulfill multiple roles. Each role should be aligned with a legitimate call in our life that expresses our true identity. The hearth call is to fulfill roles as a responsible family member—as son or daughter, father or mother, brother or sister. It is multigenerational and extends to circles beyond the nuclear unit. The community call should include participation in the local congregation; it includes roles such as member, teacher, deacon, and minister.

The marketplace call is as chaplain in a secular, pluralistic setting, but may also include being the pastor of a denominational congregation. When we understand how our roles are linked to specific calls, we can better prioritize them and minimize role conflict. Sometimes our hearth call takes priority over our vocational call, or vice versa. On some occasions, our duty as a mother or dad might trump our responsibility as a chaplain. At other times, it may be the opposite. The real source of "role conflict" is that we commonly confuse one role in life with our core identity. This error leads us to become obsessed with our "job" or a key relationship. This myopic, unbalanced perspective can cause us to become driven by that role.

How does this happen? Perhaps we always put family first to protect them from encroaching demands of our job. Or maybe we always put ministry first, thinking this is the only way to serve God. In fact, this usually means we have made a god of our vocation, and sometimes purely for the sake of success. Unmistakably, image is important, and success can open more doors for ministry.

But an inordinate drive for success and desire to please others can derail our calling, compromise our integrity, and cause us to lose focus on our identity in God. Gordon MacDonald of Denver Seminary warns, "driven" persons are usually highly competitive, abnormally busy, overly gratified by accomplishment, caught in uncontrolled pursuit of expansion, and have limited regard for integrity. He asks probing and convicting questions: "Are we driven people, propelled by the winds of our times, pressed to conform or compete? Or are we called people, the recipients of the gracious beckoning of Christ when He promises to make us into something?"[19] More often than not, "role conflict" occurs when we lose perspective about our "calling," and it is compounded by the guilt we feel for not accomplishing all we demand of ourselves for perfect job performance to satisfy what we think others expect.

In all our pathways, in vocational ministry and the rest of life, we constantly maintain an image. Though that image is external, it is not strictly superficial or unimportant. It is how others see us representing God. What is our reputation? Is it admirable and approved by Him, or is it disreputable? Every aspect of our image should derive from a legitimate role and call. In turn, it should express those values we hold at the core of our being—our identity. That image should be consistent with whom we claim to be as God's people. If our image is driven by self-gratification, our identity is self-centered. If our image is driven only by others' expectations, our identity is bankrupt, without substance, godly character, or integrity.

## Proper Alignment

A life of integrity is one that maintains the whole self—identity, call, role, and image—in proper alignment. All behaviors and actions are linked to legitimate roles, based on God-given calls, derived from our identity in God. If every aspect of our image, each role we fulfill, and each calling of life is in alignment, they are well-balanced and prioritized according to values we hold at the identity level. When we walk, talk and act with integrity, what others see outwardly is an accurate reflection of who we are inwardly. There is no role-playing just to satisfy others for self-promotion. So, hopefully we fulfill our role as chaplains in response to a genuine call to walk alongside others in pathways directed by God.

When out of alignment, we act inconsistently with our professed identity. Sometimes we behave and maintain images for which we possess no corresponding values at the identity level. This takes the form of superficial behavior, usually responding to external pressure—being driven mainly by others' expectations. At other times, we do not live out the values we profess to hold at the identity level. This takes the form of dishonesty or misbehavior—when we say that we believe a certain way, but we do not act accordingly.

---

[19] Gordon MacDonald, *Ordering Your Private World* (Nashville: Thomas Nelson, 2012), 32–38.

## A CHAPLAIN'S CALL

Consider the implications of how we answer our original question, "Who am I?" That answer motivates everything else in ministry: call, role, and image. It determines how we set priorities and how we choose to minister. Much chaplain training rightly focuses on how to "do ministry." But we should never confuse roles and image with identity—we should not mistake doing for being. This raises a critical issue concerning the vital link between our identity and our roles. That link is our calling. It begs the question: what really is the "chaplain's call"?

Chaplain ministry is not a call in itself; it is a role that fulfills but one calling of God in our lives. Again, we should remember that our essential identity is not "chaplain" or even "minister." These are roles we fulfill. They should be informed constantly by thoughtful consideration of who God calls us to "be" more than by what He expects us to "do." At this point, Paul Beasley-Murray's conclusion about the call to pastoral leadership applies equally to chaplain ministry.

> The call to pastoral leadership . . . is in the first place a call to be, rather than a call to do. . . . It is in their relationship with God that the authority of leaders is to be found. . . . Pastors therefore have no option but to major on their relationship with God. This relationship is primary. Neglect of this relationship negates ministry.[20]

## REFLECTION QUESTIONS

1. Too often, we begin our journey in ministry by asking this question: What does God want me to do? Given your reading, is this a good or misdirected question? Why?
2. What compels you to consider becoming a chaplain?
3. Why is it important to know what you believe and why before entering a ministry where you are pastor to some but chaplain to all?
4. Can you describe a situation where your work in secular settings could create a challenge to your personal integrity and religious fidelity?

---

[20] Paul Beasley-Murray, *Dynamic Leadership* (Oxford: Monarch Books, 1990), 198–99.

CHAPTER THREE

# PROFESSIONAL COMPETENCIES

## Chaplain Dick Millspaugh

If you consider professional chaplaincy a vocational choice, you might explore several questions. Do I feel called? Do those who know me well, and my faith group, affirm my sense of call? What are my interests? What are my aptitudes? What chaplaincy specialties might be a good fit for me?

Vocational testing and counseling, interviewing current chaplains and faith leaders, and researching the standards of chaplain organizations can help answer those questions. Two remaining questions are critical. What are my competencies? Am I willing to learn what I don't know?

My education in hospital ministry began when a patient ordered me out of her ward. I was a second-year seminary student and a part-time resident chaplain in a Clinical Pastoral Education (CPE) program. In the prior week, the patient had entrusted me with her fears regarding upcoming surgery to remove her lower lip, cut a flap in her forearm, and sew that flap to what remained of her lip. This procedure would leave her arm bound to her head until a blood supply returned. Then she would face more surgery. I did what I thought any competent chaplain would do: I told her of her great surgeons, the caring nurses, the excellence of the hospital, and that I was sure she would be fine.

The next week I went back to see her in the open twelve-bed unit. I couldn't find her. I looked again. Finally, I realized she must be the patient with her arm across her face, bound to her head with white bandages. I walked to her bedside and introduced myself as the chaplain. Immediately, and I do mean immediately, she yelled directly at me, "You get out of here, chaplain. You said my surgery would be fine, and it isn't. You get out of here!"

I shook. I had no idea why the patient was so angry with me. I anticipated being eliminated from the CPE program. With fear, trepidation, and incredible embarrassment, I reported the incident to my supervisor in front of other resident chaplains. They encouraged me to examine my belief that good chaplains should assure patients of excellent care and that they would be fine. My peers challenged me to consider my ministry's actual impact on the patient.

To this day, I can still picture that patient and that encounter. I thank God for her. She helped me know that I needed to understand myself better. I needed to dig deeply into my motivations and beliefs before I could understand patients and care for them authentically. This angry patient helped me discover a foundation for professional chaplaincy—the challenge of growing in competence, beginning with self-awareness and self-containment.

## WHAT ARE COMPETENCIES?

Professionals define competencies in various ways: knowledge, skills, aptitudes, motivations, and roles. For our purposes, I suggest chaplaincy competencies are behaviors that generally result in a degree of spiritual healing, comfort, insight, and acceptance. Competencies are informed by knowledge, refined by feedback and reflection, and strengthened by practice. Growing in competence requires a nondefensive eagerness to learn and the ability to look objectively and compassionately at one's attitudes, assumptions, knowledge, and performance. Seeking input from proficient, self-aware pastoral care educators increases objectivity. In contrast, persons who need to be "perfect" and compete with others to be "the best" will have difficulty accepting the honest feedback required for personal and professional growth.

The patient who directed me to leave her ward helped me recognize my lack of awareness. Because I was unaware of my motivations, I was unable to be a deep listening presence for her. I came to understand my reassurances were not so much to calm her fears but to contain my anxiety. Becoming a competent chaplain is humbling—often an uncomfortable journey toward self-awareness. I discovered that my words did nothing to help the patient experience God's comforting presence. I have since discovered that God's comfort often speaks through a transparent, vulnerable patient-chaplain relationship.

Martin Buber referred to such honest encounters as "I-Thou," in contrast to "I-It," relationships. I learned that I was treating the patient as an "It," an object, prescribing what I thought she needed. I found that chaplain ministry is rarely a matter of verbally witnessing to one's faith or giving assurances that everything is going to be OK.[21]

On the other hand, people often experience God's presence when a chaplain dares to join them either in life circumstances and challenges that raise fear, anxiety, and uncertainty, or in moments of unexpected grace that bring relief and joy.

## IDENTIFYING AND MANAGING ANXIETY

I learned that I needed to identify, be aware of and contain my own anxiety in order to be non-anxiously present with patients in their anxiety. The patient I visited feared a negative surgical outcome and, without my realizing it, triggered my own fears of uncertainty and death.

We generate anxious thoughts about the future when we anticipate a less-than-desired outcome, with some sort of negative consequence. "Performance anxiety" may occur in a given role when cultural, professional, or institutional norms are to be met—when a student must have a "C" average to pass, or a chaplain's visits are expected to help patients.

I believe students who wish to learn new material or competencies generally perform at a higher level when they can (1) identify specific thoughts that generate anxiety in the face of a specific task, (2) change behaviors and thoughts to more realistic, helpful ones, and (3) practice calming thoughts and behaviors.

Thoughts generating anxiety often predict loss of control and failure, or self-disparaging internal comments about not being good enough. For anyone who has a history of loss or trauma, where important aspects of their lives were outside of their control, this anxiety can be profound. This is especially

---

[21] Martin Buber, *I and Thou*, trans. Ronald Gregor Smith (New York: Scribner, 1958).

true for children who do not have adult coping skills. They tend to blame themselves for negative aspects of their lives over which they had no control and carry self-blame and predictions of failure into adulthood.

Then any new task may carry the perceived threat of failure, generating anxiety that makes learning or acquisition of competencies more difficult. Identifying and challenging negative predictions about future learning by examining one's actual performance takes practice. Gradually, a person can move from "I am a failure, I am never good enough, I will mess this next task up"—to—"I have passed most of my courses, even at times when I failed a test or two, so it is most likely that I will pass this one." Over time, developing this skill releases energy that can be expended on learning.

Developing self-soothing behaviors and thoughts is a next step in preparing to engage learning competencies with less anxiety. Such behaviors can be found with a little research and may include meditation, prayer, breathing exercises, seeing anxiety as excitement, and changing negative predictions to realistic positive predictions. They also include general health practices, getting enough sleep, exercise, eating well, and positive social relationships. Another powerful, soothing thought is to recognize that learning competence is a multi-stage process, as explained in the next section. Giving oneself permission to learn over time through different levels reduces the self-imposed, unrealistic expectation of performing perfectly as soon as possible.

## LEARNING COMPETENCE

Essential competencies of chaplains include behaviors that build healthy relationships of trust, honesty, fidelity, respect, mutuality, open communication, and love. This love seeks to understand the worldview of patients and joins them in discovering a path forward.

My previous patient encounter illustrates what management expert Martin M. Broadwell described as a four-level process of developing competence:[22]

---

[22] Martin M. Broadwell, "Teaching for Learning (XVI)," *The Gospel Guardian* (20 February 1969), http://wordsfitlyspoken.org/gospel_guardian/v20/v20n41p1-3a.html, accessed 21 July 2020. Broadwell was president of the Center for Management Services, Inc. He defined Unconscious Competence as a good teacher who doesn't know why he is good. I prefer the later development of this concept; one who has practiced a skill so long that the person no longer has to be conscious of

1. Unconscious Incompetence: "I don't know what I don't know."[23] I was unconsciously naive. I thought competent chaplains shared their faith and reassured patients of excellent doctors and nursing care. If you ask why sharing one's faith and assuring a hospital patient of great care may not be a sign of a competent chaplain, that is a good question. I also had to ask that question. I became aware that I had more to learn.

2. Conscious Incompetence: "I know that I don't know." My encounter with the angry patient and later clinical feedback taught me that my well-intentioned "pastoral care" may have done more harm than good. I experienced an uncomfortable dissonance between my self-image of being a competent chaplain and the reality of my incompetence. With new self-awareness, I had a choice to make. My internal insecurity and need to be perfect tempted me to see my supervisor's feedback as proof that I was not good enough. I believed I was a failure and did not deserve mentoring. I considered denying this new reality of my incompetence. I could choose to blame the patient, and defend my self-image, or I could embrace the possibility of new learning. With significant apprehension, I chose the latter, asking for honest feedback from those who knew more about chaplaincy than I did. I reflected on what I heard from my supervisor and peers and prayerfully sought additional wisdom. I asked myself several questions. How had I come to my beliefs? How had those beliefs helped me in the past? Why did they not serve me and, more importantly, my patients now? I tried new behaviors with subsequent patients and paid attention to the results. These efforts led me to learn new competencies.

3. Conscious Competence: "I am learning." As I became aware that my false reassurances grew out of my anxiety, I could consciously

---

its performance. This does not rule out a conscious, observant self who steps in to amend or correct that skill when contexts dictate revision.

[23] Initial quotes for each arena are from Seth Eisenberg, PAIRS ESSENTIALS, A PAIRS Curriculum for Successful Relationships, The PAIRS Foundation (Hollywood, FL: PAIRS Foundation, 2010–2012), 12.

decide how to calm myself. My supervisor helped me understand the difference between empathy and sympathy and feeling sorry for or compassion for the patient. Such self-examination was hard work, as I realized how much I had to learn and felt the pain of being less competent than I thought. I continually assessed my interactions, knowing that my motivation was to act in the patient's best interest and was interlaced with my personal history. I tried to treat myself nonjudgmentally, to trust that I could learn over time. When I embraced my fear and anxiety, and practiced empathic presence, I noticed my patients seemed to benefit more from my visits. They asked to see me again. As difficult as it was to grow in self-awareness, self-examination, and anxiety containment, it was all the more rewarding to see patients taking comfort from my visits.

4. Unconscious Competence: "I know it and can do it almost automatically." My competence grew, in fits and starts, certainly not in a linear way. I began to see patterns in my behavior, generated by my anxiety. I learned and practiced reflective listening. I learned to tailor my responses to patients' expressed and, at times, real but unstated needs. I had to work to let go of feeling responsible to "fix" the patient.

Chaplains become more skilled as they accept feedback from pastoral care professionals, peers, patients, and staff. Their expertise increases as they study the field and practice self-observation and reflection. After much work, chaplains may become proficient in providing spiritual care with little conscious thought and much less anxiety. That journey is grounded in growing self-awareness and acceptance of one's real, less-than-perfect self, in letting go of an idealized self. Increasing the capacity to accept oneself increases the desire to serve others and the ability to accept patients as they are. Over time, that service may expand to meet the needs of the institution and community and teach others the competencies the chaplain has learned.

## DO I HAVE WHAT IT TAKES?

How positively can you answer these questions? Do I feel called to be a chaplain? Does my faith community support my decision? Do I understand what is motivating me to consider chaplaincy? Am I open to constructive feedback and critique? Am I willing to grow in self-awareness and learn the competencies required to become a chaplain? Faith groups, board-certifying agencies, and hiring organizations establish the standards for qualified chaplains. Prospective applicants should ask these groups for their lists of competencies and how they assess and document qualified candidates.

If you intend to pursue chaplaincy education, do a self-assessment. First, write brief answers to the questions above. Second, rate yourself using the competencies described in Appendix 1. Do not be discouraged if you do not understand some of the competencies. Third, after rating yourself, consult with someone who knows you well: an educator, counselor, or pastor. Ask them to assess you using the same list of competencies and request their feedback. Comparing your ranking with theirs may give you insight regarding your level of self-awareness. Additionally, you may discover blind spots warranting your attention. If you are unconsciously incompetent in every category, you likely have much to learn about yourself and chaplaincy. That is where almost everyone begins. On the other hand, if you discover little interest in chaplain competencies, you may need to explore other vocations.

## WHO SHOULD NOT BECOME A CHAPLAIN?

Chaplaincy is not for everyone. Therefore, it begs the question: Who should seriously consider not becoming a chaplain?

- Those who feel compelled to persuade others to adopt specific religious or faith beliefs. Chaplains are often seen as authorities by those in their care. At the same time, patients, prisoners, and military personnel depend upon the goodwill of the institutions that serve them. They may feel the need to accommodate chaplains who subtly or directly coerce them to change their religious beliefs. Unilateral, unsolicited attempts to alter beliefs of those dependent upon institutional care are considered unprofessional, coercive, unethical, and abusive.
- Those who need to be the sole leader. Chaplains are team players, not autocrats.

- Those who chafe under authority. Chaplains report to faith groups, serve with the endorsement of professional associations, and work under supervision of their hiring institutions. Thus, chaplains answer to secular, professional, and religious authorities, as well as their deity.
- Those who are not lifelong learners or think they already know all it takes to be effective. Chaplaincy is an evolving profession. The requirements to maintain professional competency and to accommodate cultural needs and institutional life are continually changing.
- Those who do not wish to be accountable and refuse to document their work.
- Those who do not embrace multicultural, multifaith environments.
- Those who are unable regularly to deal with trauma, death, or life-changing conditions.

I enjoyed the blessings of being a chaplain. Chaplaincy has met my need to serve others and grow in my understanding of science, medicine, religion, spirituality, relationships, and myself. Chaplains serve in a wide variety of settings. Becoming a competent and professional, board-certified chaplain requires learning from a community of educators, peers, faith groups, educational institutions, staff, and those served. Each entity makes unique contributions to help chaplains become proficient, competent, and confident in providing pastoral care. As you explore the competencies in the appendix, blessings to you in making decisions about your vocational journey.

## REFLECTION QUESTIONS

1. Remember someone whose presence or actions consoled or strengthened you. Write a paragraph describing how you were helped by what they did, how they listened, or what they said or didn't say. Be specific.
2. How do you know when you are feeling anxious? How do you respond to others whose situation or behavior raises anxiety in you? What do you do to soothe yourself when you feel anxious?
3. Different organizations and authors approach competencies for chaplains from various perspectives. As you reflect on the list of competencies articulated by Dick Millspaugh, how does it compare or contrast with any other

list (for example, The Association of Professional Chaplains) of chaplaincy competencies?
4. From Dick Millspaugh's list of competencies, what three competencies do you believe are the most important to chaplains and why? Would your three competencies change in importance as one's primary role or level of responsibility evolve within the institution?
5. Dick Millspaugh states, "Chaplaincy is not for everyone," and lists seven questions one should answer to clarify who should not become a chaplain. Pick two and articulate whether you agree or disagree with the assessment.

## MEMORABLE MOMENT
## "CHANGE HIS CIRCUMSTANCES"

### Chaplain R. Michael Warner

While awaiting military transportation in Kampala, Uganda, I walked downtown to locate something for dinner. A beggar seemed to go unnoticed at a busy intersection among a sea of people. Since he had no legs, his situation struck me as desperate.

Watching the beggar, the Holy Spirit urged me to change his circumstances. "OK," I said to myself. "On the way back, I'll give him something." On the return trip, he was still invisible to the crowd, so I reached into my pocket and gave the beggar 20,000 Uganda shillings (about twenty US dollars). Later, I learned that amount was about one week's average wage for Ugandans. No wonder he looked at me with such excitement.

Perhaps feeling a bit self-satisfied, I pressed on toward my hotel. Within a few steps, the Holy Spirit nudged me again, "You didn't understand me ... I want to change his circumstances." I silently responded, "What? What do you mean? Lord, I don't understand. I gave him money." The Lord repeated the instruction, "I want to change his circumstances." As a foreigner far from home, I wondered how one person could change a beggar's circumstances.

Back at the hotel, my Ugandan colleague, Godfrey, suggested we learn the beggar's story and perhaps what he needed. Godfrey agreed to interpret the conversation. As we talked, a large crowd stopped to listen. We learned Sekerena (beggar's name) made his way to Kampala from Rwanda after watching the murder of his entire family. When the attackers turned their machetes on him, somehow he survived the amputation of both legs. In Kampala, his only source of income was what people gave him.

Hearing his story moved one in the crowd to speak up, "I own a business that sells cards for cell phone minutes. I'll provide you with a distributorship to sell at this intersection. You can earn up to 100,000 Uganda shillings per month."

We then discovered that Sekerena had no home. He lived in the bushes several feet away.

Someone in the crowd responded, "I own an apartment building a few blocks from here. We have one apartment open. I can give you the first three months for free. After that, you will pay 20,000 shillings per month."

But how would Sekerena move around, someone asked? One in the crowd offered, "I know where we can get a wheelchair." That kind stranger went off to get him transportation.

Sekerena wept. His world changed. He woke up that morning without hope—homeless, jobless, without transportation. He would sleep that night with newfound hope—a roof over his head, a source of income, and a method to get around.

Sekerena looked at me through tears and asked, "Why would you do this?"

I assured him, "It wasn't me, Sekerena. It was God who wanted to change your circumstances. His name is Jesus. He came to save His people."

Breaking a brief silence, one in the crowd asked, "Sekerena, would you like to learn more about Jesus? I am a member of a Catholic parish down the street. I can take you, if you like."

"Yes, I would like that very much," he said.

As the Lord does so often, multiple lives were changed as they responded to the urging of the Holy Spirit. Sekerena's life changed. Those in the crowd who heard and gave graciously changed. Perhaps others in the crowd, who witnessed God moving in Sekerena's life, changed. And indeed, God reminded an Air Force chaplain that changing someone's circumstances may involve more than giving a few dollars to a disabled beggar.

As you listen to the leading of the Holy Spirit, I wonder how God may want to change your circumstances, or perhaps how God would like to change someone else's circumstances through you.

# SECTION TWO

# WHAT ARE THE FOUNDATIONS OF CHAPLAIN MINISTRY?

CHAPTER FOUR

# SPIRITUAL FOUNDATION

### Dr. Jim Spivey

Chaplains fulfill a sacred calling to accompany and provide professional support and spiritual nurture for everyone in their distinctive, secular communities, which authorize their ministry and hold them accountable.

A "sacred calling" suggests this ministry is a holy undertaking. Chaplains are first grounded in a personal relationship with God, from whom we sense a call to divine destiny.[24] We have roots in a community of faith,[25] in which we sense a holy summons to ministerial service.[26] Like all pastoral work, chaplain ministry is not just an occupation but a "vocation" by which God calls us to a sacred trust. It is also unique. Unlike most other ministers, we serve "at large" in pluralistic institutions outside traditional parochial settings.[27]

Chaplains "accompany" people. Though we are religious leaders, we function more as shepherds who walk alongside our flocks[28]—as servant-leaders, not authoritarian chiefs.[29] We are like pilots who steer among and in front of people rather than being religious bosses who rule over them. Chaplains walk alongside others as friends,[30] for whom we should be willing

---

[24] Eph 4:4; Phil 3:14; Heb 3:1
[25] Acts 2:41–42; 1 Cor 1:2, 12; Eph 1:19–22; 1 Pet 2:9
[26] Rom 1:1; 1 Cor 1:1; 1 Tim 1:9–11; 1 Tim 4:14
[27] Eph 4:11–12
[28] John 21:15–17; Acts 20:28; 1 Pet 5:1–4
[29] Num 12:3; Mark 10:42–45; Luke 22:26; John 13:5–17
[30] Luke 24:13–35; John 15:13–15

to make personal sacrifices, as yokefellows who share their burdens,[31] and as intercessors who pray for them.[32]

Chaplains "provide professional support" in secular and religious life. We capably employ natural talents, technical skills, and spiritual gifts to help our institutions accomplish their missions with excellence and to serve as visible, vocal reminders of holy matters.[33] In our secular capacity, we should excel as administrators, staff advisors, supervisors, and advocates of our institutions. We also are religious experts who fulfill pastoral and prophetic functions and serve as ethical guides and spiritual mentors. In both institutional and religious settings, we ought to model proficiency, integrity, industry, godly character, and constructive moral influence.[34]

Chaplains provide "spiritual nurture" in three ways: religious care, pastoral care, and spiritual care. Religious care addresses the needs of specific faith groups. In doing so, chaplains function as congregational leaders who preach, teach, intercede, administer rituals, shepherd parishioners, advocate distinctive religious beliefs and mentor like-minded faith-group ministers.

Pastoral and spiritual care includes but extends beyond the faith-group setting. Pastoral care meets the practical and emotional needs of anyone in the institution. Spiritual care deals with existential matters: introspective questions such as personal identity, connectedness with others, destiny, transcendental issues, and relationship with the divine. Chaplains provide both pastoral and spiritual care in many modes. As ministers, pastors, and moral leaders, we serve, shepherd, and provide ethical guidance for the whole community. As spiritual healers, we comfort, listen, encourage, and provide a ministry of divine presence to all persons. On an individual basis, we counsel, advocate, give practical assistance, and may provide pastoral support to institutional leaders regardless of their faith-group affiliations.

Several biblical motifs serve as guides for exemplary spiritual nurturing. As "shepherds," chaplains should nourish, protect, and care for all persons in their charge—not just members of their faith group but everyone in the

---

[31] Matt 11:28–30; Gal 6:2
[32] Eph 6:18; 1 Tim 2:1; Jas 5:16
[33] Exod 31:1–6; Matt 25:14–30; Rom 12:4–8; 1 Cor 12
[34] Prov 22:29; Eccl 9:10; Matt 5:16; Col 3:23; 1 Tim 3:7; Titus 2:7–8

institution.[35] We are "servant-helpers" who minister not just to spiritual but also physical and emotional needs.[36] As "prophets," we are agents of change who model compassion, justice, and humility, who set a good ethical example, proclaim God's Word consistently, and speak with moral authority.[37] We are "healers" who bring solace to troubled souls.[38] As "heralds," we proclaim good news.[39] In appropriate contexts, we "evangelize," but our good news encompasses more than messages of spiritual salvation. It includes relieving the poor, encouraging the dispossessed, helping to free people from oppression and depression, inspiring them with a vision of hope, and giving them a sense of final purpose.[40]

Chaplains serve "everyone" because all persons are created in the image of God.[41] Each person has equal value before God, equal access to God, and equal accountability under God. Chaplains pray for everyone and share God's message in respectful, non-coercive ways with anyone willing to listen.[42] We do so in "distinctive, secular communities" where parish ministers rarely venture. The population is diverse in culture, ethnicity, and gender orientation. The religious setting is pluralistic—with many faiths and people of no faith. Chaplains respond to a divine mandate to be messengers in the everyday marketplaces of life.[43] We act as God's agents of transformation. Our immediate goal is to minister to anyone in need, regardless of background. We support every person's right to free exercise of religion and willingly accept the fact that this inevitably results in a pluralistic religious setting. Some chaplains are comfortable with this end-state and become advocates of pluralism itself. Others view pluralism as a natural consequence of free exercise and as a current condition but not as a goal. Their ultimate objective is not to sustain the

---

[35] Ps 23; John 10:1–18; 21:15–17; Acts 20:28; 1 Pet 5:2
[36] Matt 25:34–40
[37] Mic 6:8; 2 Tim 4:2; Titus 2:15
[38] Isa 61:1–2; Mark 6:12–13; Luke 10:30–37; 2 Cor 1:3–4
[39] Mark 1:14–15; Mark 6:4; Rom 10:14–15
[40] Luke 4:18–19
[41] Gen 1:27; 1 Tim 2:3–4; 2 Pet 3:9
[42] 2 Tim 2:24–25; 1 Pet 3:15
[43] Mark 16:15

status quo[44] but to fulfill a divine commission to make disciples of the God who has called them.[45]

Chaplains are employed by institutions that "authorize" and "hold them accountable." We are sent to the field by faith groups that endorse us. We maintain our "endorsement," and therefore employability, by staying in affiliation and good standing with our faith groups. However, it is the secular institution that employs and authorizes us as ministers and official representatives.

As a result, chaplains conform to organizational rules and submit to persons of authority who hold us accountable.[46] One model for this relationship is the ancient "household code" enjoining servants to obey their masters.[47] The parallel in the modern workplace is for chaplains as employees to obey employers. Yet, chaplains still come under God's authority. This raises the issue of dual loyalty and role conflict. Chaplains' first loyalty, or liege homage, should be to God.[48] Of course, we should do nothing that disobeys His Word, contravenes His will, or violates our religious consciences. And we should take care not to compromise our confessional doctrines or practices in ways that might jeopardize our faith-group endorsement.[49]

## REFLECTION QUESTIONS

1. Jim Spivey states a chaplain's ministry is not just an occupation but a vocation by which God calls us to a sacred trust. How would you define "sacred trust" and what place does it have in being a chaplain?
2. Jim Spivey stated, "Chaplains serve everyone because all persons are created in the image of God." Can you identify a group or a type of individuals who would be difficult for you to serve?

---

[44] Matt 10: 34–39; John 17:13–19; Rom 12:2; Eph 4:25
[45] Matt 28:18–20; Mark 13:10; Acts 1:8
[46] Rom 13:1–7; Titus 3:1–2; Heb 13:17; 1 Pet 2:13–17
[47] Eph 6:5–8; Col 3:22; 1 Tim 6:1; Titus 2:9–10
[48] Acts 4:19–20; 5:29
[49] 2 Tim 1:13; 3:14–15; Titus 1:9

CHAPTER FIVE

# CONSTITUTIONAL FOUNDATION

## Dr. Jim Spivey

The constitutional foundation for chaplain ministry begins with the First Amendment, particularly the first two clauses: "Congress shall make no law respecting an establishment of religion or prohibiting the free exercise thereof." The "establishment" clause forbids state-sponsored religion, while the "free exercise" clause prevents governmental infringement on religious liberty.

Originally, these provisions pertained only to the federal government. This meant states were still permitted to support government-sponsored churches with public funds. Though three states continued to do so, they eventually defunded their churches: Connecticut in 1818, New Hampshire in 1819, and Massachusetts in 1833.

Even as state constitutions were revised to strengthen guarantees of religious liberty, statutory enforcement was not uniform or rigorous. This situation began to change with passage of the Fourteenth Amendment in 1868. It forbids states to "make or enforce any law which shall abridge the privileges or immunities of citizens of the United States," or "to deprive any person of life, liberty, or property without due process of law." However, even this legislation did not guarantee uniform enforcement. That did not occur until methods of applying each right were tested for constitutionality and "incorporated" by various Supreme Court decisions.

The two religion clauses operate in tension: excessive enforcement of one can intrude on the other, especially in institutional chaplaincy. Underlying this tension is the relationship between the state as an institution and religion as a cultural phenomenon. How we view this connection depends on how we answer two questions. First, should government emphasize "free exercise" enough to encourage an environment that favors religion in general? Or should it stress "no establishment" to the point of radical secularism that distances the state totally from anything remotely religious? The first position results in a "benevolent neutrality" that encourages religion to flourish. The most extreme form of the second position is a "hostile separation" that tries to make society thoroughly secular by preventing any intrusion of religion upon it.

The First Amendment suggests government should be benevolently neutral toward religion. But if laws push this to the point of publicly funding religious groups, nonreligious persons will accuse the state of establishing a civil religion. On the other hand, if the state enforces "no establishment" too strictly, with a clinical, dispassionate mindset, it inevitably treads upon free exercise of religion.

The scope of the two clauses covers three aspects of constitutional freedom: (1) for us as individuals to believe freely and act reasonably according to our religious consciences; (2) for religious groups to express their beliefs and act corporately, unimpeded by governmental intrusion; (3) for democratic government to function effectively and without prejudice resulting from inappropriate religious intervention.

The First Amendment stands as a safeguard for religious and political freedom, while still allowing religion and politics to influence each other. This fact produces opposing views about the proper relationship between church and state. Some say the Establishment Clause requires organizational separation of church from state and prohibits state funding of religious groups.

Others say the state should accommodate people's free exercise by providing funding if this can be done fairly. There is a tension between these two positions that has produced a wide spectrum of interpretation—from "hostile separation" at one end, to a radical call for "theocracy" at the other extreme. In its numerous decisions on the subject, the Supreme Court has vacillated near the center between moderate forms of separation and accommodation, depending on the technical, legal merits of each case.

Our right to "free exercise" is not just liberty to believe but also to act on our beliefs. That right to action is explicitly stated in the rest of the First Amendment, which secures the rights of speech, press, peaceable assembly, and petition. So, we are free to preach and teach religious ideas; to publish religious material; to assemble in churches, synagogues, mosques, and temples; and to petition the government when our religious rights have been abridged. Yet, none of these rights is absolute. The Supreme Court has ruled we are not permitted to act in ways that violate proper social duties or present a grave and immediate danger to national interests.

The nature of these rights is not contractual, and their source is not the government. The preamble states six purposes of the Constitution, the last being "to secure the Blessings of Liberty to ourselves and to our Posterity." Liberty is a blessing—and blessings are not earned or negotiated through a quid pro quo agreement. They are gifts, not the result of a social contract. Nor do they originate with the government. The Constitution secures our rights and obligates the state to guard them; neither it nor government has authority to grant liberty. The Declaration of Independence states, "all men are created equal, that they are endowed by their Creator with certain unalienable Rights, that among these are Life, Liberty and the pursuit of Happiness." So, the blessings of liberty originate with God, who grants them by grace. When making this point in *The Rights of Conscience Inalienable* (1791), John Leland added, if we concede the state has the power to grant freedom, we assume it also has the right to withdraw it. Any attempt to compel or restrain individual conscience violates a basic human right and usurps God's authority.

## IS CHAPLAIN MINISTRY CONSTITUTIONAL?

Arguments have been raised against government paying chaplains to provide religious services because this violates the Establishment Clause and state-church separation. However, it is thoroughly constitutional. In most institutional settings, access to public religious services is limited. This is particularly true in closed settings such as the military. During deployment, ministry can be provided effectively only by persons hired and trained in that setting specifically for that purpose. Elimination of military chaplaincy would severely limit service members' right of "free exercise."

There is another equally cogent reason: military chaplains are indispensable to the enforcement of the "establishment" clause. As religious advisors to commanders, they work to prevent establishment of a civil religion and to protect the rights of persons who practice no religion. The same rationale applies to correctional facilities. Since the state incarcerates persons involuntarily in closed settings, prison chaplains are needed to meet inmates' religious needs and to prevent establishment.

Public institutions with chaplains conform to the First Amendment in direct proportion to the amount of oversight and funding they receive from the government and to the degree they operate as closed systems. Hospitals employ chaplains as specially trained ministers to care for people in semiclosed clinical environments. Those receiving public funds come under closer scrutiny for adherence to the First Amendment. The same is true of chaplains serving in publicly funded law enforcement, firefighting, and disaster relief agencies operating in pluralistic settings. Situations vary in the corporate world, depending on company policies, and in private hospitals and hospices, which may establish less restrictive guidelines for chaplains.

Chaplains in public institutions are obliged to protect the religious rights of everyone in those settings by facilitating everyone's "free exercise" and preventing "establishment." They do so in their roles as (1) faith-group representatives, (2) ministers to individuals, (3) chaplains to the whole community, and (4) institutional professionals.

## PROVIDING FREE EXERCISE

As faith-group representatives, chaplains provide "free exercise" by delivering faith-based ministry to members of their own denomination and people from a broader but similar religious background, such as General Protestant, Roman Catholic, Orthodox, Jewish, or Muslim. As ministers to individuals, we do so by helping, counseling, comforting, encouraging, and bringing spiritual healing to all organizational members, regardless of religious background. We also advocate for individuals with special religious needs by informing the institution and doing whatever possible to make sure those needs are met.

As community chaplains, we do three things. First, we provide for the religious needs of the whole institution beyond our faith groups. When not authorized to perform certain actions for other religious groups, we arrange for other chaplains or ministers to meet those needs. Second, for all members of the institution, we perform religious functions such as public prayer and memorial services. Third, when allowed by the institution, we may provide ministry to adjacent communities outside the institution.

As institutional professionals, chaplains provide "free exercise" by advising leaders about the religious needs of the whole institution, developing a plan to meet those needs, and making sure all members of the institution have equal access to ministry. We supervise subordinate chaplains, integrate them into the plan, ensure their rights are protected, and encourage them to provide free exercise for everyone in the institution. Regarding policies, chaplains advise leaders how to afford everyone religious freedom without compromising the mission, disturbing good order and discipline, or straining resources.

Five Supreme Court guidelines regarding the limits and extension of free exercise are helpful at this point. (1) It is permissible for persons to believe as they desire but not to act on those beliefs in ways that are illegal or inappropriate for the institutional setting. (2) Religious activities should be permitted if they are not dangerous and do not jeopardize the mission. (3) Institutional policies should be written with neutrality in mind; they should not intentionally discriminate against anyone's religious beliefs. (4) If policies infringe on religious beliefs, they should be rewritten in least restrictive, alternative ways that still allow mission accomplishment. (5) If policies cannot be rewritten to accommodate religious beliefs, the institution may retain those policies only if it has a compelling interest at stake.

## PREVENTING ESTABLISHMENT

As faith-group ministers, chaplains guard against "establishment" by not exceeding our authority or pushing our own perspective as normative for the rest of the community. We respect beliefs and practices of other faith groups and work collegially alongside their chaplains. Though permitted to share our own beliefs with others, we do not inappropriately proselytize members of other faith groups who are not seeking those answers. As ministers to individuals, chaplains do not manipulate personal encounters (counseling, comforting, helping, or spiritual healing) to push our own beliefs on others. We do not take advantage of personal relationships with leaders to advance our own religious agendas or those of our leaders. When we conduct public rites and ceremonies as community ministers, we do so with appropriate sensitivity to those present and consideration of whether attendance is voluntary or mandatory. As institutional professionals, chaplains advise leaders against policies favoring certain religions or reflecting majoritarian views that ignore the needs of religious minorities. We ensure the institutional ministry plan is designed to serve everyone's needs and require subordinate chaplains to support those policies.

Chaplains walk a fine line regarding "no establishment." We guard against preferential treatment for religious groups and protect nonbelievers against systemic religious intrusion. But we should not side with hostile separationists who disallow any institutional support of religion. As institutional professionals, we should remain benevolently neutral about specific religions and support an atmosphere that allows them an equal opportunity to flourish. As faith-group leaders, we budget for institutional resources to support religious programs that fulfill our prophetic and pastoral functions.

Our other roles regarding no establishment are more nuanced. Again, Supreme Court guidelines are helpful here. As community chaplains performing public ceremonies, we should consider the context. Is attendance mandatory or voluntary, and is it a religious or a nonreligious event? If mandatory and nonreligious, we should consider the "secular purpose" and "primary effect" tests; religious activities are allowed in such settings if they are intended to accomplish a secular purpose and if the primary effect is not to advance religion. As institutional professionals advising leaders about what support is permissible in the public arena, we should consider the "excessive entanglement" test; policies that incidentally accommodate religion may be allowed if stopping that support would excessively entangle the institution with religious groups.

## REFLECTION QUESTIONS

1. After learning that you are studying to become a chaplain, a friend at work exclaims, "If your income as a chaplain is with tax dollars, it must be unconstitutional because it violates the Establishment Clause and state-church separation." How would you respond to your friend?
2. In public ceremony settings, where mandatory attendance is required, how might chaplains adhere to their faith tenets while being appropriately sensitive to all those present?

CHAPTER SIX

# HISTORICAL FOUNDATION

Dr. Jim Spivey

When tracing the historical roots of modern chaplaincy, three facts set the parameters of the search. First, chaplains are not primarily secular agents but religious ministers; we are not priests of a civil religion, and our purpose is not to sustain an established religion. Second, chaplains are not primarily denominational agents. We represent faith groups but minister to persons of all faiths and are employed by secular institutions, not denominations. Third, we minister in pluralistic, secular settings beyond parish life. These facts suggest we should not trace modern chaplaincy to ancient and medieval religious ministries in civil, military, and hospital settings. Some of those patterns influenced modern language and attitudes about chaplaincy, but their civil-religious nature was incongruent with modern chaplaincy. We should be mindful of those patterns but not rely on them to define or defend modern chaplaincy.

## PREVIOUS PATTERNS

In the Old Testament, Levites occasionally carried the Ark of the Covenant into battle. But this was not normative throughout Israelite history, and it was theocratic in nature, not a religious ministry in a secular setting. Later, court prophets advised kings, but as part of a corrupt civil-religious establishment that compromised most prophets. Ancient pagan societies were governed by civil-religious codes administered by civil rulers who served as titular heads of priesthoods, like Roman emperors who bore the title *pontifex maximus*. Roman commanders provided soldiers with religious rites, but as part of a state-regulated cult. Constantine imported this pagan pattern into the early church. His army camps were attended by deacons and priests, and by the fifth century, Roman units had assigned priests with free-standing chapels. Invading Gothic armies were accompanied by Arian bishops. All these practices derived from state-churches headed by civil rulers, a pattern perpetuated by the medieval Roman Catholic church.

Religious hospital ministry began in the fourth century. Bishop Basil of Caesarea (d. 369) first established a hospital at his basilica and set a pattern for other eastern bishops like Ephraim of Edessa. By the sixth century there were thirty-five hospitals in Constantinople alone. The first western hospitals were established in the fifth century by Roman noblewoman Fabiola and Roman senator-monk Pammachius—a pattern continued by popes through the eighth century. During the fifth and sixth centuries the movement spread to Gaul and Spain.

The prototype for western chaplaincy was Martin of Tours (d. 397). The Hungarian son of a Roman tribune raised in northern Italy, he served in the Roman cavalry in Gaul against the Visigoths. About 361, he converted to Christianity. His encounter with a freezing beggar outside Amiens led him to cut his cloak in two and share half with the poor man. That evening, Jesus appeared in a dream, wearing the cloak and commending him from Matthew 25. This confirmed Martin's commitment to Christ, and he was baptized. After leaving the army, he became a disciple of Bishop Hilary of Poitiers. As a hermitic monk, he founded one of the earliest monasteries in France, at Ligugé, before being appointed as bishop of Tours. His half-cape, or *capella*, was kept at Marmoutier Abbey near Tours. It became a holy relic of Merovingian Frankish kings, who took it into battle and swore oaths upon it. Charlemagne relocated it to Saint-Denis Abbey near Paris. The priest who maintained it bore the title *cappellanu*, and eventually all priests serving in the Carolingian army were known as *cappellani* (Fr. *chapelains*; Eng. *chaplains*). When deployed to the field of battle, it was housed in a tent known as the *capella*—or chapel.

During the Carolingian era, two key events regularized ministry to the military. First, the Concilium Germanicum at Ratisbon (742) under Archbishop Boniface of Mainz, outlined duties of spiritual care to Frankish soldiers. This formed the legal basis for the chaplain's office in medieval Roman Catholicism. Chaplains were to carry holy relics in the field, celebrate mass, hear confession, assign penance, and not to bear arms. Second, in the mid-ninth century, Deacon Benedict of Mainz edited the most complete description of chaplain duties in canon law. Though papal policy forbade priests serving in the military, this rule, designed to prevent clergy from bearing arms, allowed some bishops to do strictly religious work: to preach, bless troops, work for reconciliation, and provide mass, penance, and extreme unction. Later, bishops and popes issued similar guidelines. Bishop Burchard of Worms (d. 1025) included guidelines for chaplains in his *Decretum*, teaching clergy how to be bishops. Bishop Ivo of Chartres's *Decretum* (1095) outlined duties of chaplains accompanying the First Crusade. At the Fourth Lateran Council (1215), Pope Innocent III authorized chaplains for the Fifth Crusade. Gregory IX in a papal bull (1238) outlined duties for Dominican and Franciscan chaplains serving in the Hungarian army.

Medieval healthcare ministry was revived under Charlemagne, who decreed (789) that all cathedrals and monasteries should run hospitals. The Councils of Aachen (817 and 836) required all collegiate churches to follow suit. During the tenth to twelfth centuries four patterns developed to provide spiritual cure for illness: monastic infirmaries, cathedral/collegiate hospitals, hospitals run by lay/religious orders, and military hospital orders supporting crusades. The Fourth Lateran Council (1215) recognized a closer relationship between physicians and clergy, but priority was still placed on spiritual cure. City hospitals emerged in the thirteenth century: clergy remained involved, but civil authorities managed them, and more emphasis was put on medical care.

State-church chaplaincy continued well into the Reformation era. One of the most notable Catholic chaplains was Ulrich Zwingli, who ministered to Swiss soldiers in service of the pope. Shaken by their loss and senseless slaughter at the Battle of Marignano, he resigned and opposed the mercenary trade but kept his pension for five years until he began the Reformation in Zurich. Ironically, he was killed at the Battle of Kappel (German for chapel) while ministering to Zurich troops defeated by a Catholic army. Protestant armies also had chaplains. During the English Civil War (1642–46) each Royalist regiment had one Anglican priest, while the Parliamentary army was served by Presbyterian, Congregational, and Baptist ministers. The Reformation changed the complexion of hospital chaplaincy. Health care in all Protestant lands became secularized. In England, the Royal College of Physicians regulated the medical profession, new hospitals came under municipal authority, and city officials became responsible for poor relief. Conversely, Catholic bishops at the Council of Trent (1545–63) implemented strict measures of accountability for hospitals. But in France, management of health care passed to the crown and the king resisted oversight by the Catholic Church.

## MODERN MILITARY

Modern chaplaincy traces its roots to the colonial American militia. The first chaplains served in Connecticut (1637), and 115 militia chaplains served in the colonial wars from 1636 to 1768. Revolutionary War chaplaincy began without denominational impetus. Recruitment was done by militia members, and most of the chaplains were their pastors. Some state legislatures like Virginia appointed regimental chaplains; others were selected by local militia commanders or ship captains. On 29 July 1775, the Second Continental Congress established the Army chaplaincy, the second oldest branch (after the infantry) of the US Army. Each regiment was to have a chaplain, who was a commissioned officer and paid $20 per month. On 28 November 1775, Navy regulations established a chaplaincy when ship captains were required to provide daily religious services and pay was fixed at $20 per month. Since the federal government did not regulate the ministry, local policies varied regarding qualifications and recruitment. George Washington required that they should (1) be gentlemen of ability and exceptional character who would influence behavior of the corps by precept and example, and (2) be able to minister to a regiment or brigade in the manner to which they were accustomed. Even before the Constitution was drafted, Washington explicitly stated his support for "free exercise" of religion in the Army.

In the 1790s, Congress renewed this level of authorization for military chaplains, but in 1808 it was changed to one chaplain per brigade. The number of brigades was increased during the War of 1812, but after the war, only one chaplain (at West Point) was authorized for the reduced standing army. Congress increased the number to twenty chaplains to cover military garrisons in 1838. In 1841, the Navy required chaplains to be ordained or licensed clergymen, but the Attorney General later ruled the Navy could not require this. During the Mexican War (1846–48), Catholic priests were allowed to serve as chaplains by presidential appointment.

In 1861, the Union Army authorized thirty chaplains for its regular corps and one for each of its 650 volunteer regiments. Regimental chaplains were commissioned and paid $1,700 per year. They had to be ordained by an acceptable denomination, approved by the state governor, elected by unit officers, and appointed by the commander. In 1862, standards were raised: endorsement required a denominational statement of good standing or five testimonials from ministers in good standing; a fitness evaluation was done after thirty days' service; and pay was lowered to $1,200 (plus a $200 allowance). Twenty-five hundred chaplains served in the Union Army. In 1861, the Confederacy authorized one chaplain per regiment, to be paid $960 per year. Between six hundred and one thousand chaplains served in the Confederate Army. Many more ministers served as voluntary camp missionaries and sparked a revival that led to 150,000 conversions. During the Civil War, Catholic priests, Black ministers, and Jewish rabbis were first commissioned as chaplains.

In 1872, Congress set the first federal standards for Army chaplains, requiring ordination or its equivalent and denominational endorsement or approval by five accredited ministers. In 1880, those standards were applied to the Navy, plus one year of pastoral experience. In 1899, Army candidates were required to pass an entry examination for moral, mental, and physical fitness. In 1908, the Navy established a Board of Chaplains to approve credentials. In 1917, Captain John Frazier was appointed as the first Navy chief of chaplains. Three years later the Army appointed Colonel John Axton as its first chief of chaplains. Chaplain ministry in the Department of Veteran Affairs (VA) traces its roots back to 1865, when chaplains were paid $1,500 per year to serve National Homes for Disabled Veteran Soldiers. In 1944, VA chaplains came under the General Commission on Chaplains and Armed Forces Personnel. The next year, Crawford Brown was appointed as the first National Director of the VA Chaplain Service, and VA chaplains were placed in all VA hospitals. The first Air Chaplain of the US Army Air Force was Captain Charles Carpenter (1942). The US Air Force became a separate branch of service in 1947, but Army chaplains continued to support the Air Force until 1949, when Major General Carpenter was appointed as its first chief of chaplains. Late in the twentieth century, Muslim, Buddhist, and Hindu chaplains were accessioned into the armed forces. Currently, the Armed Forces Chaplains Board (AFCB) oversees policy affecting religious ministry to the military services and advises the Secretary of Defense on religious, ethical, and moral matters. It is composed of the chiefs and deputy chiefs of chaplains of the Army, Navy, and Air Force.

The roots of denominational endorsement go back to 1898, when the Episcopal Church asked the government to consult with it before appointing Episcopal chaplains. In 1899 and 1901, Congress required denominations to set endorsement standards for the Army and Navy. In 1905, the US Roman Catholic bishops appointed representatives to handle appointments, and the next year, Methodist Episcopal bishops established a regulatory board. In 1914, several Protestant denominations adopted a unified approach when the Federal Council of Churches (FCC) established a six-person Washington Advisory Committee for Army and Navy Chaplains. In 1917, it was reorganized as the General Committee, representing thirty-two denominations. It accredited all Protestant candidates, who had to pass a denominational examination and possess a baccalaureate degree. During World War II, the General Committee expanded, reorganized as the General Commission on Army and Navy Chaplains, and became independent of the FCC. At that time, several other faith groups formed their own endorsement agencies.

In 1917, Pope Benedict V appointed Archbishop Patrick Hayes as Military Bishop Ordinary to lead a newly formed military Catholic diocese. Now the Roman Catholic Military Ordinariate credentials all Roman Catholic chaplains and regulates the ministry of all service members in its charge. The National Conference of Ministry to the Armed Forces (NCMAF) began as a private, nonprofit umbrella organization in 1982. It includes endorsing agents from a broad range of religious groups: Protestant, Roman Catholic, Orthodox Catholic, Jewish, Buddhist, Islamic, and Hindu. One of its standing committees, the Endorsers Conference for Veteran Affairs Chaplaincy (ECVAC), liaises between VA and American religious communities.

## MODERN HEALTH CARE

Four types of hospitals populated colonial America: (1) seaman's hospitals established by trading companies for sailors and passengers; (2) publicly funded almshouses to shelter the poor and treat contagious, mental, or chronic illness; (3) military hospitals; and (4) general hospitals to provide inpatient medical care. Hospitals were meant for lower-class or socially marginalized persons; middle- and upper-class patients were treated at home. Pastoral care in hospitals was provided by local clergy. In the nineteenth century, health care shifted from homes to hospitals of five types: (1) clinics for specialized treatment; (2) publicly funded municipal or regional general hospitals; (3) religious, nonprofit hospitals supported by denominational groups and patient fees; (4) private hospitals owned by physicians; and (5) independent, voluntary hospitals supported by public subscription and private philanthropy. Pastoral care was still provided by local clergy, not chaplains. In 1872, there were 178 hospitals in America, but during the next forty years there was explosive growth; by 1910 there were more than four thousand hospitals.

At first, pastoral care was still provided by untrained local clergy. Professional healthcare chaplaincy had no roots in previous systems; it grew out of the new "religion and healthcare" movement. Early leaders were Richard Cabot, Anton Boisen, William Keller, Helen Dunbar, and Philip Guiles. In 1925, Cabot wrote "A Plea for a Clinical Year in the Course of Theological Study," calling for seminarians to do prolonged, supervised internships in hospital settings. Boisen, a Congregational minister, started the first Clinical Pastoral Education (CPE) training at Worcester State Hospital in Massachusetts (1925). Keller, a physician, also placed theological students in a Cincinnati general hospital. Cabot, a Harvard ethics professor, medical educator, and social work pioneer, put some of his students in the first CPE program. Dunbar was a physician doing research in psychosomatic medicine. Guiles, one of Boisen's students, later taught at Andover Newton Seminary. In 1930, Boisen, Cabot, Dunbar, Guiles, and others formed the Council for Clinical Training of Theological Students (CCTTS) in Boston. Dunbar became executive director and moved the council to New York in 1932, but it split in 1935. Boisen and Dunbar remained in New York, while Cabot and Guiles stayed in Boston and formed the Institute for Pastoral Care (IPC) in 1944. In 1949, several major Lutheran groups formed the Lutheran Advisory Council (LAC) for Pastoral Care and established standards adopted by the National Conference of Certifying Associations. In 1957, a group of mostly Southern

Baptist chaplains under Wayne Oates's leadership formed the Southern Baptist Association of Clinical Pastoral Education (SBACPE). In 1967 in Kansas City, the four groups—CCTTS, IPC, LAC, and SBACPE—merged to form the Association for Clinical Pastoral Education (ACPE).

The CPE method uses intensive encounters, not books, to read "living human documents." It combines cognitive and emotive, theoretical and practical, and theological and psychological approaches to develop a realistic understanding of human nature and the art of pastoral care. The movement expanded rapidly after World War II. Original settings were mainly hospitals, where there were more pastoral opportunities than in churches. Hospitals also could afford better than churches to pay students. Until the 1950s–60s, training was largely unrelated to formal seminary training. These factors gave CPE a nonecclesiastical, secular style. The foremost CPE certifying agencies included the Association of Professional Chaplains, the National Association of Catholic Chaplains, Neshama—Association of Jewish Chaplains, Spiritual Care Association, Association of Certified Christian Chaplains, and the College of Pastoral Supervision and Psychotherapy.

Hospice chaplaincy traces its roots back to the formative work done by Dame Cicely Saunders, Elisabeth Kübler-Ross, and Florence Wald. In a lecture at Yale University in 1963, Saunders introduced the idea of specialized care for dying persons. Kübler-Ross published *On Death and Dying* (1969), which identified five stages of terminally ill patients. In 1972 she testified at a US Senate Special Committee on Aging. In 1974 Wald, Dean of Yale School of Nursing, founded the Connecticut Hospice in Branford, Connecticut, the first hospice program in the United States. The National Hospice Organization (NHO) was founded and held its first conference in 1978, the same year the US Department of Health, Education and Welfare recommended funding for hospice work. In 1979, the Health Care Financing Administration funded pilot programs, and in 1980 the Kellogg Foundation awarded a grant to develop accreditation standards for hospice programs. Congress provided Medicare support in 1982. In 1983, Medicare Hospice Regulations were published in the Federal Register, and the Joint Commission on Accreditation of Hospitals began accreditation. In 1985, states were allowed to include hospice work in Medicaid programs, and three years later, the Community Health Accreditation Program (CHAP) for hospice began. The

Department of Defense authorized funding of hospice care in military hospitals in 1991, and in 1992 the National Hospice Foundation was established. The NHO changed its name to National Hospice and Palliative Care Organization (NHPCO) in 2000 and moved its headquarter to Alexandria, Virginia, in 2008.

## MODERN WORKPLACE

Early colonial American corporate ministries were associated with exploration or local churches meeting needs of parishioners working on the frontier. Francis Fletcher, an Anglican priest, served as Sir Francis Drake's chaplain and kept a diary of their circumnavigation of the globe (1577–80). In the 1640s, Massachusetts Bay officials required employers to provide religious instruction and worship services for workers at outlying sites. Examples were Saugus Iron Works and Single Brothers' Workshop. The Saugus Iron Works (or Hammersmith Works) founded in 1646 by John Winthrop in Linn, employed immigrants, skilled workers, and indentured servants from outside Puritan society. The Single Brothers' Workshop, founded in 1769 by Moravian Brethren from Bethlehem, Pennsylvania, who settled in Salem, North Carolina, housed apprentices who learned various trades.

A nineteenth-century example in Britain was the Navvy Mission. "Navvies" worked on large civil engineering projects like canal- and railroad-building. In 1872, Elizabeth Garnett started a Sunday school to minister to them at the Lindley Wood Reservoir in Yorkshire, and Anglican vicar Lewis Evans started a fund to support the work. The movement spread until just before World War I, when navvies moved to factories or the military. Some missionaries followed them into factories as industrial chaplains. In America, the Layman Prayer Revival followed a financial panic in 1857. When Jeremiah Lanphier began missionary work in New York City, his daily prayer meetings led to a revival among businessmen that eroded barriers to religious ministry in workplaces. Today, Lanphier Press is a trademark of Corporate Chaplains of America.

David Miller, in his book *God at Work*, argues that since the late nineteenth century, a conscious effort has been made to take religious ministry into the workplace. This effort occurred in three waves. The first wave

(1890s–1945) began alongside the Social Gospel movement, but was interrupted by the World Wars and the Depression. The second wave (1946–85) emphasized lay ministry and ecumenism through the World Council of Churches under leaders like Dutch missionary Hendrik Kramer, Swiss Reformed theologian Hans-Reudi Weber, and Anglican lay-leader J. H. Oldham. The third wave (since 1985) Miller describes as the "faith at work era." According to Miller, today more major corporations allow the formation of religion-based affinity groups, the media has increased coverage of religion in the workplace, Christian colleges are offering business degrees that teach how to incorporate faith with work, and churches and parachurch organizations are training people how to do this.[50]

In the 1940s, road equipment entrepreneur R. G. LeTourneau founded the first full-time American corporate chaplaincy program at his Illinois, Georgia, Mississippi, and Texas factories. In 1949, R. J. Reynolds Tobacco appointed Clifford Peace, a former military chaplain, to provide pastoral care to employees. The United Auto Workers Chaplaincy Program began in Flint, Michigan, in the mid-1980s. Tyson Foods began its chaplain ministry in 2000. Many corporations encourage faith-based Employee Resource Groups (ERGs), while others allow chaplains to lead Employee Assistance Programs (EAPs). Some CPE programs have been established in industrial settings. Many agencies provide corporate chaplains. Foremost among them are Marketplace Ministries, founded in 1984, and Corporate Chaplains of America, begun in 1996. The National Institute of Business and Industrial Chaplains was formed in 1970 in San Diego.

## MODERN CORRECTIONAL

The history of correctional chaplaincy was influenced by colonial religious efforts to bring about penal reform. Early American prison systems were severe and punitive. William Penn's "Great Code" (1682) shifted the emphasis from harsh treatment to confinement in humane conditions. His and the Quakers' influence led Pennsylvania to become a center for penal reform. The state rewrote its code to follow Penn's pattern in 1786. The next year,

---

[50] David Miller, *God at Work: The History and Promise of the Faith at Work Movement* (Oxford: Oxford University Press, 2007).

the Pennsylvania Prison Society was formed. It pushed for prisons to become places of "correction" instead of punishment and for prisoners to have access to local religious leaders. The Walnut Street Jail in Philadelphia became the world's first "penitentiary" in 1790. The idea was to make penitence central to its corrective strategy. The goal was rehabilitative: reformation through penance. Two types of prison systems developed in America. The Pennsylvania "separate system" kept prisoners isolated in silent reflection as a means of rehabilitation. The New York or "Auburn" system modified the separate system: inmates worked silently together in daytime but were in solitary confinement at night. Ministry in prisons was done by local pastors who served without pay. The National Prison Association (NPA) was formed in 1870 in Cincinnati to spur prison reform. It adopted forty-one principles, including religious and vocational training, to rehabilitate prisoners. These standards became guidelines for prison reform throughout America and Europe. In 1876, the first facility for young offenders, a "reformatory," opened in Elmira, New York, and used many of these principles. Since 1954, the NPA has been known as the American Correctional Association (ACA).

In the twentieth century, more emphasis was placed on psychology as a means of "curing" inmates of criminality. The concept of probation was introduced, and new reform efforts were begun in New York. In 1930, Congress established the Federal Bureau of Prisons within the Department of Justice to regulate all federal correctional institutions. This entity now oversees 122 prisons with an inmate population over 152,000.

In 2000, the Religious Land Use and Institutional Persons Act (RLUIPA) was passed. It states that government will not impose a substantial burden on the religious exercise of persons confined to an institution (defined in section 2 of the Civil Rights of Institutionalized Persons Act), even if the burden results from a general rule, unless the state demonstrates it has a compelling interest at stake and the burden is the least restrictive means of furthering that interest. The law was upheld by the Supreme Court in 2006.

The American Correctional Chaplains Association (ACCA), an interfaith group, was formed in 1885 by E.C. Vines in New York as the first affiliate of the ACA, based on the ACA "Declaration of Principles," Section IX, which stresses the importance of religion in reformatory agencies. For many years membership in the ACA was only open to wardens and chaplains. The

ACCA serves as a professional organization for pastoral care personnel in the corrections field, including information-sharing networks among members and correctional administrators; formulation of standards for chaplaincy and religious programming; development and implementation of certification for correctional chaplains; advancement of the role of correctional chaplains; and communication of religious and spiritual aspects of corrections to the larger community. The American Protestant Correctional Chaplains Association, the Protestant affiliate of the ACCA, was formed in 1950. The Correctional Ministries and Chaplains Association (CMCA) was formed in 2011 to support the work of evangelical Christian correctional chaplains.

## REFLECTION QUESTIONS

1. What form of chaplaincy in your country has the most intriguing history for you? Why?
2. What is the oldest form of chaplaincy in the United States (or your particular country)? What were the circumstances that led to the adoption of this type of chaplaincy?
3. What changes within society or culture do you think will positively or negatively impact chaplains and their ministry? Explain why you believe this to be the case.
4. What would you change about chaplaincy to better meet the spiritual needs of your generation?

CHAPTER SEVEN

# THE GLOBAL NATURE OF CHAPLAINCY

## Dr. Jim Browning

In a 2003 article, Dr. John Swinton began with an emphatic statement, "These are interesting times for chaplains." He further articulated, "Chaplains will be called to account for who they are and what they do in a way that they have not previously had to."[51] Two decades later, the truth of his statement remains a clarion call for greater understanding and clarity. Chaplains continue to explain who they are, how they should prepare, what they do, and the value of what they bring.

The first edition of *The Heart of a Chaplain* focused on chaplaincy in the United States. A colleague from Australia highlighted the need for information on chaplaincy globally, spurring me to expand my research. To better comprehend how chaplains operate in countries outside the US, I created five questions and shared them as widely as I could. These questions are not comprehensive or all-inclusive. They simply provide a starting point.

Trying to comprehend the global nature of chaplaincy is indeed a daunting task. While I discovered some incredible ministries by chaplains and chaplaincy organizations, I also realized my limitations in addressing this topic. Due to this research's ongoing nature and the project's size, the answers to these questions are inconclusive. As chaplaincy is expanding globally, it is

---

[51] John Swinton, "A Question of Identity: What Does It Mean for Chaplains to Become Healthcare Professionals?," *Scottish Journal of Healthcare Chaplaincy* 6, no. 2 (2003): 2, abstract, https://www.researchgate.net/publication/255577564_A_question_of_identity_What_does_it_mean_for_chaplains_to_become_healthcare_professionals.

also changing and evolving. Can anyone truly comprehend the global nature of chaplaincy? Given language and geographical and cultural diversity, comprehending chaplaincy from a global perspective revealed an overwhelming task beyond a rudimentary perspective.

I encourage readers to consider using these questions for their own region or country.

1. What is the foundation of your chaplain programs in your region or country? In other words, why do organizations or institutions employ or support volunteer chaplains?
2. What types of chaplains exist in your area or country?
3. What kind of training, preparation, and/or credentialing do these different chaplains require before they can serve in a chaplain's capacity?
4. Are most chaplains considered full-time professionals or clergy serving in an additional role to an institution or community?
5. What makes your chaplaincy programs unique or effective in your country or culture?

The first question focuses on the foundation of chaplain programs inside one's region or country. Understanding how religion and state intersect within a country is challenging. This intersection gives insight into how secular institutions and organizations employ and use chaplains. For example, in the United States, the First Amendment to the Constitution is a foundational document supporting the integration of chaplains within federal and state institutions. The South African Constitution's Bill of Rights has a similar legal support for freedom of religion, belief, and opinion and enables chaplains to provide religious observances at state or state-aided institutions. In contrast, in France, a chaplain (*aumônier*) also offers spiritual care and support in hospitals, the military, prisons, and schools but must operate in a way that adheres to the country's strict secularism (*laïcité*).

The second and third questions explore the diversity of chaplaincy and training within an area. Chaplaincy typically represents religious bodies within the country, has some formalized religious training, and provides pastoral and spiritual care, counseling, and support in diverse settings. Most chaplains represent their faith tradition while ministering in multifaith or purely secular environments. These chaplains may also support individuals from various religious traditions or none. For instance, in South Korea, chaplaincy is predominantly Christian, reflecting the country's sizeable Christian population. In India, chaplaincy is less formalized and more diverse given the diverse religious context, including Sikh, Hindu, Muslim, Buddhist, and Christian traditions. In Japan, where secularism is a prominent aspect of their society, Buddhist priests are working in the role of chaplains inside prisons, "appointed to bring religious instruction to offenders."[52] In Israel, chaplains are primarily rabbis who provide religious services, spiritual care, and ethical guidance based on Jewish law (*Halacha*).

The fourth question reveals how regions or countries use full, part-time, and volunteer chaplains along with pay commensurate with the level of employment or the wealth of the country or organizations. Most countries have some form of hospital, military, and correctional chaplains with various levels of standardization. One interesting variation exists when institutions request a chaplain versus when a religious faith community supplies an unsolicited chaplain. A respondent from Kenya replied,

> Most organizations that have hired chaplains in Kenya were out of memorandums signed between the church and the institutions out of a need to give spiritual care. The chaplaincy positions have been shared among the different denominations in the country. The church has posted chaplains to their sponsored institutions even where the institutions have not asked for them. This has resulted in most chaplains getting frustrated because they have no one to pay their salaries.[53]

The fifth question highlights how the rapid changes in secularization within many cultures and countries affect chaplains' professional identity and practice. Jumper, Keith, and Langston, in *Chaplaincy: A Comprehensive Introduction*, state, "The future of Christian chaplaincy in America is bright, but chaplains will face greater challenges as the culture drifts further from its

---

[52] See Adam J. Lyons, *Karma and Punishment: Prison Chaplaincy in Japan* (Cambridge: Harvard University Asia Center, 2021).

[53] Email response from a chaplain associated with the Presbyterian Church of East Africa.

biblical foundations. Humanism, secularism, paganism, and individualism have been rapidly replacing God as the center of American culture."[54] The US is not alone in these cultural challenges and secularization. One sees the impact of this secularization in the use of "spiritual care providers," "pastoral carers," and "caregivers," arguing that "chaplain" is burdened by Christian lineage[55] and lacks inclusivity. Additionally, with increasing numbers of people who identify themselves as "religiously unaffiliated" or "nones,"[56] some institutions prefer "spiritual care providers" who do not identify with a religious tradition or as nonreligious (sometimes referred to as "spiritual but not religious").[57] Chaplaincy, once defined along traditional religious lines of pastoral care, is now aligning itself as "spiritual care," "creating sacred space," and "meaning-making."[58]

In a Netherlands' chaplaincy study, Visser, Zock, and Muthert highlighted this ongoing shift in positioning chaplaincy in an increasingly pluralistic world.

> Throughout the world, and markedly in the Netherlands, the professional identity of chaplains is under question because of societal trends of disaffiliation from and pluralization of religion, and of deinstitutionalization of care.
>
> Disaffiliation and pluralization challenge the field to find roles and tasks beyond traditional forms of spiritual care to remain visible and

---

[54] Mark A. Jumper, Steven E. Keith, and Michael W. Langston, *Chaplaincy: A Comprehensive Introduction* (Grand Rapids: Baker Academic, 2024), 295.

[55] See Wendy Cadge and Shelly Rambo, eds., *Chaplaincy and Spiritual Care in the Twenty-First Century: An Introduction* (Chapel Hill: University of North Carolina Press, 2022), 13–15.

[56] Pew Research Center, "Religious 'Nones' in America: Who They Are and What They Believe," Pew Research Center, January 24, 2024, https://www.pewresearch.org/religion/2024/01/24/religious-nones-in-america-who-they-are-and-what-they-believe/, accessed 10 September 2024.

[57] An increasing number of spiritual care providers are religiously unaffiliated themselves, seeking to meet the spiritual needs of groups like the humanists, atheists, and agnostics. Lawton and Cadge state, "Some people who consider themselves nonreligious and spiritual subscribe to a naturalistic spirituality that includes finding meaning and significance in the ordinary world." Amy Lawton and Wendy Cadge, "More Than 'None:' Spiritual Care by and for the Nonreligious," A Working Paper, Chaplaincy Innovation Lab, https://chaplaincyinnovation.org/resources/working-papers/nones-spiritual-care, accessed 10 September 2024.

[58] Cadge and Rambo, 1–15, 61–65.

relevant in collaboration with other professionals. They also challenge the field to develop a language and identity that includes the plurality of worldviews, but that still conveys its professional core.[59]

Their study highlights an associated issue. They and others describe chaplains' increased language use of "meaning-making." Cadge and Rambo state, as a core competency for chaplains, "First, chaplains need to be able to facilitate practices of meaning-making and to navigate worldviews in public settings."[60] While Visser, Zock, and Muthert do not dispute using the term "meaning" as the central concept in the professional identity of chaplaincy and spiritual care providers, they list three critiques of this language.

1. Meaning and meaning-making have strong cognitive and intentional connotations, which do not do justice to the lived experience of meaning and might lead to a medicalization of meaning.
2. The term meaning places the professional identity of chaplaincy in the instrumental discourse of other professions, which might lead to "abuse" of spiritual care toward external objectives such as health and (hedonistic) well-being and/or economic gain, instead of internal objectives such as faith and spirituality.
3. A focus on meaning leads to a marginalization of religion, both societally and within chaplaincy, which might negatively affect their core competence of hermeneutic understanding and worldview counseling.[61]

---

[59] Anja Visser, Hetty Zock, and Hanneke Muthert, "Positioning Chaplaincy in the Pluralistic and Multidisciplinary Dutch Care Context," *Religions* 14, no. 9:1173 (2023), https://www.mdpi.com/2077-1444/14/9/1173, accessed 7 September 2024.
[60] Cadge and Rambo, 5–7.
[61] Visser, Zock, and Muthert. They define hermeneutic competency as "'being able to clarify questions about meaning and beliefs and habits in relation to the context or situation, and being able to offer worldview counselling. This includes the ability to understand, interpret, and translate meaning in texts and images, practices and life stories, traditions and new forms of meaning-making. This takes place in relation to and in exchange with existential and spiritual questions, philosophical and ethical sources, contemporary society, faith and culture. Crucial is the ability to hear and clarify emotions and unspoken questions and implicit assumptions.' What this competency asks of the chaplain is to carefully listen to, look at, and feel what is being expressed in an encounter, to

While it is beyond the scope of this chapter to analyze each critique separately, the student would benefit from studying the analysis of their arguments.[62]

Chaplaincy is evolving and growing globally. As regions or countries adapt chaplaincy in their societies, the result is a broader acceptance and integration of chaplains. When secularization occurs within a country or culture, the need for care that addresses religious, spiritual, and psychological well-being does not diminish. Chaplains provide care, comfort, and support beyond religious tradition or faith community. Chaplains are adept at engaging with anyone and everyone, irrespective of their worldview.[63] This is particularly true in health care, where outcome-based research over the past four decades shows a strong association between spiritual beliefs and values and various healthcare outcomes.[64] Chaplains often bridge cultural and religious divides by promoting interfaith understanding and fostering mutual respect.

Institutions, organizations, and business leaders increasingly recognize the value of incorporating chaplains to enhance people's well-being.[65] Chaplains are increasingly called upon to provide ethical and moral guidance in complex situations or support in crisis or traumatic events. Finally, with the professionalization of chaplaincy through increased focus on competencies,

---

negotiate different ways of understanding what is being expressed, and to articulate this in a way that matches the situation but might shed a different light on it." This process requires integrating skills and theories from the humanities and those of the psychosocial sciences.

[62] I contend that chaplains do not need to expunge all religious or faith-based language from their communication. Chaplains, however, are to be actively present, carefully listening, observing, analyzing, and interpreting what is being expressed in every encounter while using their full range of understanding of theology, pastoral care, and the humanities. The focus of needs should not be on the chaplain but the other person.

[63] Carmen Schuhmann and Annelieke Damen, "Representing the Good: Pastoral Care in a Secular Age," *Pastoral Psychology* 67, no. 4 (2018): 405–17, https://doi.org/10.1007/s11089-018-0826-0, accessed 8 September 2024.

[64] Review the abundance of research by Christina M. Puchalski, George Washington Institute for Spirituality and Health, The George Washington University School of Medicine and Health Sciences, The George Washington University, Washington, DC.

[65] One example is MarketPlace Chaplains' "Mental Health and Moral Injury: Improving Your Employees' Well-Being through Practical Applications and Chaplaincy to Relieve Distress," White Paper Series 3, https://publications.mchapusa.com/mental-health-and-moral-injury/full-view.html, accessed 8 September 2024.

certifications, and clinical training, chaplains are increasingly integral members of interdisciplinary teams.

Education and funding are critical factors affecting the expansion of chaplaincy in different parts of the world. While religious schools offer elements of pastoral care, ethics, and practical theology, focus and methods will vary according to cultural, religious, institutional, and secularization contexts. In countries with a dominant religious tradition, education and pay for chaplains typically reflect that tradition and its role in that community. Education and training in other countries or regions with more religiously diverse or secular environments also emphasize cultural and interfaith competence but may have more significant compensation disparity. Funding challenges impact chaplains globally in several ways: government versus nongovernment funding; lack of standardization in pay and benefits; educational, training, and credentialing costs; financial capability of countries and religious institutions; competing financial priorities within institutions; institutionally paid full-time staff versus self-funded part-time volunteers; and lack of outcome-based research data used to justify chaplain services beyond healthcare. These and other factors create a wide global disparity in how chaplains function and are used.

Equally challenging in understanding the global nature of chaplaincy is realizing that similar types of chaplaincies develop and evolve differently within various cultures, regions, or nations. Sports chaplaincy offers an example. In *Sports Chaplaincy: Trends, Issues and Debates*, J. Stuart Weir states, "Sports chaplaincy should not be regarded as a homogenous entity. On the contrary, there are a range of models, frameworks, approaches and practices which fall under this generic heading." He highlights, "Moreover, the way that sports chaplaincy has developed in the US or in Australia is not the same as in the UK." The origins, models, and modus operandi are influenced by critical issues and pioneers who established a new type of chaplaincy.[66]

Notably, some chaplain organizations have a larger regional or global perspective. The resource section in this book offers additional organizations.[67]

---

[66] J. Stuart Weir, "Sports Chaplaincy: A Global Overview," in *Sports Chaplaincy: Trends, Issues and Debates*, ed. Andrew Parker, Nick J. Watson, and John B. White (London: Routledge, 2016), 9.

[67] A word of caution is in order. Having "international" in one's organizational name does not ensure the organization has a global support of chaplains. The reader is advised to do in-depth

For example, the Australian and New Zealand Association for Clinical Pastoral Education (ANZACPE, https://www.anzacpe.org.au/) is the region's umbrella organization for the associations providing Clinical Pastoral Education. Canada's leading spiritual care and psycho-spiritual therapy association is the Canadian Association for Spiritual Care (CASC/ACSS, https://www.spiritualcare.ca/). The European Network of Healthcare Chaplaincy (ENHCC, https://enhcc.eu/) focuses on healthcare chaplaincy across Europe. The Global Sports Chaplaincy Association (GSCA, https://sportschaplaincy.com/) was formed as a global "Organized Movement" with the vision and purpose of seeing sports chaplains serving with excellence in every sports community worldwide. The International Association of Chaplains in Higher Education (IACHE, http://www.iache.org/) is a network for chaplains in higher education. The International Military Chiefs of Chaplains Conference (IMCCC, https://www.eucom.mil/topic/imccc) is an annual gathering of military religious leaders worldwide. The United Kingdom Board of Healthcare Chaplaincy (UKBHC, https://www.ukbhc.org.uk/) focuses on healthcare chaplaincy, accrediting chaplains who provide spiritual care in healthcare institutions across the UK, with connections to international chaplaincy bodies.

Other US examples with a global reach include Clinical Pastoral Education International (CPEI, https://cpei.edu/) and the Association for Clinical Pastoral Education (ACPE, https://acpe.edu/). TFC Global International Ministry (TFG Global, https://tfcglobal.org/overseas-ministries/) is a trucking industry chaplaincy ministry with partnerships on two continents. The International Conference of Police Chaplains (ICPC, https://www.icpc-4cops.org/) conducts regional and global conferences to provide training and support for law enforcement chaplains with an "intentional focus on moral excellence, cutting-edge training, and effective communications to encourage every law enforcement agency to establish and maintain a powerful chaplaincy." The US National Guard's State Partnership Program has built relationships for over thirty years and includes ninety-six partnerships with 106

---

research to better understand the scope of each organization's purpose and reach. The following organizational websites listed were accessed on 10 September 2024. This list of organizations is representative and not all-inclusive.

nations around the globe.[68] The Race Track Chaplaincy of America provides and assists chaplains at horse race tracks all across the United States and has connections to chaplains in Australia, New Zealand, and Canada.

In summary, while the chaplain's role of providing some form of pastoral care, counseling, and support is typical across countries, the characterization of a chaplain varies based on the religious, cultural, and institutional/organizational contexts. In some countries, chaplains are closely tied to specific religious traditions. In others, chaplains operate within secular frameworks or serve in multifaith and multicultural settings. These differences affect how chaplains are trained, the settings in which they work, the nature of their duties, and whether (and how) they are compensated. What is common for chaplains worldwide is a growing appreciation of their work and an increasing demand for better education and training.

## REFLECTION QUESTIONS

1. From your perspective, how have the cultural and social changes in your lifetime impacted the expression of religion? Considering these changes, how should chaplains adapt their ministry approach to meet the needs of people?
2. What is the foundation of your chaplain programs inside your region or country? In other words, why do organizations or institutions employ chaplains?
3. What types of chaplains exist in your country?
4. Are most chaplains considered full-time professionals or clergy serving in an additional role to an institution or community?
5. What kind of training, preparation, and/or credentialing do these different chaplains require before they can serve in a chaplain's capacity?
6. What makes your chaplaincy programs unique or effective in your country or culture?

---

[68] National Guard, "State Partnership Program," https://www.nationalguard.mil/leadership/joint-staff/j-5/international-affairs-division/state-partnership-program/, accessed 27 August 2024.

# SECTION THREE

# HOW IS CHAPLAIN MINISTRY UNIQUE?

CHAPTER EIGHT

# ROLES, RESPONSIBILITIES, AND TASKS

## Dr. Jim Spivey

The work of chaplains is highly complex, much more so than parish ministry. Daily we perform innumerable tasks in both religious and temporal settings. In doing so, we discharge several functional responsibilities, or duties, expected by our secular institutions and our religious communities. We can group these duties into the broader category of roles we fulfill, or "hats" we wear. This is important to do. We need to see how our tasks and duties align with those roles because we typically minister differently in each distinctive context, depending on our assigned roles. The better we understand how this alignment works properly, the better we can minister effectively in the right context and minimize role conflicts that inevitably result from doing religious ministry in a secular, institutional setting.

Generally, chaplains fulfill four roles associated with four identifiable contexts where God calls us to walk and work with others. In each setting, we project a slightly different persona. First, we walk alongside persons of similar beliefs whom we serve as faith-group representatives. Second, we work alongside other members of the institution that employs us all. In this respect, we are institutional professionals. Third, people throughout the organization, regardless of religious orientation, see us as community ministers who serve everyone. Fourth, we are ministers to individuals, in either the faith-group or institutional context, and sometimes these roles overlap.

A chaplain's functional responsibilities are numerous, but there are two general types: religious duties and those not uniquely religious. This chapter describes eleven religious duties. The first four are duties as ministers, or servants, who are officially licensed religious officials. As (1) faith-group ministers, we serve the needs of like-minded believers. As (2) community ministers, we serve all persons and the interests of the institution at large. We perform religious rituals such as weddings in our capacity as (3) ministers of religious rites, and as (4) ministers of ceremonial rites, we perform official tasks such as memorial services and invocations at institutional events.

As (5) priests, we represent the presence of God and intercede for everyone we serve, regardless of context. The same is true of our (6) pastoral responsibility. Obviously, as shepherds we provide religious care for our own faith groups. At the same time, we also provide pastoral and spiritual care to the whole community by meeting the practical and emotional needs of the general population and by addressing existential and transcendental concerns. We may serve as personal pastors and confidants of institutional leaders when they allow us that privilege. In our official, technical capacity as (7) religious experts, we advise leaders on religious and ethical matters affecting the institution.

The responsibility of (8) proclamation has two dimensions. Within faith-group settings it usually takes the form of preaching about religious issues. We are also prophetic in broader institutional settings when we speak truth to power in order to effect needed change. We fulfill two duties mainly in faith-group contexts: we are (9) religious teachers who instruct the faithful and (10) evangelists who disciple others by sharing our faith. This does not mean we cannot share our beliefs in pluralistic settings, but in those cases we should do so within institutional guidelines, in voluntary situations, with the recipient's permission, and without coercion. As (11) mentors, chaplains teach, guide, and set good examples for less experienced ministers of our own faith group.

Chaplains fulfill at least fourteen functional responsibilities that are not uniquely religious. Eight of these duties deal with procedural matters. Four of these procedural duties are related to chaplains being spokespersons. As (1) advocates, chaplains speak on behalf of the institution to its own members and to external organizations such as local communities and religious groups. They also intercede on behalf of fellow workers to resolve issues and seek help from organizational officials. As (2) arbitrators, they go a step further: they help to resolve conflict between the institution and parties within its sphere of influence, including workers, their families, clients, and the communities the institution touches. We are (3) public relations agents who liaise between the institution, clients, and outside communities. Chaplains are (4) information providers who keep leaders and staff apprised of their activities and the status of their ministerial programs.

Four procedural roles deal with oversight. Chaplains are (5) administrators who manage personnel, develop operational and ministerial plans, coordinate logistics, and run institutional programs. As (6) staff members, we coordinate with other officials to plan and implement agendas to accomplish the institutional mission. Experienced chaplains are also (7) mentors of less experienced chaplains outside our faith groups but within our sphere of influence. And senior chaplains (8) supervise chaplains at subordinate organizational levels.

Six nonreligious duties are more personal in nature and closely related to our religious training and skills. Chaplains are (9) moral leaders. This responsibility overlaps with two religious duties already mentioned: religious expert and proclamation. As religious experts, our advice to leaders about religious and ethical issues provides officially sanctioned moral direction to the institution. When our duty of proclamation leads us to speak prophetically, we influence change that brings further moral clarification to that direction. At the same time, chaplains are moral leaders in a nonreligious way. When we lead by good example and sound character, our presence works as leaven, salt, and light. It is noteworthy how the presence of a chaplain in the motor pool, prison cell, or workplace can affect the way people behave, at least for the moment. Chaplains are (10) helpers: we assist individuals with life-skills and practical problems.

The next three duties are closely related. As (11) counselors we provide emotional guidance that often touches on spiritual matters. We are also (12) comforters who listen, encourage, and provide a calming "ministry of presence" wherever we go. As (13) healers, we collaborate with experts from other disciplines to maintain the holistic (physical, psychological, and spiritual) health of individuals and to promote a wholesome environment in the community at large. Finally, chaplains are also (14) crisis and trauma experts. We advise leaders how to manage emergency situations, and we intervene to help individuals through stressful times.

## ALIGNMENT OF ROLES AND RESPONSIBILITIES

### Faith-Group Representative

At the beginning of the accessioning process, it is the religious faith group that calls and endorses the chaplain. So, a key part of the chaplain's call involves ministering to persons of like faith and order. From the moment we enter the institution and assume the role of "chaplain," we project a denominational persona. While expected to minister to all members of the organization, one of our key roles is to be a faith-group minister. However, in most situations, the institution expects chaplains to broaden the tent of their faith-group ministry to include persons of similar faith and order. The fewer the chaplains, the broader our tent becomes—perhaps serving as the one Christian minister alongside a Jewish rabbi and a Muslim imam. With a few more chaplains on board, the ministry might be divided into General Protestant, Roman Catholic, Orthodox, Jewish, Muslim, and so on. With even more chaplains, denominationally specific services might be provided. Still, the tent is almost always broader than our own denomination, and we are expected to meet the religious needs of everyone in our charge. When we cannot accomplish certain functions, we provide other faith-based ministers to perform them.

Chaplains fulfill several nonreligious duties within the religious community, just as we do for the institution at large: we are administrators, information providers, helpers, counselors, healers, and comforters. But most of our efforts as faith-group representatives are spent on the following duties:

- Faith-group minister
- Minister of religious rites
- Preacher
- Priest
- Pastor
- Religious teacher
- Evangelist
- Mentor

In this role as faith-group representative, chaplains continue to maintain affiliation and contact with their own denomination and, in certain cases, may connect their members formally with its organizational structure. We also remain faithful to our confessional beliefs and practices. Generally, we operate within our own denominational guidelines, which vary between religious groups regarding functions ministers are permitted to perform. Some issues may be subjective and a matter of personal conviction; others are objectively set by our denomination. Conversely, we are also obliged to respect the liturgical and communal boundaries of other faith groups. In some religious groups, certain liturgical rites may be performed only by ministers of that order. Regarding communal limits, chaplains should not proselytize members from other faith groups.

As ministers of religious rites, chaplains perform a wide range of tasks for their faith group. These include weddings, christenings, infant dedications, baptisms, communion, funerals, memorial services, marriage renewals, and blessings. Part of our duty as preachers is to explain the sacred text, proclaim its principles, and exhort people to behave in line with its values and act on its mandates.

At the same time, we prompt in worship, lead in prayer and devotions, give spiritual direction to their congregants, and encourage them as agents of hope. As priests, chaplains lead others in offering spiritual sacrifices to God. We guide people into the presence God and help to make His presence known to them. We listen to the concerns and confessions of those seeking help and make intercession to God on their behalf. As pastors, we nurture the congregation, we provide direction as humble servant-leaders, and we protect the flock from harm. Part of this duty includes our responsibility as religious teachers to provide good scriptural instruction based on sound biblical interpretation that leads to spiritual growth and moral accountability.

In faith-group settings, chaplains act as evangelists. We should share explicitly the good news of hope and intentionally disciple those who choose to respond to this message. In certain contexts, the chaplain's message may be more narrowly expressed because the constituency is all one faith group, for example, Roman Catholic, Orthodox, Jewish, or Muslim. However, in collective settings such as general Protestant services, chaplains should present the message in broader terms, avoiding polemical issues but remaining faithful to core beliefs and not violating one's own conscience. Senior chaplains should mentor less experienced ones in the same way. If protégés are of the same faith group, mentors should not be reluctant to nurture them along confessional lines. With protégés of similar but different faiths, mentoring should be done more broadly, with sensitivity and wisdom. A fair but candid exchange of viewpoints might encourage mutual learning, but the goal should be ministerial growth, maturity, and collegiality.

**Institutional Professional**

As professionals in a secular institution, chaplains work alongside other non-chaplain colleagues to care for everyone in the organization while accomplishing the mission. In this role, we perform most of our nonreligious duties, primarily the following:

- Advocate
- Arbitrator
- Information provider
- Administrator
- Staff member
- Moral leader
- Supervisor
- Mentor (of chaplains of other denominations and non-chaplains)
- Crisis/trauma expert

We are spokespersons in various ways within and on behalf of the institution. As officials of the organization, we are advocates who promote and support its mission and values. This includes educating our own staff, other employees, and clients of the institution about its policies and procedures. Because we represent the best interests of the institution as well as the needs of workers and clients, and since we are usually respected for our fairness and neutrality, chaplains also may be called upon to arbitrate issues contested by either side. As information providers, chaplains not only keep leaders and staff apprised of religious programming; they also advise leaders as religious experts regarding ethical and religious issues affecting the institution. This includes promoting free exercise of religion and preventing religious bias. We keep leaders informed about the technical, theological nature of all religions practiced within the organization and in surrounding communities, including cultural holidays, observances, and prohibitions.

As administrators, we oversee the planning, support, and execution of religious programs for the institution. Though most of the content is religious, management is nonreligious and procedural. That is because all religious programs come under the authority of secular leadership, they are funded through an integrated institutional budget underwritten by public or corporate funds, and some of them are justified because they accomplish a secular purpose. Chaplains serve as staff members under the authority of institutional leadership. Though primarily responsible for the religious work of the establishment, they cooperate with other staff members to accomplish its secular mission. For example, military chaplains collaborate to fulfill their oath to support and defend the Constitution of the United States.

As moral leaders, we advise leaders how to strengthen the ethical climate to enhance mission performance. In the hospital context, chaplains sit on ethics committees making momentous decisions regarding prioritization of health care or termination of life. Senior chaplains also serve as technical supervisors of junior or volunteer chaplains. In the military, this is based on pyramidal levels of command. In hospital settings, supervisory chaplains oversee staff chaplains, and clinical pastoral educators supervise residents in training. In prisons and jails, typically staff chaplains supervise the work of community ministers who serve as volunteer chaplains.

As institutional professionals, we also mentor less experienced chaplains within our sphere of influence. This duty is like that of faith-group representatives, but in this case our influence extends to chaplains of all faiths, and our coaching focuses on general skills in chaplain ministry and professional development, not confessional teaching. Chaplains also mentor non-chaplains. For example, in the military, we mentor laypersons on our ministerial staff; in hospitals, we coach medical staff who also provide spiritual care; and in correctional facilities, we train laypersons, including inmates, who assist us in ministry.

Chaplains make a significant contribution as institutional professionals by serving on crisis/trauma prevention and management teams. This includes ministry in disaster settings: we come alongside people in acute, life-altering situations to provide psychological support and urgent, practical help to alleviate immediate problems. We help people cope with post-traumatic stress disorder and train other professional personnel in suicide awareness and prevention.

As institutional professionals, chaplains also perform three religious duties: we are pastors, priests, and religious experts. First, when organizational leaders allow it, chaplains should consider it a privilege to minister to them as their personal pastor. Second, as priests, chaplains should pray for all persons in leadership so everyone in the institution can lead tranquil and quiet lives with godliness and dignity. Finally, our duty as religious experts obviously overlaps with our responsibility to provide information when we advise leaders about religious and ethical matters.

**Community Minister**

As ministers in the broader institutional community, chaplains perform religious and technical functions for everyone in the organization. Many people identify the chaplain as their minister in a public way, not primarily as a denominational agent. In this role, chaplains fulfill the following duties:

- Minister of ceremonial rites
- Public relations agent
- Community pastor
- Priest
- Administrator and Information provider

As ministers of ceremonial rites, chaplains publicly perform official tasks such as conducting memorial services; leading prayer breakfasts or luncheons; and offering invocations or benedictions at formal occasions like civic activities, graduations, celebratory banquets, and dedication of facilities or equipment. As public relations agents, chaplains extend institutional influence to the outside world by connecting with local communities, external congregations, and religious denominations, along with their attendant networks.

As community ministers, chaplains perform three main religious duties: we are pastors, priests, and religious experts. First, as pastors, we are concerned about everyone's safety, health, and spiritual condition. We provide practical pastoral care, spiritual guidance, encouragement, comfort, and hope, to anyone willing to accept it. Second, the same is true of our priestly duty. Chaplains should listen attentively to everyone's concerns and be prepared to hear anyone's confessions, remembering that this is privileged and confidential communication not to be disclosed to anyone else unless legally bound to do so.

As priests, we should intercede prayerfully for all persons. We fulfill this priestly duty to everyone in the institution by manifesting God's presence wherever we go through an intentional "ministry of presence." This simple act invites the power of the divine into secular settings and injects spiritual calm amid chaos. As administrators and information providers, we produce, publish, and advertise ministry plans and make sure institutional guidelines regarding religious practices are observed.

## Minister to Individuals

Chaplains minister to all individuals, within and beyond their faith-group setting, regardless of their religious backgrounds. In this role, chaplains fulfill the following responsibilities:

- Advocate
- Information provider
- Pastor
- Priest
- Helper
- Counselor
- Comforter
- Healer

The first two are nonreligious procedural duties; the next two are religious ones; the final four, though not exclusively religious, provide skillful chaplains opportunities to provide meaningful pastoral and spiritual care. As advocates, chaplains intercede for individuals with institutional agencies to make sure their needs are addressed, and in doing so, we provide practical pastoral care. We also provide people information about organizational resources that benefit them. In both capacities as advocate and information provider, chaplains also fulfill their duty as helpers.

Again, in their role as ministers to individuals, just as community ministers, chaplains serve as pastors and priests to all members of the institution willing to receive their assistance. As helpers, we assist individuals in practical ways to access resources provided by the institution. The last three duties are at the heart of the chaplain's role as minister to individuals.

As counselors, we listen with empathy, assess needs, offer emotional support, give spiritual guidance, and provide biblical and psychological advice to resolve personal and relational problems. When unable to assess or treat severe problems, we refer individuals to other professional persons better equipped to do so. As comforters, we come alongside people in crisis to help them bear their burdens and to provide encouragement and hope. As healers, we minister to sin-sick souls, mend broken spirits, help to repair broken human relationships, and promote reconciliation with God.

## MISSION, ROLES, AND DUTIES OF CHAPLAINS

### Healthcare Chaplains

The mission of healthcare professionals is to provide holistic healing or palliative care through physical, emotional, and spiritual means. Normally, healthcare settings are more open than the military and correctional worlds. The atmosphere is a professional one, with highly trained doctors and nursing staff divided into many specialties. Compared to the military, hospital staff are stable geographically; they move voluntarily for personal or professional reasons. There are two worlds: that of hospital staff and that of patients and families. Hospital staff are at ease in their stable setting with a residential population. On the other hand, the patient population is highly transitory. The hospital may seem strangely different and intimidating for patients and families. Healthcare chaplains provide spiritual care in three settings: hospitals, hospice (palliative care), and long-term or eldercare facilities. Of the three aspects of care (religious/pastoral/spiritual), healthcare chaplains focus on pastoral care (meeting physical and emotional needs) and spiritual care (dealing with transcendental matters).

Healthcare chaplains serve three constituencies: patients, their families, and the rest of the professional healthcare staff. The most important role for healthcare chaplains is as ministers to individuals: healers who listen, comfort, and encourage through a ministry of presence; and helpers who provide personal pastoral and spiritual care. Healthcare chaplains also perform a vital role as institutional professionals: staff members who minister to the rest of the staff, serve as advocates for both the institution and patients, administer and supervise other chaplains, and advise officials on moral, ethical, and religious issues. Their primary focus is on meeting patients' needs, which are typically immediate and urgent. However, they also build long-term relationships with the staff to enhance the performance of the whole medical professional team.

Healthcare chaplains are usually the only members of that team who are religious experts and whose primary focus in holistic healing is on spiritual matters. Their primary place of ministry is not in the office or chapel but on the ward with patients. Because most patients are in the hospital involuntarily and chaplains have ready access to most rooms, chaplains must carefully observe patients' receptivity to their presence and be careful not to intrude when unwanted. An intentional ministry of presence is especially important in healthcare chaplaincy. Depending on the type of hospital, chaplains may conduct religious worship services regularly and occasionally perform religious rites. When they cannot perform rites as needed, they provide someone else to perform them.

## Military Chaplains

The mission of the military is to defend our nation and its constitutional interests. It is a relatively closed community, with the general American population having only restricted access to military installations. Military chaplains minister to service members, their families and civilian staff who support operations. They deploy with and serve military troops and contractors during overseas training and combat operations. They wear two hats: as religious ministers and as commissioned officers. They fulfill all four chaplain roles. As faith-group representatives, they conduct religious services and rites in chapels and are pastors of chapel communities, for whom they also provide religious programming. As institutional professionals, they serve on the commander's staff, advise on religious issues, and supervise ministry teams and subordinate chaplains. As community ministers, they serve the entire installation and perform ceremonial rites for all. As ministers to individuals, they provide pastoral and spiritual care, counseling, and advocacy for anyone in the community, regardless of faith background.

In garrison, military chaplains focus on service members and their families. During deployment, they concentrate on service members, while garrison support staff take care of their families at home. Chaplains are the only totally noncombatant members in military units. Though commissioned officers, they do not normally exercise command authority, except when they supervise independent unit ministry teams. Military chaplains focus mainly on two roles: faith-group representatives and institutional professionals. More than any other type of chaplain, they most closely resemble local, congregational ministers. Especially in garrison, they devote much time to leading chapel services and directing religious programming. Their duties as staff planners and advisors to commanders are equally demanding.

As faith-group ministers, they typically perform most of the religious services for their congregants. Since their members attend voluntarily, in this setting chaplains share their faith openly. During deployment, they still function as faith-group leaders, but they devote more time to staff planning and ministering to the whole community. As community ministers, they provide for the needs of other faith groups by getting other qualified chaplains or ministers to perform those services, rites, and ceremonies. In situations where chaplains serve as institutional professionals or community ministers, and when persons are required to attend involuntarily, chaplains should be cautious about how they share their faith openly. They should never abuse their authority by taking advantage of a captive audience.

## Correctional Chaplains

The mission of correctional institutions is twofold: incarceration and rehabilitation. They protect society by confining offenders in controlled environments, and they assist offenders in becoming law-abiding citizens. This is the most closed setting of all. It comprises two distinctly separate populations: inmates and correctional staff. Inmates receive ministry only from those who enter or live in the facility: the chaplain, community volunteers, or fellow inmates. Correctional staff receive ministry both in the facility and from their outside community. The environment is highly structured, regulatory, intense, stressful, and monotonous. The inmate population is culturally diverse and pluralistic, with many faith groups. Correctional chaplains minister in federal, state, county, or local facilities. At the federal and state level, many of the positions are paid; at the county and local level, most of them are voluntary and unpaid.

Chaplains minister to three constituencies: inmates, correctional staff, and families of both the inmates and staff. They operate from a truly unique position: they literally "walk the line" between inmates and correctional staff. More than any other person in the correctional facility, they speak as advocates on both sides of that line. Their most important role is as a community minister who ensures all inmates are afforded the opportunity freely to exercise their religious rights. At the same time, like military chaplains but different from corporate or healthcare chaplains, they more fully perform a balanced ministry that encompasses the other roles of faith-group representative, institutional professional, and minister to individuals. One reason for this is that the correctional world, like the military, is a closed type of institution.

Since inmates are incarcerated involuntarily, the ministry of presence and the chaplain's sensitivity about not being intrusive are especially important. At the same time, prisoners are typically receptive to all aspects of care—religious, pastoral, and spiritual. Correctional chaplains perform worship services on a regular basis and act as pastors to congregants. However, because of the pluralistic setting, they cannot perform the religious care needed by all inmates. So, much of their work is done by providing services, rites, ceremonies and religious programming through community ministers and volunteers or trained inmates called to ministry. Chaplains also serve as personal counselors, educators who coordinate life-skill classes, and experts on crisis intervention and suicide prevention. Like corporate chaplains, they serve as barometers for correctional staff to gauge and improve the conditions of the facility.

## Corporate and Workplace Chaplains

The mission of most businesses is to provide a service or commodity, usually for profit. The environment is highly competitive and stressful, with narrow profit margins and constant pressure to do things unethically to gain an advantage. Some chaplains work directly for a company; others work for an organization that provides chaplains for several companies. Many chaplains minister part-time and work for more than one business. The population may or may not be diverse and pluralistic, depending on the cultural context.

Workplace chaplains serve two constituencies: employees and management. Their daily emphasis and influence are primarily with individual employees. But they also provide pastoral care to management and represent the interests of the institution fairly to employees. The most important role of the workplace chaplain is as a minister to individuals and secondarily as a community minister. Much of the chaplain's work is done through the ministry of presence and personal counseling, which puts a premium on confidentiality. This provides employees the opportunity to be candid not only about their personal lives but also about conditions at work. It also affords chaplains a unique opportunity to speak prophetically to management, usually without recrimination, and help to improve workplace conditions. Many persons in the business world are not members of a local congregation and have no relationship with a pastor. So, chaplains have an opportunity to meet this void. Though their primary place of ministry is in the workplace, many chaplains do follow-up ministry with employees and families in their homes.

## Public Safety Chaplains

The mission of public safety (often referred to as first responders) is to defend and serve the public, usually in highly stressful, threatening, or chaotic situations. The main types are law enforcement, fire department, emergency services, and crisis intervention and disaster relief situations. These organizations are highly structured, uniform, and regulatory. The most important role of first responder chaplains is as minister to individuals, followed by being an institutional professional.

Chaplains serve two constituencies: the responders and the public. Members of the public are transitory, and their needs are temporary. Therefore, long-term ministry focuses on the responders and their families, who live and work in fixed situations. Even in disaster situations, though members of the public need spiritual care, attention should be given to caring for relief workers who are helping the public. The setting is usually highly diverse and pluralistic. First responders exist in open and closed communities. Though they reside in open neighborhoods, they work in tight-knit, closed fraternities, with rites of passage that make it difficult for outsiders to broach. In many respects, they are like paramilitary organizations. It takes great patience, skill, and conscientious but gentle effort to build bonds of trust that lead to opportunities for ministry.

## Community and Lifestyle Chaplains

Community and lifestyle chaplains minister wherever people congregate in secular venues beyond places of worship or whenever people share a similar lifestyle. The missions of these organizations vary so widely they defy categorization, but settings can be grouped into seven types: (1) institutional, (2) residential, (3) service clubs, (4) transportation hubs/networks, (5) sports, (6) leisure/recreational, and (7) affinity groups.

The **institutional** type includes educational and legislative chaplains. Educational chaplains serve at all levels but mostly in colleges and universities. They serve the whole campus—students, faculty, and staff—primarily as ministers to individuals but also as institutional professionals. Most legislative chaplains serve part-time and perform mainly ceremonial tasks, but a key role of the few full-timers is as minister to individuals. **Residential** chaplains serve in the role of community ministers, usually to stable populations in set geographical locations. These include chaplains in retirement facilities and others who manage social and civic programs to improve their neighborhoods.

Chaplains in **service clubs** perform mostly ceremonial tasks as community ministers to fraternal clubs (for example, Kiwanis and Rotary); veterans service organizations (VFW and American Legion); local civic clubs; and quasi-military associations. At **transportation hubs/networks**—airports, trucking and truck stops, seaports, and railroads—the primary role of chaplains is as ministers to individuals. They daily interact with a highly transient population but also build long-term relationships with employed staff.

**Sports** chaplains focus on two roles. As ministers to individuals, they interact occasionally with spectators at events, but, when possible, form relationships with players and support staff. They also perform religious ceremonies, and occasionally rites, as community ministers to the team. **Leisure/recreational** chaplains serve at a variety of venues: national parks, recreational theme parks, cruise ships, and other tourist sites. Their primary role is as ministers to individuals, mainly to a transient population but also to employed staff.

**Affinity groups** include people who have common interests or avocations such as bikers, aviators, or fish and game club members. Chaplains in these organizations usually perform ceremonial tasks as community ministers but often develop lasting relations as ministers to individuals.

## REFLECTION QUESTIONS

1. What is the difference between a chaplain serving in the role of a faith-group minister and a community minister? Describe key responsibilities in each of these roles.
2. Roles, responsibilities, and tasks can be both distinct and overlapping. Pick one of the roles and describe which responsibilities and tasks most excite you in a role as a chaplain.
3. In the summaries of the major types of chaplains, which is most interesting, and which is the least interesting to you? Why?
4. What role does the chaplain play as an institutional professional in providing ethical and religious advice? How might that impact the mission of the organization?
5. As moral leaders, how might a chaplain advise leaders on strengthening the ethical climate to enhance mission performance?

CHAPTER NINE

# INSTITUTIONAL LIFE

### Dr. Robert Vickers

One of the foremost challenges in chaplaincy is the adjustment to life in the institutional setting where one serves. Institutional life is significantly different from life in the local parish, and many clergy have made the faulty assumption that one is like the other. While there are similarities, the differences are enormous. Therefore, it is important to understand one's institutional setting and the uniqueness of institutional duality that places chaplains under the authority and supervision of separate entities that create role conflicts for them.

In Luke 14:28–35, Jesus admonished those interested in following Him first to consider the cost. He used two illustrations: the builder of a tower and a king preparing for battle. Both persons were determining if they had what it took to succeed. After imploring listeners to "count the cost" of their decisions before starting, He urged, "He who has ears to hear, let him hear." In the same manner, one should "count the cost" by seeking all available information and listening carefully to wisdom and advice before choosing chaplaincy as one's expression of ministry. Learning as much as possible about the pros and cons, culture, challenges, pitfalls, and expectations greatly enhances the prospects of successful and gratifying ministry.

## INSTITUTIONAL SETTING

Chaplain ministry is typically done in secular institutional settings. Healthcare, military, correctional, first responder, and corporate institutions employ chaplains for the purpose of incorporating spiritual care and a religious influence into their secular mission. Every setting is unique. Significant differences exist not only between the various types of secular institutions but also between organizations within each type of institution. Individuals entering chaplain ministry should approach each institutional setting with keen awareness of the nuances and subtleties specific to that specific organization.

New chaplains should understand from the start that they are entering a culture where unique norms, relationships, expectations, and organizational dynamics already exist. To survive, contribute, and thrive in the new setting, chaplains must have "institutional awareness" and make adjustments accordingly. They should also know their essential identity and calling and be firmly rooted in their theology before becoming chaplains. This enables them to accommodate in "accidental" matters but not compromise on the essential ones. However, some chaplains never "get it." Most of this type soon realize they are ill-matched for that setting, and they either switch to another type of chaplaincy or return to the parish.

In parish ministry, a clergyperson is primarily responsible for providing ministerial coverage for a particular denominational congregation and to other individuals who choose to become involved out of geographical convenience or simple curiosity. By contrast, the chaplain in a secular institution provides religious coverage, spiritual care, and moral support to persons from different religious faiths and to some who profess no religious faith or interest in such. Many ministerial skills learned in theological schools and refined in parish settings are transferable to secular institutional settings. Chaplains lead worship, preach, counsel, provide religious education, administer sacraments, and perform religious rituals. However, in secular institutional settings, chaplains also serve as experts on religious matters and provide spiritual care for all organization members.

Of course, one should not expect any chaplain to be totally familiar with all practices and traditions of every faith group represented in the institution. However, it is critically important that they be concerned about and sensitive to all faith needs within the institution, whether they personally believe in those faith practices. In the military setting, the expectation is that chaplains "perform" and/or "provide for" the religious needs of all members. In other settings, this expectation is also held to varying degrees.

Since every organization has a unique culture, new chaplains typically go through an informal probationary period to prove their credibility and worth before being considered a full member. I needed several months of a yearlong remote tour in the Republic of Korea to become fully accepted as part of the organization, even after having served as a military chaplain in other units for over fifteen years.

From the beginning of the tour, I was treated appropriately and with respect. However, it was very evident to me that I was "on the outside looking in." Some individuals did automatically accept me as their chaplain, but others, while acknowledging that I was filling the assigned chaplain's slot, maintained a distance and showed little interest in getting to know me or accepting what I had to offer until I had proven myself in their eyes. It took a few months. After the unit and I had trained together in the field, been involved in rigorous qualification exercises, done extensive physical activities together, and shared many difficult situations, I suddenly realized there had been a breakthrough and I was a fully accepted member of the organization.

In the early weeks, I had been able to get close to only a few members of the headquarters unit. By the end of my tour, I became significantly involved with at least ninety-five percent of the individuals in the unit. During that year together, virtually everyone experienced a crisis, either back home or in their work assignments, and being with them at their point and time of need opened doors of opportunity for ministry. Becoming an "insider" provides incredible opportunities to do ministry.

The same dynamic occurs in hospitals, jails or prisons, police or fire departments, and corporations or businesses—wherever chaplains serve. A chaplain who is new to a particular organization is unlikely to be received immediately and wholly into that culture. It takes time and resembles going through the ritual of initiation.

## INSTITUTIONAL DUALITY

One reality clergy encounter immediately upon becoming chaplains is that they are full members of two separate and distinct institutions, both of which virtually place a total claim on them. This varies by degree, depending on the type of chaplain ministry they enter.

An appreciation of the significance of institutional duality—the fact that a chaplain is not affiliated with, but is fully part of, two major social institutions—is key to understanding both the problems and opportunities of the chaplaincy.[69]

The religious institution to which a chaplain belongs holds ecclesiastical authority, and the secular institution holds commissioning, transferring, hiring and firing, and other formal authority. In cases where the secular institution is the funding source, it has the right to require that its expectations be met. It is essential that chaplains embrace the policies of both entities and seek to honor them as best as possible. In no setting should a chaplain be considered as "half clergy" and "half staff member." In reality, the chaplain is a full-fledged member of both institutions, and both of them require the chaplain's allegiance.

A vocational change might be necessary if a person cannot accept both institutions' practices, tenets, expectations, goals, or requirements. In most cases, the basic tenets of both institutions are compatible. Conflict or apparent incompatibility is often due to a misinterpretation of requirements or tenets by a commander, a supervisor, or perhaps a church official. We will address the potential role conflict below.

Most organizations are willing to accommodate the requirements of the religious institution out of respect for the chaplain and the place of religion in culture. I have witnessed only a few instances where representatives of a secular institution have been hostile or unwelcoming to the presence of chaplains. This is not to minimize the possibility, but the frequency of such negative occurrences is relatively small. It seems most secular institutions recognize and appreciate the value of chaplains and religion in the workplace. However, conflicts can occur, and when they do happen, a chaplain must seek wise counsel and navigate the issues carefully.

## ROLE CONFLICT

As chaplains are full members of two institutions that are responsible for them, inevitably clashes of ideas, values, and loyalties arise due to the nature

---

[69] Richard G. Hutcheson Jr., *The Churches and the Chaplaincy*, rev. ed. (US Government Printing Office, 1998), 5.

and expectations of two disparate roles. Misunderstandings and misinterpretations happen. These clashes may result in the powerful and potentially crippling dynamic of "role conflict," when incompatible expectations of a job or position clash and pull a person in different directions. Being full members of two all-encompassing institutions creates the likely prospect of such role conflict. Regardless of the kind of secular institutions chaplains serve, they retain full clergy status.

> The vocational identity of a minister is almost completely established by his or her church. It is the church that controls professional education, usually in denominational seminaries. In ordination it confers professional credentials. Job assignments, salary scales, vocational changes and progression, continuing education opportunities, all are determined by institutional regulation or custom.[70]

A similar all-inclusiveness is true of their institutional identity. In the military, chaplains are like all other officers in that branch of service. They receive military commissions, wear the same uniform, obey the same regulations, wear the same ranks, participate in the same training, and are salaried and assigned similar duties and responsibilities.

In health care, chaplains must pass a certification process with agencies such as the Association of Professional Chaplains (APC) and the American Association of Clinical Pastoral Education (ACPE), wear the same "uniform," and abide by the same requirements of other healthcare professionals. In corrections, similar institutional expectations for levels of training and expertise exist, along with adherence to the rules and policies of that institutional setting. In virtually every type of institutional chaplaincy, there is guidance concerning practices related to salaries, transfers, policies, and organizational expectations. It is inevitable with this institutional duality that chaplains will experience role conflict—when their role as religious ministers seems to conflict with their role as leaders within the secular institution. It is in the tension

---

[70] Hutcheson, *Churches and the Chaplaincy*, 21.

between two all-encompassing institutions, one religious and the other secular, that chaplain ministry takes place.[71]

My 1984 doctoral dissertation addressed military chaplaincy and role conflict. I surveyed numerous dissertations, studies, and articles on role conflict primarily of military chaplains but relevant to chaplaincy of all types. During the unpopular Vietnam War and in the postwar era, churches and society looked hypercritically at the role of military chaplains. The accusation frequently leveled at chaplains was that they too often adopted the military role while abdicating their clergy role. Many writers placed the military chaplaincy under close reexamination, and role conflict became a major concern. The commingling of clergy and military roles appeared to become so great that a number of churches stated the military role was "so incompatible with the clergy role as to lead them to advocate doing away with the chaplaincy."[72] In every generation since then, antagonists of chaplaincy have continued this viewpoint.

Government retains authority over all aspects of the military services, Veterans Affairs, and state-funded correctional facilities. Consequently, critics of chaplaincy constantly question the appropriateness of mixing church and state in those institutions. First Amendment concerns are always present. The legal question of the constitutionality of the chaplaincy in government settings is addressed in chapter 5, "Constitutional Foundation" and chapter 11, "Special Issues and Challenges." It is important to note that potential for role conflict not only occurs in government settings but also in every type of institution, public or private. Chaplains encounter conflict with the goals, functions, and practices in any organization.

Historically, chaplains have dealt with many "hot button" issues about which faith groups, secular institutions, and one's personal theology and ethics differ significantly. Issues such as LGBTQ rights, same-sex marriage, abortion, gender bias, and racial inequities are some that chaplains face. Chaplains should know where their faith groups stand on these matters.

For the military chaplain, potential areas for role conflict come from several issues: war and peace, church versus state, chaplains wearing rank,

---

[71] Hutcheson.
[72] Hutcheson, 22.

expectations of commanders, and the chaplain's prophetic role versus the roles of military officer and morale builder.[73] While not all types of chaplains experience these kinds of role conflict to the same extent, most of them are challenging issues in every type of chaplaincy.

Next to potential disagreement with one's supervisor, perhaps the most likely cause of role conflict is the prophetic role of the chaplain. It can be a source of powerfully meaningful possibilities for growth and development, or it may become troublesome, disastrous, and even career-ending. "Speaking truth to power" is sometimes necessary but can become costly.

The list is long of chaplains who have felt compelled to proclaim the Word of the Lord in institutional settings and have paid dearly for it. Many writers have weighed in on the criticality of chaplains embracing their prophetic role. On the other hand, others have declared it unlikely that chaplains will speak boldly with a prophetic voice because they are concerned about the negative fallout.

> How does a chaplain proclaim a prophetic gospel when he is wearing the uniform of the military, is paid by the state, and furthermore is dependent on superior officers for advancement?[74]

This dilemma is not limited to the military chaplaincy and can be an ever-present reality in any type of chaplaincy. Libby wrote that in many instances there will be only one "right" way to respond, and that reality demands agonizing prayer and appraisal on the part of the chaplain.

> It just may be necessary for the chaplain to risk asking hard questions, to include confronting behavior and thinking that indicate a lack of ethical understanding or a sense of integrity.[75]

---

[73] Robert C. Vickers, *The Military Chaplaincy: A Study in Role Conflict* (unpublished doctoral dissertation, Vanderbilt University, 1984), 46.

[74] H. G. Cox Jr., ed. *Military Chaplains: From Religious Military to Military Religion* (New York: American Report Press, 1973), x.

[75] B. W. Libby, "The Chaplain's Allegiance to His Church," *Military Chaplains' Review* 12, no. 3 (Fall 1983): 32–36.

An essential question to ask is, "how does one manage and cope with role conflict?" One must critically understand it is impossible to resolve every role conflict satisfactorily for everyone involved. In order to survive role conflict, one must be persistent, flexible, and innovative.[76]

Additionally, one must assemble as much information as possible, talk with others, and spend time in reflection and prayer. Unfortunately, the emotions around role conflict can escalate quickly, and the presenting issue that initiates the conflict often becomes lost in defensive behavior. The situation may quickly disintegrate into a contest about winning or losing. Much of the time, conflict stems more from personality clashes than from institutional policy or guidance. Studies on chaplaincy through the decades have indicated that chaplains experience significant amounts of role conflict. When this occurs, virtually all chaplains claim their first allegiance is to God.[77]

George Williams counters chaplains are more bound functionally and psychologically to their chain of command than to their ecclesiastical superiors.[78] The closeness in geographical proximity to the secular institution and distance away from the ecclesiastical institution contributes to this tendency. A consequence of that behavior, if chaplains fail to remain vigilant, is to fall into the trap of compromise as they try so hard to "become part of the team" that they go against personal and denominational values.

Awareness of potential role conflict in the secular institutional setting is critical. Hutcheson highlights the importance of recognizing and maintaining this role conflict tension. Being aware of this tension validates the different roles of clergy and officer. Without this tension, one likely has migrated too far to one role at the cost of the other. The challenge is wearing both the officer's and the chaplain's roles equally well. Hutcheson's use of the word *tension* is significant. The presence of "role tension" for chaplains can be very positive. This tension is normal and can be a healthy dynamic. Chaplains should feel tension between their interacting roles as religious ministers and professional

---

[76] Stuart Palmer, *Role Stress* (Englewood Cliffs, NJ: Prentice-Hall, 1981), 14.

[77] Robert C. Vickers, "The Military Chaplaincy: A Study in Role Conflict," *Military Chaplains' Review* 15, no. 2 (Spring 1986): 89.

[78] George H. Williams, "The Chaplaincy in the Armed Forces of the United States of America in Historical and Ecclesiastical Perspective," *Military Chaplains: From Religious Military to a Military Religion* (New York: American Report Press, 1973), 12.

representatives of secular institutions. Role tension keeps chaplains sharp, alert, focused, and effective. We can call it "creative role tension." Without it, one can get lazy or sloppy in one's work. It is much like having proper tension on the chain of a chainsaw: if the chain is too loose, it will not cut and is useless.

How does one find that point of effective and creative role tension? It comes through knowing one's theological and denominational stance. It comes from knowing oneself. It comes through building trust and connection with secular institutions. And, as one becomes part of the institutional team, working from the inside and using even unplanned and incidental opportunities to bring hope, encouragement, and help, the dynamic tension between the two roles can benefit all. Chaplains can use ingenuity to advance the goals of the secular institution while at the same time find opportunities to provide spiritual care for members of the organization.[79] One does not have to work to create role tension. It inevitably will be present. When it is not present, then it is the time to become concerned.

## ACCOUNTABILITY

Chaplains are accountable to two institutions. This is to be expected. On the ecclesiastical side, the chaplain, through the denominational endorsement process, is declared to be a minister in good standing with a faith group. This is the starting point, and a continuing relationship is imperative. Every endorsing agency maintains periodic contact with its chaplains. The faith group requires it, and the secular institution expects, respects, and supports it. Some endorsers require periodic, written reports; provide mandatory training conferences; and conduct personal visits. The maintenance of this connection secures the chaplain's relationship with the church, and it assists the faith group in keeping the chaplain updated on what is happening in the life of the denomination. Periodic communication with denominational sources and visits from church representatives are helpful in maintaining this connection.

When chaplains run into difficulty, either with the secular institution or the faith group, denominational representatives usually get involved and attempt to help bring resolution. This is discussed further in chapter 14, "The Professional Chaplain." A current challenge for churches and chaplains is

---

[79] Hutcheson, *Churches and the Chaplaincy*, 25.

their tendency to make private judgments, following their own consciences rather than staying in line with official church positions.[80] Suffice it to say that chaplains are accountable to the faith groups who endorsed them.

The secular institution also requires accountability. The expectation is every member of the institution, including the chaplain, will meet all standards and fulfill all requirements of the organization. Periodic performance reviews are used as a means of establishing goals and tracking progress toward accomplishing goals, and the supervisor holds the chaplain accountable for performance in meeting goals. Expectations are not relaxed for the chaplain. In the military, I have heard commanders say, "I want my chaplain to set the standard. I expect my chaplain to be the best officer in my unit." Leadership should expect the same standard of excellence of all chaplains in every type of institutional setting.

## ADVOCACY—TWO-WAY

The chaplain occupies a critical position in every organization. Everyone needs an advocate from time to time, and the chaplain is perfectly positioned to speak for every member of the organization, from top to bottom. Oftentimes, muted voices need to be heard for the benefit of all. If the chaplain has done a good job of gaining credibility through personal integrity, competence, and demonstrated genuine concern, the opportunity exists to make a significant impact. Additionally, the chaplain can fulfill a vital role in advocating for the organization.

Often, the organization's intended purpose and goals become lost in the everyday scrum of activity, and the members can lose sight of that for which they labor. With wisdom and sensitivity, chaplains can assist in interpreting why things are being done as they are, but only if they have gained the confidence of members at every level. When focus and direction are lost, chaplains are strategically positioned to help reset the compass for everyone.

## MINISTRY TO ALL

The chaplain is in a position to provide spiritual care to everyone in the organization, regardless of faith-group preference. The chaplain ministers not

---

[80] Hutcheson, 27.

only to those in the lower ranks but to every level of responsibility. It is sometimes thought, often erroneously, that leaders are so "put together" that they have no need for a personal relationship with the chaplain or anything the chaplain has to offer; their only need is for the chaplain to take care of the people "downline."

Some of my most meaningful and gratifying chaplaincy experiences have come from situations in which commanders, after gaining confidence in my ministry, reached out for advice, reflection about a troubling matter, or prayer for them amid a trying time. One never knows for sure the burdens leaders are carrying.

For the chaplain to present a posture of care, confidentiality, and availability opens the door for those significant and meaningful opportunities for ministry. It usually takes time to gain the confidence of leaders. The title "chaplain" and wearing of the chaplaincy emblem does not automatically open the door to leaders; it takes time and a consistent demonstration of competence and genuine concern.

In addition to providing spiritual care for all members of the organization, the chaplain has an opportunity to provide ministry to the institution itself. This means helping to infuse the organization with a heart and a conscience. In doing so, the organization can more effectively become human and responsive to human need rather than simply existing as a cold and unresponsive entity. Hutcheson lists evidence of significant organizational change as a result of chaplain ministry.[81] Just as in the military setting, all types of secular institutions benefit from chaplain ministry.

## INSIDER MINISTRY

Several years ago, Southern Baptist Mission Board published a brochure, "Going Where Others Cannot Go."[82] It provided a descriptive collage of chaplaincy in a variety of settings, all presenting chaplains as intimately involved in the totality of several different institutions. This is the essence of "insider" ministry: being one with members of the organization, not "stand-

---

[81] Hutcheson, 40–41.
[82] Joe Westbury, ed., *Going Where Others Cannot Go* (Atlanta: Home Mission Board, 1995), 8–9. This was produced by the Chaplaincy Division of the Home Mission Board.

ing on the outside looking in." As Hutcheson wrote, being an "insider" removes artificiality, grants a greater awareness of the problems faced and the life lived by chaplains' "parishioners," and provides a ready-made contact with the unchurched.[83]

To be granted entry to all work and training sites is a privilege. To be part of discussions about the health and wholeness of the organization and to be viewed as the expert in spiritual care, religion, morals, and morale of the organization is a responsibility and blessing available only to those who share the "insider" privilege. This type of ministry is often referred to as the "ministry of presence." As such, it is going with and being where the members of the secular organization work and play and sleep. Because chaplains share the experiences—hardships, victories, and defeats—along with all members of the organization, they are recognized as those who understand and can be trusted.

In past decades, on several occasions, many have attempted to "civilianize" the chaplaincy in military and other governmental settings. The challenges have come in large part because of questions about the constitutionality of supposed "government sponsorship of religion." In overruling such challenges, the Supreme Court and lower courts have recognized the importance of "insider" chaplain ministry. If chaplains were not permitted to minister as "insiders" and be an integral part of the organizations they serve, chances are remote they would be accepted as full-fledged members of the team and have any significant standing with the organizations they serve. Their value would be questionable at best. Beyond the shadow of any doubt, "insider ministry" creates the opportunity for highly effective ministry in every type of secular institutional setting.

## REFLECTION QUESTIONS

1. The largest distinction between a chaplain and a pastor is the secular institutional context of ministry. Role conflict or tension can and often occurs as a chaplain fulfills the various roles within an institution. Describe a scenario within your interest in chaplaincy where you might anticipate role conflict and how you would manage it.

---

[83] Hutcheson, *Churches and the Chaplaincy*, 39.

2. Dr. Vickers stated, "To survive, contribute, and thrive in the new setting, chaplains must have 'institutional awareness' and make adjustments accordingly. They should also know their essential identity and calling and be firmly rooted in their theology before becoming chaplains. This enables them to accommodate in 'accidental' matters but not compromise on the essential ones." What would be an example of an institutional-awareness matter that could potentially create an issue for you as it relates to your identity and calling?
3. Dr. Vickers highlights the benefits of "Insider" ministry: "being one with members of the organization, not 'standing on the outside looking in.'" From your perspective as a chaplain, what benefits and challenges could be associated with being one of the organization's members?
4. Can a chaplain overidentify with an institution? If so, what would be the impact on the chaplain in doing so?

CHAPTER TEN

# THE MARGINAL AND LIMINAL NATURE OF CHAPLAINCY

Rev. Dr. William Whitmore

It is prevalent to hear chaplains struggle with their perceived lack of importance or relevancy to an institution and its mission. Many factors can feed this perception, such as chaplains' lack of understanding of the breadth of their role and responsibilities to the institution, being poorly supported with resources, and being disenfranchised by leadership. Chaplains should not diminish the importance of the factors but must work to overcome each of these three limiting factors. However, if chaplains understand the importance of their "marginalized" positions within an institution, they can leverage their uniqueness and have a significant impact.

A fellow chaplain recently told me he felt underutilized and often overlooked by his organizational leadership due to a lack of support and, at times, being removed from decisions that directly affected his ministry and programming efforts. In short, this person felt like an outsider to the organization, even though he had served the institution for many years. At times, chaplains take this as a reflection on their abilities or question their effectiveness within a given context. Although it is easy to see its origin, I believe it misses a key element of chaplaincy. Rather than seeing the marginal nature of chaplain ministry within an organization as something to lament or overcome, what if chaplains saw their marginality as inherent and essential to effective ministry? This section will suggest that chaplaincy's marginal and liminal nature is inherent in and crucial to a chaplain's effective ministry. It will discuss the power of a liminal agent within an organization and how the chaplain embodies this role.

Two brief definitions are essential to address in this context. First, marginality refers to someone or something on the periphery of a specific group or entity. As a result of this status, the marginal being is not central to the task or goals of the larger group or body. Stephen Pattison contends that chaplaincy per se is an inherently marginal field given that, in general, chaplains are not central to the mission of the organization that they serve.[84] For example, the primary goal of a hospital is to aid individuals who are physically unwell and restore them to a place of health. While healthcare chaplains provide support and spiritual care to patients, they do not order blood work, analyze the results, and apply the findings to the patient's treatment plan. Strictly speaking, the chaplain is not primary but is in a supportive role in the central goal of an organization. Second, liminality is an ambiguous state where the individual is not in a set position within an institution. Whereas many members of an organization have clear goals and outcomes related to their position, the chaplain's work is often slightly ambiguous, with not as many explicit markers and outcomes. This is partly because a chaplain's work is mainly relational and not task-oriented. To understand how a chaplain is a liminal agent, we must first discuss rites of passage.

French anthropologist Arnold van Gennep produced the first theoretical framework for assessing and analyzing rituals in terms of their structure, frequency, and importance for times of transition. Van Gennep observed that, while the specific rituals in each setting are unique, their form and importance are consistent across contexts. In his seminal work, *The Rites of Passage*, van Gennep argues that any rite has three stages. First, the person or group undergoing the ritual experiences a rite of separation (preliminal rite), which removes the one undergoing the rite from their previous social state or norm. The rite then enters a transitional (liminal) phase. This second state is one of ambiguity, where those undergoing the ritual have separated from one entity but are not yet included in the next. After the subject has passed through

---

[84] Stephen Pattison, "Situating Chaplaincy in the United Kingdom: The Acceptable Face of 'Religion'?" in *A Handbook of Chaplaincy Studies: Understanding Spiritual Care in Public Places*, ed. Christopher Swift, Mark Cobb, and Andrew Todd (Burlington: Ashgate Publishing, 2015), 13–30.

the transitory phase, the process concludes with the rite of incorporation (postliminal). This final phase comprises the subject joining, or rejoining, the society, having undergone some form of transformational process. While all three phases are important within a ritual, van Gennep states that not all stages are developed equally or emphasized in the same way in every social context. For example, funerals emphasize rites of separation while weddings focus on rites of incorporation. Van Gennep's second phase, liminality, is of particular importance to our discussion of chaplaincy.[85] Building on the work of van Gennep, Victor Turner, a British cultural anthropologist, highlighted how rites of passage can affect or provide social change. Turner's work focused on liminality, suggesting that the transformational power of the liminal is essential for any group, society, or organization to function.

Turner broadens the understanding of liminality to incorporate entities outside of a specific rite, seeing the concept as an element of a healthy society. This entity could be an individual (such as a chaplain), festival, event, specific space, or other agreed-upon occurrence or context. For Turner, liminality connects the two poles of society: *communitas* and structure.

According to Turner, *communitas* is a relational state of equality where there is a removal of hierarchy that allows individuals from different groups in the society to be equal, whether they are social, political, or another type of differentiation. In this rite, he uses the example of a tribal chief's installation to demonstrate a period of *communitas*. In the rite described, those of lower societal status can approach the chief-to-be and acknowledge any previous wrongdoing or hardship. In contrast, the chief-to-be cannot respond and lies motionless on the ground. This type of equality would not be acceptable outside this ritual, as it would violate the group's structure. Turner states that structure, the other pole of society in his framework, is notoriously hierarchal, separating people between socioeconomic, political, or other classifications. Structure within a society not only defines individuals by these categories, deeming them more or less important than their counterparts, but also sets norms and standards that help provide order and organization to the group.

---

[85] Arthur van Gennep, *The Rites of Passage*, trans. Monika B. Vizedom and Gabrielle L. Caffee (Chicago: University of Chicago Press, 1960), 1–13.

Turner argues that no society is purely *communitas* or structure, but societies oscillate between them to remain functioning and healthy.

Turner contends that *communitas* is present where structure is not. For a shift to occur, those involved need to enter a liminal state. The liminality leading to *communitas* allows for spontaneous and relational encounters between people. One would not expect equality and transformation to arise during routine interactions between groups in a structured society; however, the ambiguity and liminality of specific people or events, such as a chaplain, allows the status quo to be transformed, even if only for a brief period. Even though *communitas* is temporal, Turner sees liminality as a lasting condition for specific groups or people.[86] He argues that the marginal person, whom the wider society may deem insignificant, can shift a community to a place of equality. I want to suggest that the chaplain's role is an excellent example of Turner's concept of a liminal agent.

Chaplains often find themselves "in between" groups and structures within a specific organization. As a result, they can fall through the cracks of the organization without a set or fixed area, which leads to chaplains feeling marginalized. Finally, as Pattison reminds us, the chaplain's position is outside the primary focus of the institution they serve, frequently leaving them on a lower rung within the organization. While this may not be true in every situation, like in the military, where a chaplain's rank and historical/legal precedent provide certain privileges, chaplains are rarely central figures within an organization's decision-making structures. As a result, chaplains often seek to build strong relationships with those in leadership, not only so they can serve them faithfully but also to have an ally within the organization. Balancing the need to receive positive attention from leadership while being aware of their position in an organization can add to the stress already felt by chaplains.

Unsurprisingly, chaplains may feel marginalized in their ministry with insufficient institutional support even though they seek to serve and provide important spiritual care to those within the institution. This position can frustrate the chaplain, particularly if the individual has shifted from

---

[86] Victor Turner, *The Ritual Process: Structure and Anti-Structure* (New York: Aldine de Gruyter, 1995), 107.

congregational ministry to chaplaincy. The faith leader is central to a congregation, but the chaplain is on the organization's margins. Those who make this shift need to be particularly aware of the difference in position and ready for this shift. However, the liminal agent remains essential to the health and well-being of a group.

Turner speaks of the power of the person who has a lesser position within the structure of a society than others who are more central to the institutional mission but still convey deep wisdom and insight within a specific situation.[87] He sees their role as vital because they are the ones who convey *communitas* to the closed entity that is a structured society. This is where the chaplain's ministry is most effective, such as leading a key ritual, in moments of pastoral care where a comforting word is transformative, providing a relational equality not always felt, or in moments of crisis where a chaplain's presence is calming. Chaplains offer a unique and essential service to those in their care. Chaplains' ambiguity and liminality allow them to move in ways others cannot, and their lack of organizational requirements give them a freedom to support where needed. As chaplains take on more elements of leadership, management, or requirements outside of caring for individuals in the community, other issues do arise that would hinder their ability to serve. For example, if chaplains also manage projects or teams outside of ministry, they become part of the structure of an organization. This could make it difficult for individuals needing a chaplain's care to seek help and be honest, as they may be worried about how their disclosure could affect their job or place in the organization. While it is in a person's nature to desire control and to feel wanted, chaplaincy thrives when these elements are not always present. In this, chaplains wait expectantly for moments to serve and care for both individuals and their organizations, understanding that by inhabiting the margins of a structured society, they can bring about *communitas*.

As liminal personae, chaplains can bring about *communitas* to a closed group in a way that others in the structure cannot provide, offering relational and pastoral support to all. This position is one of strength and allows chaplains to live out their missional witness. While Pattison is correct that the marginal position of the chaplain is a strength, his use of the term "marginal"

---

[87] Turner, *Ritual Process*, 125.

hinders his argument. Indeed, articulating feelings of marginalization is rarely, if ever, a positive; however, if chaplains can see their work as liminal, in which marginality is one unavoidable facet, they can begin to reshape and reimagine their position within their host organization. While marginality will still be present, it is not the central focus. Instead, prioritizing the benefits of liminality and *communitas* allow the chaplain to feel empowered and understand why their role will always be, in some form, on the margins. From the margins, chaplains can most effectively care for those within their organizations.

## REFLECTION QUESTIONS

1. Chaplains who serve a secular institution can feel marginalized by the institution in appreciation, support, and resources. Why do you think this is the case from reading this section?
2. Dr. Whitmore suggests that chaplains have some significant ministry opportunities because they are not central to an institution's mission. Do you agree with the author's premise? Why or why not?

CHAPTER ELEVEN

# SPECIAL ISSUES AND CHALLENGES

Chaplains face issues and challenges unique to ministry in a secular and institutional setting. Both in the preparation and execution of chaplaincy, one should become very familiar with these issues and build a cadre of professional advisors. Seeking counsel from others is an imperative, especially if one does not want to learn hard lessons the hard way. Through these different contributors, this chapter highlights several issues and challenges that can significantly impact a chaplain's ministry and offers pearls of wisdom to the reader.

# LEGAL

## Chaplain David Little, J.D.

Chaplains face several legal issues that require careful attention in their official roles. Most of these matters are situationally dependent, but others are general and occur more often. Chaplains should deal with them from legal, theological, and practical perspectives. When people are in crisis, they tend to react poorly. Sometimes these reactions turn into legal action or a remedy through legal channels. This section addresses several legal issues that can directly or indirectly impact chaplains and their ministries.

### CONSTITUTIONAL QUESTION

Are chaplains who work for the government legal? Is government-sponsored chaplaincy limited in any way? To answer these questions, one must start with the US Constitution, in both theory and practice. In theory, the government has competing systems of checks and balances. In practice, courts and laws influenced by politics and circumstances also have their say. Also, some views predating the Constitution proper (without amendments) influence this discussion.

The First Amendment to the United States Constitution states, "Congress shall make no law respecting an establishment of religion, or prohibiting the free exercise thereof; or abridging the freedom of speech, or of the press; or the right of the people peaceably to assemble, and to petition the Government for a redress of grievances."

In *Lemon v. Kurtzman* (1971), an establishment-clause case, the US Supreme Court said its prior cases promoted a three-prong "Lemon Test": "First, the statute must have a secular legislative purpose; second, its principal or primary effect must be one that neither advances nor inhibits religion. . . . finally, the statute must not foster 'an excessive government entanglement with religion.' "[88] In *Lemon*, the court held that Rhode Island and Pennsylvania statutes allowing the government to pay nonpublic schoolteachers were unconstitutional. The overall relationship between the government and the religious schools involved excessive entanglement.

Also, since differing views about "separation of church and state" are used to oppose or support chaplaincy, chaplains should understand this issue and its potential impact on ministry.

## Military

(Editor's note: In Section Five—Chaplaincy Types, Michael Berry extensively reviews "The Role of Religion in the United States Armed Forces" from its historic, moral, and legal basis.)

The US Supreme Court has not ruled on the constitutionality of military or prison chaplains. However, in *Katcoff v. Marsh* (1985), the Second Circuit Court of Appeals held that military chaplaincy does not violate the Establishment Clause.[89] Deeming the Lemon Test inappropriate in this case,[90] the court relied on the War Powers and Free Exercise clauses (and their cases), to affirm virtually all of military chaplaincy.[91]

## Health Care

*Carter v. Broadlawns Medical Center* (1988) was an Eighth Circuit case involving chaplaincy at a state hospital that had volunteer chaplain services

---

[88] See *Lemon v. Kurtzman*, 403 US 602 (1971), Legal Information Institute, Cornell Law School, https://www.law.cornell.edu/supremecourt/text/403/602, accessed 12 March 2021. For this test, the court cited: *Board of Education v. Allen*, 392 US 236, 243, 88 S. Ct. 1923, 1926, 20 L.Ed.2d 1060 (1968); and *Walz v. Tax Commission of City of New York*, 397 US 664 (1970), 674, 90 S. Ct., at 1414, https://supreme.justia.com/cases/federal/us/397/664/, accessed 2 March 2021.
[89] Emilie S. Kraft, "Chaplains," 2009, The First Amendment Encyclopedia, Middle Tennessee State University, http://www.mtsu.edu/rst-amendment/article/909/chaplains, accessed 8 Feb 2021.
[90] *Katcoff v. Marsh*, 755 F.2d 223, 228 (2d Cir. 1985).
[91] *Katcoff v. Marsh*, 237.

but wanted to hire and pay a staff chaplain.[92] The court said the Lemon Test permitted hiring but put restrictions on counseling the staff (secular purposes only) and seeing patients' medical records (only when the patient or patient's representatives allowed it).[93] Authorized chaplain's practices today, especially those involving civilian hospitals, permit walking alongside staff and supporting them. The Health Insurance Portability and Accountability Act (HIPAA) governs access to patients' medical records. It allows hospital-employed chaplains providing spiritual ministry to see those records. Chaplains of all types, especially in hospitals, must know the pertinent legal issues affecting the terrain and people they shepherd.

## CLERGY PRIVILEGE

### Federal and State Evidentiary Rules

Another legal issue for chaplains is clergy privilege. What is clergy privilege? Does it always apply? What circumstances may mitigate its usage? In various state statutes, clergy privilege, simply stated is: anything a person tells you in confidence is to be protected and not shared with others unless the person permits you to do so, or laws dictate mandatory reporting.

The clergy-penitent privilege originated in European Roman Catholic canon law, where "the seal of the confessional is 'inviolable.'"[94] In America, the privilege became viable by a New York court case, *People v. Phillips* (1813). In 1817, *People v. Smith* held Protestant ministers did not have the same confessional clergy-penitent privilege as Catholic clergy. In response, New York passed the first statute extending clergy privilege to all ministers

---

[92] *Carter v. Broadlawns Medical Center*, 857 F2d 448 (8th Cir. 1988), https://casetext.com/case/carter-v-broadlawns-medical-center-3/?PHONE_NUMBER_GROUP=C, accessed 20 July 2021.
[93] *Carter v. Broadlawns Medical Center*.
[94] F. Robert Radel II and Andrew A. Labbe, "The Clergy-Penitent Privilege: An Overview," 386, https://cdn.ymaws.com/thefederation.site-ym.com/resource/resmgr/docs/Quarterly/Archive/V64N4_Radel.pdf, accessed 19 May 2021, citing R. Michael Cassidy, "Sharing Shared Secrets: Is It (Past) Time for a Dangerous Person Exception to the Clergy Penitent Privilege?" 44 Wm. & Mary L. Rev. 1627, 1695–96 (2003).

and similar religious denominations.⁹⁵ Now, every state and the District of Columbia has some version of this law.⁹⁶

## Military

In the Armed services, chaplains must comply with the Military Rules of Evidence (MRE) and clergy privilege. MRE Rule 503 states,

> A communication is "confidential" if made to a clergyman in the clergyman's capacity as a spiritual adviser or to a clergyman's assistant in the assistant's official capacity and is not intended to be disclosed to third persons other than those to whom disclosure is in furtherance of the purpose of the communication or to those reasonably necessary for the transmission of the communication.⁹⁷

---

⁹⁵ Radel and Labbe, 385. See Cassidy, "Sharing Shared Secrets," note 3, 1638–39.
⁹⁶ Radel and Labbe, 386.
⁹⁷ "Rule 503: Communications to Clergy," from "Military Rules of Evidence," Joint Service Committee on Military Justice, https://jsc.defense.gov/Portals/99/Documents/MREsRemoved412e.pdf, accessed 3 April 2021.

> (a) *General Rule.* A person has a privilege to refuse to disclose and to prevent another from disclosing a confidential communication by the person to a clergyman or to a clergyman's assistant, if such communication is made either as a formal act of religion or as a matter of conscience.
>
> (b) *Definitions.* As used in this rule:
>
> > (1) "Clergyman" means a minister, priest, rabbi, chaplain, or other similar functionary of a religious organization, or an individual reasonably believed to be so by the person consulting the clergyman.
> >
> > (2) "Clergyman's assistant" means a person employed by or assigned to assist a clergyman in his capacity as a spiritual advisor.
> >
> > (3) A communication is "confidential" if made to a clergyman in the clergyman's capacity as a spiritual adviser or to a clergyman's assistant in the assistant's official capacity and is not intended to be disclosed to third persons other than those to whom disclosure is in furtherance of the purpose of the communication or to those reasonably necessary for the transmission of the communication.
>
> (c) *Who May Claim the Privilege.* The privilege may be claimed by the person, guardian, or conservator, or by a personal representative if the person is deceased. The clergyman or clergyman's assistant who received the communication may claim the privilege on behalf of the person. The authority of the clergyman or clergyman's assistant to do so is presumed in the absence of evidence to the contrary.

Noteworthy is the inclusion of the "clergyman's assistant," an enlisted member assigned to support the mission of chaplains.[98] Military chaplains must protect confidential disclosures made to them—no exceptions. The client owns the privilege and determines who may become privy to that information. Preservation of this trust between a military chaplain and client is critical. It is foundational for providing an invaluable safety net to those who need support and guidance.

## Health Care

How does this privilege impact healthcare chaplains (and those in Veterans Affairs) and the documentation requirement in patients' charts? How may the chaplain inform the rest of the healthcare team while protecting the patient's confidentiality? Each state's rules of evidence govern the relationship between chaplains and patients. Therefore, relevant laws in each state must be understood and followed. So, chaplains in Texas should be aware of Texas Rules of Evidence and their exceptions.[99] Chaplains serving on federal land must also

---

[98] "Rule 503: Communications to Clergy."

[99] "Rule 505: Privilege for Communications to a Clergy Member," from "Texas Rules of Evidence," Texas Judicial Branch, www.txcourts.gov/media/1448644/texas-rules-of-evidence-updated-with-amendments-effective-612020-f.pdf, accessed 22 March 2022.

>   (a) *Definitions.* In this rule:
>
>   (1) A "clergy member" is a minister, priest, rabbi, accredited Christian Science Practitioner, or other similar functionary of a religious organization or someone whom a communicant reasonably believes is a clergy member.
>   (2) A "communicant" is a person who consults a clergy member in the clergy member's professional capacity as a spiritual adviser.
>   (3) A communication is "confidential" if made privately and not intended for further disclosure except to other persons present to further the purpose of the communication.
>
>   (b) *General Rule.* A communicant has a privilege to refuse to disclose and to prevent any other person from disclosing a confidential communication by the communicant to a clergy member as a professional spiritual adviser.
>
>   (c) *Who May Claim.* The privilege may be claimed by:
>   (1) the communicant;
>   (2) the communicant's guardian or conservator; or
>   (3) a deceased communicant's personal representative.

know how federal rules apply and differ from state laws. Understanding the appropriate regulations is paramount.[100]

*Nicholson v. Wittig* (1992)[101] provides an interesting case study that directly impacts healthcare chaplaincy. In a wrongful death suit against Drs. Nicholson, Stephens, and Memorial Northwest Hospital (Houston, Texas), Mrs. Schnepel claimed the death of her husband, Ernest Schnepel, was due to the defendants' delay in treating him for a ruptured abdominal aortic aneurysm. The hospital said Mrs. Schnepel was responsible for the delay because she desired to transfer him to another hospital for surgery. Mrs. Schnepel denied having made this request. The chaplaincy-related issue concerned whether Reverend Shirl, a hospital employee who sought to give "comfort, guidance, and spiritual counseling"[102] to Mrs. Schnepel, could be forced to reveal what the family wanted to remain privileged under Rule 505 of the Texas Rules of Evidence. The Texas First Court of Appeals determined the whole conversation was privileged, regardless of its communication in front of others.[103] In doing so, Justice F. Lee Duggan cited John Wigmore, renowned Dean of Northwestern Law School, and his treatise on evidence:

1. The communications must originate in confidence not to be disclosed.
2. This element of confidentiality must be essential to the complete and satisfactory maintenance of the relation between the parties.

---

The clergy member to whom the communication was made may claim the privilege on the communicant's behalf—and is presumed to have authority to do so.

[100] "Rule 501: Privilege in General," Federal Rules of Evidence, https://www.uscourts.gov/sites/default/files/federal_rules_of_evidence_-_dec_1_2019_0.pdf, accessed 3 April 2021. "The common law—as interpreted by United States courts in the light of reason and experience—governs a claim of privilege unless any of the following provides otherwise: the United States Constitution; a federal statute; or rules prescribed by the Supreme Court. But in a civil case, state law governs privilege regarding a claim or defense for which state law supplies the rule of decision" (amended 26 April 2011, effective 1 December 2011).

[101] *Nicholson v. Wittig*, 832 S.W.2d 681 (Tex. App. 1992).

[102] *Nicholson*, 681.

[103] *Nicholson*, 688.

3. The relation must be one which, in the opinion of the community, ought to be sedulously fostered.
4. The injury that would inure to the relation by the disclosure of the communications must be greater than the benefit thereby gained for the correct disposal of litigation. 8 WIGMORE ON EVIDENCE § 2285 (McNaughton rev. 1961).[104]

However, the decision was not unanimous. Justice Michol O'Connor, who wrote the dissenting opinion, believed only the confidential part of the communication should be withheld.[105]

## Confession

The sacrament of confession is a religious act in some faith groups, primarily Roman Catholic, and has a separate privacy based on Canon Law.[106] Other religious groups may hold that a person receiving confession "stands in" for

---

[104] *Nicholson.*
[105] *Nicholson.*
[106] See "Title IV: The Sacrament of Penance," *The Code of Canon Law*, Holy See, https://www.vatican.va/archive/cod-iuris-canonici/eng/documents/cic_lib4-cann959-997_en.html#TITLE_IV., accessed 25 March 2022.

**Canon 959.** "In the sacrament of penance the faithful who confess their sins to a legitimate minister, are sorry for them, and intend to reform themselves obtain from God through the absolution imparted by the same minister forgiveness for the sins they have committed after baptism and, at the same time, are reconciled with the Church which they have wounded by sinning." **Canon 960.** "Individual and integral confession and absolution constitute the only ordinary means by which a member of the faithful conscious of grave sin is reconciled with God and the Church. Only physical or moral impossibility excuses from confession of this type; in such a case reconciliation can be obtained by other means." **Canon 965.** "A priest alone is the minister of the sacrament of penance." **Canon 978 §1.** "In hearing confessions, the priest is to remember that he is equally a judge and a physician and has been established by God as a minister of divine justice and mercy, so that he has regard for the divine honor and the salvation of souls." **Canon 983 §1.** "The sacramental seal is inviolable; therefore it is absolutely forbidden for a confessor to betray in any way a penitent in words or in any manner and for any reason." §2 "The interpreter, if there is one, and all others who in any way have knowledge of sins from confession are also obliged to observe secrecy."

God, and no other person may hear it.[107] Therefore, a chaplain should be careful when hearing the confessional statement of a patient, family, or staff member.[108] Also, one should seek guidance from experienced healthcare chaplains before charting in medical records.

### Exceptions

Clergy privilege differs in every jurisdiction. For example, the Texas Rule of Evidence 505 gives no exceptions, unlike rules governing privileges to lawyer-client (TRE 503), spousal privileges (TRE 504), and physician-patient privileges (TRE 507).[109] Chaplains should become familiar with local laws governing clergy privilege, especially regarding child sexual abuse.[110]

## EXERCISING CAUTION

Any time a situation requires the handling or execution of legal documents, any chaplain should exercise caution when asked to be involved. For instance, what happens when a patient's lack of direction gives rise to hard decisions for family or medical personnel? The family bears the brunt, and the chaplain seeks to minister. Several legal documents pertain in this situation: (1) Medical Power of Attorney; (2) Advanced Medical Directive (or Directive to Physicians); (3) Out-of-Hospital Do Not Resuscitate (OOH DNR); and (4) Declaration for Mental Health Treatment. Add to these Statutory and Statutory Durable Powers of Attorney, Do-Not-Resuscitate and Do-Not-Intubate Directives, and other palliative care directives. Chaplains must know the purposes and procedures for these legal decisions and documents.

Any chaplain involved in securing these documents should also be aware of the patient's mental authority. The patient's medical circumstances or

---

[107] Chaplain (Major) Robert C. Lyons, "A Chaplain's Guide to Privileged Communication" (master's thesis, Duke University, 10 April 2001), 25.
[108] Lyons, "Chaplain's Guide," 30.
[109] "Rule 505: Privilege for Communications to a Clergy Member." But see Texas Fam. Code Sec. 261.101 (a clergy member has a duty to report if they have reasonable cause to believe that a child's physical or mental health or welfare has been adversely affected by abuse or neglect; see also Texas Fam. Code Sec. 261.202 (in a proceeding regarding abuse or neglect of a child, evidence cannot be withheld based on clergy-penitent privilege).
[110] Radel and Labbe, "Clergy-Penitent Privilege," 386.

family situation might make this assessment difficult. As long as the patient has mental capacity, the patient's verbal instructions govern the day, even if the written instructions disagree with what the patient desires.

Each state has unique statutes and procedures, so chaplains must check the sources and be familiar with pertinent state laws. If a situation lacks proper legal documents or decisions, the state's statutes will generally rule. For instance, in Texas where I practice as an attorney and chaplain, the Texas health and Safety Code, Section 313 gives direction. Decisions rest in order of preference but as with any rule, one should be aware of exceptions:

1. The patient's spouse;
2. an adult child of the patient who has the waiver and consent of all other qualified adult children of the patient to act as the sole decision-maker;
3. a majority of the patient's reasonably available adult children;
4. the patient's parents; or
5. the individual identified to act for the patient by the patient before the patient became incapacitated, the patient's nearest living relative, or a member of the clergy.[111]

Chaplains should not minister guided only by the heart while ignoring legal or policy ramifications. They must be aware of the legal landmines so easily triggered in typical institutional settings. In such scenarios, having a trusting relationship with the institution's lawyer is an invaluable resource.

## REFLECTION QUESTIONS

1. Confidentiality between the client and the chaplain varies as it is dependent on a variety of factors. Pick a chaplain category and describe the laws or regulations that define the boundaries of confidentiality.

---

[111] Health and Safety Code, Tx Stat title 4F, §313, https://statutes.capitol.texas.gov/Docs/HS/htm/HS.313.htm, accessed 9 June 2021.

2. Confidentiality is a trust between the client and the chaplain. Given a chaplain category of your choice, what would or must you do if a client comes to you with a method, means, and intentions of committing suicide?
3. This section concludes with the statement, "Chaplains should not minister guided only by the heart while ignoring legal or policy ramifications." What would be an example of a chaplain being guided only by the heart while ignoring legal or policy ramifications?

# SOCIAL ISSUES

## Dr. Tara Dixon

Social issues span a broad spectrum of challenges and problems, which often influence many citizens and ultimately shape culture. Social issues are also interdisciplinary, crossing fields such as climate change, environmental justice, overpopulation, immigration stresses, civil rights, racial discrimination, gender inequality, access to health care, childhood obesity, bullying, suicide prevention and intervention, and poor leadership.

Chaplains navigate such social issues by carefully researching and examining interdisciplinary approaches and applying evidence-based processes to and for spiritual well-being. They must broaden their perspectives and critically review the extent of a much broader social realm. They walk alongside people from all backgrounds and faith perspectives. It is incumbent upon chaplains to familiarize themselves with the issues and stressors that may impact their embedded settings.

Chaplains walk in a capacity that does not ignore their faith-based principles while remaining truthful in the context of social issues. Chaplains are visible reminders of the Holy—both vertically in relationship with God and horizontally in relationship with one another. Of course, a chaplain's relationship with a higher power is contingent on one's faith group and the faith or non-faith perspective of individuals the chaplain is journeying with at any given moment. Chaplains, then, either extend care or accommodate for spiritual well-being in such times. Depending on the social context, both vertical (justice) and horizontal (righteousness) dimensions are critical.

Chaplains must be able to react when needed and respond appropriately. For example, though chaplains are representatives of the Holy, they are not exempt from human emotions. Chaplains feel the same hurt, pain, frustration, and even anger as everyone else. I was at home with the flu, and a call came from my boss, the Wing Chaplain. A young lady, a Non-Commissioned Officer in Charge (NCOIC) in one of my units, with whom I had spent a great deal of time journeying, had completed suicide. This news shocked me, as this person had not shown signs of distress, at least in my thinking. I reviewed months of email exchanges with her, weeks of text messages, recalling multiple conversations in which we had talked at length about family, everyday southern experiences, SEC sports, work-life balance, marriage, workplace relationships, and faith. She stopped by my office regularly to chat and pick up the latest copy of "Our Daily Bread." What did I miss? Had I been so disconnected that I failed this Airman? Was my understanding of suicide flawed? Was my comprehension of suicide too theologically constructed? I reread each email line for line; I reread each text message carefully; I even read copies of "Our Daily Bread" that I had shared with her. Nothing explained or made me feel any better about this experience.

Something within the social context leading to that suicide completion, in my opinion, failed to provide a healthy sense of purpose and belonging for this Airman. It was a learning curve that caused me to examine situations more closely and become more intentional about affirming an individual's contribution and connection to the broader social realm. I became intentional about the importance of research and adopting a working typology for dealing with social issues, particularly suicide. Durkheim's typology based on "social integration" and "moral regulation" informs my approach to suicide care.[112]

## CIVIL RELIGION

Civil religion, a term coined by Jean Jacques Rousseau,[113] is also referred to as civic religion. It comprises the religious values of a nation as reflected in public rituals, symbols, ceremonial expressions on sacred days, and holy places. It is culturally implicit because faith transcends boundaries. According to Durkheim, religious and social experience are coterminous.[114] Two long-standing

---

[112] Bernice Pescosolido and Sharon Georgianna, "Durkheim, Suicide, and Religion: Toward a Network Theory of Suicide," *American Sociological Review* 54, no. 1 (February 1989): 33–48, https://www.jstor.org/stable/2095660, accessed 18 April 2021.

[113] Ronald Beiner, "Machiavelli, Hobbes, and Rousseau on Civil Religion," *Review of Politics* 55, no. 4 (Autumn 1993): 617–38, http://www.jstor.org/stable/1407609, accessed 18 April 2021.

[114] Ruth Wallace, "Durkheim and the Civil Religion Concept," *Review of Religious Research* 18, no. 3 (Spring 1977): 287–90, https://www.jstor.org/stable/3510218, accessed 6 September 2021.

debates exist about the role of religion in society: arguments within political science and sociology. How do these arguments inform chaplaincy, and what is the role of chaplains within these constructs?

To be sure, civic religion inculcates political values within a public profession of faith. On the other hand, religion itself provides social cohesion, maintains social solidarity through shared rituals and beliefs, embraces religious-based morals and societal norms, and maintains a sense of conformity and control. The challenge for chaplains in civil society is to respond to the needs of those with whom they walk, less subjective in some ways, but fully aware of self and others, while understanding the ministerial context of shared experiences. As expressed in the introductory chapter of this primer, "Chaplains fulfill a sacred calling to accompany and provide professional support and spiritual nurture for everyone in their distinctive secular communities, which authorize and hold them accountable." In broader civil settings, they still represent a faith group, advocate for those with shared beliefs, provide for those of other faiths, and accommodate all persons of faith and no faith.

Chaplains in civil society adapt to the religious and social world, as well as surrounding culture, to provide the most impactful response to those they serve. They become comfortable with being uncomfortable when the situation demands compassion, empathy, and cultural awareness.

Finally, chaplains should be lifelong learners constantly engaged in their discipline. The ongoing changes in various faith perspectives and demographics require constant reassessment to ensure people's needs are accommodated.

## SERVING AS NONCOMBATANT

In a military context, chaplains are noncombatants who are to be respected and protected in all circumstances, as outlined by the Geneva Convention.[115] It specifies that chaplains may not be intentionally or indiscriminately attacked. Unless needed to provide religious care for prisoners of war, chaplains must not become POWs. As noncombatants, chaplains must not engage in combat. This noncombatant role is widely recognized and is a profoundly held moral constraint in the conduct of war. The principle is also a

---

[115] Geneva Convention, art. 36, 12 August 1949.

crucial underpinning of the just war theory. On the other hand, Religious Affairs Specialists (Army and Air Force) and Religious Program Specialists (Navy) are combatants who provide armed protection for their chaplains.

## REFLECTION QUESTIONS

1. Civil religion comprises the religious values of a nation as reflected in public rituals, symbols, and ceremonial expressions on sacred days and holy places. What would be an example?
2. You prepare an invocation for a civil ceremony within your institution. People are required to attend. What sensitivity should chaplains have when praying in this setting? Would your prayer change if people are not required to attend? Why or why not?

# PERSONAL BOUNDARIES AND ETHICS

## Dr. Scott Gardner

S.A.M.: this age-old acronym helps us understand what to avoid in ministry. As we consider it, we realize it is all about being a person of character, and this is easier stated than accomplished. What must we avoid? If we seek to be men and women of character and virtue—and, like it or not, chaplains are held to a higher standard—we must avoid the misuse of that which is related to sex, alcohol/drugs, and money. Temptations are all around us.

Ask any chaplain who has served any amount of time, and they will give testimony of being tempted in one or more of these areas: adultery, promiscuity, substance abuse, and money issues. I have seen chaplains disciplined (from letters of reprimand to courts-martial) for extramarital affairs, solicitation, driving under the influence of alcohol, drug addiction, and falsification of travel vouchers. Just don't do it. If you have problems, seek the help of a mentor and counseling. Bottom line: if you are going to be an effective chaplain, you must take steps to defend against these potential temptations. Enough said.

## SELF-CARE AND COMPASSION FATIGUE

An old, well-known, and frequent expression in the United States Air Force is: "Take care of the Airman, and the Airman will take care of the mission." The same is true for chaplains and their spouses. A little maintenance goes a long way. A check-up or tune-up is all most chaplains and their spouses need following a deployment or a work situation that becomes all-consuming. Some may require a more extensive overhaul by professionals, especially if post-traumatic stress is a factor. Get with your mentor and seek guidance.

While all chaplains are overworked, imagine a military member in a deployed setting. Yes, the member accomplishes the job, but the requirements of ongoing battle rhythm are intense. Now, imagine the responsibility of the chaplain caregiver, seeking to shepherd the flock. Author George Rable writes of the difficulties of a chaplain serving in the Civil War: "What the troops most valued was the human touch. In many respects, it came down to a willingness to live with soldiers and share their hardships."[116] As they were then, deployments today are tiring and draining. Everyone experiences stress in life from one cause or another. To help deal with stress, author Robert Wicks recognizes how small, daily pressures or issues can mount. While each one remains well below a level of stress, the aggregate of these common, daily pressures creates a condition called "chronic stress." Left unchecked or inappropriately managed, these pressures can lead to serious energy burnout. This condition may then require professional intervention and support. Wicks accentuates the point with a quote from Anton Chekhov, the Russian playwright who said, "Any idiot can face a crisis—it's this day-to-day living that wears you out."[117]

Burnout is a term often applied to ministry. Ministers are known to burn both ends of the candle, and many, if not most, have experienced burnout. Pastors typically do not make time for recharging. They are too busy. They are caregivers who have a hard time caring for themselves and find it difficult to allow others to care for them. Recognizing and managing symptoms and causes of burnout is essential if one is to have a ministry that is long-lasting and durable. One would be well advised to do additional study in this area.

The proverbial checklist is easy to formulate but not so easy to apply. After years of working with military members and hearing their stories, my focus targeted reintegration instead of redeployment. It was not just about coming home. It was about coming home and being effective members in the unit after deployment and, more importantly, on the home front. Military service is only for a time; families are for a lifetime.

Military members need time to reflect and rest, to refocus on their primary human relationship with their spouse, and to retreat to a place where both rest and relationship can be fostered. The resultant restoration becomes a foundation to build upon before reengaging in ministry. Rest is the starting point.

---

[116] George Rable, *God's Almost Chosen Peoples: A Religious History of the American Civil War* (Chapel Hill: UNC Press, 2010), 115.
[117] Robert Wicks, *Bounce: Living the Resilient Life* (Oxford: Oxford University Press, 2010), 24–25.

We hear of developing "coping skills" in modern culture, but how does one truly cope with such stress without aid from the divine creator who knows us from the inside out? Stress management is a hot topic. There are both "good" and "bad" stress. A host of literature deals with stress from secular and faith-based perspectives. Rest, however, is found only in Christ. With that in mind, consider the following recommendations:

1. **Rest.** Prepare for reintegration in ministry. Rest in God. Rest from work. Allow some "down time." Resist the temptation to get right back to work after a hard push or an all-consuming ministry demand. Certainly, resist the temptation to continue working at the same tempo after returning home from a high-intensity situation.
2. **Relationship.** If married, make your relationship with your spouse a priority. This is your primary community group.
3. **Retreat.** Get away. Recharge as you prepare for reintegration in ministry.
4. **Restoration** is a key to resiliency. It takes time to heal brokenness and to bounce back.
5. **Reengage** in ministry. Return to work but continue to use all these tools as you do so.

## COLLEGIALITY AND COLLABORATION

Consider the issue of religious pluralism. Chaplains must be able to work with ministers and laity whose beliefs differ from their own. They should understand and respect the religious faiths and traditions of everyone in the institution. They should also practice collegiality with fellow chaplains. Constitutional principles and historical development formed the basis of "cooperative pluralism." Hutcheson indicated that these constitutional principles and historical development preserve the interests of the government, individuals, and religious communities.

> The religious neutrality of the government is derived from the Establishment Clause of the First Amendment. The right of the individual American who is a member of the armed forces to practice the religion

of his or her choice is derived from the free exercise clause of the same amendment. The position of the first two parties of the tripartite arrangement is thus clearly staked out on a constitutional basis.[118]

## CAREER DEVELOPMENT

Reinhold Niebuhr, a popular theologian of the past century, wrote critically of his experience with military chaplains in World War I: "What I dislike about most of the chaplains is that they assume a very officious . . . attitude. Ministers are not used to authority and revel in it when acquired."[119] That is an overstatement but one that needs to be heard and appreciated. In my thirty years as a chaplain, I ran into my share of chaplains whose rank seemed to be more important than their religious insignia. Applequist explains the reason for chaplains having rank and wearing a uniform.

> Before and during World War I there were chaplains who had no rank, and they found, as did the Red Cross men, that they were often regarded by the military as accessories with no standing and of questionable value. When things needed to be done for the men, the chaplains had no power that would provide a basis for action. . . . Rank was given to chaplains to introduce order into a confused situation and to give the chaplain a legitimate voice within "the establishment."[120]

Serving as a chaplain means wearing the larger hat of a cleric and the smaller one of an officer. We are there to serve and to do so as servant leaders is a challenge. Career development is important, as the military is an "up or out" institution. However, being overly consumed with promotion means being less focused on the importance of ministry as our primary concern. Find a mentor and an example to follow: an older, wiser chaplain or senior enlisted leader to show you the ropes. Make an effort to meet with your mentor regularly. Don't choose a peer. Select a leader at least one rank above your own. As

---

[118] Richard G. Hutcheson, *The Churches and the Chaplaincy* (Atlanta: John Knox Press, 1975), 117.
[119] Reinhold Niebuhr, *Leaves from the Notebook of a Tamed Cynic* (San Francisco: Harper and Row, 1980), 20.
[120] Ray A. Applequist, *Church, State and Chaplaincy* (Washington, DC: General Commission on Chaplains and Armed Forces Personnel, 1969), 38.

you learn more regarding career progression, details will become clearer. They include which educational or credentialing opportunities are necessary, when to apply and complete them, which assignments or job opportunities are essential, and at what point in your career to apply for them. It is not unusual for others to be looking out for you when you are completely unaware.

Good leaders watch for certain skill sets and personality traits in those they put in significant positions. They want their chaplains to develop in order to handle more responsibility and to care for others who accomplish the mission of the institution. So, they watch your job performance and seek to prepare you for future job opportunities. The point is that you don't need to be overly concerned about career progression. Do your job. Minister to those within your scope of responsibility. Listen to your mentor, and be a mentor to someone else when the time comes. Chaplaincy is a unique ministry in which not every minister can excel. Trust God, study hard, pray often, mentor and be mentored, and serve well.

## REFLECTION QUESTIONS

1. Dr. Gardner references author Robert Wicks and his statements of "how small, daily pressures or issues can mount. While each one remains well below a level of stress, the aggregate of these common, daily pressures creates a condition called 'chronic stress.' Left unchecked or inappropriately managed, these pressures can lead to serious energy burnout." Give an example of how small daily pressures or issues can mount. Then, suggest a strategy for relieving the building of stress.
2. Dr. Gardner suggests five recommendations for renewal. Pick one of the five and describe how you might implement his suggestion.
3. What opportunities and challenges might exist for you as you work with ministers and laity whose beliefs differ from yours? How do you see yourself striving to understand and respect the religious faiths and traditions of everyone in the institution?
4. Dr. Gardner concluded, "Chaplaincy is a unique ministry in which not every minister can excel." Do you think a minister/rabbi/imam could excel within a local religious setting and still fail as a chaplain? Why or why not?

# UNDERSTANDING PERSPECTIVES: AN IMPORTANT JOURNEY

## Dr. Tara Dixon

Chaplains are called to minister to everyone, regardless of their faith background. In organizations, people often come from various religious backgrounds or may not adhere to any faith. How do we navigate these spaces? How do our experiences shape how we interact and provide spiritual care for those we serve? These are complex questions that lack easy answers.

In my previous writings, I used diversity, equity, and inclusion (DE&I) to demonstrate an organization's commitment to being an inclusive workplace. As I have researched this topic extensively and with my work in the United States Air Force, I have altered my approach to this important subject. Despite this shift, the essence of chaplaincy and its relationship to diversity remains consistent.

The field of chaplaincy is not immune to diversity issues, underscoring the importance of self-examination, empathy, communication, collaboration, and fostering diverse perspectives in the workplace.

By shifting a focus from diversity to a more individualized and chaplain-centered approach, we can explore how our personal values, beliefs, and biases influence our leadership from a spiritual perspective. We can enhance our relationships with others by first understanding ourselves more deeply.

## UNDERSTANDING SELF

In my first assignment as an active-duty military chaplain, I encountered a situation highlighting my need to understand myself and others. A service member walked into the chapel and wanted to see a chaplain. At that time, I was the only chaplain in the building. The individual was so upset that he decided to speak with me; although I could tell, being an African American, I was not the person he had hoped to find. As we engaged in this counseling session, he grew more comfortable with me and shared his real issue. The person explained how he had to confront his bias toward African American military personnel, specifically some in his work section. He had been raised to believe that African Americans did not have a strong work ethic. However, the people he worked with demonstrated something much different that challenged his worldview. At the end of our session, he returned to work with a changed mindset and a deeper appreciation of his coworkers. This change could not have happened without this individual changing from an inward mindset to an outward mindset. Likewise, it would not have been easy for me to engage a person who had strong feelings and opinions about African Americans without having an outward mindset.

Arbinger Institute distinguishes between having an inward mindset, which is self-focused, and an outward mindset, which prioritizes others.[121] As chaplains, we need to cultivate an outward mindset. This means we need to truly understand ourselves through self-reflection and assessment that goes beyond the surface level. Our values may evolve as we gain new experiences and insights. We must be consciously aware of our values and ensure they remain personally and professionally consistent. For example, if I have identified one of my values as "faith," I am more likely to see the value of faith in someone else or, at the very least, provide the proper spiritual care based on that assumed value.

One night during my Clinical Pastoral Education (CPE) residency at San Antonio Military Medical Center (SAMMC), the emergency room paged all specialties to report to their location. Chaplains are considered essential for a trauma response in this medical setting. Upon arriving at the trauma bay, I encountered a young Hispanic man, around nineteen years old, who had jumped off a bridge and was brought to SAMMC for emergency treatment. Following a thorough medical examination, the doctors determined that he was not going to survive. As a chaplain, it was my duty to address the situation from a religious and spiritual perspective. The young man was unresponsive and had no identification on him. Being aware that a significant number of Hispanics in San Antonio are Catholic, I understood the importance of providing spiritual care that would hold value for his family.

---

[121] "Diversity, Equity, and Inclusion (DEI) in the Workplace," Arbinger Institute, https://arbinger.com/diversity-equity-inclusion/, accessed 12 April 2024.

Once we identified him and notified his family, I wanted to ensure that his chart reflected the spiritual care, last rites, and other religious practices. Additionally, as a mother of a similarly aged child, I acknowledged the emotional impact of this situation on me. I collaborated with my Catholic Priest colleague to ensure that the appropriate spiritual care was administered and documented for this individual. While some may view this response as standard, it necessitates an outward-focused and inclusive mindset of diverse perspectives to care effectively for and establish meaningful relationships with others.

## EXPANDING OUR HORIZONS

Chaplains are trained in theology and work as religious professionals. Our faith perspectives usually align with our endorsing agencies, leading to a tendency for people to worship separately based on their beliefs. This can make connecting with those with different theological views challenging. However, in our role as chaplains in various settings such as the military, hospitals, hospices, sports, and other institutions, we interact with individuals with diverse beliefs. Chaplains must be open-minded, empathetic, and respectful of differing viewpoints rather than imposing their beliefs on others. However, change can be challenging, and it takes time for individuals to recognize and appreciate the value in those different from themselves.

I have encountered numerous uncomfortable situations that have tested me personally and professionally. One Sunday, shortly after relocating to a new military base, my husband and I decided to attend a chapel service to familiarize ourselves with the worship service as it would be part of my responsibilities. As we entered the fellowship hall, an individual approached us and bluntly commented, "We won't like you here." I was taken aback by the statement and sought an explanation. The person proceeded to explain that at that chapel, they were not accustomed to "running around the chapel and jumping over pews." Unsure how to react, I debated between feeling offended or seeking clarity. Opting for the latter, I delved deeper into the conversation. It became apparent that the individual assumed that I practiced the described behaviors due to my affiliation with the African Methodist Episcopal denomination, which was not the case at all. This experience highlights the importance of broadening our perspectives, particularly as chaplains.

## BUILDING BRIDGES

As a chaplain, I am exposed to different perspectives. By strategically engaging in various settings, I can be a change agent for the situation. Remembering advice from elders in my community about not burning bridges, I now understand its importance. Chaplains uniquely foster improved relationships between diverse groups and individuals, facilitating better understanding and interactions. Our task is to bridge gaps and emphasize our shared humanity. Despite our differences, many of us grapple with feelings of inadequacy and alienation, leading to self-isolation and communication barriers. Effective communication is crucial for nurturing understanding and collaboration. It is also essential for creating inclusive environments where everyone feels appreciated and respected.

In the past, I struggled with fitting in on a team where each member had their distinguished responsibilities. When I expressed my discomfort with conducting traditional worship services due to feeling out of place, the Wing Chaplain candidly addressed the issue. He stated, "It would be difficult to explain why the only woman on the team who happens to be African American does not preach." While it might have been a challenging conversation, his honesty was invaluable in promoting open communication and understanding.

## NURTURING COMMUNITY

To create a nurturing community, we must be deliberate in our efforts. Chaplains wield the ability to exemplify the virtues we preach, fostering communities built on trust, accountability, and respect, regardless of our faith perspectives. Failing to subject the organizations we serve to critical evaluation could result in a culture of conformity and restricted thinking. My most significant personal and professional growth occurred when I was encouraged and free to express my thoughts openly. In these supportive environments, individuals are more likely to feel empowered to contribute without fear of dominant voices overshadowing their perspectives during decision-making processes.

Chaplains possess the authority to promote and cultivate a culture of equality and inclusivity across various facets of life. Increased understanding of others is possible when we deepen our understanding of ourselves and hold ourselves responsible. Self-awareness is a crucial element of personal development, and by neglecting internal reflection, we miss out on the richness of human connection.

Self-evaluation is essential for those committed to treating others with dignity and respect. Reflecting on a memorable experience, I recall receiving a teacup from my eldest daughter adorned with the phrase, "As long as everything is exactly the way I want it, I'm totally flexible." This gift served as a wake-up call, revealing a tendency to maintain rigid perspectives with my family dynamics. Recognizing this behavior at home prompted me to reflect on my conduct in professional settings. I realized the importance of adjusting my approach to be more receptive to diverse ideas and contributions.

## REFLECTION QUESTIONS

1. Dr. Dixon opens this section by stating, "Chaplains are called to minister to everyone, regardless of their faith background." Do you agree with this statement? If so, what challenges can you imagine arising as you seek to be a chaplain to all?
2. Why is self-reflection essential for inclusive spiritual care? How can limited emotional intelligence impact spiritual care?
3. How can we ensure inclusive spiritual care? Why is spiritual care a personalized service? Why is it a community service? Why is it a subgroup (race, gender, economic, age, and so on) service?

# PROFESSIONAL

## Dr. Jim Browning

Early in my chaplaincy career, I learned a valuable lesson distinguishing between "being in a profession" and "being professional." In one of my assignments, I served at the Air Force Chaplain Corps College, where we provided initial training for ministers and enlisted personnel, qualifying them to perform as chaplains and religious affairs airmen.

Meeting new airmen, who had just graduated from basic training, we chaplains wanted to put at ease those anxious enlisted persons, who likely were encountering their first officer. Reading their name tags, I would say something like, "Airman Jones, what is your first name?" The airman would reply, "Airman Jones reporting. Sir (emphasis on sir), my first name is John, sir." The airman would be rigid, standing at attention, looking forward, and wanting to get quickly past this officer and back into the classroom. I would respond, "Well, John, welcome." He then would hurry away. I felt proud of my pastoral care offerings until a technical sergeant instructor explained how we undermined the airmen's intensive basic training with our unprofessional welcome. It was a lesson about professionalism I carried with me throughout my career. I learned the difference between being "a professional" and "being professional."

Most institutions and individuals recognize chaplains as professionals because of their calling, education, ethical standards, discipline, knowledge, and skills. Effective chaplains adhere to a code of ethics and understand both written and unwritten rules of behavior. They hold themselves accountable to their denomination, profession, and institution. By adhering to expected institutional norms and not taking liberties so often afforded chaplains, we present ourselves both as "members of a profession" and as "professionals." To ignore these expectations is to reduce our effectiveness within the institutions we serve.

Being a professional is who you are. Being professional is what you do and, very importantly, how others view you in what you do. Ignoring what the institutional culture defines as professional negatively impacts ministry effectiveness. Being a professional and being professional are both important. We must carefully hold with integrity the standards of each.

Being a professional chaplain is about preparation. It starts with a vocational call, a heart for chaplaincy, and a solid academic foundation. Added to this preparation is enhancing one's skills with specific competencies. Being a professional implies a high level of capability that includes continual learning and being a lifelong student who stays current with new ideas and information. It also builds on the legacy of character, integrity, and dedication of those who have gone before us. We must never accept a level of mediocrity caused by stagnation or laziness.

Complementary to being a professional chaplain is being an institutional professional. Chaplaincy involves balancing competing demands between living out one's allegiance to God and adhering to institutional requirements. This tension can be challenging to navigate without a mentor's wisdom and guidance.

Being professional within chaplaincy starts with humility. Pride and arrogance undermine a chaplain's work. Being professional is about teamwork. Those "out for themselves" become isolated and ineffective. Being professional involves continually learning about the institutional culture and operating within its boundaries and expectations.

Being a professional is joining a long legacy of individuals who have done what it takes to prepare with education, training, skills, expertise, knowledge, and experience. Whether one serves as a volunteer, a part-time, or a full-time paid chaplain, being professional is how we choose to behave in practice, judgment, principles, and ethics.

## REFLECTION QUESTIONS

1. Dr. Browning distinguishes between "being professional" and "being in a profession." What do these mean to you, and how are they different?
2. Dr. Browning lists several aspects of being a professional. List these and select two to discuss their importance.
3. Does "being a professional" change with the different categories of chaplaincy?
4. As it relates to "being professional," why is it important to know the culture and ethos of an institution?
5. How might one unintentionally communicate a lack of "being professional"?

# STAMINA FOR THE LONG HAUL

## Dr. Jim Browning

In chapter one, I stated that an effective chaplain's ministry was to "sojourn" with others, walk alongside them, understand their stories, and discover a deeper understanding of God and our response to Him. In these relationships, chaplains build connections with others, sometimes for a moment and other times for a long duration. In these connections, we share another's joys, challenges, difficult times, or deep sadness. Walking with others so burdened or traumatized is a sacred journey where they often find support in our ministry. In our caring and authentic walk with others, we, too, can become exposed to their suffering, hurt, and pain. Occasionally, the relationship or situation can impact the chaplain so significantly that the chaplain has little to nothing to offer.

Most have all heard words like "compassion fatigue," "burnout," "post-traumatic stress," and maybe a new term for many, "moral injury." These are not separate and distinct issues but likely reflect an impact continuum. Chaplains and ministers are often subjected to traumatic events or a cumulative impact that creates what I call "scarring of the heart." For a caregiver or chaplain to ignore their own physical, mental, emotional, or spiritual exhaustion is to invite a callous response to others, a loss of empathy and compassion, and a downward spiral toward stress-related illnesses.

Chaplains are not the only ones impacted. Ministers, doctors, nurses, mental health providers, social workers, first responders, and many others can be overwhelmed by the crisis or needs of others. How does one develop and maintain stamina for the long haul? How do chaplains maintain an awareness about themselves so that they seek help and support at the appropriate time? What should chaplains do to provide some protection against spiritual, mental, and emotional exhaustion? As we think about a chaplain's stamina for the long haul, it is essential to understand the difference between a sprint and a marathon. You cannot run a marathon in a sprint.

This topic receives high marks when I speak at national conferences or teach students in class. Why? As chaplains, we prioritize caring for others and often neglect caring for ourselves (and our families). Most chaplains find it easier to care for others than for themselves. Caring for oneself may appear selfish and self-centered. However, if the chaplain is depleted, little is left to offer others. A chaplain can fake it for a while, but eventually, exhaustion overcomes the best of intentions.

When presenting this topic at national conferences, I first emphasize the need to care for oneself before caring for others. In reality, these should happen concurrently with each other. For instance, hospital chaplains, moving from room to room, should take stock of themselves in the hallway before entering the next room. In between caring for each patient, a chaplain is wise to pause and note the impact of the visit. Otherwise, the chaplain can unknowingly carry the impact of the previous engagement into the next visit. Sometimes, I found it necessary to step off the patient floor to have a moment of reflection and prayer or to unload some of the emotional pain I felt with the help of a friend. With self-awareness, one builds stamina by being intentional in how we care for ourselves, others, and the institution. To have staying power for a long and productive career as a chaplain, one should not lose focus on these five areas: self-awareness, care for yourself, care for your family, care for your constituents, and finally, care for the institution.

## SELF-AWARENESS

Numerous books and articles express the need to care for yourself to avoid burnout, compassion fatigue, and any physical, emotional, mental, or spiritual symptoms of overload or exhaustion. Building stamina for the long haul begins with a great deal of awareness. While not an exhaustive list, I humbly offer some personal insights:

- Have you identified your own time/energy killers?
- Do you chase unnecessary "squirrel" moments?
- Are you in line with your boss's/institution's priorities, or are you bucking the system to get your way?

- Are you working in "lone ranger" mode because you have no other team members or have failed to build a team focused on the mission?
- Can you make better use of volunteers?
- Are you delegating, or have you failed to trust others to do their job?
- Are you leading your team with a good vision, mission, and objectives, or are you micromanaging?
- Are you empowering people to do their job?
- Do you affirm others for their job well done, or do you want all the accolades?

## CARE FOR YOURSELF

- Stay connected to your spiritual moorings. Do not neglect your religious disciplines. Read your sacred text, pray, meditate. Seek those who will walk with you when God seems distant or silent. Trust and find spiritual stillness, for example Proverbs 3:5–6 or Psalm 46:10.
- Pay attention to your physical, emotional, relational, and spiritual health. Do not ignore the depletion of your resiliency. Do what is necessary to reduce your stress—exercise, see a movie (diversion), enjoy a cup of ice cream (comfort food), take a minute "vacation," permit yourself to cry or scream (emotional release), breathe, stretch.
- Resist mediocrity and strive for excellence, but not perfection.
- Be your best and give your best each day. Recognize when you cannot. Pause to refresh and renew. Don't be afraid to seek professional help.
- Be and work as part of a team. Be collegial and collaborative. Chaplaincy is not a competitive sport.
- Guard your character and your integrity. Avoid taking shortcuts or succumbing to temptations. A single wrong decision can end a lifetime of effort and ministry. Given the right circumstances, we are all vulnerable.

- Reaching out to others is not a sign of weakness. Acknowledging your need for help is a healthy step in realizing your limitations and accepting needed support.
- Be a lifelong learner. Read, study, explore. Be open to new ideas and ways.
- Celebrate every day as the gift it is. Do not count the days; make the day count by making a difference.

## CARE FOR YOUR FAMILY

- Build and protect time with your spouse, family, or close friends. Have a regular date with your spouse and each child. Your family needs your care and support.
- Achieving a balance between family and work is an endless teeter-totter effort. Any pressure on either side causes an imbalance. Instead of seeking balance, determine what "centers" you. Decide what your pivot point is for all other activities to evolve. Once identified, this central pivot point informs and supports how you engage in life's various aspects, decisions, and actions. Your actions and emotions will be validated if you are honest about what "centers" you.
- Your ultimate legacy will likely not be accolades and achievements but your family. Be careful not to sacrifice your family to achieve a temporary status.

## CARE FOR THE CONSTITUENTS

- At the center of your ministry should be God's heart pulsing through your heart. Sometimes God uses what we think is a mundane conversation to create a significant effect in another person's life. Pay attention to the small, still voice within as you engage others.
- Be authentic.

"When I learned of this book's publication, my first reaction was 'It's about time!' *The Heart of a Chaplain* is a masterful, comprehensive work that is long overdue. The chaplaincy in all its applications owes a debt of gratitude to the creators and collaborators who made this dream come true."

—**Dondi E. Costin**, PhD,
President, Liberty University; Major General,
US Air Force; 18th Air Force Chief of Chaplains (Ret.)

"The second edition of *The Heart of a Chaplain* is an extensive and powerfully thorough overview of chaplaincy and its many disciplines. It is the best example of highlighting the difference between a job and a heartfelt call to ministry. This book is the premier resource for every chaplain and leader in all chaplaincy disciplines and settings."

—**Randall "Randy" E. Kitchens**,
Chaplain, Major General, USAF, 20th Chief of Chaplains,
2nd Space Force Chief of Chaplains (Ret.)

"*The Heart of a Chaplain* lays the foundations of chaplaincy in an engaging and informative way; its honest and straightforward applications of skills are enforced by precise personal applications demonstrating specific employment amongst the people chaplains serve. This is a powerful resource for chaplaincy and is an invaluable tool to have in your hands. It is 'powerful,' 'exhilarating,' 'informative,' and inspirational."

—**Michael W. Langston**, PhD
Professor of Chaplaincy & Practical Theology
Columbia International University

"*The Heart of a Chaplain* is an ideal text for those exploring a chaplaincy vocation, faith groups who endorse clergy for chaplaincy positions, and seminaries interested in training chaplains. The book addresses the uniqueness of chaplaincy and chaplains' roles; the wide field of chaplain positions; historical, US Constitutional, and faith foundations for the vocation; and qualifications and competencies for professional success. To be mentored by multiple chaplain experts individually would be impossible; this text allows the readers to learn from the thirty-seven chaplain authors who are experts in the field."

—**Rev. Dr. Jan McCormack**, BCC, ACPE CE,
Chair of Chaplaincy and Pastoral Counseling Programs,
Denver Seminary; coauthor of *The Work of the Chaplain*

"I have read *The Heart of a Chaplain* and loved it. First, it covers all aspects of chaplaincy ministry. Second, it preserves the rich history of the clinical pastoral education movement. Third, it should be required reading for anyone considering chaplaincy and be placed in every seminary library. This book closes the existing gaps for institutional administrators."

—**Dr. Joe Gross**,
Chaplain and Director (Ret.), Pastoral Care & Counseling,
Baylor Health Care System, Dallas, Texas

"Professional chaplaincy engages ministry with broad lenses, refusing to be pigeonholed to one religious tradition or particular service field. Therefore, a thorough study of a full breadth of professional spiritual care is needed. *The Heart of a Chaplain: Exploring Essentials for Ministry* is a practical resource for understanding the width and depth of this wonderful service in honor of the Holy."

—**Chaplain Joe Perez**,
Past President of Association of Professional Chaplains,
Chief Mission & Ministry Officer for Baptist Health System

"The second edition of *The Heart of a Chaplain* is a practical guide to understanding who chaplains are, what they do, and how they minister in very unique settings. Chaplains serve in places where other ministers can't serve! This book does a wonderful job explaining the various types of chaplain ministry and the steps involved in pursuing a call as a chaplain. I am thankful for the individuals who contributed to this book and have created a resource for individuals and schools that train our chaplains. This book is a must-read for anyone serious about answering the call to chaplain ministry!"

—**Todd Combee**,
MDiv, Director/Endorser,
Baptist Chaplaincy Relations

"*The Heart of a Chaplain*, 2nd ed., continues the legacy of the first edition. Dr. Jim Browning and Dr. Jim Spivey build on their comprehensive introduction to the chaplain profession with a masterful synthesis of factual information and engaging stories. Each section and contributor encourage readers to be authentic, courageous, and disciplined as they passionately pursue their calling. It is at the top of the reading list for all IMF chaplains."

—**Tony Duck**, M.R.E., BCC, CPES, BC-MS, BC-GRS,
Vice President—Chaplain Ministries, International Ministerial Fellowship

"I emphatically endorse this book! *The Heart of a Chaplain* lit a fire in my own heart with a renewed passion for my own service as a chaplain. It is the definitive book available for explaining chaplaincy. It should be a required part of chaplain introductory courses at every level of education. It should be in every chaplain's library. No aspect of who and what it means to be a chaplain is left out. By using those who are subject-matter experts in the intricacies of this profession, they have presented a thorough look at this invaluable calling. I plan to purchase a copy for every chaplain endorsed by the Evangelical Chaplains Commission and would encourage every endorsing body to do the same."

—**Steve West**,
Director of Chaplaincy for the National Association of Evangelicals,
author of *The Bronze Scar: Understanding How PTSD Feels*

"The first task I gave to my unit or agency chaplain was to meet me every Monday to hear my concerns and pray me into the week. You see, in addition to all your many responsibilities, you are your leader's chaplain too. I believe this book will help prepare you for all facets of your ministry, to include giving you the courage to knock on the door of your commander, director, secretary, or commissioner. Offer to hear their significant burdens and plans, and offer to pray for them on the spot. They need you, whether they know it or not."

—**Major General Mark S. Inch**,
US Army (Ret.); 15th Provost Marshal General;
9th Director of the Federal Bureau of Prisons;
and 12th Secretary of the Florida Department of Corrections

"Dr. Jim Browning and Dr. Jim Spivey have gathered the wisdom of an outstanding group of colleagues who have nurtured many of today's frontline caregivers and leaders in chaplaincy. The pages that follow will be invaluable and thought provoking for men and women exploring chaplaincy for the first time, as well as those who have many years of ministry experience."

—**Mike Mullender**, PhD, BCC,
Vice President and Chief Mission & Ministry Officer for
Baylor Scott & White Health

"This thoughtful and practical collection encourages clergy and prospective clergy to follow God's call as they explore opportunities in chaplain ministry. Drawing on their extensive experience and adding present-day applications, the thirty-seven contributors of *The Heart of a Chaplain* share their ministry insights in a way that will enlighten, encourage, and answer the questions of every person considering service as a chaplain. If you're ready to walk with God toward ministry as a chaplain, this is the book for you!"

—**Cecil R. Richardson**,
Chaplain, Major General, USAF;
16th Air Force Chief of Chaplains (Ret.)

"Crisis happens. What can be done about it? *The Heart of a Chaplain: Exploring Essentials for Ministry* elaborates on the many facets and contexts of chaplain service. Chaplains operate outside the confines of their place of worship, necessitating the development of competencies and skills that are not customarily addressed within seminary training (crisis and suicide intervention, critical incident stress, multicultural competency, and many others), which speaks to the specialized study required in addition to theological training. It was an honor to contribute to this much-needed work. This pivotal work will impact the twenty-first century and beyond."

—**Chaplain Ken Schlenker**,
Founder and Executive Director of RKM Crisis Team, dba CAREForce

"Chaplaincy resources introduce us to the transformational work of professional chaplaincy, including correctional chaplaincy. With more than two million people who are incarcerated in the US, loved ones of the incarcerated, those who work in law enforcement, victims of crime, and those who are returning to your neighborhoods upon release from custody, we all have the call to respond in faith. As one who has served as a county jail, state prison, and federal prison chaplain since 1996, I encourage you to open your heart and faith to the gift of correctional chaplaincy. For when you do, you too can become a part of God's continued restorative justice with individuals and wider communities."

—**Chaplain Heidi Kugler**,
Chief Chaplaincy Administrator for the Federal Bureau of Prisons
*Note: Opinions expressed are those of the author and do not necessarily represent the opinions of the Federal Bureau of Prisons or the Department of Justice.*

- Learn to see those who are unseen (for example, learn the janitor's name. Speak to them when you see them. Ask them about their family. Show appreciation for what they do.)
- Show dignity and respect to all. Discover the richness of diversity. Learn their stories. Listen.
- Invite others who are different from you to help you broaden your perspective and understanding. Be slow to react and quick to appreciate different perspectives.
- Be patient in building relationships.
- Be actively present, especially amid a crisis.

## CARE FOR THE INSTITUTION

- Learn the institution's mission, vision, and objectives. What does the institution need from you? What do you need from the institution?
- Pay the rent, which means meeting your boss's or institution's needs before exploring your own creative interests. Manage the institution's priorities by effective time management. Ask yourself what you "must do, should do, could do." Keep a running list and review it at the end of the day. Start your new day doing the most important "must do" first. Did your boss interrupt you and change your priorities? It's OK. Keep a running list. (You get the picture.)
- Embrace the training the institution requires.
- Learn to speak the institution's language to explain more effectively how your ministry relates to its mission and objectives. Understand your return on the institution's investment.
- Be a good follower to later become a good leader. Be loyal to and supportive of your boss and mission. Be professional, diplomatic, and courageous to share your perspective with your boss. Remember, one day, you may also have leadership responsibilities and will need the support of others.
- Be willing to do the job that nobody else wants.

- Be politically savvy but not political. Understand the political issues but act apolitically.

Someone once told me, "Ministry would be a great job if you did not have to deal with people." Circumstances and needs can be exhausting to those who care for others. To have the endurance needed for a career as a chaplain, one must pay attention to the issues of self-awareness and caring for oneself, others, and the institution.

## REFLECTION QUESTIONS

1. A car's instrument panel gives numerous alerts when fuel, oil, or tire pressure is low. What indicators in your life provide you with a warning for energy, maintenance, or adjustments? Which indicators do you tend to ignore?
2. What have you found that works best for you to recharge your physical, mental, emotional, or spiritual well-being?
3. The author stated, "To have staying power for a long and productive career as a chaplain, one should not lose focus on these five areas: self-awareness, care for yourself, care for your family, care for your constituents, and finally, care for the institution" and provided in each a short list of insights. In each area, select and explain which statement resonates the most with you. What would you add to the list?

# MEMORABLE MOMENT
## "A UNIQUE PRIVILEGE"

### Dr. Lorraine Potter

My earliest, most significant pastoral experience as a military chaplain—worth all the challenges I, as the first woman military chaplain, faced throughout my thirty-one-year career—was during my remote, unaccompanied assignment to Osan Air Base, Korea in 1975. I had been on active duty for two years and found myself at a location in the initial stages of integrating women into this isolated location.

It was Christmas Eve 1975. This memorable and "holy" experience forecasted the incredible opportunities yet to come in my military service and ministry. The gift of the Holy Spirit was powerfully present on a remote mountaintop radar site in Korea. It was COLD. None of us would have chosen to be there on this special night. Many came feeling the loneliness and homesickness this special holiday exaggerates. We gathered in a small unheated stone chapel to celebrate and proclaim the good news of God's unending love found in the birth of Jesus in Bethlehem centuries ago.

A Roman Catholic priest and this female Baptist chaplain jointly led this worship service with about fifty American, French, and Korean soldiers and airmen present.

Remember, this was 1975. We read the Scriptures of Jesus' birth—in English, French, and Korean. We sang Christmas carols simultaneously in all three languages. What an angelic sound. The priest served the Eucharist to Roman Catholics at one end of the altar, and I served Holy Communion to Protestants at the other end. Inside the chapel, we could hear "the still small voice of the holy baby's cry." Outside, the strong wind hummed a majestic hymn of "Peace on Earth, Good Will to Men."

Far from home, we all experienced the delight and warmth of the Lord's presence and our oneness as children of the "King of Kings, the Lord of Lords." "FOR GOD SO LOVED . . . THAT HE GAVE . . ."

At this time in history, no place else could I, a woman pastor, have had this unique privilege and pastoral experience but in the United States military.

CHAPTER TWELVE

# FREQUENTLY ASKED QUESTIONS

When one considers a ministry as a chaplain, questions naturally and frequently arise. One typically raises a question with "As a chaplain, . . ." This section seeks to answer many common questions from students and inexperienced chaplains. These fourteen questions are not exhaustive. We asked chaplains with diverse backgrounds and extensive experience to share their wisdom and insights. While some of the questions could have generated a lengthy response, we limited our contributors to a single page. Their brief answers highlight some challenges and opportunities for chaplains. We encourage the reader to review the list of contributors for each author's background and experience as each response is contextually based.

### 1. Can I Volunteer as a Chaplain?
### Dr. Gene Wilkes

Can you serve as a volunteer chaplain while working full-time elsewhere? Absolutely. I served as a volunteer chaplain for my local police and fire departments for thirteen years while the senior pastor of a local church. I have recently returned to active volunteer chaplain status while serving at B. H. Carroll Theological Institute as President and Professor of New Testament and Leadership.

To volunteer effectively, you must know how much time you can legitimately serve and not overcommit to the detriment of your family or full-time job. I currently limit my chaplaincy availability to weekends, as our other volunteer chaplains serve on local church staffs. During my first experience as a volunteer police and fire chaplain, we were fortunate to have four active volunteer chaplains, so we were on call only one week a month, which was not overwhelming to my schedule as the pastor of a church. Currently, we have five volunteer chaplains, which allows greater flexibility and mobility of schedules.

As a volunteer chaplain, one gains access to invaluable experiences and training. We are often called to make death notifications or be with family members of suicide or homicide victims while officers and medical examiners do their jobs at the scene. Although rare, when an incident involves many people, we help calm and serve both those affected and involved in the incident. Being trained in such methods as critical incident stress debriefing, we lend support to the on-scene first responders. Membership in groups like the International Conference of Police Chaplains is invaluable, as they provide annual and periodic training.

Serving one's local community in this way allowed me to exercise my faith appropriately in the community and to "keep my feet on the ground" in pastoral ministry with real-life situations that people experienced day in and day out. My service in the community enhanced my service in the church. I also had the opportunity to build relationships with police officers, who came to trust their chaplains as I ministered to them in various ways and shared special events (for example, weddings, dedications).

Chaplains also minister to dispatchers as they often do not hear "the rest of the story" of a particular call. By periodically checking in with the dispatchers, chaplains can hear their stories and encourage them as they deal with the emotional impact of being exposed to too many tragedies.

I am fortunate to live in a community where both the department and the community value chaplain services. While the community has become very diverse in ethnicity and religious preference, the chaplain's role remains an essential service for first responders and those who protect and serve the citizenry. Being able to volunteer as a chaplain enriches my ministry and allows me to give back to the community.

## 2. Why Did You Leave the Ministry?
## Chaplain Charles Cornelisse

This question about leaving the ministry is more common than one would think. I entered the parish ministry and the military chaplaincy in the Reserves in the mid-1980s. At that time, chaplaincy was not nearly as commonplace as it is today. When I was in seminary, I vividly recall talking with my childhood pastor about my intention to enter the military chaplaincy and his response. He asked, "Why would you want to leave the church?" I don't recall my verbal response, but I remember how puzzled and frustrated I was at his lack of understanding and appreciation for chaplaincy. I was not "leaving the church." Instead, I was entering an extension of the church into the world.

What does happen when someone enters the role of a chaplain? No matter what type of chaplaincy they enter, chaplains become an extension of their church or religious body. Their loyalty belongs to their faith community and the organization they are serving. A military chaplain is an excellent example of that dual loyalty.

Ministers may only serve as military chaplains if and when a recognized group or denomination completes the required endorsement form. In essence, a religious organization (for example, church, synagogue, mosque, temple) loans its pastors, rabbis, or imams to the military. Should chaplains lose their endorsement, for whatever reason, the military must release them from their commitment and return them to their religious organization. For example, the Roman Catholic Church often recalls priests and assigns them to their respective civilian parishes.

Chaplains' church membership will typically reside with their last faith community before entering service as a chaplain. The responsibility of maintaining membership in good standing depends on the mutual relationship between chaplains and their religious faith community. Since chaplains are usually not attending or serving in their off-base/civilian faith community, it can become a matter of "out-of-sight, out-of-mind." Fortunately, most chaplains will have the integrity to keep in touch with their respective faith communities and endorsers, thereby maintaining good ecclesiastical relationships.

## 3. Who Pays the Chaplain for Services?
### Dr. Dennis Leedom

While chaplains receive their training, ordination, and endorsement within the context of a local church or faith group, once professionally hired, the institution or a servicing company receiving the spiritual or pastoral care pays the chaplain.¹²² Chaplains are paid as employees or as contractors. Other chaplains must raise their own funds or serve in a volunteer status to provide care to a specified group. So, who pays the chaplain for services? It depends, and the chaplain needs to be aware of all determining variables.

Military chaplains serve as officers in a branch of the armed forces and receive base pay and other benefits commensurate with their military rank. Healthcare chaplains typically serve as salaried employees of a specific hospital or healthcare system.

Likewise, the federal, state, or local government in charge of running the correctional facility may hire chaplains as salaried employees. In both healthcare settings and correctional facilities, compensation and advancement depend upon factors such as the institution's size, years of experience, level of education, and scope of duties. Part-time employment is also available in the chaplaincy career field.

Military chaplains, serving part-time in reserve or national guard units, typically minister bi-vocationally in a local church. Similarly, bi-vocational ministers can be employed part-time as PRN (as needed) chaplains by a healthcare organization or correctional facility. PRN chaplains are typically paid on an hourly basis without benefits and serve according to the varying needs of the hiring institution. Other types of chaplains' pay is dependent upon the arrangements with the institution, company, or group served. Last but not least are the volunteer chaplains, who receive the payment of "Thank you, chaplain, for being there. You were a godsend."

## 4. Does Government Payment Violate Church and State Separation?
### Chaplain Karen Diefendorf

This frequently asked question reflects a fallacious application of "separation of church and state," a concept that does not exist within the Constitution. The actual guidance on this issue is in the First Amendment clause: "Congress

---

[122] For instance, Marketplace Chaplains provides a personalized and proactive employee care service through Chaplain Care Teams. The hiring company or corporation voluntarily uses this service and contracts ethnically diverse ministers as full-time or assignment-based chaplains, depending on company locations and numbers of employees served.

shall make no law respecting an establishment of religion, or prohibiting the free exercise thereof." Note the two competing requirements: no establishment and free exercise. Thus, Congress cannot choose to give preference one over the other to ensure the intent of the amendment.

For instance, in most cases, the use of tax dollars to support religious functions has been deemed unconstitutional because it would most likely "preference" one faith group over another, the layman's way of understanding the Establishment Clause.[123] However, in 1984, the US District Court for the Eastern New York ruled that a paid Army chaplaincy (obviously paid with tax dollars) was **not** unconstitutional because the government must ensure the free exercise of religion and noted that there are times when one of the two competing clauses must take precedence.[124] It also stated that under the War Powers Act, Congress has the right to organize the military however necessary, including the use of government-paid chaplains.

Army chaplains (as do all military chaplains, but this case sued only the Army) serve as government employees who (1) ensure the free exercise of religion for soldiers by either performing or providing for religious rites, (2) are inherently governmental, that is, they serve in their advisory capacity to commanders as one who guarantees free-exercise opportunities for their soldiers, and (3) protect against violating establishment by ensuring no one religious group is "preferenced."

## 5. Can You Evangelize and Preach the Gospel?
## Chaplain Judy Collins

One of the fundamentals of chaplaincy is to meet people where they are, regardless of their faith preference. Although endorsed and held doctrinally

---

[123] Michal S. Ariens and Robert A. Destro, *Religious Liberty in a Pluralistic Society*, 2nd ed. (Durham, NC: Carolina Academic Press, 2002). This book compiles court cases by type challenging religious liberty through 2002.

[124] *Katcoff v. Marsh*, 755 F.2d 223, 228 (2d Cir. 1985). See also, Israel Drazin and Cecil Currey, *For God and Country: The History of a Constitutional Challenge to the Army Chaplaincy* (Hoboken, NJ: KTAV Publishing House, 1995). Drazin, an Assistant Chief of US Army Chaplains (USAR), was also an attorney and advisor to the army during this lawsuit. The plaintiffs were asking the courts to decide on whether a paid chaplaincy violated the establishment clause. Ironically, the courts never directly answered that question.

accountable by specific faith communities, chaplains are trained to be fellow sojourners with unique training to guide and comfort those in need. Chaplains preach according to their conscience, faith perspective, and doctrinal tenets. Yet, they also remain sensitive to the pluralistic makeup of any gathered group. It is considered unethical for a chaplain to judge or proselytize. Chaplains can still openly share their faith story, but it should be in response to the recipient's initiating interest. It is unethical to try to convert persons unless they have opened the faith conversation themselves. As a sojourner, we walk alongside others who are seeking to find meaning.

Consider what to do if a family is worried about a patient's salvation. They ask the chaplain to present their idea of saving knowledge to the patient, hoping a profession of faith will be made at the bedside. The chaplain struggles to reassure the family while encouraging the patient wherever that person is on the faith journey. Some suggestions:

- Be honest with the family about the chaplain's role to show a presence of love, compassion, and reassurance. Agree to meet with the patient, telling of the family's concern, and use the opportunity to ask the patient to share their faith journey. The chaplain can listen and offer help if wanted.
- Encourage the family to tell the patient directly of their concern. Remind them that pushing the issue is not productive but breaks down relationships, stunts reflective thought, and can confuse the patient.
- Recognize the family's anxiety. Listen to their concerns, offer to pray for the whole family, and voice their concerns collectively, asking for peace and harmony.

Chaplains are called to be a presence for justice, compassion, love, and peace, which applies to all faith groups. The chaplain's most important role in this ministry of purpose and presence is to be the vehicle of God's love.

## 6. Can Chaplains Pray in Jesus' Name?
### Chaplain Mark Grace

The short answer to this question is yes. A chaplain is free to pray with individuals according to the chaplain's religious convictions, provided they agree to prayer in the first place and give consent to the particular form of prayer or other religious ritual offered.[125] Thus, it may be surprising that many people who do not identify with any religious tradition accept prayer from a chaplain.[126]

The slightly longer answer would ask whether the chaplain's personal theological convictions allow for any variation in expressing a prayer. For example, does the chaplain believe that only prayers prayed "in Jesus' name" are heard by God? Then it becomes more critical that the person being ministered to has a chance adequately to consider and give informed consent to prayer (or any other religious ritual) offered in that fashion.

I offer my prayers by saying, "I pray these things in the name of my Savior Jesus, and I invite you to pray in the name of that which is sacred to you." In a small group or individual setting, I follow a brief description of this practice with the simple question, "Are you comfortable if I pray that way?" If the response comes back in the negative, then rich conversation and the potential for a deeper relationship often ensues.

Like so many other questions about spiritual care, the answer must focus on the person's needs. Additionally, the chaplain's goals for a visit should always include the desire to cultivate relationships, foster trust, and pave the way for other caregivers down the line.

## 7. Are You Required to Perform Rites & Rituals for Other Faith Groups?
### Chaplain Judy Collins

One of the exciting opportunities of chaplaincy is learning about the rituals and customs of other faith groups. While this knowledge can open doors to

---

[125] "Common Code of Ethics for Chaplains, Pastoral Counselors, Pastoral Educators and Students," Professional Chaplains, 2004, https://www.professionalchaplains.org/files/professional_standards/common_standards/common_code_ethics.pdf. Standard 1.3 "Demonstrate respect for the cultural and religious values of those they serve and refrain from imposing their own values and beliefs on those served."

[126] Fiona Timmins et al., "The Role of the Healthcare Chaplain: A Literature Review," *Journal of Health Care Chaplaincy* 24, no. 3 (July–September 2018): 87–106, DOI: 10.1080/08854726.2017.1338048, accessed 7 September 2021.

deeper and more meaningful relationships, it also presents challenges. For example, if the chaplain is from a Baptist background and is asked to baptize an infant, how should one respond? The role of the chaplain is to meet people where they are and to be present for their needs. But how can this be done with integrity when the actual definition of baptism differs from one faith group to another? Can a chaplain be all things to all people? No, that is not feasible.

If a chaplain performs a baptism or any other ritual outside the chaplain's doctrinal boundaries, it is not only personally unsatisfying but also dishonest and placating to the others involved. Chaplains should not be forced by an institution or individual to perform any rite or ritual beyond the tenets of the chaplain's beliefs or endorser's guidance. When unsure and time allows, a call to one's endorser might help the chaplain sort out the issue.

Alternatives exist. First, chaplains can reach out to their community to find a minister of similar belief who can conduct the ritual. Ministers of all faith groups are usually very accommodating to meet the needs of their own. Another option would be to explain to the family that the chaplain cannot conduct a baptism in the strictest definition of their faith group, but other rituals might be possible. One option is a "blessing" that celebrates the baby and encourages the parents. Another choice is a "naming ceremony" honoring the baby's new place in the family.

Finally, chaplains might look at their own beliefs and reconsider. For example, if asked to bless a home, can a chaplain, though unfamiliar with this ceremony, still embrace it theologically? Good chaplains grow and evolve in their faith, modeling what they ask of others. While chaplains are entitled to their convictions and must maintain the integrity of their values, it is vital to acknowledge the beliefs of others and find creative ways to help meet their needs.

## 8. Do You Compromise by Working with Non-Christian Groups?
### Chaplain Mark Grace

I worked in a denominationally connected healthcare setting for more than thirty-three of my thirty-seven years as a chaplain. During that time, I often heard the assertion, "We have to be uncompromisingly Christian in everything we do." Sometimes that assertion meant that we ought to be very sure that the ethical stances we took concerning business or medical issues reflected our deep commitment to Christ's teachings.

Sometimes that assertion was another way of reminding everyone around the table that non-Christians should get used to the status quo and refrain from asking for consideration and support for their religious traditions and practices. On those occasions, my response was, "How about if we also worry about being unapologetically just and compassionate? Unswervingly committed to respecting the dignity and inherent worth of everyone we care for and everyone who has joined hearts and hands with us as members of our staff?"

No healthcare institution, small or large, could survive by serving only individuals who belong to the sponsoring religious group. How about that for an ad campaign: "The very best in health care . . . for Christians?" In addition, healthcare institutions hire individuals from every conceivable religious and nonreligious perspective because we could not offer lifesaving care by restricting ourselves to hiring only Christian care providers.

Every day, hundreds of times per day, all over the world, Christian ministers collaborate with non-Christians to ease the burden of suffering humanity. If working to relieve the suffering of a human being by contacting a beloved rabbi, a trusted priest, or a fellow member of a mosque seems like compromising one's convictions, then chaplaincy is probably not the best career match. On the other hand, interfaith collaboration can become the occasion for providing a more influential Christian witness to the whole community one serves. It may also challenge and inspire us to redouble our personal Christian commitments.

## 9. Are You Legally Bound to Report Sexual Abuse?
### Chaplain Judy Collins

At some point, most chaplains will face the tragic disclosure of a sexually abused person. As it relates to confidentiality, all chaplains must understand reporting requirements according to federal and state jurisdictions and regulatory requirements. Chaplains must protect confidential communication revealed during their duties unless given informed consent by the person who made the communication or unless required by law. Chaplains should know in advance what resources are available and what courses of action are necessary when confronted with such a disclosure.

If the victim is a child or an impaired adult and admits to being sexually abused, the first call should be to the police. A chaplain may be required by law to do so as a mandatory reporter. If the victim is a child or an adult who is mentally impaired and does not admit to being sexually abused, but evidence and testimony suggests so, a chaplain should call either Child Protective Services or Adult Protective Services to handle the case.

Again, the law may dictate to report abuse. If the victim is an adult who will not admit to it but shows signs of being sexually abused, the chaplain can offer to call Adult Protective Services for help. Adult victims have the right to refuse this service, so chaplains should give them other resources to access, such as crisis hot lines, violence support groups, and professional counselors.

For some chaplains, the requirements of sacramental confession are paramount and prevent any disclosure without permission of the abused individual. If prevented from disclosure, the chaplain can still encourage the victim to report the abuse personally. Knowing which local resources are available, a chaplain can offer to "walk with the individual" to secure needed help and support.

Though laws vary from state to state, chaplains everywhere should ensure victims are safe, get them the help they need, and walk with them through the process. It is a painful journey that requires expertise beyond the typical training most chaplains receive. The ministry of presence and comfort from a trusted chaplain can be an invaluable part of the healing process.

## 10. How To Mitigate Family Tension Regarding DNRs
### Chaplain Judy Collins

The Do Not Resuscitate (DNR) order is a medical and legal document used to communicate a patient's (or a surrogate's) desire or decision to reject life-sustaining interventions. All family members do not always accept this desire or determination.

This scene is too familiar in hospital life. A family caregiver has decided to withdraw life support for a loved one based on what the caregiver believes are the wishes of the patient. Other family members arrive and challenge the DNR decision. A scene of arguing and blaming follow until family members retreat, angry and/or sullen. In the angry exchange, one might hear family members express emotionally laden statements like "You are killing Mom if you turn off her respirator," "You just want Dad's money," "We must continue treatment. I prayed. God has to heal him."

This type of incident is why hospitals encourage patients to have an Advanced Directive, such as a Do Not Resuscitate order. Chaplains can be very helpful in this process, saving a great deal of family heartache at the end of a patient's life. All chaplains should have a thorough understanding of Advanced Directives and the skill to help families understand how to navigate through the process.

The most logical DNR medical decision, seemingly so clear to health professionals, is not as easily reached by emotionally wrought families. First, chaplains should help families set a cooling-off period to process facts. Second, they can remind families of the goal of allowing their loved one to be at peace. They can help loved ones face the finitude of life by asking them to reflect upon the patient's wishes and previously discussed courses of action. Hopefully, this will stir comforting memories that are helpful and directive. Third, if the patient and family have a faith-based perspective, the chaplain can offer support through prayer or rituals. It is also a good idea to contact their faith leader for help, as a source of authority and respect.

Despite a chaplain's best efforts, family tensions can continue long past the hospital. However, a chaplain can assist a family to pause and reach what is medically best for the patient. The chaplain can often facilitate reconciliation and see new harmony emerge, bringing something good from a painful situation.

## 11. Explain the Coexistence of God and Suffering
### Dr. Lindell Anderson

An intense pastoral encounter on a mountain overlooking the A Shau Valley in Vietnam, fifty-one years ago, confronted me with my need to grapple with the mystery of suffering. Several young soldiers bombarded me with demanding questions, cursing God, heaven, and earth after a fellow soldier in their squad stepped on a booby trap and lost both legs. They demanded an answer to questions like, "What kind of blankety-blank God would allow such a tragedy?"

Their repeated use of God's name and references to God's absence caught my attention. One side of me yearned to defend God, but at the same time, I longed to comfort those youthful soldiers. Later I realized they needed to be seen, heard, and understood as they searched for meaning and God. They also needed me to be a reminder of God's presence. As I have reflected on that experience, I believe the God of Suffering was present, even though the soldiers believed He was absent.

Helping people discover the presence of God in suffering without exacerbating their sense of alienation is one of the most significant challenges chaplains face. Aligning ourselves with God through Jesus Christ in prayer will increase the likelihood we make an empathic connection with a patient.[127] We cannot fully know the mind of God concerning suffering. Job's friends claimed to know the mind of God and they went searching for his sin. Answers such as "God is punishing you," "It is God's will," or "He is testing, teaching, or warning you" seldom fit the particulars of their situation.[128]

The best interpretation of suffering comes from those suffering and not from the chaplain. Nevertheless, the purpose of suffering is often unclear and confusing when patients are suffering.[129] Our role as chaplains is to help patients weigh their explanations for suffering and assess if their answers are helping or hurting them.

However, as Jeffry Zurheide warns, we need to be cautious not to wrest such a notion as "it is God's will" or "it is punishment for my sin" from the hands of the sufferer.[130] If their answers are hurting them or reflecting poorly on God's goodness or greatness, then a chaplain needs tactfully to challenge

---

[127] Jeffry R. Zurheide, *When Faith Is Tested: Pastoral Responses to Suffering and Tragic Death* (Minneapolis: Fortress Press, 1997), 5.
[128] Richard C. Eyers, *Pastoral Care Under the Cross: God in the Midst of Suffering* (St. Louis: Concordia Publishing House, 1994), 29.
[129] Eyers, 47.
[130] Zurheide, *When Faith Is Tested*, 20.

their understanding of God and suffering. Our ultimate understanding of God's mind and the meaning of suffering is our redemption as revealed in Jesus Christ and Scripture.

## 12. Can You Bear Arms for Self-Protection?
## Dr. Jim Browning

Bearing arms for self-protection is a critical issue for police and military chaplains. This question is easy to debate in class but challenging to adhere to in a life-threatening situation. For example, a deployed chaplain could be visiting a Forward Operating Base (FOB) when the enemy attacks and breaches the protective barrier. Now isolated from others, does the chaplain secure and discharge a weapon in self-defense?

The policy of the institution dictates what a chaplain is allowed to do. The Department of Defense policy is a firm no for the military chaplains.[131] A defiant military chaplain who ignores this policy jeopardizes the noncombatant status of all military chaplains. For law enforcement chaplains, each department sets its policy, guidelines, and appropriate training for this situation.

This topic generates hot debate in the safety of a classroom. Knowing official policy is not enough but should be processed emotionally, socially, mentally, and spiritually. A chaplain should not wait until the heat of the moment to decide what one would do in a situation of self-defense.

If you cannot abide by and be at peace with the institution's policy, you need to find a new venue for chaplain ministry.

---

[131] Joint Guide 1-05 Religious Affairs in Joint Operations (1 February 2018), https://www.jcs.mil/Portals/36/Documents/Doctrine/jdn_jg/jg1_05.pdf, accessed 28 August 2021.

Geneva Convention for the Amelioration of the Condition of the Wounded and Sick in Armed Forces in the Field (commonly referred to as Geneva Convention I) identifies chaplains as protected personnel in their function and capacity as religious ministers. Service regulations further prohibit chaplains from bearing arms and classify chaplains as noncombatants. See Articles 4, 6, 7, 9, 10, 11, 24, 28, and 47 of the Geneva Convention (I) for more information regarding treatment of chaplains in the context of the Convention.

## 13. Must You Obey Orders in Violation of Your Religious Beliefs?
### Dr. Jim Browning

Must you obey the dictates of a commander or a boss if they are contrary to your religious beliefs? The easy answer is no. However, both the leader and the chaplain should first strive to find a religious accommodation that supports the institutional mission.

Religious accommodation is a principle embodied in the very fabric of our nation and public policy for civilians and military members. The US Equal Employment Opportunity Commission states,

> The law requires an employer or other covered entity to reasonably accommodate an employee's religious beliefs or practices, unless doing so would cause more than a minimal burden on the operations of the employer's business. This means an employer may be required to make reasonable adjustments to the work environment that will allow an employee to practice his or her religion.[132]

The Department of Defense (DOD) also supports all service members' rights to observe the tenets of their religion or to observe no religion at all.

> [The DOD] . . . will accommodate individual expressions of sincerely held beliefs (conscience, moral principles, or religious beliefs) which do not have an adverse impact on military readiness, unit cohesion, good order and discipline, or health and safety. A Service member's expression of such beliefs may not, in so far as practicable, be used as the basis of any adverse personnel action, discrimination, or denial of promotion, schooling, training, or assignment.[133]

---

[132] US Equal Employment Opportunity Commission, "Religious Discrimination" (2021) https://www.eeoc.gov/religious-discrimination, accessed 8 August 2021.
[133] DOD Instruction 1300.17 Religious Liberty in the Military Services (2020), 3, https://www.esd.whs.mil/Portals/54/Documents/DD/issuances/dodi/130017p.pdf, accessed 8 August 2021.

A chaplain must be adaptable and flexible to support the institutional mission. However, seeking wise counsel from one's denominational endorser or mentor helps to know where to draw the line.

## 14. What Does a Chaplain Do After "Retirement"?
### Dr. Jim Browning

This post-retirement question is valid to ask even at the beginning of one's chaplain ministry. How individuals understand the start of a career often helps determine how they will approach the finish.

When I was halfway through my military career, my supervisor told me I should seriously think about and plan for retirement. Was he giving me a hidden message? Was he telling me I should dust off my civilian skills, as I would be getting out sooner than expected? No, Chaplain Jim Barlow, a Catholic priest I deeply admired and respected, was mentoring me to think about a post-military chaplaincy career. I did not fully understand it then, but he was very insightful. To ignore the "what's next after retirement" question is to reach the end of an assignment and flounder without direction.

Most chaplain positions have a distinct start and finish. The middle is the race, the effort one seeks to finish well. What happens in the middle is a career that can be stimulating, exhilarating, exhausting, and rewarding. But what happens right after one reaches the finish line and accepts the accolades of a grateful institution for the years served?

A wise friend suggested a retiree should get a tricycle at retirement. A tricycle has two small wheels and a big one. Then he said, "The three wheels are location, job, and money. The rider picks which of those three becomes the big steering wheel. One might move closer to family, take a job regardless of what it pays, or seek any job that pays the desired amount." I understood his lesson.

Yet, for one called of God to ministry, this analogy ignores God's irrevocable call and His direction in our lives (Romans 11:29, Proverbs 3:5–6). If you find your identity in God, then your calling to ministry does not end when you take off the chaplain's uniform. The place of ministry may change, but deeply embedded in each of us is an awareness that God is still working in and through us.

The location and focus of ministry may change, but not the calling. Moses is a great example. God prepared him with multiple years of experience for the next leadership task. With a willingness to be open to a very different type of setting and a continual sensitivity to God's direction in our lives, our past and present experiences may very well be the preparation for our next ministry assignment.

## REFLECTION QUESTIONS

1. Which of these questions resonates the most with you? Why?
2. What question do you have that was not addressed?
3. Can one serve as a chaplain while working full-time elsewhere? How?
4. Why do some people view entering chaplaincy as leaving the ministry? What would you say to someone who asked you that question?
5. Regarding interfaith interactions, what strategies do you think are most effective for maintaining your religious integrity while respecting and serving individuals from different faith backgrounds?
6. In what ways do you see your role as a chaplain evolving, especially in terms of long-term career or postretirement plans?

# MEMORABLE MOMENT
# "THE CHAPLAIN IN ME"

### Dr. Jan McCormack

Upon my retirement as a US Air Force Chaplain in 2000, Denver Seminary hired me to create an MDiv degree with a chaplaincy specialization. Although still endorsed by my ABC-USA denomination for Institutional Chaplaincy, I am no longer working in the field as a chaplain. I am not a university or seminary chaplain. I am a tenured professor educating future chaplains and supervising CPE units.

However, you can take the chaplain out of the field, but you cannot take the chaplain out of me. I engage student, faculty, staff, and administrative concerns by providing pastoral care to any individual whose crisis is similar to those I encountered in the military and hospital chaplaincy settings. I have worked with seminary personnel and students concerning relationships, careers, medical issues, domestic violence, mental illness, suicide, and mass casualty situations. Perhaps one of the differences for me is that, in addition to providing pastoral care with a person seeking my care, I also typically educate the person on counseling and interventions skills.

An MDiv–Chaplaincy Specialization student (I will refer to her as Beth) had been in a class where I lectured on counseling skills for domestic-violence situations. Beth called me in a panic, asking for advice. She shared that she had been studying at a table outside the library when another unknown female student, Sue (not her real name), walked past the library table. Beth noticed that Sue seemed upset, so she greeted her and asked if she was OK. Sue joined her and poured out her heart about her relationship with her seminarian husband, Tom (again, not his real name). As Sue shared how Tom was treating her, Beth immediately believed Sue might be in an emotional domestic violence situation. His behavior appeared to be escalating, with Tom checking Sue's phone and throwing things in their campus apartment. Beth listened, empathized, and ascertained that Sue did not appear to be at immediate risk of physical abuse as of that moment. Beth asked Sue if she had another place where she could go, even temporarily, where she could feel safe. Sue said her parents lived close by, and they would come to get her. They exchanged phone numbers, and Sue went back to her apartment.

Beth called me to see if she did the right thing and if she had to report the conversation to authorities. I assured her that she had provided good pastoral care. Although this situation did not fall under a mandatory-reporting situation, it did involve a couple living in campus housing. I counseled Beth to contact the dean of students and report what had happened. The dean could then assess the situation and intervene to ensure Sue's safety if necessary. I then contacted the dean and informed her of what I knew secondhand about the couple's situation and what I'd counseled Beth to do. The dean and I consulted on a care plan for the couple, for Sue herself, and for Beth. We agreed that the dean would take over responsibility for the couple and for Sue, while I would continue to support Beth, whose experience level was inadequate for such a difficult situation. Beth followed my counsel and contacted the dean, who took over responsibility for the couple's care. Beth's engagement with the dean resulted in a de-escalation of the situation and a plan to help the troubled couple.

Beth subsequently called to tell me that she had met with the dean to share her involvement with Sue. I complimented Beth for her proactive care for Sue, seeking advice from me, and reporting her concerns to the dean. Later, I met with Beth and was able to discuss important issues like confidentiality, the need to draw appropriate boundaries, not interfering with those with responsibility to assist, and the importance of being a friend, not a counselor.

Even though I am now a tenured seminary professor and no longer function in the role of a chaplain, the skills I learned as a chaplain inform my educational approach in working with students, faculty, staff, and administration. These skills have made me a better educator and proved critical in designing our MDiv-Chaplaincy and Pastoral Counseling Programs at Denver Seminary, Littleton, Colorado. The chaplain in me remains, regardless of my current job title and responsibilities.

CHAPTER THIRTEEN

# CALLED TOGETHER INTO MINISTRY

## Mr. Scott Collins

My daughter and I exchange glances, knowing what is coming is anything but ordinary. Judy begins another story about her day as a hospital chaplain. Judy tells her narratives with ease and comfort, in the same manner most people talk about going to the grocery store or doing laundry. Her dinnertime stories are always far from predictable. Because I make my living as a professional storyteller, I have always been fascinated with Judy's stories about her chaplaincy. Like most people on the frontlines, chaplains often do not see the interesting and unique aspects of their work, much less their heroics.

Most of my wife's stories begin with a benign opening phrase such as, "We had something interesting happen today." Her more memorable stories illustrate facets of chaplaincy that pull the curtain back for her family and allow us to peek backstage at the drama that, to chaplains, is all in a day's work, but makes a layperson feel proud and reflective.

One such story: As she made her way through the hospital, visiting patients, Judy heard her name called from a nearby room. Taking a slight detour, she walked in and greeted the patient who'd called her, with the patient's mother standing by the bed. The chat was pleasant and reassuring. The patient asked Judy to pray for her. The three ladies held hands and Judy prayed. "When I closed the prayer with 'amen,' I felt her hand go limp and she died," Judy told us that night at the dinner table.

Reflecting on that story years later, a few things strike me. First, the patient knew Judy's name. She called out to her from her hospital bed. In only a short time as a patient, she had already built a relationship with Judy. Second, there was trust—spiritual trust. Trusting a person to show up on time for a meeting is one thing, but trusting a chaplain with your dying moments is entirely different. Third, while the story was then, and remains today, compelling to me as a layperson, it is one of many similar stories Judy and most chaplains could tell nearly every day. And finally, not long after Judy told that story with compassion and empathy, an event occurred that would shake our family for the rest of our lives—the death of a family member, my dad. As a board-certified, CPE-trained professional chaplain, Judy was better prepared for this than I was.

I was not ready for my father's death. I arrived at the hospital the day before Good Friday. Dad lived in a nursing home and had been admitted to the hospital for COPD, something that had been happening regularly. My trip home had been planned long before Dad went to the hospital, so when I arrived, I was surprised to find him in such bad shape. My brother, a local pastor, had spoken with Dad's doctor, and she'd told him she was not optimistic.

Later Thursday afternoon, the doctor came by the room and told us she doubted Dad would make it through the night. This was not surprising news, but a shock nonetheless. My brother and I stepped into the hallway and discussed what we should do. We wondered if one of us should stay all night in the room, so I called Judy for her advice.

For the first time, my wife became my chaplain. I was lost, with no idea what to do or say. When I told her the news from the doctor, I asked if one of us should spend the night in the room with Dad. Years later, her answer still echoes in my head.

"No one should ever die alone," she said. "Yes, you need to spend the night with your dad."

Dad made it through the night and died the next morning. It was the first and only time I have witnessed death as it happened. I will always be grateful to Judy for her advice, delivered as both a chaplain and a spouse.

Throughout our marriage and Judy's career as a chaplain, I've learned that, sometimes, institutions diminish the value of a chaplain or the chaplain feels that way. In a hospital or other setting where doctors, nurses, and other caregivers rush around tending to physical illnesses and saving lives, there have been times when Judy felt a need to prove herself or her value. I remember what Father Mulcahy, the TV chaplain on the series *M\*A\*S\*H*, once said to a doctor: "When you lose someone, you've lost a life. When I lose someone, I've lost a soul."

Through the years, I have kept mental notes on observations about chaplaincy:

1. **Chaplaincy is a career.** Friends sometimes reach out to Judy, saying they want to become a chaplain. Perhaps the friend has had a bad experience on staff at a local church, or has experienced a traumatic life event. In reaction, the person feels the need to become a chaplain. When we talked about those instances, it became evident to me that a career change is not the answer and will not bring the internal healing the person seeks or needs.

2. **Chaplaincy is a calling.** A career and a calling are two distinct things. A career is a job done with a high level of professionalism. A calling is a deeply held response that ultimately leads to a profession. Both are essential in the field of chaplaincy and pastoral care for an individual to be successful and to survive the mental and spiritual demands and stresses. Watching Judy through the years, I have seen times when her calling sustained her, and other times when focusing on her career emboldened her to do her job well and professionally.

3. **Chaplaincy is a profession.** More than a career, chaplaincy is a professional discipline requiring extensive training, from the proper graduate education to additional specialized training like Clinical Pastoral Education (CPE) units. Along the way are endorsements and board certifications. From a spouse's perspective over more than three decades of marriage, I have become aware of the ongoing need for training and retaining professional standards. Chaplaincy is much more than praying at a patient's bedside.

4. **Chaplaincy has its place.** I joke with friends and colleagues that "I don't have to be a chaplain because I married one." This is my way of saying Judy is the nice one in our marriage. At times, it has felt like

she was being my chaplain and we had to talk about how her training fit into our marriage. I have come to appreciate how the insights her chaplaincy gives her can positively affect me and our marriage. Still, I believe both spouses need to have a clear understanding about the guardrails in a marriage.

5. **Chaplaincy has an intuitive side.** Intuition is critical for chaplains. Like all professions, experience builds intuition. Knowing when to do certain things (and when to not do them) as you perform your role is invaluable in any profession. For a chaplain, these things include knowing when and how to enter a hospital room, a prison cell, an office cubicle, a foxhole, or anyplace where people work or live; when to pray, or not; what to say and when to say it. While a person can be trained to succeed in those areas, I have observed the value of intuition. Often it is attributed to experience, but just as often it is in the DNA of Judy and other chaplains I have observed.

6. **Chaplaincy is inside out, outside in.** Being a chaplain is who Judy is, both inwardly and outwardly. Her chaplaincy is an outlet for who she is at her core, and the ministry functions she performs every day are expressions of herself. She is a kind and giving person, willing to put the needs of others ahead of her own. I have often walked into the kitchen to find her working away on her signature Dr Pepper cakes, only to be informed they are not for me. "The surgery department has had a tough week," she'll say, "so I thought this might cheer them up."

Judy received an opportunity to serve as chaplain at a local hospice in Fort Worth not long after we married. Her role at the hospice was my initiation into chaplaincy, or at least into being married to one.

The hospice served patients across Fort Worth and Tarrant County, and Judy had a standing invitation from the Fort Worth Police Department to escort her any time, night or day, to any place where she might not feel safe, something I never imagined a chaplain needing. In a vicarious way, I experienced hospice chaplaincy, hearing stories about patients dying from lung cancer lying in bed and continuing to smoke while sucking on an oxygen tube with a tank nearby. Despite Judy's reminders that oxygen tanks were highly explosive, patients usually demurred, reminding her they were going to die soon anyway. She had to remind them that she, however, was not.

We learned lessons that helped our marriage during those years. Along with visiting patients in their homes, Judy hosted grief groups for survivors. We absorbed insights she gleaned from talking to widows who lacked a driver's license or access to the bank account after their husbands died, or to widowers who had no idea how to cook, run a dishwasher, or grocery shop without their wives. One of those insights became real the time we hosted a grief group for an end-of-class cookout at our home. Each group member had been assigned a task for the meal. An elderly gentleman assigned to bring condiments handed Judy gallon containers of mayonnaise, ketchup, and mustard. Eyes downcast, he said he had no idea how much to bring, because his late wife had always done that sort of thing. We vowed to learn from these survivors, whether it was wives who had lived their lives totally dependent on husbands, or husbands completely lost without wives. More than thirty years later, those experiences and lessons continue shaping our marriage.

Spiritually, I gained a new understanding for grief and loss. The annual grief service Judy organized and hosted became an event I looked forward to every year. It was humbling and sobering to see so many who had lost loved ones, and to feel their loss in a palpable way during those moving services.

For more than three decades, Judy has served in healthcare chaplaincy. Regardless of her place of service, she has become a friend to hospital staff, serving as their chaplain as much as for patients. Whether it is performing weddings, funerals, or baking cakes for them, anytime I enter her hospital I am besieged by "friends" I have never met. My involvement has been limited primarily to participating in fundraising 5K runs or attending the Black-Tie Ball. On the occasional visit to the hospital as a patient, I remind myself I am the chaplain's husband and everyone knows it, meaning I must always be on my best behavior, regardless of how much pain I am in.

During the years Judy served as a hospice chaplain, I would periodically ask what was the worst way to die. She had seen patients die from nearly every cause, but I had never witnessed death aside from television or movies. Judy's answer was ALS—amyotrophic lateral sclerosis, or Lou Gehrig's Disease. She would talk about patients whose minds were trapped inside bodies that refused to work any longer. Our conversations about ALS gave me a lifelong fear of the disease.

Then in 2020, Judy came home with reports of hospitals overrun with patients on ventilators, morgue trucks in hospital parking lots, face masks, social distancing, remote working. All of it just kept coming. By then, the coronavirus pandemic was raging across the globe. I left my office in mid-March of 2020 to work from home. On the other hand, Judy continued her normal routine, yet nothing was normal about her work at the hospital. With fear at their backs, hospital staff across the world became "frontline heroes." Rightfully so, doctors and nurses were lauded for their heroic efforts, donning face masks and shields, along with gowns and gloves, what we all came to know as PPE—personal protective equipment. They put their lives on the line every minute of their shifts.

A stark reality of COVID-19 was isolation, from office workers working from home to individuals quarantining for long stretches of time. Humanity's interconnectedness was broken. Nowhere was that isolation more profound or more painful than for COVID-19 patients and their family members. The raging infectiousness of the disease meant families could not be with those suffering and dying from the virus. A bridgeless chasm. But chaplains like Judy became the bridge to reconnect patients with families. With mobile devices donated by local churches, family members could finally see and talk to a sick relative. Judy became a messenger, carrying information back and forth, giving patients and family members a sense of togetherness.

I will never forget the evening Judy arrived home from the hospital after their first COVID-19 death. Her description of what she had seen from behind a window left little doubt that ALS was no longer the worst way to die. Hearing her description of the violence COVID-19 wreaked on the body was stunning and sobering. For the first time during the pandemic, I became aware of the vital role chaplains played during the crisis, to patients, families, and hospital staff, all living with acute fear and overwhelmed by fatigue. Day after day, chaplains like Judy delivered news of death to family and friends. Personal belongings of the dead had to be thoroughly sanitized before being returned to survivors, a task often assigned to the chaplain.

Some ten months into the coronavirus pandemic, Judy and I tested positive for COVID-19. While we cannot be certain, it likely came home with her from the hospital. The fear we had seen grip others now gripped us. My bout with the virus proved worse than Judy's, so she immediately kicked into chaplain mode, making sure I was OK, even driving me to the hospital emergency room one morning, sitting in her car in the parking lot for nearly three hours while they treated me.

We have sought ways to accommodate our mutual callings and careers. We have worked hard, emphasizing the mutual parts of our marriage and our careers. We have each taught the other, which means we each have been the teacher as well as the student. A key to the success of our marriage has been active involvement in our local church, a place of mutual ministry and common ground.

Our pastor observed that "Knowledge is knowing a tomato is a fruit. Wisdom is not putting it in a fruit salad." Years of marriage help Judy and me define and maintain lines between our individual callings, careers, and professions. Our knowledge of each other helps us know when to talk about our work, and wisdom guides what we say.

## REFLECTION QUESTIONS

1. Scott Collins kept mental notes about chaplaincy and listed six observations. Pick one of his observations and describe how you agree or disagree.
2. How would you rank these six observations from most to least important? Explain your order.
3. Describe the importance of having your family's support as a chaplain. How might this affect a chaplain's ministry? Will this impact differ depending on the category of chaplaincy?

# SECTION FOUR

# WHAT ARE THE QUALIFICATIONS FOR CHAPLAINS?

CHAPTER FOURTEEN

# THE PROFESSIONAL CHAPLAIN

## Dr. Eric Whitmore

What does it mean to be a professional chaplain? Do you have to be paid to be considered a professional? Must you have a specific call to chaplain ministry? How do we become professionals? We debate these questions within academia and the institutions we serve but rarely find a good answer. In this chapter, I hope to shed some light on how you can be a professional chaplain and participate in the chaplaincy profession.

Two definitions suggest that a professional is "someone who does a job that requires special training, education, or skill" or "someone who is a member of a profession."[134] The word *profession* comes to us directly from Latin and means "publicly to declare." In Middle English, the word was used to describe vows to a religious order. Today, evangelicals often require adherents to profess Christ—that is, to publicly declare their faith. In these situations, a profession requires a lifelong commitment to a specific group of people.

In this light, a professional is one who adheres to the rules, mores, and ethics of a specialized community. In modern terms, professionals not only have a vocation (calling) and education or certain skill sets, but they also take further steps to become more involved in the life of an institution or career field. For example, if you earn a civil engineering undergraduate degree, you are qualified to work for the public works planning department of a local

---

[134] *Merriam-Webster* online, s.v. "professional," https://www.merriam-webster.com/dictionary/professional, accessed 29 September 2021.

city. However, neither your education nor your job makes you a professional. When you decide to commit more time and effort learning more about engineering, keeping up with the latest research, joining regional and national professional organizations, and pursuing a CEC (Civil Engineering Certification), then you might consider yourself a professional in your field.

Chaplaincy is no different. Anyone can become a professional chaplain. Anyone can learn more about pastoral care in a specialized setting. Anyone can develop skill sets to share the love of Christ in places other ministers cannot go. That said, anyone can get a job as a chaplain, but not everyone is a professional chaplain. To be a professional chaplain requires preparation and qualification as well as becoming part of the guild of chaplains.

## PREPARATION AND QUALIFICATION

Preparing and becoming qualified to serve as a chaplain at a professional level takes a high level of intentionality, persistence, and a determination to learn and prepare. One crucial element of preparation for professional chaplain ministry is acquiring the proper education and training.

### Theological Education

Many institutions require formal theological education for placement as a chaplain, whether full-time, part-time, or PRN (*pro re nata*: fill-in or on call). Typically, formal theological education takes place at the undergraduate or graduate level, and every hiring institution has different expectations for chaplains. No single standard for hiring chaplains exists, and each organization, government, or company develops its own requirements. For example, the minimum requirement set by the federal government for chaplains is a master of divinity or equivalent graduate degree.[135] However, there is no agreement among the federal departments about how many credit hours are required. The Department of Defense (DOD) requires seventy-two hours, but the Federal Bureau of Prisons (FBOP) requires eighty hours.

Many large healthcare systems have similar educational requirements. Smaller systems (hospice care in particular) do not have stringent constraints

---

[135] Equivalency is determined by the hiring institution.

for theological training. While the smaller systems may desire a chaplain to have an MDiv, they often hire chaplains without graduate degrees. In the healthcare world, experience and Clinical Pastoral Education (CPE) units can be as important as education.

Correctional institutions rarely require graduate degrees outside the federal system, but they usually require a bachelor's degree or equivalent experience in pastoral ministry. States and local correctional systems have a wide variety of hiring requirements for chaplains, both paid and volunteer.

## Informal Training

While not everyone can earn a formal university or seminary degree, everyone can be a lifelong learner. Many schools, churches, and institutions provide chaplain training, workshops, and certificates, and a professional chaplain should seek these opportunities. For example, if you want to learn more about spiritual care after natural disasters, you can find many courses to take, books to read, and webinars to join.[136] As you learn more about disaster spiritual care, you may join others in responding to events in your community and help your church minister beyond its walls.

Many institutions provide volunteer chaplains with certification and safety and spiritual-care training. You cannot enter a federal prison as a volunteer without taking the Federal Bureau of Prisons training and interviewing with a federal chaplain. If you want to serve in the county jail as a chaplain, most likely the sheriff will require extra training before letting you meet inmates. Most hospitals require their pastoral care volunteers to take in-house courses before allowing them unfettered access to patients.

If you want to be a professional chaplain, always be on the lookout for ways to increase your knowledge and hone your skills as a pastoral care provider. Read a wide range of books that educate you about theology, counseling, psychology, and pastoral ministry. Learn more about your ministry location and the needs of your clients and staff. If you want to be a professional military chaplain, read books on military history and doctrine. If you want to be a professional healthcare chaplain, read books on medical ethics.

---

[136] A good reference is Dan Franklin, *Disaster Spiritual Care: A Training Manual for Spiritual Care Providers* (independently published, 2017).

If you want to be a professional corrections chaplain, read books on prison culture. Read anything that teaches you more about your ministry environment so you can become more effective in it.

## Clinical Training

Clinical Pastoral Education (CPE) is an important starting point for healthcare chaplaincy. While some hospitals and hospice companies do not require CPE for employment, most mid-size to large systems require at least one unit of CPE as a baseline, and many require four to eight units.

When I was about to graduate seminary, I realized I was not called to be a pastor. I was a military chaplain candidate working as a federal prison chaplain intern, and I decided to try hospital ministry to see where God would take me in my chaplain journey. My professor suggested I take a unit of CPE, so I applied for an extended unit. After seminary, I continued CPE training with the Veterans Affairs healthcare system and completed four units of residency. CPE taught me three valuable lessons. (1) I was challenged to care for people on the worst days of their lives. (2) My faith and practice were challenged by my peers, and I learned what I really believed and why. (3) I learned that I did not want to be a full-time hospital chaplain.

On the surface, CPE provides training and education for chaplains in healthcare settings. Below the surface, CPE is a process of self-learning that can be painful, challenging, and wonderful. It is designed to push you to your limits and challenge your assumptions, ethics, theology, and being. Through personal supervision, group accountability, and personal reflection, you learn more about yourself, your call to ministry, and your environment in a very short time. CPE is not just education or a job. It is learning.

Many organizations offer CPE. Many hospitals are affiliated with the Association for Clinical Pastoral Education (ACPE). Other CPE programs include the College of Pastoral Supervision and Psychotherapy (CPSP), the Institute for Clinical Pastoral Training (ICPT), Clinical Pastoral Education International (CPEI), and Canadian Association for Spiritual Care (CASC). All programs use a similar model of personal reflection, theological formation, and honing pastoral competencies.

Here are the basic types of CPE programs you might want to consider.

| Type of CPE Unit | Schedule | Notes |
|---|---|---|
| Basic or Summer Unit | 10–12 weeks, full-time | Not paid |
| Extended Unit | Part-time. Once a week for 6–8 months plus on-call | Not paid |
| Residency | Full-time. 10–12 week units. One year, 4 units | Stipend provided |
| 2nd-Year Residency (Fellowship) | Full-time. One year, 3–4 units | Stipend provided. Requires 4+ units of CPE. Can be specialized |

Note that this list is not exhaustive. Many programs are now online and provide supervision without group reflection. Most programs keep to the standard of at least four hundred hours of service, training, and education per unit.

PRN training is also an important supplement to CPE. PRN chaplains provide part-time and on-call services ad hoc for hospitals. Often, hospitals pay PRN chaplains a small retainer fee plus hourly wages if chaplains are called in after hours to offer care to patients and their families. As part of their part-time employment, hospitals require more clinical training post-CPE for PRN chaplains. This training includes healthcare safety, institutional HR courses, and specialized care training (ER, oncology, palliative care, and so on).

## Professional Training

To participate in an institution's life requires extra training within the institution. For example, military chaplaincy requires a plethora of courses to become and remain part of the military family. From basic officer leadership courses to combat training, military chaplains receive many opportunities to learn about their profession and culture. Army chaplains begin their career with the Chaplain Basic Officer Leadership Course (CHBOLC), which includes officer leadership and military chaplain training. The Navy and Air Force separate their officer and chaplain entry-level training. In these services, military chaplains attend the Navy Officer Development School (ODS) or the Air Force Officer Training School (OTS) with other officer candidates, then they attend a chaplain-specific course (Basic Chaplain Leadership Course and Basic Chaplain Course, respectively).

After basic training, military chaplains continue to attend various classes to maintain their commission. Unit-level training, garrison/base-wide exercises, service-wide diversity training, pre-deployment field training, and post-deployment debriefings are just a few examples of the types of military training chaplains are required to attend.

In addition to these courses, military chaplains are expected to maintain their professional military education (PME). Each military branch has a different set of courses, but the concepts are similar. The DOD states:

> The PME system is a progressive educational continuum guiding an officer's individual development over time. The continuum structures the development of Service and Joint officers by organizing PME into educational levels and linking those levels so that each builds on the experience, self-development, and learning mastered previously.[137]

While these courses are voluntary, a chaplain typically will not progress in rank (and therefore remain in service) without them.

Federal and state healthcare and correctional institutions also offer various leadership courses. Most of them are voluntary, and they provide a great way to learn more about your ministry environment. Although not as formalized, non-governmental healthcare and correctional chaplains should seek out professional courses that promote a deeper understanding of the culture of their institutions. Healthcare chaplains might take a course in "Return on Investment" (ROI) so

---

[137] Chairman of the Joint Chiefs of Staff Memo CJCSI 1800.01F, Officer Professional Military Education, 15 May 2020,6.PME Continuum, https://www.jcs.mil/Portals/36/Documents/Doctrine/education/cjcsi_1800_01f.pdf?ver=2020-05-15-102430-580#:~:text=PME%20Levels.,Services%20during%20an%20officer's%20career, accessed 29 September 2021.

they can better create metrics for their departments as they seek more funding from hospital administrators. Correctional chaplains might take a correctional officer leadership course to learn more about their officers and their needs.

Other forms of chaplain ministry require professional courses. Disaster Spiritual Care chaplains must attend Federal Emergency Management Agency (FEMA) courses to procure certification and remain current in the disaster recovery policies and procedures. National Incident Management System (NIMS) training is often required by organizations that provide certified chaplains associated with the National Voluntary Organizations Active in Disaster (NVOAD) as well as various local and regional agencies.[138]

## Denominational Training

As you seek to be part of institutional ministry, do not forget your local church, denomination, or other faith-group affiliation. Remaining active in your faith group is a crucial part of chaplain ministry, and many denominations provide (even require) annual training, continuing education, and religious instruction. Participation in the life of your faith group also gives you a level of accountability as you work beyond the four walls of your church. Check with your local church or denomination to determine how best it can equip you for chaplaincy.

For example, Baptist Chaplaincy Relations (BCR), a ministry supported by the Baptist General Convention of Texas and the Baptist General Association of Virginia, requires its chaplains to attend annual training at least once every three years. At the annual training, BCR provides skill-based continuing education and "best practice" informative sessions for chaplains to upgrade their knowledge base, maintain currency, and share new ideas. In addition, BCR also offers an online cohort for seminary students pursuing military chaplaincy to introduce them to military ministry and culture.[139]

---

[138] A full list of required courses can be found at the Crisis Resiliency Team website: https://texascrisisresiliencyteam.org/crisis-response-training/, accessed 29 September 2021.

[139] See www.texasbaptists.org/chaplaincy. The editors and writer acknowledge the impact and mentorship of Ch. Dr. Bobby Smith, the first endorser of Baptist Chaplaincy Relations. His material in the first edition was woven into this section only to reduce redundancy. This compilation does not diminish Dr. Smith's wisdom and impact. He is missed by many.

## CREDENTIALS AND ENDORSEMENT

Another crucial element of preparation for professional chaplain ministry is acquiring credentials and becoming endorsed to serve in your chosen field. While two distinct elements, they work together to prepare you for ministry and employment.

### Credentialing

The word *credential* comes directly from Latin (*credere*) and relates to the concept of trust and believability. If you have credentials, you can be trusted as a professional. A physician has a medical degree and a state license; an attorney has a law degree and qualifies at the state bar; and professional engineers have a degree, pass two years of competency exams, and earn a state license. Chaplains, however, do not have standardized credentialing. While many institutions require basic theological education and ecclesiastical endorsement, they do not define other credentials, especially faith-group licensing, ordination, or commissioning. Even within my own faith group (Baptist), we do not agree on which credentials should be required for our pastors or chaplains. On one hand, the institution cannot tell a faith group which credentials are important. On the other hand, faith groups often struggle with their own credentials, especially in free-church Protestant traditions.

Also, many faith groups do not include licensing or ordination. For example, the Church of Jesus Christ of Latter-Day Saints (LDS) does not ordain clergy but provides chaplains to various institutions. Many faith groups have formal, lengthy, and strict requirements for credentials. The Roman Catholic church, for example, requires a priest to complete his ordination before becoming a chaplain, and in the United States, this usually takes up to nine years of formal education. Check with your local church or faith-group representative to determine the required credentials.

### Ecclesiastical Endorsement

Many chaplain employers require endorsement, which is the primary credential for chaplains. How do we define endorsement? It is often easier to explain what endorsement is not rather than what it is. Endorsement is not a credential such as ordination or a commission provided by a church or denomination. Endorsement is not a certification that validates your chaplain proficiency. Endorsement is not a license to perform chaplain ministry. Ecclesiastical endorsement is validation from a faith group that you are a professional minister who can serve as a chaplain within a specific institution.

Endorsement is only for a specific ministry role at a specific location. It is not a generic or blanket certification that you can take to any institution for employment. Your faith group tells your future employer or volunteer supervisor that you represent your church body at that location. Endorsement does not necessarily allow you to perform all the rites and rituals of your faith group, but it does verify that you share the faith and practice of your endorsing body.

## Endorsement Benefits

While not every institution requires chaplain endorsement, you should still seek it. Endorsement provides important benefits for your chaplain ministry. First, it provides a high degree of accountability. No one likes a "lone ranger" chaplain who is not affiliated or supported by a local church or denomination. Endorsement allows you to maintain a relationship with your faith group. Second, endorsement provides high-level support and helps hold your institution accountable. As a watchdog for governmental and nongovernmental agencies, your endorser will protect your religious freedom and provide you with "top cover" in many circumstances. Third, your endorser will offer continuing education to keep you current in your profession. Finally, and most importantly, endorsers provide pastoral care for you and your family. No minister should work in a vacuum, and endorsers can step in as pastors to chaplains when times get tough.

## Role of the Endorser

The endorser manages the requirements and endorsement of the faith group. The relationship between the chaplain and the endorser is vital because of the pastoral care and support the endorser provides. Additionally, the endorser supports the chaplain with professional training, continuing education, and mentoring opportunities from experienced senior chaplains of the same faith group. Regardless of institutional requirements, all chaplains should benefit from and have the recognition and support of their endorsers.

Endorsement establishes a relationship with the faith group based on four pillars: integrity, character, responsibility, and accountability. Integrity and character are inward realities of personal and faith-group ethical beliefs that become outward realities of practice in all life circumstances. Responsibility and accountability assure the protection of the chaplain's rights, the institution, and persons receiving the chaplain's ministry.

In addition, endorsers should commit to the following:

- Be available to provide pastoral support.
- Make visits to endorsed chaplain.
- Serve as an advocate for the chaplain and chaplaincy.
- Pray for the ministry of all chaplains.
- Provide annual training and continuing education for chaplains.
- Stand with the chaplain and the chaplain's family in times of distress or emergency.

## Maintaining Your Credentials

Each endorsing agency requires their chaplains to maintain their credentials. Each faith group includes different obligations. Here are some possible requirements to maintain endorsement:

- Annual fees or regular financial gifts
- Field reports and updates
- Training attendance
- Church attendance
- Annual visit with endorser
- Maintain denominational or clergy status

## Ministerial Experience

To be employed as a chaplain, you must meet all the requirements of the hiring institution. Experience is one qualification that can be difficult to acquire. Like most entry-level positions, you need experience to get a job, but you cannot get experience without a job. This can be even more difficult if you are not a pastor or called to be a pastor. How can you get ministerial experience to get hired by your institution? Let us examine a few ways to equip yourself.

1. Health care chaplaincy
   - Take at least one unit of CPE (or more)
   - Volunteer as a chaplain at a nursing home
   - Ask your pastors to serve as lead care provider to visit people in the hospital or go along with them on their visits
   - Pastor a church

2. Correctional chaplaincy
   - Volunteer at the local or county jail
   - Participate in mission outreach to the homeless (many homeless have been in prison and will help you understand the culture)
   - Take at least one unit of CPE
   - Pastor a church

3. Military chaplaincy
   - Volunteer at a funeral home, VA cemetery, or nursing home
   - Volunteer to lead young adult or youth groups
   - Pastor a church, young adult, or youth group

Hospitals and hospice companies are looking for clinical experience. Correctional institutions are looking for pastoral experience. The military seeks pastors with experience in preaching, teaching, counseling, pastoral care, and leadership. Also, many institutions require two years of paid, full-time pastoral experience.

Your faith group will also have requirements for experience, particularly if you seek endorsement, credentialing, or certification. Many denominations require that you pastor a church before becoming a chaplain. Others require CPE or similar experience before supporting your chaplain application. Rarely will a faith group endorse you for a specific chaplain position without some level of experience.

What is not considered as ministerial experience for chaplaincy? Here is a short list of what does not qualify you to serve as a chaplain:

- Media director at a local church
- Children's minister
- Music minister
- Church administrator
- Ordained deacon/deaconess

While these roles are significant to the function and ministry of a local congregation, unless they include substantial pastoral care duties, they are not considered essential for chaplain experience.

**Ministerial Résumé**

You must document your ministerial experience so your future employer or volunteer supervisor can readily see the breadth and depth of your ministry. While many institutions have their forms to validate experience, you should still compile a solid résumé for ministerial positions. Ministerial résumés are different than secular ones. Secular résumés do not include photos, family information, or personal/theological insights. Ministerial résumés often include pictures of you and your family, personal information, and reflective statements or essays.

## THE GUILD—ENTRY AND SUSTAINMENT

Professionalism does not exist in a vacuum. You cannot become a professional without a community that sets and maintains standards, ethics, and norms. We call this "the guild." The guild concept is an old one. In the European Middle Ages, artisans and merchants would gather in cooperative associations to support each other and achieve common goals. These societies became powerful entities that drove entire economies and became the foundation for modern banking, investing, and professional organizations.

The guild of chaplains does not exist in any official capacity, but its threads can be found in many faith groups, theological schools, endorsement agencies, and affinity groups. You might encounter the guild in a seminary, a CPE program, or a military chaplain course. You might hear similar theological themes from both a correctional chaplain and a hospice chaplain.

## Access to Institutions

Why become part of the guild? The guild of chaplains gives you access to the institutions that employ chaplains. If you develop relationships with other pastoral care providers, chaplains, and pastors, you will find out the needs of the community, institutions, and churches. As you discover needs, you can work to meet them. Then, as you enter the institution, you can provide the best possible care to meet the needs of its members.

However, your requirements also need to be met. The institution cares about itself and its goals but does not always care about yours. The guild can help you develop without help from the institution.

When I was an Air Force chaplain, I knew that the service did not care about my theological stances about marriage. My personal view is that marriage is only between one man and one woman. As same-gender marriage became legal in the military, my personal view was incompatible with the law. However, the Air Force does not force chaplains to marry couples and upholds free exercise of religion. Therefore, although I disagreed with public policy, I was able to serve as a chaplain and even preach about behavior outside a biblical view of marriage. The need of the Air Force was that I care for airmen and their families and perform or provide for their religious rites and rituals.

However, as I struggled with the change in culture in the Air Force, I felt isolated and alone in my theology and worldview. I realized the need to reach out to others in the guild who would support me even if they disagreed with my perspective. I had good friendships with LDS chaplains (who do not support same-gender marriage) and progressive Presbyterian chaplains (who do support same-gender marriage). Together, we forged an agreement to encourage each other through the difficult days of change.

Not only might you and the institution diverge, the needs of the faith community can also conflict with the institution. In my example, I had the support of my chaplain endorser. BCR published a policy letter in 2013 outlining its expectations for chaplains about same-gender weddings.[140] Because my faith group did not agree with my institution's view of marriage, my denomination was willing to offer "top cover" in support of my beliefs. Many

---

[140] Basically, the document states that BCR chaplains should not perform same-gender weddings and should love everyone as Jesus did.

of my chaplain friends did not get similar support and had to forge their own policy on the issue.

The guild can help you get into an institution and remain there. Use the guild to help you balance your needs with those of the institution and your faith group.

## Professional Organizations

Professional organizations will help you become and remain an informed, skilled, and educated chaplain. They are a physical manifestation of the chaplain guild, and you should seek ways to get involved in your specific cognate group. See the resources section at the end of the book for a sample list of popular groups you can join. All these professional chaplain organizations require a membership fee and provide frequent training, communication, and other benefits.

# MENTORING

Part of being in the guild of chaplains is to pass on your experience to others, especially the newest and youngest chaplains. Many ways exist to help a protégé, and all of them require time and effort to promote the success of the ministry, the individual, and the guild.

Every chaplain should have a mentor. You will not succeed in your institution (much less in ministry) if you refuse to be mentored or equip a protégé for chaplain ministry. There are many biblical models of mentorship. Elijah mentored Elisha, Nehemiah mentored the Israelites, Priscilla and Aquila mentored early churches, and Barnabas mentored Paul, who mentored Timothy, who mentored others. All these types of mentoring have one thing in common: personal and professional relationships. We must develop and maintain mentoring relationships to become the ministers that God called us to be.

Mentors also offer a bridge between personal and professional relationships. As pastoral leaders, mentors share experiences, skills, and insights without judgment or expectation. Mentors are safe role models, motivational leaders, and confident edifiers, encouraging protégés to pursue their calling and professional socialization.[141]

The best mentoring is organic and derives from established relationships. It works best when the protégé picks the mentor, not the other way around. If you are a new or aspiring chaplain, seek out mentors. If you are an older, wiser chaplain, make yourself available but do not force mentoring on others.

The only way for the guild of chaplains to succeed in the future is to have a succession plan. You can promote the guild in one important way. You can train others to replace you. Too often, ministers get locked into "their" ministry or focus on what God is doing with and through themselves. While this is honorable, it is not the entire story of ministry. If you are like the pastor who believes it will fall apart when he leaves the church, you need to reconsider your calling and ministry role. If you are like pastors who think they love congregants more than God, you need to get on your knees and pray for forgiveness. None of us is irreplaceable. None of us loves others more than God does. All we can do is serve faithfully and pass on what we learn to others who follow.

Prepare your institution for your departure. Prepare your protégés for their opportunity to lead. Prepare yourself to begin another phase of life and ministry. The guild of chaplains will thank you.

## REFLECTION QUESTIONS

1. What about being a chaplain appeals to or excites you?
2. What are the credentialing requirements for your chaplain position? What would be the benefits of incorporating endorsement into your ministry, even if it is not required?
3. How might you promote the guild of chaplaincy? What groups can you join?
4. What is the value of having a mentor? Who is your mentor? Who are you mentoring?

---

[141] Julia Pomerenk and Heather Chermak, "Using Mentoring to Encourage Others (and Ourselves)," *College & University* 92, no. 2 (April 2017): 31–36.

# CHAPTER FIFTEEN

# THE CHAPLAIN AS A MORAL GUIDE

## Dr. Gary Clore

As chaplains, we have the unique opportunity to witness a wide range of human behavior, from the most challenging to the most inspiring. Embracing this role means immersing ourselves in these experiences, striving to embody the highest moral and ethical standards with the guidance and grace of God. It is a privilege to walk this path and positively impact those we encounter. As chaplains, it is crucial to recognize that our behavior, actions, and attitudes are constantly being noticed by many. The way we present ourselves in front of others holds immense significance. As ambassadors of the Holy, people seek to see if our lives reflect our words. This is our moment to demonstrate that we genuinely live out the values we preach and truly "walk the talk." We can inspire others through our actions and be a shining example of sincerity and dedication.

As chaplains, we represent God and serve as spiritual and moral role models for those under our care. It is paramount for us to set a positive example and live out our beliefs with authenticity. Our mission is abundantly clear: to remain steadfast in our relationship with the Divine, prioritize our moral compass, and uphold ethical standards in every aspect of our lives. This responsibility is awe-inspiring and one we wholeheartedly embrace with passion and unwavering commitment.

Every individual has the potential to be an ethical thinker—asking pertinent questions, making sound decisions, and striving to live conscientiously. As chaplains, we must first tend to our ethics and morals. In doing so, we embody the timeless metaphor of shepherds who guide the flock. By nurturing our own moral and ethical lives, we can better guide and lead others.

The concepts of ethics and morals share similar meanings. According to Merriam-Webster, ethics relates to "the principles of conduct governing an individual or a group" and "a set of moral issues or aspects (such as rightness)."[142] Morals guide us to do the right thing, encouraging good behavior and ethical conduct. These terms are often used interchangeably and are tied to the distinct characteristics of a specific group—attitudes, customs, or beliefs about what is right or wrong as well as positive and negative behavior. It is genuinely captivating how these concepts shape our understanding of behavior. It is wonderful to explore how these principles influence our actions and interactions.

To fully grasp the concept of a moral guide as a chaplain, it's crucial to delve into the meanings of *ethical* and *moral*. The dictionary typically defines *ethics* as "relating to morals." Similarly, it relates *morals* as being "concerned about ethics." Lacking precision in their definitions, they highlight the interchangeability of ethics and morality. *Ethic* originates from the Greek word *ethos*. *Moral* stems from the Latin word *mores*, both signifying something distinct about a specific group of people—their attitudes, customs, or beliefs regarding right and wrong; good, better, best versus bad; what is virtuous rather than what is vice. As a result, the chaplain's responsibility as an ethicist is to keenly observe and contemplate these attitudes, customs, beliefs, and behaviors.

Chaplains consider delving into Socratic thinking (look up Socratic thinking, an excellent assignment) at a higher ethical level, which entails engaging in deep discussions to discern the most appropriate actions rather than simply describing standard practices. These conversations revolve around exploring the concepts of good and evil, the qualities of virtuous individuals and communities, ways to cultivate virtue in people, and the essence of genuine happiness. Ethics plays a crucial role in our everyday lives, influencing how we handle our finances and time, build quality relationships, interact with others, and navigate our choices in our personal and professional spheres. By embracing this approach, we can navigate life with integrity and purpose, contributing to a harmonious and fulfilling existence.

Chaplains are pillars of strength, drawing on their unwavering faith to guide their decisions and actions. They embody the essence of ethical leadership and

---

[142] *Merriam-Webster* online, s.v. "ethic," https://www.merriam-webster.com/dictionary/ethic, accessed 14 November 2024.

theological wisdom, their moral compass intricately intertwined with their deep-rooted beliefs. Through their profound connection with God and extensive theological training, they earnestly contemplate what is right and good, shaping their character as they serve their communities. Empowered by God's grace, they live by moral principles, instilling hope and guidance in the hearts of those they serve, be it in the marketplace, hospitals, prisons, the military, or any other setting that calls for their invaluable support.

The pastoral role of the chaplain centers around "guidance," representing knowledge and wisdom. As spiritual and religious leaders, chaplains bring expertise as professionally trained theologians, counselors, and ethicists. They earn trust through unwavering integrity and reliability, prioritize open and transparent communication, and empathize and understand. Additionally, they maintain strong ethical discipline, possess unique knowledge and wisdom, respect the autonomy and responsibility of others, provide confident leadership with humility, and consistently learn and seek help and advice. They also teach out of experience, knowledge, and wisdom, and cultivate the miracle of dialog that draws people to inquire, seek, and consider a Holy God who is ultimately the One who can speak through us and our behavior.

Imagine a seasoned tour guide on a Holy Land tour, passionately highlighting the sacred sites and their rich historical and theological significance. A fantastic guide is a treasure trove of knowledge, radiating pride while leading and mentoring others with their expertise! This experience creates an inspiring and potentially transformative experience for everyone involved. This example beautifully shows how an exceptional guide combines genuine care with deep expertise, sharing valuable insights and thoughtful perspectives that uplift and engage everyone they encounter. What an incredible journey that can be! Chaplains are responsible for using their pastoral leadership knowledge, skills, and behaviors to guide the people in their ministry context.

## TOOLS

In addition to theological training, pastoral leaders can benefit from honing specific skills to offer moral guidance effectively. Like a shepherd's staff, what modern tools do chaplains have to serve as moral guides? I suggest the following:

1. a model for making moral decisions
2. principles of decision-making
3. three contexts of decision-making
4. three types of leadership of ethical decision-making in organizations
5. three types of spirituality contributing to the development of moral guidance
6. four chaplain core capabilities

Mastering these pastoral leadership skills will empower chaplains as moral guides in their ministry context, enabling them to fulfill their roles more effectively. Embracing these skills will undoubtedly enhance their ability to impact positively those they serve. These will provide chaplains with the necessary tools and principles to navigate confidently and sincerely the complexities of moral guidance while fostering understanding and positivity along the way.

## Tool #1: A Model for Making Moral Decisions

This is a continuous and circular effort.

> **Step 1: Define the Problem.** Identify the issue to ensure you are addressing the right problem.
> **Step 2: Collect Relevant Information.** Gather data from both internal and external sources to guide your decision.
> **Step 3: Generate Alternatives.** Brainstorm potential solutions or courses of action.
> **Step 4: Assess the Alternatives.** Compare each option's pros and cons, considering costs, risks, benefits, and implications.
> **Step 5: Make the Decision.** After weighing all the alternatives, choose the option that best fits your goals.
> **Step 6: Put the Decision into Action.** Implement the chosen solution, carefully planning for successful execution.
> **Step 7: Review the Decision.** Once the decision is implemented, evaluate the outcomes and make any necessary adjustments.

## Tool #2: Principles of Decision-Making

A. Principle of **A**utonomy: Embracing and honoring personal agency and responsibility.
B. Principle of **B**eneficence: Dedication to pursuing the greatest good.
C. Principle of **C**onfidentiality: Upholding privacy and protecting individuals with discretion.
D. Principle of **D**o No Harm: Aspiring to assist most nobly and effectively to do no harm or the least harm as autonomy and beneficence are factored into a decision.
E. Principle of **E**quity: Combining with what is *fair* to determine what is *just*.
F. Principle of **F**airness: Pursuing justice through moral discernment as you consider what is also equitable. Equity and Fairness must always be used in tandem to determine the ethical principle of justice and to understand "what is just."
G. **G**ood principles provide **G**ood decisions: Achieved through careful consideration of all moral principles, allowing the principles above to compete with one another to understand the process of making the best decision possible.

The A, B, Cs with D, E, F, and G provide a helpful mnemonic that beautifully illustrates the principles shaping chaplains' approach to offering compassionate and wise support. The four principles of biomedical ethics, established by Beauchamp and Childress, namely Autonomy, Nonmaleficence, Beneficence, and Justice, are the cornerstones of healthcare practice, commonly called the Four Pillars of Ethics. As chaplains understand and embrace these universal principles, they provide profound moral guidance in their ministry, offering impactful and ethical support to those in need.[143]

## Tool #3: Three Contexts of Decision-Making

All decisions have these.

---

[143] Tom L. Beauchamp and James F. Childress, *Principles of Biomedical Ethics*, 4th ed. (New York: Oxford University Press, 1994).

1. **Personal Context:** This involves self-awareness of our thoughts, desires, strengths, and weaknesses. For example, it is setting an alarm to wake up on time for work, allowing enough time for personal hygiene, and factoring in commuting time.
2. **Social Context:** This pertains to how we interact with others, whether we are team players, leaders, followers, or responsible individuals, and whether our behavior is constructive or destructive. For instance, it is balancing work and school to improve our lives while learning to cope with others in similar situations.
3. **Situational Context:** This concerns where we are and the decisions we face personally and socially at this specific time and place in our lives. For example, it is managing finances to avoid using credit cards, striving to be debt-free, and finding time for personal improvement and spiritual growth.

Chaplains should be aware of three critical contexts in ministry whether in the marketplace, military, prison, hospital, or elsewhere. Awareness of these three primary contexts can serve as a moral compass, helping us and others understand their situations and providing them with the strength and direction we need.

## Tool #4: Three Types of Leadership of Ethical Decision-Making in Organizations

1. **Rules-based ethics.** All members must deeply understand the organization's rules and regulations in ministry contexts. This ethical code underscores the significance of being well-versed in the laws and expectations governing the organization. Commonly known as compliance ethics, all members must be familiar with and adhere to these rules. Noncompliance may result in disciplinary measures; however, it is essential to approach this with the Golden Rule in mind: "Do unto others as you would have them do unto you." By comprehending and abiding by these guidelines, you will serve as a moral compass and positively influence the organization.

2. **Mission-based ethics.** Organizations typically have mission and vision statements. As a moral guide, the chaplain must know these statements, understand how to interpret them responsibly, and consider how to be an appropriate leader of the mission/vision as they reflect on their theological and ethical training.
3. **Ends-based ethics.** The organization has goals and objectives customarily communicated as part of its purpose. The military's focus may be war readiness, the prison's focus may be corrections, and the hospital's focus may be healing. As leaders, chaplains must understand the organization's purpose, goals, and objectives. Chaplains are leaders and need to understand the organization's mission to provide moral guidance aligned with that mission.

Decisions are made daily in the organizational ministry contexts, and all three types of leadership are involved in ethical decision-making. As the chaplain, you can monitor these contexts and, with your expert situational awareness, may have the moral temper needed to help the organization's individuals, units, and leaders. When there becomes an imbalance between these ethical streams, you could be the wisdom, advice, and insightful encourager.

## Tool #5: Three Types of Spirituality Contributing to the Development of Moral Guidance

1. **Human Spirituality** reflects the essence of humanity, emphasizing our true nature, our capacity for personal growth, and the profound experiences that shape our existence. It is inclusive and open to a diverse range of beliefs. Moral guides recognize the challenges of navigating different belief systems and the implications of such systems. An example of human spirituality is atheism, a philosophy that is quite the opposite of Divine spirituality.
2. **Divine Spirituality** emphasizes a deep connection to religion and a spiritual way of life, involving a strong belief in God and active participation in spiritual practices. Balancing this with communal life and actively nurturing faith through worship and spiritual disciplines is crucial. This is the pathway to knowing God and helping people

in your ministry context navigate human and cultural spirituality to grow toward knowing the Holy One, Almighty God.

3. **Cultural Spirituality** focuses on the social aspect of spirituality within a religious community, highlighting the rich history and traditions of one's faith. Chaplains need to understand the unique cultures they interact with and acknowledge each one's narratives as valuable.

Understanding the three types of spirituality can significantly enhance our ability to communicate and connect with others on a spiritual level. This approach ensures that terminology, definitions, and applications resonate consistently across diverse communities. Armed with these insights, it becomes crucial to delve into more targeted inquiries, such as recognizing and comprehending spiritual expressions in individuals and groups and respectfully advocating for these spiritual beliefs. Understanding the three types of spirituality provides a valuable tool for understanding where individuals are in their spiritual journey within the cultural framework of one's organization and with the Divine. These types of spirituality coexist harmoniously and offer a meaningful framework for self-reflection and empathizing with others, fostering an optimistic approach to spiritual growth and interpersonal relationships. Chaplains can use this knowledge to improve their ethical awareness of themselves and others in their connection with God, thus becoming more effective moral guides and leaders.

## Tool #6: Four Chaplain Core Capabilities[144]

1. **Provide:** Providing professional religious ministry through worship services, religious education, weddings, funerals, and other religious rituals and rites.
2. **Facilitate:** Facilitating the religious needs of our people from other religious traditions by identifying their needs and coordinating support from other chaplains, civilian clergy, and lay leaders.

---

[144] The US Navy Chaplain Corps highlights these as their core capabilities; however, they are universally applicable for chaplains providing spiritual and pastoral care to the people in most organizations.

3. **Care:** Caring for our people with dignity, respect, and compassion, regardless of an individual's beliefs, and making informed and professional referrals. Chaplains are available with confidential counseling to ensure that service members and their families have the spiritual resilience to cope with the inevitable hardships of military life.
4. **Advise:** Advising commanding officers, organizational leaders, and individuals who need wisdom on the accommodation of religious needs; on the moral, ethical, and spiritual well-being of our people; and on religious matters that affect the command's mission.

As chaplains, we have the excellent opportunity to witness a rich tapestry of human experiences! Chaplains must embody strong moral and ethical values guided by their faith. Others closely observe our actions and attitudes, making it all the more important to reflect our beliefs in everything we do. By living authentically and demonstrating genuine care, we can uplift those around us and serve as inspiring spiritual and moral examples. Our mission is bright and clear: to deepen our relationship with the Divine, stay true to our moral compass, and wholeheartedly embrace our responsibilities, showcasing our dedication and enthusiasm in all aspects of our lives as moral guides!

## REFLECTION QUESTIONS

1. How do you understand the similarities and differences between the definitions of *morals* and *ethics*? Provide an example of each. What challenges do you anticipate in your commitment to maintaining high ethical standards?
2. In what ways can a chaplain, as a moral guide, use the Socratic method to help others explore profound questions about virtue and ethical living?
3. As moral guides, chaplains must "walk the talk" to demonstrate authenticity and integrity in their ministry. How can you ensure that your actions align with your words as a chaplain? What could compromise this alignment? How might you hold yourself accountable for this effort, especially when faced with difficult situations?
4. How can a chaplain navigate a dilemma when doing the right thing conflicts with the values or directives of their institution? Can you identify ways to enhance your leadership by employing the tools of a moral guide to address this dilemma and support and guide others?

## MEMORABLE MOMENT
## "INVESTING MY LIFE INTO OTHERS"

Ch. Todd Combee, Director/Endorser,
Baptist Chaplaincy Relations (BCR)

It is the type of phone call I dread. A couple in my church received word that their grandson was killed in a single-car accident. He was a college student at Mississippi State; his parents lived in Georgia, and his grandparents lived in Virginia. Emotions were running high, and everyone was shocked by the news. I went to see the grandparents and ministered to their needs. They wanted to head down to Georgia to be with their daughter; however, they knew their daughter was already planning to travel to Mississippi. How could we minister to this grieving family spread over three states? I remembered that one of our endorsed chaplains serving in the Mississippi Army National Guard was also a faculty member at Mississippi State. I contacted him, hoping he could provide ministry support for this family. He was already aware of the student's death and knew the family from their time on the school's faculty. He connected with the family and supported them through this excruciating experience. I continued ministering to the grandparents back in Virginia. The Lord provided the people and the resources to minister to this grieving family across three states! Chaplain endorsement is about building relationships and walking with our chaplains through their ministry and lives.

Baptist Chaplaincy Relations (BCR) exists to endorse, support, and train military, healthcare, corrections, public safety, and other chaplains who relate to the Baptist General Convention of Texas (BGCT) and the Baptist General Association of Virginia (BGAV). As an endorser, I provide ecclesiastical endorsement through a process that affirms to an employer or organization that a chaplain or pastoral counselor has met all the basic requirements of the denomination to practice ministry in a specialized setting. Basic requirements include personal, spiritual, and professional accountability; educational, moral, and ethical standards; ability to work in a pluralistic environment; doctrinal stability; and active membership in a local church.

We have an Endorsement Council elected by the BGCT Executive Board, which serves as the endorsement agency for the BGCT and the BGAV. In the twenty-two years of our existence, we have endorsed close to twelve hundred chaplains, with almost six hundred currently serving full-time, part-time, or as a volunteer in one of nine chaplain disciplines. Along with my position as the Director/Endorser, our BCR team consists of four part-time Associate Endorsers who provide pastoral care and support to our chaplains and their families, two annual training opportunities, administrative support, and who serve as liaisons between the BGCT/BGAV and our chaplains.

I retired from the United States Army in 2014 after thirty-four years of military service. I spent four years on active duty in the Adjutant General Corps before transferring to the Army Reserves as a Chaplain Candidate while attending seminary. That was followed by twenty-six years as a chaplain in the Virginia Army National Guard and the Army Reserves. I also served as a minister in four local congregations in North Carolina and Virginia from 1984 to 2020 before leaving full-time church ministry to become an Associate Endorser with BCR. I assumed the role of Director/Endorser in May 2023. I share my background with you so you can better understand how and why I do what I do as an endorser. I have always seen my calling into ministry as an opportunity to proclaim the lordship of Jesus Christ and to care for the people God has entrusted to me as both a pastor and a chaplain. I genuinely believe that being a pastor allowed me to be a better chaplain, and being a chaplain enabled me to be a better pastor! I now have the privilege to serve as a pastor to chaplains and their families.

It all seems so simple: make yourself available to God's leading and learn to follow that calling to the best of your ability; then watch what God will do! I am still amazed at what I get to do as an endorser. I invest my life into the lives of our chaplains and celebrate their achievements, victories, and family joys. I am also honored to walk alongside them as they experience heartaches, disappointments, family struggles, and even failures. I grieve when a chaplain shares their frustration in getting passed over for a promotion or being hurt during a long separation due to an overseas deployment. My heart breaks for them when I hear the anguish in their voice as they talk about a son or daughter making poor decisions and the pain it causes in their family relationships.

I rejoice in the birth or adoption of a child, and I am saddened by the news of a cancer diagnosis in a family member.

One of our Navy Active Duty Chaplains recently invited me to his promotion ceremony. He treated me as an honored guest, inviting me to share several meals at his home, conducting an office call with his chief of staff, allowing me to offer a prayer at his promotion ceremony, and taking me on a tour of a nuclear submarine and an aircraft carrier! I was so overwhelmed by his genuine hospitality, and yet he was the one who kept thanking me for coming to see him. When the time came for me to leave, this chaplain put his hand on my shoulder and offered a prayer for *me* and my family. That's the heart of a chaplain, and I will always cherish that moment!

On a recent summer vacation to Florida, I wanted to gather our chaplains in the Orlando area for dinner. I invited chaplains and their spouses to meet at a specific restaurant on a Thursday evening. We had one chaplain and his wife, who drove from Tampa, and another chaplain and his wife drove from Jacksonville. They both traveled several hours to share a meal for an evening. I was honored by their presence. A healthcare chaplain from the area also came. She kept saying how wonderful it was to meet other BCR chaplains and to realize that she was not the only one in the area. When she attended our latest training event in Dallas, she still smiled and talked about the dinner we shared in Orlando.

The little things often make the biggest impressions in our lives. That's what gives me pleasure and satisfaction as an endorser!

# SECTION FIVE

## CHAPLAINCY TYPES

## CHAPTER SIXTEEN

# HEALTHCARE CHAPLAINCY

### Chaplain Mark Grace

"Do you work here?" the woman asked, peering at my badge with a frown of puzzlement or disapproval. It was impossible to tell which.

I smiled and responded, "Yes, I'm one of the chaplains employed by the hospital." As the doors closed and the elevator began to ascend, she asked the inevitable follow-up question. "Just exactly what is it that you do?"

"Lots of things," I said. "I offer friendship, a listening ear, prayer if that is meaningful, among other things. Nearly all of what I do involves supporting people emotionally and spiritually as they cope with whatever it is that brought them here."

She paused and said, "I don't know how you do it. It must be depressing working with all that pain."

"It can be, for sure, but it is also incredibly instructive, fulfilling, and inspiring. I feel privileged to be able to help so many courageous people, especially at a time when it may mean everything to them." The elevator slowed to a stop at my floor, and I prepared to leave, murmuring a good-bye as the doors opened. As I stepped out of the elevator, I fished a business card from my pocket and offered it to her, saying, "Here. Just in case you know someone who needs the support."

Her eyes filled with tears, and she grasped my hand in both of hers as she responded, "We are just here for some tests. My dad is dying. I'd give anything to have someone to talk to, but I doubt you make house calls."

I hesitated a moment, then stepped back on the elevator before the door could shut. "Call that number. We have chaplains working with faith communities and in hospice care all over the area. I'll do my best to connect you with someone who can help you shoulder this burden."

## OVERVIEW

Every day around the world, healthcare chaplains are having similar conversations. Every day, people are cast upon the shores of pain and suffering with little awareness of their deep internal needs for support and compassion. In addition, the psychological, conceptual, and spiritual baggage that suffering individuals bring with them into these settings is almost limitless in their variety.

And as the above vignette illustrates, most people have a limited idea of what it is that chaplains might offer them. They often do not possess the energy to entertain one more healthcare worker with a load of questions and a clipboard. Or they are weary of vague platitudes and pep talks. To make matters worse, these platitudes often reveal a painful lack of knowledge and understanding, perhaps even a lack of basic interest, in the critical details of a person's life.

Chaplains (and ministers) of all types will likely encounter these kinds of issues and problems. What makes healthcare chaplains unique is their ministry requires them to be familiar with an intimidating array of specialized healthcare settings. In addition to more general knowledge about those settings, chaplains must also master technical terminology, models for diagnosis and treatment, regulations, and disease processes, as well as the psychological, emotional, and spiritual aftereffects of those disease processes. They also must understand and work effectively within the specific organizational cultures wherein they carry out their ministry.

Because of their role as healthcare team members, chaplains can advocate directly for the spiritual, emotional, and relational needs of the people to whom they minister. They are familiar with the individuals' unique needs and have taken the time to prepare themselves to help and not harm the individuals. In addition to ministry with patients and their family members, healthcare chaplains, especially in the age of pandemics, must understand and be equipped to respond to the emotional and spiritual needs of the other members of the healthcare team. Most important of all, these chaplains ought to have received training and have demonstrated professional competence in working with people who represent a wide range of social, ethnic, and religious identities, as well as people of many different national origins, ancestries, and sexual orientations, with a wide variety of medical conditions and physical, developmental, and mental challenges.[145]

## A BRIEF HISTORY

The idea of creating a professional role and standards for healthcare chaplains' certification began in 1939 when Russell Dicks addressed the American Hospital Association on "The Work of the Chaplain in the General Hospital." Primarily due to Dicks's and physician Richard Cabot's efforts the Chaplains' Section of the AHA was formed in 1946. In that same year, sixteen chaplains also came together to form the Association of Protestant Hospital Chaplains, the precursor to the Association of Professional Chaplains.[146]

"Today, there are more than 10,000 healthcare chaplains in the United States, most with master's degrees, rigorous hands-on training, and board certification. Almost two-thirds of the country's hospitals make chaplains available."[147]

## A DAY IN THE LIFE OF . . .

This section's title represents an inside joke for anyone who has worked in healthcare chaplaincy long enough to have been interviewed by a friendly journalist intent on knowing a "typical day" of a healthcare chaplain. The answer that most working chaplains would love to be able to give might go

---

[145] "Common Standards for Professional Chaplains," Association of Professional Chaplains, 7 November 2004, https://www.professionalchaplains.org/Files/professional_standards/common_standards/common_standards_professional_chaplaincy.pdf, accessed 21 September 2021.

[146] "A Brief History of the Association of Professional Chaplains," Association of Professional Chaplains, https://www.professionalchaplains.org/content.asp?pl=24&sl=31&contentid=31, accessed 21 September 2021.

[147] A. Abrams, "Hospital chaplains stick to the heart of the job amid health care industry changes," Religion News Service, 31 May 2019, https://religionnews.com/2019/05/28/hospital-chaplains-stick-to-the-heart-of-the-job-amid-health-care-industry-changes /, accessed 21 September 2021.

something like the following: "Visiting patients/clients/residents and their family members in my assigned areas, working with those facing death or with the families of those who have died, doing some group education and support for people in my specific setting or in the community, having meaningful, supportive conversations with my colleagues who are also directly caring for my patients/clients/residents and their families, and regularly conducting multifaith services involving a variety of staff to encourage and strengthen our coping."

The day-to-day reality is chaplains in most settings must chart their work with patients and attend multidisciplinary meetings focused on the care of patients in a given area. They are required regularly to take in-services and educational events deemed essential for every staff member. They must participate in various meetings to make schedules, solve problems, set goals, and improve morale. Every healthcare challenge is to balance, every day, work required to keep the hospital doors open while also caring effectively for the people who come through those doors.

A 2018 review of the international literature on the role of healthcare chaplains noted the activities most often engaged by them included specifically religious interventions: (1) hearing of confession or amends, (2) affirmation of one's faith, (3) theological reflection and exploration, (4) performance of a religious rite or ritual, (5) provision of a religious item, (6) offer of a blessing, (7) prayer, and (9) other spiritual support.

Frequently used interventions that did not necessarily carry religious meaning for the patient/client/resident were: (1) crisis intervention, (2) ethical consultation/deliberation, (3) life review, (4) emotional support, (5) patient advocacy, (6) counseling, (7) bereavement, (8) meditation, and (9) empathetic listening. The authors noted at several points that prayer was significant to people whether they shared the chaplain's faith or even considered themselves religious. Prayer was ranked high in the order of interventions utilized by chaplains. Also important were their roles as members of institutional ethics councils and in offering ethical consultation to patients and family members, either individually or as members of a larger ethics team.[148]

---

[148] Fiona Timmins et al., "The Role of the Healthcare Chaplain: A Literature Review," *Journal of Health Care Chaplaincy* 24:3 (2018): 87–106, DOI: 10.1080/08854726.2017.1338048, accessed

## A MINISTRY OF COLLABORATION

The price of being a viable member of a healthcare team composed of highly qualified and certified professionals is documentation, communication, and collaboration. These actions necessarily take time away from the activity that almost every working chaplain finds most fulfilling: direct ministry with people in need. Being a healthcare team member also requires a willingness to stay current with the literature in one's field, participate in research to demonstrate the effectiveness of one's work, and learn better ways to accomplish that work. This willingness to share one's work with the rest of the healthcare team in the form of in-services and educational events inevitably results in more effective and efficient ministry as one's colleagues better understand how and when to refer cases to the chaplain.[149] And as the advent of COVID-19 has shown us, it also means being able to stop on a dime, reassess, revise, and reinvent the kinds of ministry a chaplain might offer.[150]

## HEALTHCARE CHAPLAINCY SPECIALITIES

While most healthcare chaplains provide ministry in hospitals, healthcare chaplaincy happens in an impressive range of settings. In the general acute care hospital setting, a chaplain may choose to focus on one of a plethora of specialties, provided the institution served allows for such specialties in spiritual care.

As for settings outside the traditional hospital, chaplains may serve in specialty hospitals that focus on one kind of patient care such as cardiac surgery, cardiologic care, physical medicine and rehabilitation, cancer treatment, free-standing surgery, or free-standing emergency treatment, among others. Eldercare chaplains serve in nursing homes, assisted living facilities,

---

21 September 2021.
[149] J. P. Vlasblom, J. T. van der Steen, D. L. Knol, and H. Jochemsen, "Effects of a spiritual care training for nurses," *Nurse Education Today* 31:8 (November 2011): 790–96, https://pubmed.ncbi.nlm.nih.gov/21146259/, accessed 21 September 2021.
[150] Anne Vandenhoeck, "The Impact of the First Wave of the Covid-19 Pandemic on Chaplaincy in Health Care: Introduction to an International Survey," *Journal of Pastoral Care & Counseling* (March 2021), https://journals.sagepub.com/doi/full/10.1177/1542305021992044, accessed 21 September 2021.

and specialized Alzheimer's and dementia units. Chaplains also work as staff members in free-standing substance disorder clinics, eating disorder treatment centers, and other settings focused on subspecialties in behavioral medicine.

Also, healthcare chaplains may work exclusively with local faith communities to support ministers, educate congregations, and train and coordinate the efforts of spiritual-care liaisons who then provide spiritual and practical support to medically at-risk and underserved individuals. Hospice chaplains travel extensively to provide spiritual care to the dying and their families in rural and urban settings. Chaplains may also work directly with physicians in office practices as well as in outpatient clinics. In some settings, chaplains focus exclusively on staff support. They also provide spiritual care in settings devoted to the care of developmentally and cognitively challenged individuals.[151]

## WHAT DOES IT TAKE?

What does it take to become a healthcare chaplain? The question about qualifications, education, training, and certification requirements was previously straightforward: ordination, endorsement by a recognized religious body, a master of divinity degree from an accredited theological school, at least four units of clinical pastoral education (CPE) accredited by the Association of Clinical Pastoral Education, and board certification from the Association of Professional Chaplains.[152]

Thanks to increased emphasis on chaplaincy among faith traditions whose practices of educating and training adherents vary widely, today's conversations about credentialing reveal a much wider variety of possible avenues to credentialing. As an example, the relatively new Spiritual Care Association

---

[151] L. VandeCreek and L. Burton, eds., "Professional Chaplaincy: Its Role and Importance in Healthcare," *Journal of Pastoral Care* 55(1) (Spring 2001): 81–97, https://pubmed.ncbi.nlm.nih.gov/11303456/, accessed 21 September 2021.

[152] "About Certification and the Application Process," Board of Chaplaincy Certification, https://bcci.professionalchaplains.org/content.asp?pl=25&sl=26&contentid=26, accessed 21 September 2021.

recognizes credentialing from fifteen separate chaplaincy certifying bodies.[153] While the oldest and largest certifying body, the Association of Professional Chaplains, continues to provide the most significant number of credentialed chaplains in health care (about four thousand), the variety of possible avenues to credentialing are increasing every year.

A career in healthcare chaplaincy does not necessarily have to wait to complete four CPE units and pass a board certification committee or exam. As the situation demands, entry-level chaplaincy roles, on-call, and PRN (*pro re nata*) typically require much less education, training, and certification. Often, one may begin working for a healthcare institution with only one unit of CPE. These requirements vary widely, as do rates of pay and the number of hours it is possible to work with those minimal job qualifications. However, such opportunities often afford individuals pathways to increased experience and mentoring while completing other board certification requirements.

## IS IT WORTH IT?

One recent study of job satisfaction among US professional healthcare chaplains reported that 82 percent of the more than one thousand chaplains surveyed reported they were highly satisfied or very highly satisfied with their work. This score compared favorably with other members of the healthcare team.[154] As with most studies and statistics, the article's conclusion is only the beginning of the conversation. Like many other forms of chaplaincy, healthcare chaplaincy is a highly stressful and rewarding occupation. Healthcare chaplains will seldom find themselves on stage as the star of the show. They often find themselves working in the most difficult and painful circumstances possible, dealing with death far more than other healthcare team members. They may sometimes feel under-appreciated and under-resourced in a profession of healthcare leaders who have yet to connect the dots between their

---

[153] "About Board Certification," Spiritual Care Association, https://www.spiritualcareassociation.org/requirements-for-board-certification.html, accessed 21 September 2021.

[154] K. Crossley, "Professional Satisfaction among US Healthcare Chaplains," *Journal of Pastoral Care & Counseling* 56(1) (March 2002): 21–27. https://doi.org/10.1177/154230500205600104, accessed 21 September 2021.

own "healing for the whole person" rhetoric and the chaplain's genuine and increasingly well-researched contribution to whole-person care.

On the other hand, this author's experience is that most healthcare chaplains would say their deep love for and satisfaction with their work sustains them when recognition or influence is lacking. These chaplains often name the following reasons: the joy of working with highly dedicated professionals from a wide variety of disciplines, the intense sense of fulfillment that comes with having stood in the breach with someone at the worst moment of their lives, the joy of being able to contribute to the lives of their colleagues on a multidisciplinary team, the challenge of engaging an environment that demands excellence, and the conviction that what they are doing somehow embodies the essence of their faith-compassion in action.

# HOSPITAL CHAPLAINCY

## Chaplain Mark Grace

"They won't let me in. I am sitting here in my car in the hospital parking lot. I brought Annie (not her real name) to the emergency department, and they told me I couldn't stay with her." Sounds of weeping punched through the speaker of my phone, and I can tell you with confidence that it was a sound no one wants to hear. When Annie's mother spoke again, her voice, though choked with tears, was filled with determination, tinged with frustration and anger. "I couldn't think of anyone else to call. Is there anything you can do?"

Thousands of different stories could easily illustrate the essential nature of hospital chaplaincy. This experience will always rise to the forefront of my memory when I describe what it is like to be a hospital chaplain. Events like this one, although rare, were not unknown in the years preceding the global pandemic. Now they are all too common.

## COMPANIONS IN THE FIERY FURNACE: A JOB DESCRIPTION

Hospital chaplaincy shares many of the same qualities as described in the above introduction to healthcare chaplaincy. Working as a hospital chaplain involves the readiness to provide care, compassion, and support to individuals enduring unimaginably painful circumstances in the most challenging situations. A hospital chaplain does not get to say, "Come to my office on Monday morning, and we can talk about it," or sometimes even, "I will be there in a few minutes." Skilled care doesn't just mean in-person care; sometimes, one must provide care immediately over the phone or in a video conference call.

Chaplains are frequently called upon to provide crucial information and guidance and to engage problem-solving skills in tandem with emotional availability and spiritual care to those overwhelmed by fear, anger, panic, and shock. Hospital chaplains are called to cultivate insight into legal, regulatory, and organizational dynamics and then to use that insight to advocate for the people they serve. And they provide such care, problem-solving, and advocacy almost entirely for individuals they have never met before.

As I prepared to write this chapter, I interviewed my wife, Linda Wilkerson. After thirty years, she retired a few years ago as a chaplain and certified spiritual-care educator. She spent nineteen of those years as director of pastoral care in one of the most challenging hospital environments in the nation, the Parkland Health and Hospital System in Dallas, Texas. She made two emphatic statements. The first was, "Hospital chaplaincy requires individuals who are comfortable providing care in a wide range of circumstances and settings." No matter how specialized a chaplain may become, very few hospitals have a staff large enough to afford a chaplain the luxury of doing the same kind of ministry every day in the same setting. Hospital chaplains are required to demonstrate a high degree of adaptability to changing circumstances as well as unusual levels of resilience in the face of steadily increasing demands. The rate of change and the corresponding demands for adaptability and resilience have only increased in the face of the global pandemic in 2020.[155]

Few ministry settings encompass a greater diversity of linguistic, ethnic, national, social, economic, gender expressions, sexual orientation, and medical diagnosis. Many times every day, the success or failure of hospital chaplains' ministries will rise or fall upon their capacity to connect with individuals who are very different from them.[156]

Linda's second statement was, "What most people underestimate about hospital chaplaincy is the degree to which profoundly effective ministry routinely happens at the most unexpected times." Theologically, ministers often speak of the reality of *kairos*, the right, proper, or appropriate moment seized amid *chronos*, or time's repeating cycles arising out of the interaction of an almost infinite range of causes.[157]

---

[155] Wendy Cadge, "The Rise of the Chaplains," *The Atlantic* (24 September 2020), https://www.theatlantic.com/ideas/archive/2020/05/why-americans-are-turning-chaplains-during-pandemic/611767/, accessed 24 August 2021.

[156] "Common Standards for Professional Chaplains," Association of Professional Chaplains, 7 November 2004, https://www.professionalchaplains.org/Files/professional_standards/common_standards/common_standards_professional_chaplaincy.pdf, accessed 24 August 2021.

[157] Abarim Publications' Free Online Dictionary of Biblical New Testament Greek, "καιρος" (2017), https://www.abarim-publications.com/DictionaryG/k/k-a-i-r-o-sfin.html, accessed 22 August 2021.

In the above sense, operating in an acute-care general hospital setting is often like putting on a diving suit and descending three hundred feet into the ocean. The water pressure people experience at that depth is unimaginable to those who have never operated in such an environment. Diving at three hundred feet demands attention to every detail. The smallest of actions can result in catastrophe. Conversely, such diligence in the hospital setting can preserve health and save lives.

In the same way, the pressures that individuals routinely experience in hospital environments can be unbelievably intense. Chaplains are called upon to operate with a clear sense of the many causative factors unique to the individual, social, emotional, spiritual, and medical situations encountered and to trust in the power of applying the proper intervention at the right time.

Five minutes of attentive, compassionate care offered in a pre-surgery visit can make all the difference for that patient. The same can be said of pastoral care offered to patients or family members in a dozen different hospital settings. As the sociologist Arthur Frank, twice a survivor of a life-threatening illness, states, "The voices that speak to us at particular moments in our lives, especially during transitions or crises, imprint themselves with a force that later voices never quite displace."[158]

Most chaplains would tell you they desperately need more time to spend with patients and family members and having more time to devote to them would improve the overall levels of care they can provide. However, I am also confident they would agree this little-noted aspect of spiritual care comprises one of the hallmarks of chaplaincy in modern hospitals.

The skill of clinical judgment is critical because of the immense variety of encounters in hospitals. In the strictest sense, the term "clinical judgment" refers to the "cognitive or thinking process used for analyzing data, deriving diagnoses, deciding on interventions, and evaluating care."[159]

This problem-solving, decision-making, and critical-thinking process is at the heart of the professional practice skills section of the "Common

---

[158] A. W. Frank, *The Wounded Storyteller: Body, Illness, and Ethics* (Chicago: University of Chicago Press, 2013), 49.
[159] *Medical Dictionary for the Health Professions and Nursing*, s.v. "clinical judgment," 2012, https://medical-dictionary.thefreedictionary.com/clinical+judgment, accessed 22 August 2021.

Qualifications and Competencies for Professional Chaplains."[160] (See Millspaugh's excellent discussion of competencies in chapter 3 of this book.) In a slightly broader sense, clinical judgment represents the point at which hospital chaplains bring their engaged and self-aware presences to fluid and changing circumstances so as to respond in highly effective ways to the particular needs of the individuals they are serving.

There are no one-size-fits-all resolutions for the pain and suffering that hospital chaplains (or any chaplains) encounter. For instance, hospitals and other healthcare providers and their spiritual-care departments routinely generate scripts for specific situations and high-priority communications to patients and their family members. These scripts should be utilized whenever possible for clarity and consistency. However, a script is only the beginning of the conversation. Every new encounter brings new challenges and opportunities for the chaplain, not based on what is likely to happen or what happened in the last visit, but what is occurring in the unpredictable, present moment. The fact that these interactions occur between strangers adds a further note of uncertainty. That uncertainty requires attentiveness, skill, respect, and reverence on the part of the chaplain.

Hospital chaplains must function as effective team members on the healthcare teams to which they belong. Like other healthcare chaplains, they have the opportunity and challenge to minister to patients, family members, and virtually every member of the facility staff. With the advent of the pandemic, chaplains across the country have seen a dramatic rise in the number of staff members seeking spiritual, emotional, and moral support from hospital chaplains.

Hospital chaplaincy also requires chaplains to develop comprehensive programs of spiritual care. Sometimes these programs are limited to specific patient care areas, such as nursing floors or intensive-care units. Sometimes, the chaplain is called upon to assess needs, set priorities, and develop programs for an entire hospital.

---

[160] In 2016–2017 five board-certifying organizations agreed on and published the "Common Qualifications and Competencies for Professional Chaplains," https://www.professionalchaplains.org/files/2017%20Common%20Qualifications%20and%20Competencies%20for%20Professional%20Chaplains.pdf, accessed 21 July 2020.

Like other healthcare chaplains, hospital chaplains cultivate the skill of assessing spiritual and emotional needs. Chaplains must stay up to date in reading and integrating the literature related to the hospital environment, the overall impacts of illness, injury, and hospitalization on individuals, and the current state of research in hospital chaplaincy. When possible, they should engage directly in research about the care they provide. Chaplains have traditionally expressed reluctance, even a great deal of resistance, to researching their work, ostensibly because some feel the work of the Spirit cannot be quantified by a set of numbers.

> But if the profession is to survive, chaplaincy needs to embrace evidence-based spirituality as its primary language . . . because decisions about health care are determined by data and the people who are grounded in that "language." When chaplains can speak the same language as their colleagues, then they will be able to more fully integrate into patient care and serve effectively and confidently.[161]

Hospital chaplains daily confront the necessity of measuring important things about their ministry even as they commit themselves to the transcendent reality that God is present at every point in their work, doing far more than can be measured or imagined.

Like other healthcare chaplains, hospital chaplains also serve as spiritual and religious advocates for patients and family members. Such advocacy forms an essential element in effective ministry. It includes but is not limited to the chaplain's determination to help the healthcare team understand their patients' religious and spiritual motivations. Without the advocacy of the chaplain, these motivations can become points of misunderstanding and estrangement from medical personnel rather than enhancing a healing alliance between patients and their healthcare teams. Chaplains also document their care in the medical record to communicate spiritual and other care priorities to the medical staff.

---

[161] "Measuring Pastoral Care Performance," *Health Progress: The Journal of the Catholic Health Association* (May–June 2018), https://www.chausa.org/publications/health-progress/article/may-june-2018/measuring-pastoral-care-performance, accessed 24 August 2021.

Many hospital chaplains serve as the de facto organizers of hospital ethics committees, even though someone else may carry the title of leader for such efforts. Even when that is not the case, chaplains are still highly involved in all phases of the work of these committees. "Chaplains provide spiritual care and support to patients, families, and hospital staff. What may be less familiar is that chaplains also help mediate decisions among patients, family members, and clinical teams."[162]

Many people in health care routinely underestimate the public ministry of chaplains. This ministry often helps shape the organizational culture of patient-care areas and an entire hospital or health system. Chaplains take the initiative to provide nonsectarian prayers in organizational gatherings, unique blessings for healthcare team members, stress-relief programs such as "tea for the soul"[163] or "code lavender."[164] Chaplains often write for hospital publications, providing education about spiritual care to other healthcare team members, informing hospital staff of support available to them, and providing inspiration and comfort as staff seeks to cope with unusual stress and pressure. Interfaith services support the hospital and community's life and are especially relevant during stressful or crucial times.

A last, but increasingly important, dimension of hospital chaplaincy, is the chaplain's role on palliative and supportive-care teams. These teams of specialist physicians, nurses, social workers, and chaplains are mandated to care for patients living with serious illness and who need additional support in the face of such illness.[165] Palliative care is a chaplaincy specialization recognized and certified by reputable professional chaplaincy certifying bodies.

---

[162] Susan Harris, "Chaplains' Roles as Mediators in Critical Clinical Decisions," *AMA Journal of Ethics* 20(7) (July 2018): 670–74, https://journalofethics.ama-assn.org/article/chaplains-roles-mediators-critical-clinical-decisions/2018-07, accessed 24 August 2021.

[163] "Nurturing Caregivers with 'Tea for the Soul,'" Boulder Community Health, June 2017, https://www.bch.org/latest-news/2017/june/nurturing-caregivers-with-tea-for-the-soul, accessed 23 August 2021.

[164] J. E. Davidson et al., "Code Lavender: Cultivating Intentional Acts of Kindness in Response to Stressful Work Situations," *EXPLORE* 13(3) (2017): 181–85. DOI: 10.1016/j.explore.2017.02.005, accessed 23 August 2021.

[165] "Palliative Care," World Health Organization, 5 August 2020, https://www.who.int/news-room/fact-sheets/detail/palliative-care.

# A DAY IN THE LIFE: BOUNCING FROM PILLAR TO POST

While there is no typical day in the life of a hospital chaplain, the daily ministry is commonly based on a set of practices and priorities for optimal care, seeking to be at the right place, at the right time, providing needed care for as long as possible. A hospital chaplain's day may begin with an event called "morning report," when the chaplain on call the night before briefs the oncoming chaplain(s) about ministry that took place during the night, as well as other hospital events of note. Since the start of COVID-19, chaplain managers are also likely to attend a "house- (hospital-) wide huddle" devoted to updating medical staff on the number of cases and deaths, their impact on the availability of beds, and shifting plans. Daily priorities in care vary among hospital chaplaincy departments, depending on the department's staffing.

Typically, chaplains prioritize (1) patient deaths and medical emergencies, (2) patient and family requests for visits, and (3) staff referrals. Staff levels permitting, chaplains will round daily on intensive care units and through the emergency department, with care and attention given to staff support and patient care. Documenting patient care takes up a significant chunk of time in all the above situations. Many chaplains also facilitate support groups for specific patient populations or more general grief- and bereavement-support groups.

After reading the contents of this chapter, one might ask, "Why would a person ever want to sign up for a vocation as demanding and stressful as hospital chaplaincy?" The answer can be summed up as follows: hospital chaplains tend to be ministers who want to be in the thick of things. They thrive on a high-demand environment that calls upon them to bring their best and are often quickly bored by less demanding settings. They love working with other highly skilled professionals. Paradoxically, they tend not to need to be the center of attention, but find their greatest satisfaction in making a difference for suffering people at their moment of greatest need.

# LONG-TERM CARE CHAPLAINCY

## Chaplain David Mann

Long-term care (LTC) is a range of services and support persons may need for their care as they age. About 60 percent of aging people will need some assistance with routine functions like getting dressed, driving to appointments, or making meals.[166] The ultimate goal of long-term care is fostering an individual's independence as much as possible while enhancing the quality of life. This encompasses many facets of care. Though the dominant thinking about long-term care centers on the nursing home, it must also include independent living facilities, assisted living facilities, memory care facilities, long-term acute care facilities (LTACs), and at times rehabilitation care and mental health/psychiatric care facilities. Continuous Care Retirement Communities (CCRCs) may provide care at each of the previously listed levels.

### MEETING SPIRITUAL NEEDS

Many long-term care facilities now recognize the importance of having a clinically trained chaplain on staff. The chaplain is available to provide spiritual care on an ecumenical basis. Chaplains are an essential part of the team's long-term care for residents and their families. A primary responsibility of the long-term care chaplain is to assist people in transitioning into a different phase of life with their faith and spiritual practices intact.

Residents at most long-term care facilities across the United States come from many faith traditions and a lifetime of participating in some form of worship. Chaplains coordinate and often lead group meetings and worship services, are available for one-to-one ministry, address spiritual issues related to end-of-life care, and minister to grieving families. Additionally, they provide education about and assist in preparing Advance Directives.

Chaplains of long-term care facilities find various ways to journey and connect with residents. Spiritual connections may come through leading worship services and Bible studies. Paying attention to the residents' preferred

---

[166] See "LongTermCare.gov" at https://acl.gov/ltc, accessed 5 April 2021.

style of worship can also assist in building spiritual trust with residents. A chaplain must be sensitive to spiritual needs while refraining from proselytizing. A caring chaplain strives to learn the spiritual-care practices important to each resident and incorporates those practices into a meaningful worship experience. Though the chaplain may lead most of these activities, local faith-group leaders are always welcome to visit and conduct specialized services.

A chaplain's ministry can center around storytelling, reminiscing, and activities beneficial to assist residents in building a sense of community. Perhaps the most significant way to provide spiritual care is through one-to-one interaction, thus learning the individual's personal story and spiritual needs.

Being part of an interdisciplinary team is an integral part of the success of any spiritual-care program in a long-term care facility. As coworkers discover the spiritual needs of their long-term care residents, they make referrals to the chaplain, who provides a pastoral presence, a listening and empathic ear, words of encouragement, and a word of prayer. A chaplain should learn how to use the gift of pastoral presence, when effective ministry occurs while remaining silent. It is of utmost importance for the chaplain never to have a "one-size-fits-all" pastoral approach, but to take time to learn every resident's individual needs and spiritual concerns.

Chaplains can also be a tremendous resource for family members and serve as liaisons between residents and families. When family members cannot visit, they may call on the chaplain to check on their loved one. With the growing availability of video conferencing, the chaplain may utilize this technology to assist families and residents in staying in touch with one another.

End-of-life care, funeral planning, and bereavement follow-up for family and friends are significant parts of any chaplain's responsibility. At times, the chaplain may assist an individual in naming fears and regrets and come to a sense of peace with God and family. Grief support before and after death is of significant importance. When a death occurs, the chaplain offers support and comfort for the family and often assists with plans and arrangements. The chaplain may sometimes take part in or lead a funeral or memorial service. In many long-term care communities, chaplains hold an annual memorial service to remember each resident who has died during the previous year.

Equally important, chaplains also provide emotional, pastoral, and spiritual support to the employees of the facilities, especially after the loss of someone they have cared for daily. Chaplains may become their pastors or counselors for those not involved in a faith community. For some workers, approaching their chaplain with a question or concern may be less threatening than going to their pastor. A chaplain should learn to listen and offer counsel without judgment. As with long-term residents, the staff may come from various faiths or no faith tradition at all. An effective chaplain finds ways to make spiritual connections regardless of their background.

A well-trained chaplain is an essential team member who provides spiritual care to anyone in the long-term care community. Ministry opportunities with residents, families, and staff abound. The chaplain needs to be sensitive to any spiritual needs that arise daily. Sometimes this opportunity comes in conversation, a word of encouragement or blessing, a crisis, the need for prayer, or some other form of support. Long-term care may include long-term relationships. The chaplain who is sensitive to spiritual-care opportunities will find journeying with individuals in the long-term setting both rewarding and fulfilling.

# DEMENTIA CHAPLAINCY

## Chaplain Ben Boland

When I started serving as a chaplain with people living with dementia, I made two assumptions: Dementia was primarily memory loss, and I was there to help. Both proved to be gross oversimplifications. While dementia does cause memory loss, it also impacts thinking, communication, and the ability to perform everyday tasks.[167] Arguably more importantly, dementia is often a disease of social abandonment.[168] As I spent more time with people living with dementia, Jesus' ministry with lepers came into sharp relief. Leprosy in the first century was an umbrella term for various skin conditions. Dementia in the twenty-first century is an umbrella term for a range of neurological diseases. People with leprosy and dementia are typically treated as outcasts and segregated from society.

For example, a few years into my dementia chaplaincy journey, I was in the secure unit and introduced myself to a woman I had not previously seen. She explained she was packing up her mother's room following her death. I offered my condolences and apologized for not having introduced myself previously. She replied, "Oh, this is the first time in over two years I have been here as mum did not recognize me." As a chaplain and as a son whose father often does not recognize me due to dementia, I understand the trauma that dementia can cause for loved ones. I also know that people flock to visit and engage with babies—who do not call anyone by name. Yet people often treat dementia as highly contagious!

Leprosy is highly contagious, yet Jesus not only loved people living with leprosy, he engaged with people living with leprosy and touched people living with leprosy. As a chaplain, I work to follow Jesus' example by moving toward, not away from, people living with dementia.

---

[167] Dementia Australia, *The Dementia Guide: For People Living with Dementia, Their Families and Carers* (Sydney: Dementia Australia, 2019).

[168] Warren A. Kinghorn, "'I Am Still With You': Dementia and the Christian Wayfarer," in *Still Waters Run Deep: Theological Reflections on Dementia, Faithfulness and Peaceable Presence*, ed. John Swinton and Elizabeth MacKinlay (Milton Park: Routledge, 2024), 98–117.

"Moving toward," however, assumes I am the "helper," which is my second assumption and has two flaws. First, it assumes I can help. Two residents in my first secure unit taught me how wrong I was. Mary spent much of her waking hours walking around the unit asking "Am I OK?" at thirty-second intervals. As the new chaplain, I saw this as an opportunity to help. I tried all the dementia best practices I could find; I walked with her, held her hand, and sang with her. I tried simple reassurances. "Yes, you are OK, safe, and loved." I tried spiritual options. I prayed with her and recited John 3:16, saying we are OK because of Jesus' love. I may have impressed the staff and other residents with my perseverance, but I did not provide discernable help to Mary. Finally, out of desperation rather than strategy, I replied to the incessant "Am I OK?" with "You are beautiful." Mary stopped, smiled, and preened, and that smile lasted for about two minutes. Then she would again ask, "Am I OK?" This experience taught me that my ability to "help" would often be very small; in this case, giving Mary a minute of smiling.

The second flaw with viewing myself as the "helper" was that it assumed I was the person who had something to give. Just down the hall from Mary lived Frank, a retired Baptist minister, so I offered to pray with him. I prayed a textbook dementia ministry prayer—short and concrete. Then Frank prayed. His prayer had a depth, power, and richness beyond anything I had ever heard. It was not me who helped Frank but Frank who helped me!

## THEOLOGY OF CHRISTIAN DEMENTIA CHAPLAINCY

Scripture teaches that people are incredibly diverse, and their characteristics change over time. For example, a newborn is almost totally dependent, while a person in middle life is likely to be highly independent and, in later life often experiences increasing dependence. The Bible attributes a person's worth not to external characteristics (for example, beauty, race, and presentation) or internal characteristics (for example, agency, wisdom, and intelligence) but to a threefold doctrinal position that applies to all people:

1. All people are created by God.
2. All people are created in God's image.

3. All people are so valuable God died to bring them back into a relationship with Him.

This doctrine implies that whatever a person does, owns, or believes, one's value does not change with God. What gives people value, purpose, and meaning is not the what but the who—God. Scripture is also very clear about how humans are to engage with one another: people are called to love people, including people who are struggling.[169]

## THE PRACTICE OF CHRISTIAN DEMENTIA CHAPLAINCY

Christian Dementia Chaplaincy is, therefore, loving people affected by dementia. While Christian love includes practical care, chaplains' love can aim to provide LARP:

| | |
|---|---|
| **Learning** | Learning about dementia, about how best to care for people impacted by dementia, and most importantly, from people living with dementia. |
| **Assuring** | Encouraging people living with dementia, their loved ones, and staff that while dementia can take many things, it cannot stop them as human beings from being loved by others. |
| **Religious** | Facilitating prayer, worship, and engagement with Scripture. |
| **Pastoral** | Providing pastoral care through tools such as presence and listening. |

---

[169] Ben Boland, "Should Churches Stop Providing Aged Care?" Eternity, August 19, 2021, https://www.eternitynews.com.au/australia/should-churches-stop-providing-aged-care/, accessed 11 September 2024.

The mechanics of LARP are beyond the scope of this chapter; suffice it to say LARP will include tools such as music,[170] words,[171] and love.[172]

When I met Polly, she was living in the dementia unit. My early interactions with her were somewhat distant as she was antagonistic to faith. Using LARP, I had a framework for engaging her. Over time, she began to respond to my simple pastoral care in the corridor. Because she enjoyed music, she started intermittently attending my dementia church service. Next, she became a regular at the secure unit and the main care home worship service. Then she encouraged other residents to come, too, and told me, "I don't know what happened. I was never interested in God, but now I love attending church."

I look forward to dancing with her in eternity.

---

[170] Kirsty Beilharz, *Music Remembers Me: Connection and Wellbeing in Dementia* (Sydney: HammondCare, 2019).

[171] Ben R. Boland, "Creating a Church Service to Facilitate Belonging for People Living with Dementia—Seven Principles and a Service Guide," *Stimulus* (2025); Lindsay Pelloquin and Jaye Keightley, *Celebrating the Seasons in Residential Care Homes: A Service for Every Week of the Year* (Rugby: Paul Thomas group, 2022).

[172] Jane Marie Thibault and Richard L. Morgan, *No Act of Love Is Ever Wasted: The Spirituality of Caring for Persons with Dementia* (Nashville: Upper Room Books, 2009).

# HOSPICE CHAPLAINCY

## Dr. Dennis Leedom

Hospice chaplaincy provides a unique and meaningful opportunity to minister to terminally ill patients and their loved ones during the final months and days of their lives. Although death and dying are not easily discussed in our modern culture, the hospice chaplain supports the patient in bringing their earthly life to a close with peace and dignity. Depending upon the patient's needs, this can include a review of life events and accomplishments, forgiveness and reconciliation of old wounds, encouragement and reconnection with God, and letting go of their "treasures on earth" as commanded in Matthew 6:19. The hospice chaplain's ministry also includes support of close friends and family members who are grieving the loss of the patient.

## THE HOSPICE TEAM

The hospice chaplain performs ministry within the context of an integrated healthcare provider team comprised of a physician (medical director), registered nurse (case manager), licensed medical social worker, hospice chaplain, and certified nursing assistant. The hospice team operates under a medical license granted by each state and conforms to federal guidelines and regulations published by the Centers for Medicare and Medicaid Services (CMS).

These regulations require each member of the hospice team to assess the patient's needs, establish a formal plan of care that prescribes interventions and frequency of visits, and document progress over time. In addition, the hospice chaplain formally participates in a periodic review of patient status led by the medical director. As such, the hospice chaplain is vitally integrated into the patient's overall care that addresses a continuum of physical, social, and spiritual needs.

## THE HISTORY OF HOSPICE CARE

The term "hospice" comes from the Latin word *hospitium*, meaning hospitality, shelter, or place of rest. By the eleventh century, the Roman Catholic

Church had extended the meaning of *hospitium* to include a place of caring for the sick, wounded, and dying. The modern hospice organization took form during the mid-1960s in the United Kingdom and appeared in the United States by the mid-1970s.

Over the next several decades, the fields of medicine and health care formally integrated hospice care into a continuum of care throughout a person's life. Medicare, Medicaid, and most private health insurance policies cover hospice care benefits. Organizations such as the National Hospice and Palliative Care Organization (NHPCO), the North American Nursing Diagnosis Association (NANDA), and CMS work to define, prescribe, and regulate medical, social, and spiritual services to terminally ill patients.

## THE INTEGRATED HOSPICE TEAM

The generally recognized goal of end-of-life care is for the patient to experience a "good death"[173] that maximizes the peace and dignity of the individual. This end-of-life care implies the requirement to address the patient's physical, social, and spiritual needs in a holistic manner. The nurse case manager employs prescribed medicines and other medical interventions to manage the physical pain and other symptoms associated with the patient's disease process.

The case manager also arranges necessary medical equipment to be brought into the home, such as hospital beds, safety equipment, and oxygen tanks. The medical social worker works with the patient and close family members to set up a medical power of attorney, funeral and body-donation plans, and other legal arrangements needed at the time of death. The social worker also acts as a counselor to resolve family disputes and achieve supportive care for the patient in the final days.

The certified nursing assistant typically supports the patient in personal hygiene tasks such as bathing, oral cleansing, and skincare. The hospice chaplain broadly attends to the religious and spiritual needs of the patient and close friends or family members. In some cases, a local church, synagogue, or

---

[173] Jordan Rosenfeld, "The 11 Qualities of a Good Death According to Research," Quartz, July 2016, https://qz.com/727042/the-11-qualities-of-a-good-death-according-to-research, accessed 8 December 2020.

other religious organization already supports the patient. While not replacing this support, the hospice chaplain serves as a voice of experience, guiding the patient and family through the course of the dying process. In other cases, the hospice chaplain serves as the only representative of God available to patients who no longer actively practice their faith.

Of particular importance to the hospice chaplain is the topic of spiritual distress—a condition that can be as significant as physical pain for many terminally ill patients. While once defined in strictly religious terms, spiritual distress has been given a more existential emphasis by the postmodern culture within which the hospice chaplain operates. In its current state of usage within the medical community, spiritual distress (as reflected in the form of anxiety, depression, and feelings of low self-worth) is defined as "the impaired ability to experience and integrate meaning and purpose in life through connectedness with self, others, art, music, literature, nature, and/or a power greater than oneself."[174] Simply stated, connections to the world that once gave life meaning and significance are no longer sufficiently intact to provide the person with a sense of peace. Given that each person develops a unique set of connections in life, the hospice chaplain must carefully understand how a patient's framework of meaning and significance is affected by advancing age and terminal illness.

This understanding of the patient's framework involves considering both the patient's religious faith and sense of worldly responsibilities and accomplishments in life. As the patient's disease progresses, the hospice chaplain must also remain keenly aware of how losing control over daily life impacts the patient's sense of worth and dignity. Throughout the process of dying, the hospice chaplain comes alongside patients to help them let go of the things of this world while strengthening their faith connection with God. Mindful of the strength and maturity of the patient's faith in God, the hospice chaplain helps the patient to navigate the spiritual transition from this world to an eternal relationship with God. This ministry is performed primarily through active listening, sensitivity to the patient's religious background, and gentle reflection, rather than through proselytizing.

---

[174] North American Nursing Diagnosis Association, *Nursing Diagnosis: Definitions and Classification 2009–2011* (Oxford: Wiley-Blackwell, 2011).

## PREPARATION OF THE HOSPICE CHAPLAIN

The hospice chaplain is a subset of healthcare chaplaincy that typically requires the individual to complete at least one unit of Clinical Pastoral Education (CPE). This education program prepares the chaplain to work within a clinical setting, conform to the operational requirements of a healthcare organization, and heighten their sensitivity to performing ministry within a multi-cultural, multifaith context.

Since most hospice patients spend their final days at home, hospice chaplains must balance the need to work on an integrated healthcare team with the concept of maintaining an independent travel and visit schedule. Hospice chaplains must be careful to perform strictly within their functional boundaries yet serve as representatives of the entire healthcare organization when visiting in patients' homes. As chaplains become familiar with typical medical symptoms and conditions, they serve as another set of "eyes and ears" that can alert nurse case managers or medical social workers to emergent conditions affecting patients' physical health and safety.

Likewise, the hospice chaplain might receive occasional comments from other team members regarding the patient's spiritual condition. Feedback from different team members represents one of the key advantages of being part of an integrated team. Finally, the hospice chaplain must be comfortable working within a system that requires careful documentation of the ministry, including assessing the patient's spiritual issues, developing an appropriate plan of care, and tracking changes and progress.

## SATISFACTION AND FRUSTRATIONS

Serving as a hospice chaplain brings both satisfaction and frustration. Hospice chaplains can experience gratification knowing that their ministry presence contributes to the peace and dignity of dying patients. They can also experience frustration knowing that some patients die without reconciliation with God. In this regard, hospice chaplains must simply view themselves as servants of God called to be faithful to the needs of others.

Since the hospice chaplain serves as part of an integrated healthcare team, the actions and influence of the chaplain impact the image and integrity of the overall organization. The hospice chaplain must conform to the highest ethical and professional standards of the healthcare industry, in addition to being faithful to God's calling to chaplaincy. Patient families give very positive feedback, generally taken after the patient's death, about the hospice chaplain's contributions. This feedback, in turn, can affect the amount of monetary compensation awarded to the healthcare organization by CMS.

Hospice chaplaincy provides an opportunity to serve others at a most critical and stressful time of their lives. The bonds formed between the hospice chaplain and patients during their period of care will sometimes extend to the privilege of conducting a funeral or memorial service. Grateful families complement the internal feeling of satisfaction as the hospice chaplain reflects over a life of helping others leave this world with peace and dignity.

# VETERANS ADMINISTRATION (VA) CHAPLAINCY

## Chaplain Dick Millspaugh

My understanding of God's call grew out of a church youth group meeting. The presenter stated that our call would be at the intersection of our interests and skills and the world's needs. I liked God's inclusion of the real me and the real world in my call. I was interested in science, religion, and in serving the world.

Following my sense of God's call led me through many twists and turns and opportunities. I served as a local pastor for eleven years in four different churches, twenty years as the Director of Chaplain Services in a Midwest hospital, and thirteen years as Chief of Chaplain Service at the VA Hospital in San Diego.

Because of my background and experience, I believe it is essential for anyone interested in VA chaplaincy to understand the following: (1) What do VA hospital chaplains do? (2) What makes VA chaplaincy unique? (3) Who should avoid VA chaplaincy? (4) What are the qualifications of a VA chaplain?

### WHAT DO VA CHAPLAINS DO?

While VA chaplains provide the services performed in general hospital ministry, VA hospital ministry is unique, delivered in a specialized setting.[175] VA chaplains offer clinical services as desired or requested by the veteran. Proselytizing is strictly forbidden. VA chaplains ensure that religion is not imposed upon veterans and ensure the veterans' constitutional right to exercise their religion freely.

### WHAT MAKES VA CHAPLAINCY UNIQUE?

The VA healthcare system is a nationally integrated system of 1,255 healthcare facilities, including 170 hospitals and 1,074 clinics. The roots of that

---

[175] For a full description, see "VA Chaplains—Comfort, Support, Lead, Advocate, Counsel, Mediate and Educate," US Department of Veterans Affairs, www.patientcare.va.gov/chaplain/What_Do_Chaplains_Do.asp.

system extend back to Abraham Lincoln, who authorized post-Civil War care for Union soldiers and sailors. VA chaplains serve local VA hospitals. The National VA Chaplain Service determines qualifications for VA chaplains, provides for their continuing education, and establishes standards for local VA chaplaincy programs. VA chaplains connect by phone, email, or telecommunication, for support or consultation on any pressing issue. The VA National Ethics Center also provides education on medical and institutional ethics and is available for ethics case consultation.

The VA uses an integrated electronic medical record in which VA chaplains document spiritual screenings and assessments. The electronic record allows chaplains to see documentation from multiple disciplines as they prepare each patient's spiritual-care plan. Similarly, other care providers can review the chaplain's notes as they do their care planning.

VA Medical Centers are federal institutions. They do not represent or advocate for or against any set of particular religious beliefs, nor directly compete with other hospital systems.

## VA Hospitals Serve Veterans Only

Except in cases where humanitarian assistance is required, veterans are VA hospitals' only patients. VA patients feel a kinship and loyalty to other VA patients as bonds developed with their "military family, brothers and sisters" during their military service. The history of "having had each other's backs" creates alliances that may be stronger than family, resulting in patients often being protective of each other during and following treatment. Veterans claim their VA hospital as their home. They embrace their nation's care in return for the service they offered to their country. Staff also consider veterans as family and find meaning in honoring them for their service. Chaplains, as full team members, are privileged to join this kinship. Chaplains may establish long-term relationships with veterans who continue to use "their" VA hospital. For me, serving veteran patients is the highest privilege of the VA chaplain. I catch my breath when a veteran says, "Chaplain, I have never told anyone this before, but . . ." Veterans provide chaplains a high privilege when they reveal spiritual or emotional trauma that no one should have to bear alone.

## VA Hospitals Are on the Cutting Edge of Veteran Issues

VA Hospitals focus on veteran issues: moral injury, identity formation following military service, post-traumatic stress, suicide prevention, military sexual trauma, alcohol and drug addiction, traumatic brain injury, vocational rehabilitation, hospice and palliative care, and prosthesis issues. The VA is a leader in these areas, presenting VA chaplains as full members of specialty treatment teams, with opportunities to grow in specialization.

## VA Chaplains Walk in the Footsteps of Military Chaplains

Military chaplains, who at times put their own lives in danger serving military men and women, are revered for their commitment. Troops respect chaplains in their ministry to individuals, leadership, and the institution. Chaplains speak truth to power and can advocate a particular need to leadership. Military chaplains' commitment to confidentiality earns service members' highest respect and makes the military chaplain highly trustworthy to hear the most delicate and wrenching aspects of the human story. The VA chaplain shares this trust and high regard earned by military chaplains as service members enter the VA system to receive health care.

## The VA Is Not a Military Installation

Military chaplains working in the VA will find a significantly different culture. Those expecting a formal command structure will find a more participatory governance style. As compared to the military, the VA culture will also have some differences in what is considered intolerable or unacceptable. Additionally, the VA evaluation system is not directly tied to advancement like it is in the military. The military emphasizes evaluations as they form the core determination for promotion. This promotion system creates enormous stress for military personnel. Because fewer opportunities exist for VA chaplains to advance in positions, annual evaluations are important as learning tools, and influence pay raises, but are not conduits for advancement.

Military chaplains will find confidentiality within a VA hospital different from the strict "absolute" confidence between the chaplain and the client. Within the VA hospital ministry, confidentiality is understood broadly as strict confidence based on the need to know in order for the patient to receive the best care from the healthcare team. Therefore, VA chaplains must introduce themselves as members of the treatment team and be aware that they adhere to the safeguards of the Health Insurance Portability and Accountability Act and the ethical imperatives of the chaplaincy profession. The VA chaplain must decide how much of what transpires between the chaplain and the patient is relevant to the treatment team's need to know to provide the best care to the patient. If a chaplain believes the information revealed in the chaplain-patient relationship is essential for one or more treatment team members to know, that chaplain will inform the patient of why their doctor, nurse, or another team member should know that information to provide better care. The chaplain will then encourage the patient to share the information with the appropriate caregiver or give the chaplain permission to do the same. Following that conversation, the chaplain will determine whether or not to chart the information for the treatment team, or if more appropriate, simply share the information verbally with only a specific team member.

Civilian chaplains working in the VA facility may also have a steep learning curve. If they wish to gain veterans' trust and understand their needs and orientation, civilian chaplains need to understand the unique culture engendered in military service.

## VA Hospitals Require Continuing Education

The Department of Veteran Affairs established a culture and standards that promote, support, and require continuing education. Opportunities to learn, grow, and teach abound for the VA chaplain. Also, VA hospital affiliations with medical schools create opportunities to stay current with medical knowledge. Priceless are the opportunities to learn across disciplines from highly skilled and committed professionals and veterans themselves.

## The Warrior to Soul Mate Program (W2SM)

Though not in all VA hospitals, the Warrior to Soul Mate Program is nine hours of in-service training in intimate communication skills for veterans to strengthen relationships with their significant others. Intimate relationships often suffer from the sacrifices of military service. Rebuilding those relationships takes intentional commitment and skills training in intimacy, self-disclosure, and authentic communication. W2SM has led thousands of veterans and their partners to deepen their relationships in ways that disrupt the loneliness, isolation, and spiritual pain that may contribute to suicide, drug abuse, homelessness, depression, and anxiety. Chaplains, along with other multidisciplinary members, have developed this program.

## WHY AVOID VA CHAPLAINCY?

First, avoid VA chaplaincy if you need to be seen as the key person in leadership. Chaplaincy in specialized settings requires initiative, flexibility, unique knowledge, and an ability to work among various vocations and professionals. Chaplains in specialized settings must earn the respect of their coworkers by productive contributions to the organization. Second, avoid VA chaplaincy if you need to proselytize. The VA forbids proselytizing. Period. VA chaplains educate staff and visitors about the veterans' right to be free from proselytization. VA chaplains provide religious services and religious discussions, but only with the patient's permission or at the patient's initiative. Third, avoid VA chaplaincy if you hate paperwork, continuing education, or being a team player. People reluctant to report, document, and work with an electronic record or who prefer not to be accountable should avoid VA chaplaincy. Working for the VA means committing time to do paperwork. VA chaplains have to tolerate a sacrifice of direct patient care time to meet these requirements. A VA chaplain must participate in continuing education and be a team player. Therefore, VA chaplaincy is not for the individual who only wishes to do patient care or is threatened by learning new ways to provide services. Fourth, avoid VA chaplaincy if you are averse to change. Change is constant in the VA, with leadership changes, professional organizations, mandates, and National VA Chaplain Service policies. VA clinical chaplains serve veterans whose spiritual and religious traditions are diverse and ever-changing.

## WHAT ARE THE QUALIFICATIONS OF A VA CHAPLAIN?

The qualifications to apply for a VA chaplaincy position change from time to time, so it is best to contact the National VA Chaplain Service about current qualifications and application processes.[176] Successful applicants will:

1. Have a given number of years of professional experience after completing a master's of divinity degree or its equivalent.
2. Be a United States citizen.
3. Have four units of Clinical Pastoral Education.
4. Be competent in writing and speaking English.

The VA does not accept volunteer chaplains, nor does it require prior military service to apply to be a VA chaplain.

## SERVING THOSE WHO SERVED

I served more than twelve years as a VA chaplain. I never imagined myself in VA chaplaincy, yet I am so grateful and honored to have attended to the spiritual needs of veterans. I have spoken with veterans who served their country as their patriotic duty. They served as a response to their understanding of God's call, who served because of their sincere effort to build peace. They sacrificed to protect their homeland and their family tradition. However, I have also spoken to veterans who discovered that serving their country was different than they expected. They struggle with guilt and ambivalence toward their country for what they have done or were ordered to do.

In serving as a VA chaplain, I have served my country with integrity and integrated my interests in science and religion. Becoming a chaplain called me to look deeply within myself, to become aware of my woundedness, to hold myself with compassion, and seek healing. Professionally, I believe God called me into hospital chaplaincy to learn how to hold others with the same compassion God has for me. Therefore, God's call unfolded as an invitation to love patients and to love myself. For this double blessing, I continue to be grateful.

---

[176] For additional and updated information regarding Chaplain Services within the Veterans Administration, the reader is strongly encouraged to contact the National VA Chaplain Service at 202-461-1625, https://www.patientcare.va.gov/chaplain/index.asp, or 810 Vermont Ave. NW, Washington, DC 20420-0001.

## MEMORABLE MOMENT
## "BEN"

### Chaplain David K. Mann

The murky air smelled of his pipe being laid aside upon my arrival. Only a tiny amount of light peered through the slightly opened drapes. It was just enough for me to see the silhouette of his face, just enough to see the whites of his eyes, and when he smiled, to see his teeth illuminated against his dark black skin.

I was feeling particularly anxious. Being raised in a predominately white town in north-central Alabama, I had limited contact with people of color. As I sat in this darkened living room, I was fighting the voices of my past and my upbringing. I had always professed not to be prejudiced. Yet I was aware of my discomfort. This was my third visit with Mr. Green. We talked for a while, about nothing in particular. It was a struggle to discuss his terminal cancer, his faith, or even his family. My previous two visits had not gone very well, and I feared this visit would fare no better.

As a second-year resident in the Clinical Pastoral Education Program of Baptist Health Systems, I was learning to get in touch with and, if necessary, to confront my feelings. I was also learning a patient's vulnerability may depend on my vulnerability as well. "What could it hurt?" I asked myself. "This visit could not get any worse."

My 275-pound body seemed so timid, so unlike the burly fellow I knew I was. I had to resist the ever-pressing urge to say a prayer and leave. That would be the easy thing to do. Then, finally, after drawing a deep breath of the murky, thick air, I mustered all the courage I could find. Almost before I knew what had happened, I said it. "Mr. Green, I know this visit isn't going very well. I am feeling very anxious. It is hard to talk to you. I guess part of that is because I have never really been around black people. I'm fighting the urge to leave. I want to be of pastoral help to you, but I do not know how. I know that I feel uncomfortable in your home, and I want to be honest with you. I don't know what you are going to do with what I've just said, but . . ."

In my fear and anxiety, I would have probably rambled on in my loquaciousness. However, Mr. Green, with his deep laughter, stopped my own muffled and nervous voice. My urge to leave was so intense that I had to clutch the arms of my chair. Until now, Mr. Green had been a man of little effect and certainly a man of few words. Then, through the laughter came a heartfelt, honest reply.

"Well, son," he said, "it's not every day that I have a young, white preacher boy sitting in my living room either."

My anxiety quickly turned to laughter. I had heard his vulnerability and his blessing. As we confronted our fears of color and age and laughed together, a beautiful friendship was born. In the weeks ahead, we had many opportunities to talk. I came to know Mr. Green as Ben, a man with a big heart facing head-on his fear of death and his faith struggles.

During those weeks, Ben talked of wanting to be healed. In every visit, he requested prayer for the same. Finally, one day Ben informed me that God would heal him, but not in the way he had sought. He had come to see death as his friend and the doorway into eternal healing. Just weeks before he died, Ben's frail and emaciated body lay in a hospital bed. We had come a long way. Spiritually, Ben seemed to glow with peace. As I left that visit, I reached over to hug him.

"I love you, Ben."

"I love you, too, David."

Together we cried. Nothing would hold back our tears. We had indeed come a long, long way. I knew Ben would always be a part of my heart. A few weeks later, I stood in a little black Baptist church in Mulga, Alabama, and shared this story as part of Ben's funeral. Again, no force could have held back the laughter nor the tears.

> There is no *distinction between* Greek and Jew, circumcised and uncircumcised, barbarian, Scythian, slave and freeman *(Black or White)*, but Christ is all, and in all.
>
> —Colossians 3:11 (italics mine)

## REFLECTION QUESTIONS

1. How do misconceptions about chaplains' roles impact their ability to interact with healthcare staff, patients, and families? How might a chaplain help counter these misconceptions to clarify their role and build rapport?
2. Healthcare chaplains typically face the emotional burden of working with suffering and the fulfillment of offering support. How might a healthcare chaplain build resilience while maintaining one's sense of purpose amid suffering or tragedy?
3. As a multidisciplinary team member, how might a chaplain advocate effectively for patients' and staff's spiritual and emotional needs?
4. Significant connections in life that bring about a sense of meaning and purpose are often stored mentally in the form of salient life narratives or stories. How can the chaplain use the initiation and structuring of conversations with the patient?
5. Several assessment instruments have been developed and used in the healthcare setting for identifying and quantitatively scoring a specific patient's spiritual distress level. These instruments are intended to support an empirical, evidence-based approach to health care, much like the physiological assessment instruments used by physicians and nurses. What are the practical limitations of using these instruments with terminally ill patients? Is it meaningful to reduce the idiosyncratic nature of spirituality across different patients down to a common set of factors? To what degree can these instruments support differential diagnosis and development of an individual care plan?

CHAPTER SEVENTEEN

# MILITARY CHAPLAINCY

## Chaplain Jay Johns

You're awakened at 0430 by a siren that signals a mortar attack on your base. After taking cover and then receiving the "all clear," you dress and go to the dining facility to share breakfast with hundreds of your comrades in arms. On the way back to your room, one of the soldiers walks with you to discuss how he's going to work through the difficulties he's having in his marriage because of the seven thousand miles separating him from his new bride. Shortly after encouraging the soldier, you make your way over to the assembly area to visit and pray with the platoon that is about to go on patrol "outside the wire."

At noon, you catch a ride on a convoy headed to a small forward operating base that hasn't seen a chaplain in a couple of weeks. Circulating through the ranks, you speak with as many soldiers as possible and focus on a few that lost a buddy to sniper fire last month. They mostly want to talk about how much they miss their friend, but their pain is palpable as each of them struggles with the question, "Why did he die, and why did I survive?"

There are no good answers to this question, so you listen and sit in the moment with them. You wonder whether the passage of scripture you shared with them at the end of the visit helped them at all, but you leave the base hoping that somehow your presence brought them a sense of hope and comfort amid a very dark time.

Back at your base, you spend an hour or so preparing your message for Sunday's chapel service. You plan to infuse a sense of meaning into the life of your congregation, but this seems daunting given the high operational tempo and frequent combat losses in the unit. After praying for God's wisdom, you put pen to paper and try to apply timeless truths to a very time-bound moment. How does "Fear not, for I am with you. Do not be dismayed, for I am your God. I will strengthen you, I will help you, I will uphold you with my victorious right hand"[177] translate to a twenty-year-old who will face grave danger multiple times over the next week? And after a late dinner, you're summoned to the medical aid station to visit three soldiers injured in a roadside bombing.

Thankfully, all three are conscious and will survive the attack. As the soldiers await a helicopter flight to a more robust treatment facility, you have the chance to pray with each and give a human touch in the name of God that somehow soothes their terrified souls. As the night draws to a close, you kneel next to your bunk and thank God for the privilege of serving and for the strength to face tomorrow's challenges.

If this sounds at all meaningful, then military chaplaincy might be your calling. Part of the excitement of chaplain ministry is the opportunity to serve in places where clergy typically have limited or no access and in some places that cry out for a divine touch. Like no other arena, combat lays the soul bare. The military chaplain is there, ready to care for those who have volunteered to serve and protect their nation. What is a military chaplain, and why do we need them? What are the duties of a military chaplain? What are the various avenues of service within this calling? What does the career trajectory of one choosing this path look like? These are the questions we will attempt to answer in this introduction to military chaplaincy.

## OVERVIEW

A military chaplain is a religious ministry professional serving as an officer in one of our nation's military services under the endorsement of a religious organization.[178] The First Amendment to the US Constitution guarantees the right to the free exercise of religion. But how might US military members enjoy this right when the nation they defend has sent them into a combat situation thousands of miles from home? How will they be able to participate

---

[177] Isa 41:10
[178] Department of Defense Instruction 1304.28, "Guidance for the Appointment of Chaplains for the Military Departments," 11 June 2004.

in the rites/ordinances/sacraments so vital to the observance of their religion if their pastor, priest, rabbi, or imam is still on the home front? Title X of the US Code safeguards the right to the free exercise of religion for service members by providing for military chaplains who serve alongside soldiers, sailors, marines, airmen, and members of the Coast Guard across the full spectrum of operations.

Though military chaplains enjoy the right to the free expression of their own religious convictions,[179] it is a mistake for them to think of themselves as "missionaries in uniform." While chaplains should adhere to the standards of their respective endorsing agencies, they must understand their purpose in the Armed Forces is to ensure the free exercise of religion for every service member.

A Protestant chaplain assigned to a military unit cannot, for example, conduct Mass for the Catholic members of that unit. However, it is the responsibility of the unit chaplains to coordinate appropriate chaplain coverage (in this case, finding a Catholic chaplain) for those in their care. A Catholic chaplain, approached by a member of his unit who wants to speak to a Jewish chaplain about deepening his faith, cannot simply say, "I'm not a rabbi." Instead, he must find a way to coordinate that conversation with a fellow chaplain. Because of the need for continual collaboration, military chaplains develop collegial relationships with each other across religious and denominational affiliations. These relationships allow them to find the right chaplain for the right circumstance so that all military members have their religious needs met in a timely manner.

Even though chaplains are members of the clergy, many conversations in which service members engage their chaplains are not religious in nature. Most recruits enter the military at the age of eighteen and serve a four-year enlistment. They are still wrestling with their direction in life at this young age. Often this involves questions about career prospects, the need for further education, or even how they will get through a self-inflicted complication, such as managing the aftermath of a bad decision. Having developed the legacy and reputation of trustworthiness, chaplains are often the source of

---

[179] Department of Defense Instruction 1300.17, "Religious Liberty in the Military Services," 1 September 2020.

life and career guidance for those seeking direction. During these conversations, chaplains should represent themselves authentically for who they are and what they believe.

Additionally, chaplains are free to bear witness to their faith journeys to those who have asked about their beliefs. In the first military unit in which I served as a chaplain, I encountered a sergeant who would glare at me with arms crossed when we were anywhere near each other. His standoffishness continued for a solid year. Then one day he knocked on my office door and asked to speak with me about a personal issue. I told him I was glad to see him, but I was also surprised to see him because he had never spoken with me before, even in passing. His response to this was, "I was just watching you to make sure I could trust you." That conversation about a personal issue led to many other discussions about faith and one's purpose in life.

## ROLES AND RESPONSIBILITIES

Military chaplains have a wide range of responsibilities, making this ministry particularly appealing to those averse to getting "stuck in a rut." Chaplains serve as staff officers to unit commanders.[180] In this role, they advise the commander on the impact of religion on various operational considerations and unit morale as affected by religion. As religious leaders, chaplains conduct religious education activities (leading a unit Bible study or a marriage enrichment retreat, for example), perform weddings and memorial ceremonies, and lead chapel services. Because of their noncombatant status, chaplains do not bear arms. Consequently, an enlisted service member is assigned to the unit chaplain to provide armed protection in a combat environment and operational and administrative support. Chaplains supervise (and often mentor) these personnel, ensuring they receive the best possible professional development.

Because so much of the effectiveness of chaplain ministry depends on relationships, military chaplains circulate as much as possible among unit members. The potential locations for pastoral conversations are almost

---

[180] The unit commander is the person ultimately responsible for every person, dollar, and piece of equipment in the organization. The religious support program of the unit is the responsibility of the commander; implementation of the program is the responsibility of the chaplain.

endless: on the flight line or in the hangar; at any number of workstations on a ship or aircraft carrier; on a jump during airborne operations training; on a road march while carrying a heavy rucksack; in the motor pool with the mechanics; in the dining facility with the cooks; or on the track during physical fitness training.[181] Getting to know one's "flock" in a military unit is as important as a pastor becoming familiar with the congregation. The most effective chaplains are intentional about becoming integral to their military units.

Some chaplains have prior military experience (as pilots, logistics officers, mechanics, or in the infantry, for example) before becoming military chaplains.[182] Others enter the military as chaplains with no previous military experience at all. However, before entry as military officers, all military chaplains possess an advanced degree and substantial experience as religious professionals (in the parish or other ministry settings).

As military doctors and lawyers enter service as fully credentialed professionals, so do chaplains. Because of their educational and ministry-experience requirements, chaplains are typically ten years (or more) older than their officer peers who enter military service (usually at the age of twenty-two), just after graduation from a service academy,[183] a Reserve Officers' Training Corps program, or an Officer Candidate School that commissions enlisted personnel.

---

[181] Physical fitness is important for military chaplains. Each service has a height/weight standard, as well as standards for physical performance. Given the rigors of the combat environment, these standards help ensure one's ability to thrive in demanding conditions.

[182] My own journey as a military chaplain began at the suggestion of a neighbor of mine in seminary housing when I was a master of divinity student. Having no clear direction on ministry direction other than "I know God wants me to be in seminary right now," I pursued my studies diligently. I changed apartments one year and lived two doors down from Al, who had been drafted during the Vietnam War and had become a practicing Christian under the ministry of his unit chaplain. After his enlistment, Al left the Army, completed his bachelor's degree, and entered seminary with a view toward becoming an Army chaplain. He mentioned to me one day, "You ought to be an Army chaplain; it would be a great fit for you." At that point, I didn't even know the Army had chaplains. I filed that information away for several years but did, indeed, end up serving as a career Army chaplain.

[183] The US Military Academy (West Point) produces Army officers; the US Naval Academy produces Navy and Marine Corps officers; the US Air Force Academy produces Air Force officers; and the US Coast Guard Academy produces Coast Guard officers.

Though the learning curve might appear steep for the new chaplain with no prior experience, a passion for the military culture goes a long way toward building confidence. One of the best pieces of advice I ever received from a senior chaplain was this: when you enter a unit, ask unit members about their jobs, and then ask them to describe how their work fits into the larger mission of the unit. This demonstrates the chaplain's interest in unit personnel and provides the new chaplain with a personalized education regarding the workings and structure of the military.

## A TYPICAL DAY AT HOME STATION

What might a typical day at the home station look like?[184] It might begin with physical training with the unit at 0630. After showering and eating breakfast, the day at the office starts at 0900, when you catch up with some administrative work. At 1000 you attend the Command and Staff meeting, followed by a counseling appointment with a unit member at 1115. At noon you meet a fellow chaplain for lunch to discuss the chapel service you're leading on Sunday. After lunch, you circulate through the unit workstations visiting with your flock. A couple of people you have casually engaged really need to talk about something going on; the first has a seriously ill parent; the second is dealing with the consequences of a bad decision. At 1500 you're scheduled for premarital counseling with a couple whose marriage you'll perform next month. After the session, you answer some emails requiring your attention and then review the slides you will brief tomorrow during suicide-prevention training. Some duty days may end around the dinner hour, but given the military adage "train to standard, not to time," there may be days when the work lingers into the evening.

One must understand that the primary responsibility of the military is to fight and win the nation's wars. During peacetime, the military constantly trains in preparation for effectiveness in war. Though no sane human being hopes for war, we understand that it is necessary to fight at times. Even in the absence of conflict, the nation demonstrates its military strength through training exercises designed to dissuade those seeking aggression against the nation. The bottom line is this: when people join the military as chaplains,

---

[184] "Typical" is dependent upon duty station, type of unit, and training/deployment cycle.

they are not joining a corporation or a movement. A military chaplain becomes part of a vast juggernaut whose sole purpose is national defense. In their role, military chaplains provide ministry to the nation's sons and daughters who fight and sometimes die in our nation's wars. During World War II, General George C. Marshall, chief of staff of the Army, said it best, "The Soldier's heart, the Soldier's spirit, the Soldier's soul, are everything. Unless the soldier's soul sustains him, he cannot be relied on and will fail himself and his commander and his country in the end."[185]

Caring for the souls of those willing to put themselves in harm's way and the willingness to minister in potentially life-threatening situations is the privilege of every military chaplain. This career is certainly not for everybody, nor should it be entered into lightly or unadvisedly. It is, however, profoundly rewarding.

## AVENUES FOR SERVICE AS A MILITARY CHAPLAIN

If one senses God's direction in this calling, what are the avenues of entry? Three military services have a chaplain corps. The Army Chaplain Corps assesses, equips, and trains chaplains for ministry to soldiers. The Air Force Chaplain Corps does the same for airmen and members of the US Space Force. The Navy Chaplain Corps provides chaplains to sailors, US Marines, and Coastguardsmen. The military services retain their own cultures. Although there are similarities in chaplain duties across the services, the ministry within each service is unique.

Within these three chaplain corps (Army, Navy, and Air Force), three components provide ministry opportunities for the military chaplain. The first is the Active Component (Component One), meaning that one's full-time job is the service chaplaincy. Though engaged in the on-post/base chapel community, an active-duty military chaplain does not serve as a leader of a civilian religious congregation. Active-duty military chaplains must be prepared to live in various locations (including overseas) throughout their careers, potentially moving every two to three years. The lack of family life

---

[185] Brian Hill, "Chaplains Help Fort Leonard Wood Soldiers, Civilians Reflect on Spiritual Readiness," US Army, June 9, 2022, https://www.army.mil/article/257413/chaplains_help_fort_leonard_wood_soldiers_civilians_reflect_on_spiritual_readiness.

predictability and stability (changing of schools for children, disruption in spouse employment, and other considerations) may steer some away from the Active Component. For others, the travel and adventure[186] are a bonus to the employment security afforded to Active Component members.

A second possibility is service in the National Guard (Component Two). Only two of the three services contain a National Guard component (Army and Air Force). National Guard forces serve under the authority of each state's governor (in Title 32 status), though the president of the United States may mobilize them for federal missions. Most members of the National Guard serve part-time, typically with duty one weekend per month and two weeks of training in the summer. Governors may call upon the National Guard to support missions as diverse as fighting floods and wildfires, quelling civil unrest, and assisting hurricane-relief operations. Service in the Guard allows chaplains and their families to put down roots in a local community and the chaplain to serve as a leader of a civilian congregation.

However, since 2001, the Guard has often been mobilized for active duty and employed in combat operations. When members of the Guard are mobilized or deployed, their families usually stay in place. Family Readiness Groups, organized by the unit but primarily staffed by spouses (on a voluntary basis) of those deployed, serve as support and information-flow mechanisms for the mobilized/deployed families.

Another possibility for service in the military chaplaincy is through service in the Reserves (Component Three). The Army, Navy, and Air Force offer service opportunities in the Reserve. Navy Reserve chaplains provide chaplain ministry to Navy and Marine Reserve units. Reserve forces are members of the federal service (Title X) who serve on a part-time basis like their Component Two counterparts. Reserve chaplains also enjoy the opportunity to put down roots and serve as leaders of civilian congregations. However, Reserve status does not imply immunity to disruption. Like the Guard, the Reserve also has been mobilized often for active duty and employed in

---

[186] Each service has bases and installations worldwide. Whether in the Continental United States (CONUS), or Outside of the Continental United States (OCONUS, which includes Alaska, Hawaii, and all stations abroad), military communities are typically cohesive because of the contribution of each member to a shared mission.

combat operations; Family Readiness Groups are in place to provide family support to the families of mobilized/deployed reservists.

While the Army, Navy, Air Force, and Marine Corps are part of the Department of Defense, the Coast Guard is part of the Department of Homeland Security. Navy chaplains provide ministry to active duty and reserve Coast Guard Forces. Because the Coast Guard operates under Title 14 of the US Code, it may be utilized in operations more akin to law enforcement than to national defense (though both occur).[187] Consequently, it enforces all applicable federal laws on the high seas and waters within the territorial jurisdiction of the United States. It administers laws and promulgates and enforces regulations to promote the safety of life and property along the entire US coast, including Alaska and Hawaii.[188]

## CAREER TRAJECTORY

For the first several years of one's career, a military chaplain will provide direct ministry to a unit of several hundred personnel. As discussed earlier, the chaplain is the staff officer responsible for executing the commander's religious program in the unit. Execution (doing) is the operative word for the junior chaplain. In the early years of one's career, a chaplain will provide plenty of pastoral counseling, religious education, outreach activities, crisis intervention, chapel ministry, weddings, marriage enrichment events, and other initiatives that will fill a schedule to the brim. These activities are those in which the chaplain should have been thoroughly trained in graduate-level theological education. It is the work to which we believe God calls.

However, a time comes in this "up or out"[189] military structure that requires a chaplain to view administration as ministry. The longer one serves

---

[187] The Posse Comitatus Act is a federal law enacted in 1878, which limits the powers of the federal government in the use of federal military personnel to enforce domestic policies within the United States. Federal (Title X) forces may not engage in law enforcement activity. As mentioned earlier, National Guard forces may engage in law enforcement activity under the direction of a state's governor (Title 32 status).
[188] "Missions," United States Coast Guard, www.mycg.uscg.mil/Missions/.
[189] In the military, one must be capable of attaining increasing levels of responsibility. At certain points of their careers, military chaplains are considered for promotion to the next rank. With the attainment of rank comes increasing levels of responsibility, to include leading people and

in a military career, the less one conducts "direct" ministry. The more senior the chaplain is, the more the chaplain must focus on setting the conditions for the success of subordinate chaplains. A military chaplain will spend nearly ten years at the entry-level rank (O3, short for Officer 3).

This rank is Captain in the Army and Air Force and Lieutenant in the Navy. Success during this decade will mean promotion to O4 (Major in the Army and Air Force and Lieutenant Commander in the Navy). Direct ministry to members of higher echelon staff members still occurs. However, the O4 chaplain's primary focus is developing and overseeing entry-level chaplains (usually three or more) and ensuring they have the resources and training necessary to perform their mission. It is helpful to think of this stage of ministry as "leading and developing people."

After about five or six years, success at this level leads to promotion to O5 (Lieutenant Colonel in the Army and Air Force, and Commander in the Navy). We might think of this level of ministry as "managing systems." Though some O5s serve as senior chaplains in operational commands (with still more subordinate chaplains to lead and mentor), most serve in any number of logistical, administrative, or personnel billets that facilitate the operation of junior chaplains. For example, junior chaplains focus on direct ministry to the members of their commands in their first units.

They have little time to think about such questions as: "How will the chaplain corps deliver the most effective training at their institutional training centers? How will the service gain the necessary resources and funding to deliver enterprise-wide marriage enrichment programs over the next decade? How will the chaplain corps manage its personnel system in such a way that, worldwide, the service has the right chaplain, at the right place, at the right time?" These are problems with which O5s struggle.

Success at the O5 level leads to selection for O6 (Colonel in the Army and Air Force, and Captain in the Navy). Ministry at this rank involves "shaping the enterprise," or setting conditions for success for the operation of the entire chaplain corps. Here, they might find themselves as the senior

---

managing systems. Failure to promote to the next rank decreases one's longevity in the military system and limits one's ability to affect the military culture through strategic leadership. Said another way, there is no "career" for a chaplain who, through failure to promote, stays at the entry level of the organization and does not demonstrate potential for increased responsibility.

chaplains of large military installations or high-level commands, overseeing the operation of several chapels, a large budget, and hundreds of chaplains. Another O6 chaplain might serve at the Office of the Undersecretary of Defense, drafting Department of Defense-wide religious support policy directives. Another might be the Executive Officer for one of the Chiefs of Chaplains, managing the day-to-day operations of a large chaplain staff working at the Pentagon.

For there to be continued joy and a sense of calling throughout one's career, one must learn to embrace the reality that the work of leadership and administration is the ministry of senior chaplains.[190] This work is demanding but rewarding, and the ability to shape the culture of the chaplain corps is not something to be overlooked. As young pastors seek out and even emulate those who have walked the long road of ministry with excellence and integrity, young military chaplains will seek out senior chaplains who have kept the spark of passion and calling alive and have demonstrated integrity and humility on the journey through the ranks.

## NOT FOR THE FAINT OF HEART

Accepting a call to military chaplain ministry entails a commitment to a way of life and immersion into the culture of a particular organization. This career is not for the faint of heart and undoubtedly inadvisable for those whose spouses cannot embrace the prospect of occasional family separation. There will be times when the military spouse worries about the safety of his or her loved one. There will also be the occasional missed birthday, anniversary, or holiday.

For those so called, the military chaplaincy provides a profound opportunity to minister to those courageous sons and daughters of the nation who

---

[190] Early in my career, a senior chaplain told me, "You need to learn to see administration as ministry, because you'll be spending the bulk of your career doing administration." Though I didn't fully understand it at the time, I came to see the wisdom of his words. In roles as diverse as Career Management Officer for the Army Chaplain Corps, Operations Chaplain for US Forces-Afghanistan, and Executive Director of the Armed Forces Chaplains Board, when asked what my job entails, I would often respond by saying, "I'm involved in things that junior chaplains don't even know exist, so that they're successful doing all of the cool things I got to do when I was younger, like jump out of airplanes and lead unit Bible studies."

have assumed tremendous responsibility for our national defense. While serving God and country, chaplains and their families become engaged in a vital mission dating back to 1775.[191] One would be hard-pressed to find a more rewarding, challenging, and exciting ministry in which to devote one's career.

---

[191] The Second Continental Congress authorized chaplains to serve in the Continental Army with a bill passed 29 July 1775. Since then, chaplains have served with distinction in every armed conflict. Nine chaplains have been awarded the Congressional Medal of Honor.

# THE ROLE OF RELIGION IN THE UNITED STATES ARMED FORCES

## Michael Berry

(**Editor's note:** While this section centers on US law, students outside the United States should research and have a familiarity with their country's laws as they relate to chaplaincy.)

Attempts to secularize America's military have existed for as long as America has had a military. Amid increasing diversity, some question the role religion should or may permissibly play in the military. This chapter attempts to address the role of religion in the United States Armed Forces from the historic, moral, and legal basis.

## THE HISTORICAL FOUNDATIONS OF RELIGION IN THE MILITARY

Since the United States' founding, American civil and military leadership have taken deliberate steps to meet the religious needs of the military and to prevent it from becoming a purely secular entity. The founders were no strangers to government provision of religious support. For example, in 1789 the first federal Congress passed a law providing for the payment of legislative chaplains.[192] Nearly two centuries later, the Supreme Court upheld the constitutionality of those legislative chaplains, concluding that it "is not . . . an establishment of religion" but rather "a tolerable acknowledgement of beliefs widely held among the people of this country."[193] Today, in continuance of the first Congress' policy, the government directly funds the salaries,

---

[192] *Journal of the First Session of the Senate of the United States of America*, August 28, 1789 (Washington: Gales and Seaton, 1820), 67. See also "An Act for allowing compensation to the Members of the Senate and House of Representatives of the United States, and to the Officers of both Houses (c)," in *The Public Statutes at Large*, vol. 1, September 22, 1789 (Boston: Little & Brown, 1845), 70–71.

[193] *Marsh v. Chambers*, 463 U.S. 783 (1983).

activities, and operations of more than 4,500 military chaplains.[194] Despite periodic legal challenges, the Supreme Court "has long recognized that the government may (and sometimes must) accommodate religious practices, and that it may do so without violating the Establishment Clause."[195] This includes military chaplains.

It is important to note that while paid chaplains may constitute an official acceptance of or authorization for the presence of organized religion in military life, chaplains are the personification—not the limits—of such religious expression. In other words, if the government pays chaplains to perform religious exercises, it may also approve other forms of religious expression that are distinct from a formal chaplaincy, including service members' religious expression.

Perhaps no individual had a more significant influence in shaping our nation's armed forces than George Washington, its first Commander-in-Chief. He made known his convictions on the importance of religion within the military early in his career while serving as a young colonel during the French & Indian War (1753–1763). Throughout that time, he repeatedly requested religious support for his troops,[196] explaining:

---

[194] As of June 2006, there were 1,432 Army chaplains; 825 Navy chaplains, and 602 Air Force chaplains, for a total of 2,859 regular-duty chaplains. Additionally, there are 433 chaplains in the Army Reserve National Guard, 500 chaplains in the US Army Reserves, 237 chaplains in the US Navy Reserves, 254 in the Air National Guard, and 316 in the US Air Force Reserves, for a total of 1,740 reserve chaplains. This makes a combined 4,599 federally funded chaplains in the regular and reserve military. From information provided from the office of then-US Congressman Bobby Jindal (LA) on September 28, 2006.

[195] *Corporation of Presiding Bishop v. Amos*, 483 U.S. 327 (1987).

[196] Washington made at least six separate pleas for chaplains, including five times to Virginia Governor Robert Dinwiddie and once to Virginia Governor John Blair. These occasions included to Governor Dinwiddie: September 23, 1756; November 9, 1756; November 24, 1756; April 29, 1757; and June 12, 1757 (*The Writings of George Washington*, 39 volumes, ed. John C. Fitzpatrick [Washington, DC: Government Printing Office, 1931], 1:470, 1:498, 1:510, 2:33, 2:56); and to Governor Blair: April 17, 1758 (Fitzpatrick, 2:178). He also wrote a letter to John Robinson, speaker of the House of Burgesses from 1738–1766, on this issue on November 9, 1756 (Fitzpatrick, 1:505).

Common decency, Sir, in a camp calls for the services of a divine, and which ought not to be dispensed with, altho' the world should be so uncharitable as to think us void of religion.[197]

Washington's British superiors refused each of his requests. But Washington believed so firmly that religious exercises and activities were essential to the well-being of his troops that he periodically undertook to perform those duties himself, including reading Scriptures, offering prayers, and conducting funeral services.[198]

Future presidents and legislators followed Washington's lead, laying a solid foundation for religious expression in the military. After the Battles of Lexington, Concord, and Bunker Hill, it became evident that reconciliation with Great Britain was unlikely. In response, Congress officially established the Continental Army and explicitly recommended that "all officers and soldiers diligently to attend Divine Service."[199] Similarly, Congress instructed America's fledgling Navy that "commanders of the ships of the Thirteen United Colonies are to take care that Divine Service be performed twice a day on board, and a sermon be preached on Sundays."[200]

America's second Commander-in-Chief, John Adams, was no less insistent that religious expression be promoted in the military. Known as "The Father of the American Navy," Adams's presidency saw the US Navy grow from its humble origins, as an organization composed mainly of privateers,[201] into a formidable fighting force capable of defending the nation. During the Navy's ascendency under his watch, Adams instructed his Secretary of the Navy, Benjamin Stoddert, on the importance of a Navy chaplaincy:

---

[197] George Washington to John Blair, April 17, 1758 (Fitzpatrick, 2:178).
[198] See, e.g., Jared Sparks, *The Writings of George Washington*, vol. 2 (Boston: Russell, Odiorne, & Metcalf, 1834), 54; E. C. M'Guire, *The Religious Opinions and Character of Washington* (New York: Harper & Brothers, 1836), 136; Washington Irving, *Life of George Washington*, vol. 1 (New York: G. P. Putnam & Co., 1855), 128–29, 201; C. M. Kirkland, *Memoirs of Washington* (New York: D. Appleton & Company, 1857), 155; Hon. J. T. Headley, *The Illustrated Life of Washington* (New York: G. & F. Bill, 1859), 60.
[199] June 30, 1775, *Journals of the Continental Congress*, 34 volumes (Washington, DC: Government Printing Office, 1905), 1:112.
[200] November 28, 1775, *Journals of the Continental Congress*, 3:378.
[201] A private citizen authorized by the government to serve aboard military naval vessels.

> I know not whether the commanders of our ships have given much attention to this subject [chaplains], but in my humble opinion, we shall be very unskillful politicians as well as bad Christians and unwise men if we neglect this important office in our infant navy.[202]

Congress responded favorably to President Adams's desire by establishing and providing for naval chaplains, reissuing the naval regulations it established during the Revolutionary War, requiring that Divine Service be performed twice daily aboard all naval vessels, and that a sermon be preached each Sunday.[203]

With this foundation firmly established, the tradition of religious expression within the military carried well into the twentieth century. For example, shortly after taking office and during the military build-up preceding World War II, President Franklin Roosevelt declared:

> I want every father and every mother who has a son in the service to know—again, from what I have seen with my own eyes—that the men in the Army, Navy, and Marine Corps are receiving today the best possible training, equipment, and medical care. And we will never fail to provide for the spiritual needs of our officers and men.[204]

During World War II, President Roosevelt apparently became even more committed to preserving the spiritual fitness of the military. So committed was Roosevelt, he directed, at government expense, the printing and distribution of the Bible to troops along with his exhortation that "I take pleasure in commending the reading of the Bible to all who serve in the Armed Forces of the United States."[205]

---

[202] John Adams to B. Stoddert, July 3, 1799 (*The Works of John Adams*, 10 volumes, ed. Charles Francis Adams [Boston: Little, Brown and Company, 1853], 8:661–62).
[203] "An Act for the Better Government of the Navy of the United States," April 23, 1800, Art. II, *The Public Statutes at Large*, vol. 2 (Boston: Charles C. Little and James Brown, 1845), 45.
[204] Franklin D. Roosevelt, "Fireside Chat," *The American Presidency Project*, October 12, 1942.
[205] *The New Testament of Our Lord and Savior Jesus Christ, Prepared for Use of Protestant Personnel of the Army of the United States* (Washington, DC: US Government Printing Office, 1942), letter by Franklin Roosevelt inside front cover.

Following World War II, with the emergence of communism as the preeminent threat to American and Western European democracies, the battle for ideological superiority commenced. President Harry Truman, wanting assurances that American service members were prepared to combat communism, convened a commission to examine the role of chaplains and spiritual faith in the military. The commission reported:

> One of the fundamental differences dividing this world today lies in the field of ideas. **One side of the world, to which we belong, holds to the idea of a moral law which is based on religious convictions and teachings. The fundamental principles which give our democratic ideas their intellectual and emotional vigor are rooted in the religions which most of us have been taught. Our religious convictions continue to give our democratic faith a very large measure of its strength.** The other side of the conflict has organized its idea upon a rejection of moral law and individual dignity that is utterly repugnant to any of our religions. Indeed, it has been necessary for the totalitarians to attack and stifle religion because such faith represents the antithesis of everything they teach.
>
> **It follows, therefore, that if we expect our Armed Forces to be physically prepared, we must also expect them to be ideologically prepared. A program of adequate religious opportunities for service personnel provides an essential way for strengthening their fundamental beliefs in democracy and, therefore, strengthening their effectiveness as an instrument of our democratic form of government.**[206]

The commission's report was not unfounded. During and after World War II, the US Army surveyed thousands of soldiers about their attitudes toward military service. In 1949, the US Army's Research Branch, Information and Education Division, produced a three-volume record of the survey's results.[207] In volume 2, *The American Soldier, Combat and Its Aftermath*, the US Army surveyed its officers and enlisted service members about the

---

[206] *The Military Chaplaincy: A Report to the President by the President's Committee on Religion and Welfare in the Armed Forces*, October 1, 1950 (Washington, DC: 1951), 1–2 (emphasis added).
[207] Samuel A. Stouffer et al., *Studies in Social Psychology in World War II*, 3 volumes (Princeton: Princeton University Press, 1949).

importance of prayer. Among a list of options that included "thinking that you couldn't let the other men down" and "thinking that you had to finish the job in order to get home again," World War II veterans most frequently identified prayer as their source of support during combat. It is, therefore, reasonable to conclude that a permissive religious climate was essential to America's combat efficacy during World War II.

The preceding anecdotes are but a sample of the hundreds of historical examples establishing a clear and unambiguous message: the practice of permitting, encouraging, and at times requiring, religious expression within the armed forces was instituted by those who first won America's independence. And, despite multiple challenges, it has continued uninterrupted since then.

## LEGAL CHALLENGES TO RELIGIOUS EXPRESSION IN THE MILITARY

Legal challenges to the constitutionality of religious expression within the military may take various forms. However, the substance of the argument is generally similar: because service members are representatives and agents of the federal government, service member religious expression necessarily implies governmental endorsement of religion, thereby violating the Establishment Clause of the First Amendment. Although courts have repeatedly rejected this argument as discussed below, the unique nature of the military and its mission[208] means that courts often apply the First Amendment to service members differently than in other contexts. In contrast to civilian society, individuals have less autonomy in the military. Obedience to orders, good order, and discipline are vital to a military force capable of fighting and winning wars. The United States Supreme Court repeated this on multiple occasions:

> The military need not encourage debate or tolerate protest to the extent that such tolerance is required of the civilian state by the First Amendment; to accomplish its mission the military must foster instinctive

---

[208] See *Parker v. Levy*, 417 U.S. 733, 743 (1974) ("It is the primary business of armies and navies to fight or be ready to fight wars should the occasion arise.").

obedience, unity, commitment, and *esprit de corps*. . . . The essence of military service "is the subordination of the desires and interests of the individual to the needs of the service." . . . "Within the military community, there is simply not the same [individual] autonomy as there is in the larger civilian community."[209]

And:

While the members of the military are not excluded from the protection granted by the First Amendment, the different character of the military community and of the military mission requires a different application of those protections. The fundamental necessity for obedience, and the consequent necessity for imposition of discipline, may render permissible within the military that which would be constitutionally impermissible outside it.[210]

Nevertheless, even the military's mission to fight and win wars, which necessitates obedience to authority, good order, and discipline, does not absolve it from ensuring the constitutional right to religious expression. In fact, one court stated that the military not only *may* accommodate religious expression, but it *must*.

In 1985, the United States Court of Appeals for the Second Circuit decided the case of *Katcoff v. Marsh*.[211] In *Katcoff*, two Harvard Law School students challenged the constitutionality of the US Army's chaplaincy, arguing that government provision and funding of chaplains in order to provide for religious practice violated the Establishment Clause. The court rejected that argument, reasoning that, because of the rigors of military life, a service member's ability to practice their religion freely would be stifled unless the military provided chaplains.[212] Importantly, the court held that the Constitution "*obligates* Congress, upon creating an Army, to make religion available to soldiers who have been moved by the Army to areas of the world where religion of their own denominations is not available

---

[209] *Goldman v. Weinberger*, 475 U.S. 503, 507 (1986).
[210] *Parker v. Levy* (1974) at 758.
[211] *Katcoff v. Marsh*, 755 F.2d 223 (2d Cir. 1985).
[212] *Katcoff v. Marsh* (1985) at 234.

to them."[213] The principle *Katcoff* exemplifies is now embodied in official DOD policy. Joint Publication 1-05, Religious Affairs in Joint Operations, states:

> US military chaplains are a unique manifestation of the nation's commitment to the values of freedom of conscience and free exercise of religion proclaimed in her founding documents. . . . Uniformed chaplaincies are essential in fulfilling the government's, and especially the Department of Defense's (DOD's), responsibilities to all members of the Armed Forces of the United States.[214]

In other words, without a military chaplaincy, Congress would be unable to ensure service members' rights under the Free Exercise clause.

American service members assigned to austere environs or forward-deployed experience this reality daily. They cannot freely exercise their religion by virtue of their military service. Generally speaking, service members assigned to a base in Europe or Japan, or a remote outpost in the Middle East, cannot attend services at their church, synagogue, mosque, and so on. Thus, military chaplains provide an invaluable service that our forefathers understood to be a bulwark of liberty—military chaplains facilitate the free exercise of religion as guaranteed by the First Amendment.

But the challenges to the chaplaincy and chaplains' religious expression did not stop with *Katcoff*. In the 1990s, Congress considered a legislative override to President Clinton's veto of the Partial-Birth Abortion Ban Act. Seeking to present a unified voice in support of the congressional override, the Catholic Church in the United States engaged in a "Project Life Postcard Campaign," which began in 1996. The campaign consisted of Catholic priests throughout the country—including the Archdiocese for Military Services—preaching to their parishioners against the "partial-birth abortion" procedure. Priests encouraged parishioners to sign postcards urging their elected representatives to vote to override President Clinton's veto.

---

[213] *Katcoff v. Marsh* (1985) at 234 (emphasis added).
[214] "Religious Affairs in Joint Operations," Joint Publication 1-05, November 20, 2013, at I-1.

In response, the Judge Advocate General of the Air Force—the highest-ranking attorney in the Air Force—issued an opinion letter prohibiting participation in the postcard campaign. The Army and the Navy[215] subsequently issued similar guidance to their chaplains.

Father Rigdon and Rabbi Kaye, a Roman Catholic priest and Jewish rabbi, respectively, were US Air Force chaplains. Believing that partial-birth abortion was a significant issue to their denominations and congregations, both chaplains wanted to take part in the postcard campaign. But the Air Force prohibited them from doing so. In 1996, Father Rigdon and Rabbi Kaye sued the Secretary of Defense, alleging that the military's prohibition on military chaplains encouraging their congregants to contact Congress in favor of the Partial-Birth Abortion Ban Act violated the Religious Freedom Restoration Act.[216] In 1997, the United States District Court for the District of Columbia ruled in favor of the chaplains.

The court's rationale was straightforward:

> When chaplains are conducting worship . . . they are acting in their religious capacity, not as representatives of the military or . . . "under the color of military authority." . . . Military chaplains do not invoke the official imprimatur of the military when they give a sermon; they are acting in a religious capacity, and therefore, it is wholly appropriate for them to "advance their religious beliefs" in that context.[217]

Thus, not only does the First Amendment's Free Exercise Clause require the provision and funding of military chaplains, it also prohibits censorship of their speech when performed in their religious capacity. When chaplains perform their religious duties—whether delivering the Sacraments, preaching from the pulpit, or counseling the penitent—they enjoy enhanced First Amendment protection compared to their military colleagues.

---

[215] The US Marine Corps does not have an independent chaplains corps. The US Navy provides chaplains for the US Marine Corps. The US Air Force provides chaplains for the US Space Force.
[216] *Rigdon v. Perry*, 962 F.Supp. 150 (D.D.C. 1997).
[217] *Rigdon v. Perry* (1997) at 160–61.

## MILITARY RESTRICTIONS ON RELIGIOUS EXPRESSION

As *Katcoff* and *Rigdon* demonstrate, religious expression in the military does not run afoul of the First Amendment to the Constitution simply because it amounts to government acceptance or approval of such religious expression. *Rigdon*, however, did not define the limits on the military proscription of a chaplain's nonreligious speech. Nor did the court disturb the Supreme Court's holding in *Parker v. Levy*, which arguably grants the military greater authority to curb nonreligious speech.[218] Indeed, it is not difficult to imagine many scenarios in which the needs of the military conceivably outweigh the right of free exercise. Nevertheless, the Constitution, federal law, and military regulations require a careful balancing of these interests.

Because the fundamental concept of the "needs of the service" being greater than the "desires and interests of the individual" is central to how courts view service members' religious liberties, the right to religious expression in the military is not without limitation. The Department of Defense and each of the five military service branches have policies that govern how the military must accommodate the religious needs of service members. The notion that military commanders retain the authority and discretion to maintain good order and discipline, military readiness, and mission capability, are embedded in those policies.

For example, the US Army policy states, "The Army will approve requests for accommodation of religious practices unless accommodation will have an adverse impact on unit readiness, individual readiness, unit cohesion, morale, discipline, safety, and/or health."[219]

The US Navy and Marine Corps policy states the "Department of the Navy policy is to accommodate the doctrinal or traditional observances of the religious faith practiced by individual members when these doctrines or observances will not have an adverse impact on military readiness,

---

[218] *Parker* involved an Army medical specialist who, in protest against the Vietnam War, encouraged soldiers to refuse to deploy to Vietnam for political reasons.
[219] AR 600-20 of March 18, 2008, ¶ 5–6a.

individual or unit readiness, unit cohesion, health, safety, discipline, or mission accomplishment."[220]

The US Air Force policy is perhaps the most restrictive of the service branches on this subject. It states, "Leaders at all levels must balance constitutional protections for an individual's free exercise of religion or other personal beliefs and the constitutional prohibition against government establishment of religion."[221] Paradoxically, the same regulation also states that "all Airmen are able to choose to practice their particular religion" and that Airmen "should confidently practice [their] own beliefs."[222] But even then, an Airman's "right to practice [their] beliefs does not excuse [them] from complying with directives, instructions, and lawful orders."[223]

Clearly, the right to engage in religious expression in the military is not unfettered. Military commanders retain substantial discretion in leading, training, and regulating the conduct of their subordinates. This restriction even extends to expressive conduct.[224]

## LIMITATIONS ON MILITARY AUTHORITY TO CENSOR EXPRESSIVE CONDUCT

Although *Greer v. Spock* upheld the authority of military officials to restrict speech in furtherance of military objectives, it did not grant carte blanche to the military.[225] Indeed, military commanders who engage in censorship in an arbitrary and capricious manner, even under the guise of military necessity, may find themselves on the losing end of a lawsuit. Such was the case in *Nieto v. Flatau*.[226]

Jesse Nieto's son, Marc Nieto, was an American sailor killed in the Islamic terrorist attack on the USS *Cole* in 2000. Mr. Nieto, a retired US Marine,

---

[220] SECNAVINST 1730.8B of October 2, 2008.
[221] AFI 1-1 of August 7, 2012 at ¶ 2.11.
[222] AFI 1-1 at ¶ 2.12.1.
[223] AFI 1-1 at ¶ 2.12.2.
[224] See *Greer v. Spock*, 424 U.S. 828 (1976). It holds that the military ban on partisan political activity is consistent with military objectives and does not violate the First Amendment.
[225] *Greer v. Spock* (1976) at 839. It concludes that the policy was "objectively and evenhandedly applied."
[226] *Nieto v. Flatau*, 715 F.Supp. 2d 650 (E.D. N.C. 2010).

worked as a civilian contractor at Marine Corps Base Camp Lejeune, North Carolina. In response to his son's death, Mr. Nieto began displaying various decals on his vehicle to honor his son's memory and to express his views criticizing Islam and terrorism.

In 2008, Camp Lejeune officials began receiving complaints that Mr. Nieto's decals were offensive. Colonel Richard Flatau Jr., the base commander, responded by ordering Mr. Nieto to remove his decals, citing Camp Lejeune regulations prohibiting "extremist, indecent, sexist, or racist messages on . . . motor vehicles in any format."[227] When Mr. Nieto refused to remove the decals from his vehicle, Camp Lejeune officials ordered him to remove his vehicle from Camp Lejeune and banned him from the base and all other federal installations until he complied. Mr. Nieto sued, arguing that Colonel Flatau applied the base regulation against him in an arbitrary and capricious manner and that he engaged in viewpoint discrimination.[228]

The court agreed with Mr. Nieto, holding that because Camp Lejeune officials permitted some decals to be displayed, they could not arbitrarily pick and choose those decals that were not permitted simply because some may find their message offensive.[229] Specifically, pro-Islam messages were permitted, while anti-Islam messages were not. Importantly, the court stated, "while the military may have greater leeway in restricting offensive material in furtherance of securing order and discipline among its troops, it may not do so in a manner that allows one message while prohibiting the messages of those who can reasonably be expected to respond."[230] This form of censorship is referred to as viewpoint discrimination, and it is unconstitutional.[231]

Thus, even when a military regulation authorizes a commander to prohibit certain forms of speech in order to maintain good order and discipline, commanders may not engage in viewpoint discrimination against religious expression.

---

[227] *Nieto v. Flatau* (2010) at 652.
[228] *Nieto v. Flatau* (2010) at 656.
[229] *Nieto v. Flatau* (2010).
[230] *Nieto v. Flatau* (2010).
[231] See, e.g., *Rosenberger v. Rector and Visitors of the Univ. of Virginia*, 515 U.S. 819 (1995).

## CHALLENGING ALLEGED CONSTITUTIONAL VIOLATIONS BY THE MILITARY

Inevitably, the question arises: What recourse or remedy is available to a service member whose constitutional rights are violated by the military? It is a question courts have yet to address in a comprehensive and satisfactory manner. The unfortunate result is the lingering misconception that *no* recourse is available. This subsection attempts to dispel that myth.

In 1986, the Supreme Court decided the case of *Goldman v. Weinberger*.[232] In *Goldman*, the Court held that the US Air Force did not violate the First Amendment rights of an Orthodox Jew and ordained rabbi who served in the Air Force by prohibiting him from wearing his yarmulke while indoors and on duty. The Court held that the regulation at issue reasonably and evenhandedly regulated attire in a manner that accomplished the military's need for uniformity and discipline.[233] Although Mr. Goldman did not prevail on the substance of his constitutional claim, his case is notable because it stands for the proposition that service members *can* sue the federal government for violating an individual's constitutional rights.

Just three years earlier, and in contrast to *Goldman*, the Supreme Court decided *Chappell v. Wallace*,[234] in which it held that enlisted service members could not sue to recover damages from superior officers for constitutional violations during military service. The Court's rationale was that, because of the unique and special nature of the military, Congress created a separate system of justice for service members under the Uniform Code of Military Justice (UCMJ).[235] If the Court were to craft a judicial remedy exposing officers to personal liability to those they command, it could severely undermine the unique nature of military life. Moreover, because Congress—to whom the Constitution delegates control over the armed forces—had not provided a cause of action and remedy for constitutional violations by individual officers, any judicially created remedy would be inconsistent with Congress's

---

[232] *Goldman v. Weinberger* (1986).
[233] *Goldman v. Weinberger* (1986) at 510.
[234] *Chappell v. Wallace*, 462 U.S. 296 (1983).
[235] *Chappell v. Wallace* (1983) at 302–04.

authority in military matters.[236] In other words, the *Chappell* Court held there is no military analog to a *Bivens*[237] action, meaning enlisted service members may not sue their superiors for constitutional violations. Subsequent Congressional action, however, renders continued reliance on *Chappell* misplaced.

Ten years after the Supreme Court decided *Chappell*, Congress passed the Religious Freedom Restoration Act of 1993 (RFRA).[238] Although a subsequent decision limited RFRA's reach to only the federal government,[239] RFRA nevertheless prohibits "a government" from substantially burdening a person's free exercise of religion unless it can demonstrate a compelling interest that is implemented in the least restrictive way. RFRA creates a cause of action against "a government" that is unable to satisfy this standard. By its own terms, RFRA defines "a government" as including "a branch, department, agency, instrumentality, and official (or other person acting under color of law) of the United States."[240] Thus, post-*Chappell*, Congress *did* create a cause of action for constitutional violations by individuals. Accordingly, *Chappell*'s validity is questionable, at best. And although it may be difficult to prevail against an individual military officer on a constitutional violation claim—for example, the officer may claim qualified immunity—it is clear that RFRA creates a cause of action for such claims.

Therefore, service members who are victims of constitutional violations *can*, in fact, sue the United States, the responsible individual, or both.

## CONCLUSION

American service members voluntarily surrender many freedoms and liberties upon entering the military. Religious freedom, however, is not one of them. Religion and faith have played integral roles in America's military

---

[236] *Chappell v. Wallace* (1983) at 304.
[237] See *Bivens v. Six Unknown Named Agents*, 403 U.S. 388 (1971). It provides for monetary damages as a remedy for injuries resulting when federal officials violate an individual's constitutional rights.
[238] 42 U.S.C. §§ 2000bb – bb-4.
[239] *City of Boerne v. Flores*, 521 U.S. 507 (1997).
[240] 42 U.S.C. § 2000bb-2(1).

since before our founding. Today, service members continue to enjoy broad, robust First Amendment rights. Service members are free to engage in religious expression consistent with their faith. The authority and discretion of military officials to curb such expression is not unfettered. And those who find themselves the victims of First Amendment violations may allege constitutional claims against those responsible.

## REFLECTION QUESTIONS

1. Give an example of a historical figure's impact and influence on the role of religion in the military. How does your understanding of this history help explain to others why chaplains serve the military?
2. What are the primary legal arguments for and against the presence of religious chaplains funded by the government in the military?
3. Mr. Berry argues that religious presence in the military contributes to moral guidance and resilience among service members. How does this moral guidance serve to strengthen our nation's democracy? Do you agree with this perspective?
4. In what ways does the military attempt to accommodate religious expression among its military personnel?
5. Reflect on your views of the importance of religion in your life. How might it influence your views on religious presence and expression in a structured, hierarchical organization like the military?

# ARMY CHAPLAINCY

## Chaplain Jay Johns

In the previous section, I gave a broad overview of military chaplaincy. Though there are significant similarities in the chaplain corps of all branches of service, each retains its ethos. This section focuses specifically on Army chaplaincy, along with its opportunities and challenges.

Within our military, there is a healthy degree of interservice rivalry. One well-circulated quip among those in uniform claims only two military services: the Army and the Navy. The Air Force is a corporation, while the Marine Corps is a religion.[241] All joking aside, each military service has its own distinctive culture. Deciding to "marry the military" is a bold endeavor. Ensuring chemistry in that relationship between you and your chosen service makes the journey even more exciting. I have served joyfully for over twenty-six years as an active-duty Army chaplain. Though I have chaplain friends and colleagues in each of the military services who love what they do, I make no apologies for my enthusiasm, dedication, and love for the Army chaplaincy, as it holds a special place in my heart.

The mission of the United States Army is "to deploy, fight, and win our nation's wars by providing ready, prompt and sustained land dominance by Army forces across the full spectrum of conflict as part of the joint force."[242] Chaplain ministry in the Army is nested within the larger Army mission: the chaplain corps seeks "to build Army spiritual readiness to deploy, fight, and win our nation's wars by providing reliable and relevant world-class religious support, as a unique element of the Army . . ."[243] Its motto, *Pro Deo et Patria* ("For God and Country"), captures the spirit of the calling of those dedicated to this ministry.

The word *soldier* is often used as a catch-all term for anyone serving in uniformed national defense within American culture, likely due to the sheer number of soldiers in the military compared to the other branches of

---

[241] The US Space Force, now its own military service, is served by US Air Force Chaplains.
[242] "The Army's Vision and Strategy," US Army, https://www.army.mil/about/.
[243] "Chaplain Corps," US Army, https://www.army.mil/chaplaincorps/#org-about.

service.²⁴⁴ Or it may harken back to childhood, when children form up in squads to "play soldier" in imaginary battles against malign armies. I do not recall anyone from childhood playing "airman" or "sailor," though playing "Marine" was fairly serious business. Throughout history, US soldiers have sacrificed mightily to preserve our nation's freedom. At the risk of oversimplification, my advice to anyone considering Army chaplaincy is to make sure you love God and soldiers, because these will be the focus of your life.

The Army chaplain's "flock" consists of soldiers and their family members, as well as Department of the Army Civilians²⁴⁵ for whom you will provide a vast array of direct ministries. Being an integral asset to the unit is one of the most appealing aspects of the Army chaplaincy. Whether your calling leads you to the Active Component, the Army National Guard, or the Army Reserve, you will embark on a similar journey.

Imagine you have just completed your basic course and sign in to your first unit, which likely is a battalion of about five hundred soldiers. At this point, you have attained the rank of first lieutenant and will promote to captain within six months. Your immediate supervisor is the Battalion Executive Officer, a major responsible for coordinating all staff activities. However, your Battalion Commander (a lieutenant colonel) is the person who gives your "marching orders."²⁴⁶ Though you are the only chaplain in the unit, your Brigade Chaplain (a major at the next higher headquarters) serves as your technical (chaplain) supervisor and ideally as your mentor. Your peers in the unit are the Company Commanders (typically three), as well as fellow staff officers overseeing personnel, intelligence, operations, logistics, and communications. Your Unit Ministry Team (UMT) consists of yourself and

---

²⁴⁴ There are over one million soldiers in the three Army components. See https://www.army.mil/soldiers. To provide a scale, all other services and components combined have 1.3 million personnel. See https://www.statista.com/statistics/232330/us-military-force-numbers-by-service-branch-and-reserve-component/, accessed March 2021.

²⁴⁵ Some Army organizations employ career civil servants within their ranks. Though they do not wear the Army uniform, Department of the Army Civilians are vital to mission accomplishment and provide stability through institutional memory in units where soldiers normally spend two or three years before moving to a new duty station.

²⁴⁶ Chaplains serve on the commander's personal staff. In this role, they plan and execute the Command Master Religious Program (CMRP) and advise the commander on matters of religion and morale.

your Religious Affairs Specialist. This soldier (a specialist or sergeant) serves as your vehicle operator, administrative and logistics coordinator, and armed protector.[247] The Religious Affairs Specialist, an enlisted military member trained to serve in this role, is the only soldier for whom you have supervisory responsibility.

Your office is located near battalion headquarters and the rest of the staff. This allows you to learn from them even as you serve them as chaplain. You spend hours each day near the soldiers in your unit, many of whom live in the barracks near battalion headquarters. The most effective chaplain engagement is "ministry of presence." Instead of sitting in your office waiting for soldiers to drop by and talk, you have the opportunity and obligation to engage them as much as possible. Some of the most effective sites for pastoral conversations include field exercises, road marches, the motor pool, the dining facility, and countless other situations.

While sleeping in the woods and sharing hardships, particularly during inclement weather, you seize opportunities to engage your flock and create a bond of trust that is difficult to describe to those who have not experienced it. Some of the most valuable time I spent as a junior chaplain was in the field on exercises with whatever section might be training at any given time. The best affirmation I received in those early years in my infantry battalion was to hear a soldier say, upon seeing me at a field site, "There's my chaplain."

Though your commander may want to know about counseling trends and morale in the unit, you must be careful to guard the trust soldiers have placed in you. Military chaplains must protect privileged communication: whatever a service member[248] confides to a chaplain must not be divulged to anyone without that person's permission. This privilege guarantees a person can confide in a chaplain whatever may be occurring in life without fear of consequence. While it is entirely appropriate to inform the commander about marriage counseling trends or general issues with which soldiers may be struggling, it is never acceptable to divulge specifics of any case or names

---

[247] Chaplains are noncombatants who do not bear arms. In hostile environments, the Religious Affairs Specialist is responsible for the armed security of the UMT.

[248] This privilege also applies to family members and Department of the Army Civilians.

of people whom the chaplain has counseled.[249] Effective chaplain ministry is built upon trust. This trust is built over time, but it can be destroyed in an instant.

One of the benefits of the Army chaplaincy is the opportunity to serve in many different types of units. In your time as a captain (approximately nine years), you may serve in a wide range of battalions: infantry, armor, aviation, logistics, military intelligence, signal, special forces, and medical. Though your work is similar in each organization, you discover that each type of unit has its own culture.[250] It is completely natural for chaplains to gravitate over time toward soldiers in specific military occupational specialties. Ever since starting my career in a light infantry battalion whose motto was "Travel light; freeze at night," I have held a particular affection for those soldiers who are the "tip of the spear" in Army warfighting.

If you can imagine yourself in one of these scenarios, then you might also be thinking, "This sounds like a perfect fit for me. How do I sign up?" There are three avenues of service in the Army chaplaincy: the Active Component, Army National Guard, or Army Reserve.[251] Several times each year, the Army Chaplain Corps holds Accessions Boards to bring qualified applicants into the Army. Minimum requirements for consideration include holding a master of divinity degree, endorsement from an ecclesiastical agency, professional ministry experience, and passing a medical examination and a security check. The likelihood of being selected varies from board to board, depending on how many applicants are in the pool and how many chaplains the Army needs for its manning requirements. Those pursuing Army chaplaincy some-

---

[249] I have seen several chaplains erode the credibility of the chaplaincy and destroy any trust they might have built in their units by carelessly discussing counseling matters with unit leaders. When this occurs, their intent is usually not malicious. They may be too eager to prove their worth to unit leaders and try to demonstrate their expertise by discussing a problem they helped to solve in such a way that it becomes apparent whose problem they were engaging.

[250] As a captain, I served in infantry, forward support, and aviation support battalions.

[251] The Army also offers the Chaplain Candidate Program, designed for those interested in service as an Army chaplain but who are still pursuing their graduate degrees. Chaplain candidates serve in the National Guard or Reserve and work as commissioned officers (staff specialists in the rank of second lieutenant) under the supervision of the unit chaplain. For more information about this program, see https://www.goarmy.com/chaplain/become-an-army-chaplain/candidate-program.html.

times feel overwhelmed by the sheer volume of paperwork associated with the application process. Some become discouraged because they have heard erroneous or outdated information from others who have inquired about the process. The bottom line is: get your information from the right source,[252] and be prepared to demonstrate commitment to the rigorous application process.

Once accessioned into the Army Chaplain Corps, you will receive your initial training at Fort Jackson, South Carolina, at the Chaplain Basic Officer Leader Course (CHBOLC). This eight-week course (conducted three times each year) prepares you to enter your first unit as a trained and confident religious leader. At CHBOLC, you will learn Army Warrior tasks, basic officer skills, leadership, and how to operate in field and garrison environments.[253] Perhaps most importantly, you will develop friendships with your peers at CHBOLC that will endure throughout your entire military career and into retirement.

The benefits are numerous but serving as an Army chaplain can be difficult. The Army is America's main ground force. It is committed to securing terrain in military operations and is vital to effective peacekeeping operations. Soldiers often operate in dangerous and austere conditions. As the shepherd of soldiers, you'll accompany them wherever they go throughout long days, family separations (including missed birthdays, special occasions, and holidays), and continual preparation for what we all hope never arrives—war. If married, Army chaplains need their spouses to be supportive in this challenging but joyful endeavor. Love and stability at the home front keeps a soldier focused and grounded while deployed overseas.

My own journey into the Chaplain Corps began with my selection to serve in the US Army Reserve in 1991. After one year, I applied for active duty. Though I believed I was a quality candidate, the Army was in a drawdown phase following Operation Desert Storm and was accessioning very few chaplains for active duty. I was rejected but reapplied three months later. I was rejected again. Though I believed God had called me to active duty, I

---

[252] Go to the chaplaincy recruiting site at https://www.goarmy.com/chaplain.html. A chaplain recruiter will shepherd you through the application process once you have made contact.
[253] The CHBOLC course description may be found at https://usachcs.tradoc.army.mil/courses/chbolc/.

wrestled with the thought that perhaps I had misunderstood God's direction and should stay in the Reserve and remain as pastor of my church. I applied for active duty a third time in 1994 and was accepted. Looking back at that time of confusion and rejection, I see God's timing was perfect: I would not have been ready for the challenges of active duty in 1992. I certainly learned perseverance through that two-year process.

People often ask me if I believe I made the right decision in my choice of career. My answer is this: if you had handed me a pen and notebook thirty years ago and told me to sit under a shade tree for an afternoon and create my dream job, I could not have come close to this life the Army chaplaincy has afforded me. The Army chaplaincy is a perfect fit for me. I knew it nearly thirty years ago, and I believe it still. My prayer is that you will find that perfect fit for yourself within your calling to ministry, possibly as a chaplain in the US Army.

# NAVY, MARINE CORPS, AND COAST GUARD CHAPLAINCY

## Chaplain James Denley

If you enjoy both adventure and ministry, being a chaplain in the Sea Services is for you. The Sea Services consist of the US Navy, US Marine Corps, and the US Coast Guard, which provide numerous venues and opportunities for God to work through you as you support service members and their families. The Navy recruits qualified ministers to become commissioned officers to serve as chaplains in all three of these services. The naval customs and traditions that define the Sea Services add to this adventure.

As a lighthearted indicator of how unique the Sea Services are, who has a better vocabulary? In the Army and Air Force, stairs are stairs, but in the Sea Services, they are "ladders." Walls are "bulkheads," doors are "hatches," and hallways are "passageways." When a chaplain embarks aboard a helicopter, the helicopter is renamed the "Holy Helo."

Consider, too, the long naval tradition of having a shipboard-wide Evening Prayer broadcasted on the ship's public address system, the 1 MC. Every evening, the crew pauses to hear an encouraging prayer from their chaplain. On my ships, the Evening Prayer occurred just before Taps, or ten p.m. Each night the Boatswains Mate of the Watch spoke over the 1 MC, "Taps, taps, lights out in five minutes. Stand by for the Evening Prayer." It gets better. On aircraft carriers, every pilot's landing (or trap) is graded for precision. Any pilot who lands during the Evening Prayer receives a "holy upgrade" (extra credit). As you can see, the chaplain is a fully integrated part of naval customs and traditions.

Before diving deeper into this chapter on ministry in the Sea Services, I **strongly** recommend reading Dr. Jim Spivey's chapter "Spiritual Formation and the Call" (chapter 2) and Chaplain Jay Johns's section, "Military Chaplaincy" (chapter 17). The first one introduces an overarching principle that I describe as knowing who you are and Whose you are, a critical personal and professional goal for every chaplain in the Sea Services. You will need to be a steadying presence. You will be your best if you understand yourself, your ecclesiastical doctrine, your relationship with God, and your pastoral identity and authority. In Chaplain Jay Johns's introductory section, you will find a broad description of many foundational principles that underline and contribute to the military chaplain's role.

## HELPFUL INTRODUCTORY GUIDELINES

This introduction addresses some guidelines grounded in professional naval chaplaincy[254] and naval tradition. Additionally, we will focus on the tactical ministry performed aboard ships, battalions, and small units. By the end of this section, you should have an excellent orientation to naval chaplaincy in its many permutations.

**1. Fully appreciate your command's mission and its operational environment.**

The duty of every naval officer, including the chaplain, is to understand your command's mission and its operational environment. Wherever assigned within the Sea Services, you will be a member of a command with a specific mission, a unique operating environment, and special tasks to accomplish to be ready to "execute the mission." You will need to understand the scope of your command's mission and how your command meets its mission requirements. Within this landscape, you will be responsible for the Commanding Officer's (CO) Command Religious Program (CRP), which incorporates all religious activity sponsored by the command.[255]

---

[254] Secretary of the Navy, Instruction 5351.1, Change Transmittal 1, "Professional Naval Chaplaincy," 2 July 2015, https://www.secnav.navy.mil/doni/Directives/05000%20General%20Management%20Security%20and%20Safety%20Services/05-300%20Manpower%20Personnel%20Support/SECNAV%205351.1%20CH-1.pdf, accessed 27 September 2021.

[255] Secretary of the Navy Instruction 1730.7E, Religious Ministry within the Department of the Navy, 11 March 2019, https://www.secnav.navy.mil/doni/Directives/01000%20Military%20Personnel%20Support/01-700%20Morale,%20Community%20and%20Religious%20Services/1730.7E.pdf and Chief of Naval Operations Instruction 1730.1E, "Religious Ministry in the Navy," 25 April 2012, https://www.secnav.navy.mil/doni/Directives/01000%20Military%20Personnel%20Support/01-700%20Morale,%20Community%20and%20Religious%20Services/1730.1E.pdf, accessed 27 September 2021. Commandant of the Marine Corps Order 1730.6F with Administrative Change, "Religious Ministry in the Marine Corps," 16 August 2018, https://www.marines.mil/Portals/1/Publications/MCO%201730.6F%20Admin%20Change.pdf?ver=2018-08-24-065538-480,

When I was the senior chaplain aboard USS *Enterprise* (CVN-65), a nuclear-powered aircraft carrier, the ship was tasked with conducting a burial at sea for several Navy veterans. It took weeks of on-again-off-again planning to find a window of opportunity to conduct the ceremony. We wrestled with flight schedules, weather conditions, sea states, and training requirements. Finally, a window of opportunity presented itself.

The CO signed a plan of action for the burial at sea, which included actions by those in the propulsion plant, bridge team, and aviation department. The bridge team positioned the behemoth aircraft carrier so the wind and sea had the least effect on the ceremony. Only twenty-five personnel of the thirty-five hundred aboard the "Big E" gathered by #4 Elevator for the ceremony, but the entire crew knew about this time-honored tradition. As we lowered the #4 Elevator to as close to the sea as possible, the CO asked me how long the burial would take. A medical evacuation helicopter was inbound, and the elevator needed to be back up before the helo arrived with a seriously ill patient. Our rehearsals had run for about forty minutes.

I told the CO we would finish in thirty-five minutes without rushing, but fewer if necessary. He said thirty-five minutes would work. From the announcement on the 1 MC of "All hands bury the dead," to "Secure from burial at sea," it was thirty-five minutes. We were on time. If the CRP team hadn't understood how the "Big E" operated, the burial could have delayed the inbound flight and endangered the patient. Understanding the mission and operational environment is essential for every event on board a warship, even the events comprising the CRP.

## 2. Speak up when you have something to contribute. Don't be timid.

The best model for understanding the Sea Services' fundamental structure is the intricate interactions on a warship's bridge at sea. It is a formal environment, but surprisingly egalitarian.

---

accessed 27 September 2021. Commandant of the Coast Guard Instruction 1730.4C, "Religious Ministries within the Coast Guard," 9 March 2012, https://media.defense.gov/2017/Mar/06/2001707724/-1/-1/0/CI_1730_4C.PDF, accessed 27 September 2021.

The formality looks like this. When the CO enters or exits the bridge, the Boatswain's Mate of the Watch announces, "The Captain is on the bridge," or "The Captain is off the bridge." When I opened the hatch to the bridge to visit the bridge team or say the Evening Prayer, I always asked, "Permission to enter the bridge?" No one ever said "No," but the custom to ask permission goes back centuries. Formality and courtesy are the threads that tie together personal interactions throughout the Sea Services.

Another custom on the warship's bridge, which extends to all naval leadership, is communicating critical information. Perhaps you've heard the saying, "If your boss wants your opinion, he/she will give it to you." In the best naval tradition, it is precisely the opposite. Leadership expects you to speak up and not be timid if you have something important to share—every voice matters.

Consider, for example, this typical interaction on the bridge. The officer of the deck (OOD, in charge of navigation) tells the helmsman, "Come left ten degrees." If anyone sees a potential danger to the left, that person must speak up. A lookout might report, "Officer of the Deck, I hold a small surface vessel at one thousand yards off of the port bow." Perhaps the OOD already knew this and planned to shift the rudder momentarily. Perhaps not. But the OOD is going to thank the lookout who spoke up. Chaplains are no exception when serving in the Sea Services. Speak up respectfully, clearly, and confidently. And professionally present your comments in support of your command's mission.

## 3. Be a student of religion.

Being a perpetual student of religion is essential for four reasons. First, as a Navy chaplain, you are likely to be the only chaplain available for extended periods. Many will not have access to ministers of their own faith. A chaplain's job is to provide an empathetic and knowledgeable conversation about their religious needs when the service member may be experiencing pain or personal loss.

Here is a typical example. Aboard a ship or in a battalion, approximately 20-25 percent of personnel will be Roman Catholic. Obviously, you will not directly meet those specific needs unless you are a Roman Catholic priest.

However, a chaplain facilitates the spiritual development of all personnel. Therefore, it is essential to the Catholic personnel and command's readiness for the chaplain to have a working professional knowledge of Catholicism. With that knowledge, a chaplain is extremely helpful to Catholic service members who are rediscovering their spiritual roots, a common need for many young people. Perhaps one of your Marines didn't complete the Catholic confirmation process. Helping her focus on receiving her first communion might be the most critical step you take to deepen her faith and build her spiritual resilience. Being a student of religion will pay big dividends for your people and the command's readiness. After all, every mission depends on reliable people, and faith is vital to personal growth and well-being.

Second, being a student of religion is important when advocating for those who need an accommodation to practice their faith properly.[256] I once had a sailor who was well known aboard my ship for his Christian faith. One day his Leading Chief Petty Officer (LCPO, a senior enlisted leader) dropped by my office with a "chit" (special request form) from this sailor, who wanted extra time off to celebrate Sukkot (Feast of Tabernacles). The LCPO knew what I knew: Sukkot is a Jewish holiday. He did not realize that the kind of Christianity the sailor practiced defined itself as both Jewish and Christian. The sailor observed Jewish and Christian holidays. Knowing this fact helped us address the request's legitimacy and resolve an issue that otherwise could have been thorny. Most importantly, from a chaplain's perspective, the sailor's chain of command was provided the needed information and fully supported him. The sailor's religious freedom was honored, strengthening his spiritual resilience.

The third reason to be a student of religion is because units deploy to or visit many overseas places. A ship in the Mediterranean Sea might visit places that are as religiously different as North Africa (predominantly Muslim), Italy (Roman Catholic), Greece (Greek Orthodox), and Israel (Jewish). Along the Pacific Rim, ports are heavily influenced by Buddhism, animist religions, localized adaptations of major world religions, and any number of Christian

---

[256] Department of Defense Instruction 1300.17, Religious Liberty in the Military Services, 1 September 2020, https://www.esd.whs.mil/Portals/54/Documents/DD/issuances/dodi/130017p.pdf?ver=2020-09-01-151756-730, accessed 27 September 2021.

missionary outreaches. In such environments, the CO needs to understand the ground rules for the crew's interactions with local people. Is a religious festival something that the crew should avoid? Are there religious rules for interactions between men and women? Would the local mosque welcome American service members? Usually, the US State Department helps the CO with fundamental questions, and chaplains should read these briefs. Still, as a student of religion, a chaplain should have a more refined picture of the cultural issues the crew might face. During the pre-deployment period, a chaplain will know the command's schedule and should be able to prepare accordingly. Such awareness highlights a chaplain's value to the command's mission.

The fourth reason is that the operational environment (training or "real world" operations) is diverse. The following vignette shows how the principles of understanding the command's mission and of speaking up about something important can work together. Once during an operational briefing for a training event, the Special Forces team on board described how they had observed a small town for three days. The team planned a mock daylight infiltration. The town was quietest just before sunset. They planned to infiltrate the town in two days, just before sunset. As I listened to the brief, I waited for someone to point out a significant and known fact. They planned their mock infiltration for the hour before sunset on a Friday in a Muslim town. The town would be abuzz with activity as the mosque (center on their map) opened its doors for worship. I eventually spoke up and explained the dilemma for the infiltration team. Aside from a bit of egg on the faces of the junior officers who had planned the mock infiltration, the senior leaders (as expected) said, "Thanks for mentioning that, Chaps." They reworked their plan, and off they went.

## 4. Swap your public persona for a family role.

As the pastor of a church, you can typically afford to have a public persona. You can decide when and how you will present yourself. That is not possible in the tactical environment of the Sea Services, where you usually are in an expeditionary environment. Think of camping out for weeks or months with hundreds of congregants. Think of living at sea for months with your congregation and coworkers.

It was a big step for me to transition from being the pastor of a small church. As a civilian pastor, I could prepare myself for Sunday worship, hospital visits, or dinner at our house. But at sea, I saw sailors to whom I sought to minister everywhere I went—even when I was seasick, missing my family, or angry because something got under my skin. I needed to learn a new set of skills. I had to decide that I was a member of a very large, very diverse, and, overall, very gracious family.

Over time I learned to become a family member. We went through everything together. A crew member might observe, "Chaps, you look troubled. You all right?" With a controlled level of transparency, I might respond, "Yes, I'll be OK. I just heard a disturbing story. How about you? How are you doing?"

I was a brother to some. A father to others. Even a goofy uncle to those who found my personality or faith amusing. But always their pastor, sick with the flu or not. Same with the Marines in the field. We slept next to each other, ate whatever we had, shared snacks and stories and humor and sadness. But always their pastor. Sometimes this is called "incarnational ministry." I like that phrase. You will be a representative of Jesus even when you and your people are soaked to the bone from a storm, sweating in tropical heat, or looking for any heat you can find. That's the swap: persona for family—incarnational ministry.

## 5. Have a professional demeanor about you.

Perhaps we all agree that good ministers should have a sense of humor and not take themselves too seriously, be generous with their kindness, and handle conflicts with grace. For a Navy chaplain, these are necessary qualities. What you do on the bow of the ship will be repeated on the stern of the ship. What you say on one end to a group of Marines will become a legend on the other end. And this next point is very important. Your professional demeanor must be genuinely consistent with who you are and Whose you are. You grow into it. You cannot fake it.

The issue is not that everyone is looking and listening. They certainly are. But they look and listen because they need your example, your faith in God, your balance in life. They know you are living through what they are living. If you can approach stress and strain with a good attitude fueled with faith, they will grow in their faith. I've never seen a ship's crew or a platoon of Marines trust a chaplain who complained to them or about them, who became angry with them, or who refused to walk with graciousness beside them. Your professional demeanor is enormously important to the spiritual growth of everyone who observes you.

## 6. Two Stories of "Who you are and Whose you are."

*Story #1: It worked out.* "Maritime interdiction operations" (boarding commercial ships to check for contraband) take a long time from beginning to end. It works like this. A small boat from your ship takes a boarding team to the commercial vessel, they conduct their inspections, and your warship stands guard.

During one of these multi-hour operations, a crowd gathered outside the bridge to watch the operation. I was out there, too, when the CO told the executive officer (XO, second in command) to clear the area. The XO gave some orders, and people quickly cleared out. As the ship's chaplain, I wanted to keep a shepherd's eye on the operation and spend a few rare peaceful minutes talking with the CO about how he was doing. I am always a pastor, and I had my reasons for remaining in place. The XO stepped off the bridge and said, "That goes for you, too, Chaps. Off the bridge wing." I stood perfectly still as my brain and heart wrestled with the XO's direct order and what I saw as my role as the chaplain. I was relieved when the CO turned to the XO and said, "That's OK, XO. The chaplain knows how to handle himself out here."

Based on who I was and Whose I was, I made a risky decision. Fortunately, it worked out. I chatted with the CO about his family and how he was doing. And we discussed the well-being of our boarding crew that had been very busy lately. I stayed on the bridge wing well past dark until the boarding crew was safely back on board. Mission accomplished: theirs and mine and God's.

*Story #2: Learn from your mistakes.* Every military branch has a custom like this: the junior troops eat first, junior to senior. One evening in the field with my Marines, we got "hot chow" (food in heated containers) instead of the day-in and day-out Meal, Ready-to-Eat (MREs). We were indeed happy to see the hot chow arrive.

Thinking over who I am and Whose I am, I decided it was a good idea to be the last to eat, both as a gesture of kindness and as their spiritual leader. But that is not the custom. The senior officer and senior enlisted leader eat last. That is the custom. So, as I delayed getting in the cue, I held up the line. There were four people senior in rank to me, plus the sergeant first class. One of the senior officers grabbed me by the elbow and said, "It's your turn to eat, Chaps," and ushered me to the chow line.

As a chaplain, you make countless spur-of-the-moment decisions. In situation after situation, you will ask yourself how best to glorify God through your actions. In reflecting on my misapplied Christian virtue to put others' needs first, I inadvertently put myself in a position of superiority. We do not always get it right, and we learn from our mistakes, big and small. Having a sense of humor and not taking yourself too seriously will make every "oops" more comfortable for everyone. This will make it easier to embrace the lesson, as well. Ten minutes after we ate our hot chow, my faux pas was forgotten except by me, the student.

## UNEXPECTED DOOR OPENINGS

Navy chaplains, imprinted by their culture, find the smallest units of Sailors, Marines, and Coastguardsmen in their area and visit them. If one follows this rule, unexpected doors will open for ministry.

I've conducted worship services on a nuclear missile submarine far from its homeport. My family and I sang carols on Christmas Eve with an isolated Special Forces unit. I've flown into an active volcano in a Marine Corps helicopter with volcanologists collecting data. I've ridden on tugboats, the unsung heroes of port operations, to encourage their crews. I made friends with the six crew members of a Coast Guard buoy tender in the Philippines. I've conducted funerals in locations you could hardly find on a map, helped feed the poorest of the poor, ministered to celebrities, and been an honored guest in the humblest of dwellings.

Although limited in scope, this section gives you an accurate, albeit brief orientation to chaplaincy in the Sea Services. If you feel like the ministry opportunities are endless, you are right. Keep these few basic guidelines in mind, and you will do very well.

# AIR FORCE, SPACE FORCE, AND CIVIL AIR PATROL CHAPLAINCY

## Dr. Steven Richardson

I went to college to study biology and mathematics but lost my passion for both subjects. Near the end of my second year, I was desperate for direction. Taking a canteen and a Bible into Mark Twain National Forest, I fell on my knees and vowed not to leave until I knew God's will for my life. After several days, I contacted my dad and told him I believed God was calling me to enter the ministry as an Air Force chaplain.

Let me share a little more about my father for you to understand what happened next. My dad served a church in Wisconsin when he accepted his commission as an active-duty chaplain. He eventually led all Air Force Chaplains as the USAF Chief of Chaplains. My father's love for God and airmen was contagious. My father always had a twinkle in his eye, a smile on his face, and a bounce in his step when he led worship services, visited airmen in their work centers or greeted Security Forces at the base's entry gate. I treasured the opportunities to gather with more than 150 young airmen in a chapel annex as he taught them the Bible. I loved joining him as he connected with airmen any time, any place.

When I told him about my life-changing decision, Dad spent the next hour trying to talk me out of becoming a chaplain. He spoke about the stress of constantly sharing other people's burdens, the exhausting hours, the challenges of multidenominational and multifaith ministry, and the hardships my future family would face due to the constant moves. He wanted to ensure I followed God rather than just following him. But I knew what I needed to do. For the first time in my life, I had a sense of calling, a purpose, and a passion. I felt the fire of a chaplain ministry burn deep within me.

As you consider the Air Force as your ministry loci, I highlight the following issues: the process, the mission, the ministry, and three guiding imperatives.

## EMBRACE THE PROCESS

The journey to become a military chaplain can be long and arduous. One should embrace the process, knowing you take one step at a time. The Air Force expects applicants to meet specific educational and experiential requirements.[257] While not mandatory, anyone potentially interested in Air Force chaplaincy should consider applying for the Air Force Chaplain Candidate Program.[258] This program enables seminarians and students in other professional religious schools to explore and evaluate their compatibility and potential as an Air Force chaplain. When accepted, one is commissioned as a second lieutenant and typically trains during the summer. Upon graduating from seminary and obtaining an ecclesiastical endorsement, one may apply for an appointment in the Air Force Reserve, Air National Guard, or Active Duty.

An applicant's desire to become an Air Force chaplain does not guarantee entry. The Air Force chaplain accession process is influenced by many factors, selects according to the needs of the Air Force, and chooses candidates who are best qualified. Being accessed for the Reserve, Guard, or Active Duty requires persistence and determination to get through all the necessary steps.

Another avenue of ministry (and experience) is as a Civil Air Patrol (CAP) chaplain, a nonpaid volunteer in the Civil Air Patrol. The Civil Air Patrol Chaplain Corps primarily provides pastoral care and support to CAP members throughout a senior or cadet membership. The Chaplain Corps conducts religious services, assists CAP personnel when making death/serious injury notifications, acts as a moral and spiritual example/influence for cadets, conducts the CAP character development program for cadets, and provides spiritual assistance during CAP missions.[259] Anyone interested should engage an Air Force Chaplain Corps recruiter, who will help to understand and navigate the process.

Attending the six-week Basic Chaplain's Course at the Air Force Chaplain Corps College of Air University in Montgomery, Alabama, introduces the chaplain candidate or newly commissioned chaplain to the unique culture

---

[257] For information about USAF Chaplaincy, see https://www.airforce.com/careers/specialty-careers/chaplain.

[258] See https://www.afrc.af.mil/About-Us/Chaplain/Chaplain-Candidate/, accessed 12 May 2021.

[259] CAP's accession requirements are similar to those in the active duty, reserve, and guard. CAP however has larger numbers of slots for appointment.

of the Air Force and Space Force. It helps one to transition from a civilian to a military ministry. It also prepares chaplains to work as a team with clergy of various faiths. Students learn about military funerals, funds management, interfaith worship, inclusive chapel programs, ministry in a readiness environment, chaplain administrative responsibilities, and counseling skills.

## UNDERSTAND THE MISSION

The mission of the US Air Force Chaplain Corps is to inspire the readiness of Airmen, guardians,[260] and their families through unparalleled soul care, leader advisement, and religious liberty.[261] The top priority for an Air Force chaplain is the free exercise of religion. The Chaplain Corps exists to ensure that those who raise their right hand to support and defend the United States Constitution have the same free exercise of religion privileges afforded civilian citizens. When individuals commit to "support and defend," they are pledging service and self-sacrifice, qualities often bred and nurtured by their families and faith communities. Anyone willing to take such an oath must have their constitutional rights guaranteed and supported. Chaplains support those who desire to gather for a prayer service, a Catholic mass, an Orthodox feast, a Hanukkah celebration, or Islamic Friday prayers, sometimes in remote places and under austere conditions.

As a new chaplain, I quickly learned young men and women entering the military are spiritually hungry. Although many have never had any form of Christian or religious education, they are excited to meet chaplains and often bombard them with questions about faith and spirituality. They want to hear something positive amid the world's negatives; they yearn to hear God loves them, has a plan for their lives, and offers hope for their future.

General Giulio Douhet, an Italian military theorist and proponent of airpower's inherent flexibility, inspired the phrase, "Flexibility is the key to airpower."[262] Flexibility is also the key for an Air Force chaplain ministering

---

[260] Military personnel serving in the US Space Force are called "Guardians."
[261] "Fact Sheet," Fairchild Air Force Base, https://www.fairchild.af.mil/Information/Fact-Sheets/Indextitle/B/, accessed 22 May 2021.
[262] Giulio Douhet, *The Command of the Air*, trans. Dino Ferrari (Air Force History and Museums Program, 1998), https://media.defense.gov/2010/Sep/24/2001329765/-1/-1/0/AFD-100924-017.pdf, accessed 5 October 2021.

to service members, their families, and support personnel in the Air Force and the Space Force. No two assignments are the same. The people, mission, and needs differ from command to command, location to location, and unit to unit. Air Force chaplains strive to understand service members in all circumstances while enriching and strengthening their spiritual lives. For an Air Force chaplain, ministry means being there: being there when recruits step off the bus at basic training and head to the barbershop; being there when young pilots take the aircraft up by themselves for the first time; being there in a war zone when the troops arrive, scared and wondering what their future holds; being there to counsel with a young couple just beginning their journey "till death do us part"; being there at the altar when young men or women step forward to make a profession of faith; and, of course, being there when hearts grieve, tears flow, and warriors need wise counsel.

## ENJOY A RICH AND DIVERSE MINISTRY

Air Force ministry means providing pastoral care for the hurting, preaching with passion and excellence, and counseling with insight. It means helping warriors reintegrate into their families following a deployment. It means leading resiliency training programs and retreats and conducting weddings and memorial services. Amazingly, it is common for all those activities to occur in a single week. Chaplains spend many hours and long days with those in their circle of care—praying, encouraging, strengthening, and loving them as a "visible reminder of the Holy."

Each military branch has a rich history, legacy, traditions, and ever-changing missions that shape and influence its ethos. Chaplains must learn their respective military service history, mission, and culture to be effective. The Air Force separated from the Army Air Corps and became a distinct service on 18 September 1947, when President Harry S. Truman signed the National Security Act. The US Space Force (USSF), established by signed legislation on 20 December 2019, is the newest military service.

The US Air Force affords chaplains fantastic opportunities to work in various ministry contexts, acquire advanced degrees, and learn from senior chaplain mentors. Air Force chaplains must learn to function as part of a multidenominational team ministry. In addition to working at a base or command level, chaplains may work directly for a commander or support unique groups like Special Forces and Intelligence.[263] These are unique opportunities to lead a two-person team as members of a squadron or group apart from the base chapel team. It is often the first opportunity for a chaplain to shoulder the full responsibility for an entire unit's "soul care" and supervise an enlisted Religious Affairs Airman as part of a Religious Support Team (RST).

Air Force chaplains are subject to a high rate of deployments. Mission objectives and personnel rotation cycles determine the length of the deployment. While being away from one's family can create personal challenges, ministry in deployment locations can provide vibrant ministry opportunities. Air Force chaplains and Religious Affairs Airmen transform ordinary places in the harshest environments into sacred places of worship and hope. Chaplains offer prayers in guard towers and briefing rooms, worship services in aircraft and tents, and counseling in the privacy of a forgotten office or the back of a cargo plane. Chaplains face all the perils of war as they provide "ministry of presence or purpose" in the most volatile regions on earth. Chaplains encourage the living, pray for the wounded, and minister to the dying.

People may speak of "combat chaplains," but this term is an oxymoron. Air Force chaplains are noncombatants. They do not carry or use weapons. They do not fly aircraft, guard the perimeter, or gather intelligence on the enemy. As ordained clergy, military chaplains provide ministry for combatants: praying, counseling, preaching, and offering spiritual ministry to men and women in crisis.

## SAFEGUARD THREE IMPERATIVES

As you consider becoming an Air Force chaplain, permit me to share three things my dad told me. First, hold tight to your faith. You do not have to compromise your message or rein in your passion for God. You are a chaplain called by God and endorsed by a specific religious faith group to minister to military people. Do not let anything distract you from the ministry God has given you. For example, if you are a Christian chaplain, you represent Christ

---

[263] The Air Force has established a variety of resiliency programs. One example, inspired by the United States Special Operations Command's Preservation of the Force and Family Program, was "True North." This initiative embedded mental health professionals, physiologists, physical therapists, and a religious support team within high-risk groups of a wing.

and the Christian faith. It is the same for Jewish and Islamic chaplains as they represent their faith group equally. You are not a morale officer who tries to make people happy and comfortable. God calls you to make a difference. You are to make disciples and help them grow in their faith.

Second, do not neglect your own spiritual life. Chaplains bring a word from God, strengthen marriages, support families, and help singles build a foundation of faith. But if the chaplain's spirit is weak, that person will be poorly equipped to help others. Learn the art of running into the arms of God. Nourish your faith. If your spiritual well goes dry, you cannot bring living water to the thirsty.

Finally, take care of your family. "God first, family second, ministry third . . . no exceptions." The old witticism states, "If the military wants you to have a family, they will issue you one." On the contrary, the Air Force expends a great deal of leadership energy and money to care for and support families. The Air Force is known to be the most family-friendly of all the military services. Unfortunately, chaplains can easily focus so much on their career or ministry that they unintentionally sacrifice their own family. As the Air Force values families, chaplains must also prioritize their own families, second only to God.

My family has come full circle. Just as I was involved in my dad's military ministry, now my sons play guitar for the chapel services, help with the teen ministry, and work with the children while I lead worship services or marriage enrichment events. Even though our children have moved nine times in the past twenty-one years, being a part of the Air Force Chaplain Corps family has been as instrumental in their spiritual development as it was in mine so many years ago. If God calls you and your family to serve and minister in the Air Force Chaplain Corps, we look forward to having you as part of our Air Force family.

# MEMORABLE MOMENT
# "A LIGHT AMID THE DARKNESS"

### Dr. Jim Browning

Most chaplains attend to survivors of a tragedy. Typically, a chaplain will assist others in informing a parent or spouse of their loved one's death. Experiencing their immediate anguish cuts deep into your own heart and can lead to a cumulative burden of experiencing the grief of others. When the Army Field Mortuary personnel at Baghdad International Airport requested me, I was not sure I could face the sting of death again. A very dark dread came over me as I entered the mortuary tent. I was not sure if I could personally get through it, let alone minister to the three Army personnel who were grieving over the death of their two battle buddies.

This brush with death was not my first experience. Nor was it my last in my nearly twenty-nine years as an Air Force chaplain. Throughout my career, I would be the "visible reminder of the Holy" for many grieving at the loss of life. Within two months of my active-duty career, I assisted in supporting the search and recovery team that retrieved the four dismembered bodies of a KC-135 plane in-flight explosion and crash and participated in helping the families and friends with a memorial. I had many other events to follow: a U-2 plane crash killing one, a helicopter crash killing six, several vehicle/motorcycle crashes, an airman's murder of his commander, numerous suicides, and the list goes on and on. I also served at Dover Air Force Base, where my responsibilities included organizing and providing spiritual care and support to grieving families and the Charles C. Carson Center for Mortuary Affairs staff.

In my time at Dover AFB, we cared for the remains of fifteen mass casualties' events, including the USS *Cole* terrorist bombing, the 2003 Space Shuttle *Columbia* explosion, and the Pentagon 9/11 terrorist attack. Additionally, in my deployments, my team or I would help honor the remains of those killed in action in Iraq and Afghanistan. After an honor guard would load the flag-draped cases on air transport to the States, we would be inside the plane's cargo hold and offer a prayer. These events, involving approximately 680 casualties, created a cumulative effect that deeply scarred my heart.

So, when the request came, it was all I could do to force myself to go back into the dark presence of body bags. I honestly did not want to do it. Yet I knew I had to meet this request. The mortuary personnel asked me to come immediately as several soldiers had accompanied two of their fallen battle buddies. The soldiers wanted me to come and pray for them and their fallen comrades' families. I wondered if I could function as a seasoned Air Force chaplain called to support the Army chaplaincy's "nurture the living, care for the wounded, honor the fallen." The immediacy of their request mandated I perform this solemn role. The responsibility fell to me alone. Reluctantly, I had to embrace it.

Entering the makeshift mortuary, I already knew the layout and the personnel as I had previously visited them. Upon entering, I saw the traumatized faces of three soldiers who stood as a silent sentry to their fallen. After engaging them pastorally and hearing their specific request, I cleared my actions with the mortuary personnel.

I slowly unzipped the body bag of both soldiers, just enough to expose their faces and the upper portions of their bodies. A roadside explosion had killed them. I joined them in a circle. We stood for a long moment in silent prayer, and then I offered a prayer for these fallen warriors' families and these grieving battle buddies. After the prayer, I closed the body bags and spent a long time listening to these men. My ministry was one of presence and support. They thanked me for my prayer and my supportive care of them and their fallen friends. They left to return to their mission.

I stood silently as I again had to process a death experience. Wiping the tears from my eyes, I recognized what a solemn privilege of representing Christ, who also cried beside the graveside of his friend.[264] Just as He was visibly moved by the grave's darkness, so was I. Somehow, we all found the strength to push forward. Others depended upon us. We had a job to do. We all left, knowing this experience would deeply impact each of us. Later that day, I prayed over their flag-draped cases after an honor guard loaded them on a C-17 plane for their return to Dover and their families. This time, I had

---

[264] John 11:35

seen the fallen and spoken to their grieving battle buddies. Once again, the sacred calling to accompany and provide professional support and spiritual nurture for these grieving men humbled me.

Life happens. Sometimes, it is dark and ominous. Chaplains are often called to walk into the midst of the storm and its darkness. We have the solemn and precious opportunity to bring a "visible presence of the Holy," a light into the midst of the darkness.[265]

## REFLECTION QUESTIONS

1. Military chaplains are "pastors to some" but "chaplains to all." What issues might arise as chaplains seek to meet the pastoral and spiritual needs of officers and enlisted?
2. How can a chaplain's presence impact military personnel in combat or high-stress situations?
3. What would you advise new military chaplains to do to maintain their spiritual health and resilience while constantly tending to the emotional and spiritual needs of others?
4. Considering the broad range of duties performed by military chaplains, what qualities do you think are essential for someone serving in this capacity? Why?
5. Of the different branches, which type of military chaplaincy most interests you? Why?

---

[265] Matt 5:14–16

CHAPTER EIGHTEEN

# CORRECTIONAL CHAPLAINCY

## Dr. Vance Drum

The first day I walked into my prison chaplain's office in 1985, I looked around and knew why I was there. The hippie-era, 1970s wall poster, left by the previous chaplain, still spoke wisdom to all who entered: "Today is the First Day of the Rest of Your Life." I was there to bring hope and provide options for a better way of doing one's life. I discovered all of that was true and much more I didn't then know. Although I had already served as a volunteer chaplain in the Dallas County (Texas) Jail, I had much more to learn about ministry to the incarcerated.

It wouldn't be easy. The hundred-year-old Eastham Prison—America's Toughest[266]—in East Texas, former residence of Clyde Barrow (of the Bonnie and Clyde gang), had a well-deserved reputation for being a violent, end of the road, worst of the worst of America's prisons. But God had called me to be there, and I stayed twenty-seven years. It would be quite a trip.

Tom Beckner describes incarceration well as like being in "the belly of a great whale. . . . The chaplain sits in the belly, greeting those who arrive with respect as fellow children of God gone seriously astray and offering them comfort, care, and good counsel during their stay."[267]

---

[266] Daniel Pedersen, Daniel Shapiro, and Ann McDaniel, "Inside America's Toughest Prison," *Newsweek* (6 October 1986): 46–61.

[267] W. Thomas Beckner, *Correctional Chaplains: Keepers of the Cloak* (Orlando: Cappella Press, 2012), 76.

## OVERVIEW

What is a professional correctional chaplain? Early in my prison chaplaincy ministry, my Director of Chaplains Emmett Solomon, the previous Eastham chaplain who had left the poster, encouraged chaplains to attend the American Correctional Association conferences. I did and in 2007 presented a workshop there on the subject: who is a professional chaplain to the incarcerated. I wrote: "A professional correctional chaplain is one who, with specialized knowledge and extended training, is called and compensated to facilitate religious services and provide pastoral care to incarcerated persons of all faiths in an institution."[268] Correctional chaplains have two primary missions in their work on behalf of the incarcerated: (a) facilitate the free exercise of religion and (b) provide opportunities for moral rehabilitation and life management learning.

## FREE EXERCISE OF RELIGION

Inmates confined to an institution do not lose their constitutional right to practice their religion because of their confinement. The First Amendment to the US Constitution states: "Congress shall make no law respecting an establishment of religion, or prohibiting the free exercise thereof."[269]

Courts have historically ruled that prisoners have the right to exercise their faith.[270] State governments provide and compensate chaplains to facilitate this fundamental religious liberty guaranteed by our country's founding document. In addition, in its standards for accreditation of correctional

---

[268] Vance Drum, "Professional Correctional Chaplains: Fact and Fiction," workshop, American Correctional Association Congress of Correction, 13 August 2007, Kansas City, MO, http://www.correctionalchaplains.org/, accessed 28 September 2021.

[269] See https://www.archives.gov/founding-docs/bill-of-rights/what-does-it-say, accessed 28 September 2021.

[270] For example, see *Cutter v. Wilkinson* (2005), https://www.law.cornell.edu/supct/html/03-9877.ZS.html, accessed 28 September 2021. This Supreme Court case upheld prisoners' religious rights articulated in the Religious Land Use and Institutionalized Persons Act of 2000 (RLUIPA), https://www.justice.gov/crt/religious-land-use-and-institutionalized-persons-act-0, accessed 28 September 2021.

facilities, the premier professional association in US corrections, the American Correctional Association, requires the presence of facility chaplains.[271]

How does free exercise of religion in corrections work? In 2005, the Supreme Court upheld the Religious Land Use and Institutionalized Persons Act of 2000 (RLUIPA),[272] which noted that religious exercise in prisons requires unique safeguards for proper enforcement. The Court gave four requirements for facilitating the First Amendment in prisons:

- **Sincerely held belief.** The inmate must have a sincerely held religious belief.
- **Substantial burden.** Government must not impose a substantial burden on free exercise.
- **Compelling governmental interest.** If an incarcerated person's religious exercise is to be restricted, there must be a compelling governmental interest in doing so. The most common compelling interest is in guaranteeing the safety and security of the institution.
- **Least restrictive means.** If religious exercise is to be restricted for incarcerated persons, it must be done with the least restrictive means to secure the government's compelling interest. In an analogy: if a fly swatter will do the job, do not use a hammer.

Correctional leadership (executive leadership, attorneys, directors of chaplains) must make numerous policy and procedure decisions on facilitating free exercise of religion in their institutions. There are currently more than four hundred self-identified religions among the inmate population in Texas, all seeking congregational accommodation. The problem is how to provide for "free exercise" for different faith groups within the walls of a facility in a given week. Outside of prison, persons may congregate anywhere—in a facility, in a house, under a tree—and they may worship at any time. But in prison, time and space limitations are complicated issues. Many states

---

[271] American Correctional Association, Department of Performance-Based Standards and Accreditation, "Performance-Based Expected Practices for Adult Correctional Institutions," Standards #5-7-F-4512—5-7-F-4513, 5th edition, 2018.
[272] *Cutter v. Wilkinson* (2005).

have accommodated the "free exercise" by placing numbers of denominational faiths with similar core beliefs under ten to twenty larger, congregating umbrella groups.

For example, Protestant Christian denominations are typically grouped in one worship service. It works. In the prison worship experience, commonalities of all denominations are emphasized and each group's distinctions are deemphasized. All Protestant Christians hold certain religious beliefs in common. They worship together and express their essential unity at the same time. As my director of chaplains, Emmett Solomon, often said, "If you get the Ten Commandments and the Sermon on the Mount mastered, you've come a long way down the road toward doing what's right."

Chaplains, free-world volunteers, and inmate peer ministers[273] approved by the chaplain—all teach what they believe. Because the inmate population is religiously diverse, a well-rounded chaplaincy program will express various denominational viewpoints. In the Protestant group, clergy from various denominations will minister, and each service will reflect the "flavor" of the minister's faith. The chaplain will take care to instruct all ministers not to disparage other religions or races. That is against prison policy, and the "no disparaging" rule must be strictly honored. Additionally, ministers should be careful not to emphasize continually denominational distinctions in a way that causes inmates who believe differently to feel excluded. A chaplain should conduct worship services, so all present find them meaningful and spiritually edifying.

## MORAL REHABILITATION AND LIFE MANAGEMENT PROGRAMS

A second central mission of chaplains, no less important than facilitating free exercise, is to provide moral rehabilitation and life management opportunities through rehabilitation and reentry programs. In the United States, there are vast numbers of people who have little to no exposure to prosocial, healthy ways of doing one's life. Many have never learned it is wrong to steal

---

[273] See www.prisonseminaries.org for information on the Prison Seminary Model and inmate peer ministers.

because they were not in church growing up; their homes may have been amoral, dysfunctional, or abusive; and public schools did not teach much about the difference between right and wrong. Stealing your neighbor's stuff, as well as other moral issues, may never have been discussed as being wrong as they grew up. Statistics show that children of prison inmates are up to five times[274] more likely to go to prison than those whose parents were not in custody. One distinctive feature of correctional chaplaincy is the development of effective programs that give inmates an awareness of other, better ways to live than going in and out of prison.

One substantial benefit of moral rehabilitation programs is that they help reduce recidivism: the rate of return to prison. Currently, the Texas recidivism rate is one of the lowest in the nation at 21 percent after three years out of prison. Texas has closed ten prisons over the past ten years, and the prison population has declined by about 35,000.[275]

Many ways of doing moral rehabilitation programs exist. One of the most visible and impactful initiatives is the Prison Seminary Model. In this nationwide program, qualified inmates volunteer to be trained in a four-year, accredited seminary degree program, after which they are transferred throughout the state's prisons to become ministers to their fellow prisoners. Effects of the program at Louisiana's formerly notorious Angola Prison were researched and found to positively transform individual prisoners and the violent Angola prison culture.[276]

Faith-based dorms, or Character-formation Housing Areas, are another means of training in moral values and effective life management. In these housing areas, correctional officials group inmates "to offer support for offenders who desire to incorporate religious faith and practice in a group setting."[277] Rehabilitation and reentry courses are a central part of the

---

[274] H. Zehr, "Justice for Children Whose Parents Are in Prison," Eastern Mennonite University, Zehr Institute for Restorative Justice Blog, 10 December 2010, https://emu.edu/now/restorative-justice/2010/12/10/justice-for-children-whose-parents-are-in-prison/, accessed 5 October 2021.

[275] Texas Department of Criminal Justice, Office of Executive Services, https://www.tdcj.texas.gov/publications/index.html#Executive, accessed 4 January 2021.

[276] Michael Hallett et al., *The Angola Prison Seminary: Effects of Faith-Based Ministry on Identity Transformation, Desistance, and Rehabilitation* (New York: Routledge, 2017).

[277] "Annual Review of Fiscal Year 2017," Texas Department of Criminal Justice, https://www.tdcj.texas.gov/documents/Annual_Review_2017.pdf, accessed 4 January 2021.

program, which continues for six to twenty-four months. After completing the program, graduated inmates are distributed throughout the facility to help transform the environment with prosocial influence.

Another type of program is the Big Event. A group, perhaps a large one, of free-world volunteers conducts a big event, or series of events, perhaps over multiple days, in the facility or on a recreation yard. One example is the Kairos program, a short course in Christianity designed primarily for non-chapel participants. Other significant events may bring in professional athletes or other performers to testify how God has changed their lives. The purpose is to let inmates know that God loves them, the volunteers care about them, and there are other ways of doing their lives than their previously chosen paths.

Family ministries, including marriage seminars, parenting classes, and family events (Day with Dad, Day with Mom), provide a time when family members come into the facility for a volunteer-directed, all-day event. Typically, inmates and family alike long remember it as an enriching experience.

Other programs include many varieties of addiction recovery. One of the best known, Celebrate Recovery,[278] is a ministry begun in California's Saddleback Church. This six-month, faith-based course covers issues such as divorce, sexual abuse, codependency, domestic violence, and addictions to alcohol, drugs, sex, gambling, and food.

Moral rehabilitation and successful reentry are goals of many state departments of correction, as seen in the Texas Department of Criminal Justice mission statement: "to provide public safety, promote positive change in offender behavior, reintegrate offenders into society, and assist victims of crime."[279] Chaplains help provide valuable opportunities for personal and spiritual growth. It is meaningful for the chaplain and potentially life-changing for the inmate.

## SHOULD YOU CONSIDER CORRECTIONAL CHAPLAINCY?

Being a correctional chaplain is not for everybody. Working with jail detainees or convicted prisoners can be stressful. However, if God calls one to be

---

[278] See www.celebraterecovery.com, accessed 28 September 2021.

[279] www.tdcj.texas.gov, accessed 28 September 2021.

a correctional chaplain, it is one of the most rewarding vocations one can choose. That was my experience. I loved my work and never burned out in my thirty-eight years as a chaplain working behind bars.

Minimum qualifications for correctional chaplains vary from state to state.[280] In most states, they consist of a combination of education (usually a bachelor's or seminary master's degree) and ministerial experience (usually between one and three years). Most states require ordination and ecclesiastical endorsement. Some states require Clinical Pastoral Education (CPE) or other supervised ministry experience for initial hiring or promotion.

Successful correctional chaplains possess several attributes. The first is to care about what happens to people. God loves guilty prisoners, and chaplains, as God's representatives, should too: "Then they cried to the Lord in their trouble, and he saved them from their distress."[281] At the same time, chaplains must be aware of boundaries: the rules and regulations of the jail, prison, or juvenile facility; state and federal laws; and personal boundaries, which must not be violated. A chaplain without boundaries will not long continue in this vocation.

Effective chaplains are not territorial. They work collaboratively with other facility chaplains and recruit and welcome good chaplaincy volunteers. They affirm and supervise inmate peer ministers. In an era of tight state budgets, the number of hired chaplains is insufficient, but volunteer help adds to the correctional ministry from outside and within the prison.

Chaplains also understand they are members of the team. They work in collaboration with their chaplaincy, administrative, and security leaders. They are flexible as needed. Chaplains are relational. They care and support both staff and inmates. Their "ministry of presence" is felt throughout the facility.

Finally, chaplains have a spiritual core. They have wisdom from being in touch with God and God's people. They are empathetic listeners, educated in their profession, who prayerfully make wise decisions, show respect toward all, and endeavor to continue learning.

---

[280] Beckner, *Correctional Chaplains*, appendix.
[281] Ps 107:13

# FEDERAL BUREAU OF PRISONS CHAPLAINCY

## Chaplain Joe Pryor

Two dates are never far from my thoughts when I reflect on my twenty-one years as a chaplain in the Federal Bureau of Prisons: Sunday, November 4, 1990, when I started my ministry at the Federal Correctional Institution in Tallahassee, Florida, and Friday, November 12, 2011, when I walked out of the door in the Central Office in Washington, DC, for the last time.

Both days were emotional for me. The first date evoked fear and anticipation, as I had never spent more than a few hours ministering in a prison and had little clue as to what trials and challenges awaited me. The last date was an unexpected shock to my system. Anticipating moving on to new challenges and leaving the stress of my position as Chief Chaplain behind me, I did not expect to break down in tears when I read through the congratulatory letters my fellow chaplains had sent me. As the Chief Chaplain, I saw myself as "their" chaplain. No longer was that the case. I also took time to reflect on the journey I had as a chaplain and remain aware to this day of the challenges my fellow chaplains still face in federal prisons all across the country. More so than any other ministry I have personally encountered, chaplains in the Federal Bureau of Prisons form a kinship and fellowship that stretches beyond their careers.

## A COMPLEX COMMITMENT

As a federal prison chaplain, I served in low and high-security institutions, a female medical center, and regional and central office positions. I have witnessed dozens of other dedicated chaplains offer pastoral comfort to grieving and struggling prisoners regardless of whether or not they were people of strong faith or no faith at all. Providing ministry, regardless of one's faith (or lack thereof) is the hallmark of being a chaplain in the Federal Bureau of Prisons. Chaplains are called to minister to every person, inmate, or staff in their institution. It is a ministry of constant presence.

Federal prison chaplains regularly dine with prisoners to celebrate holy days with a ceremonial meal. They hear the call to prayer from Muslims and witness the blowing of the shofar by the Jews. They marvel at the meaningful dances of the Native Americans and the reverence of Mass by the Catholics. They tiptoe past the quiet meditation of the Buddhists and rejoice with Protestant Christians in songs of praise. They sway to the reggae rhythms of the Rastafarians and appreciate the devotion to the earth of the nature-based religions.

While chaplains hold firmly to their faith and call to ministry, they must be committed to protecting the religious freedoms of all faiths even when those faiths stand in stark contradiction and are often diametrically opposed to their own beliefs. In protecting the religious freedom of others, chaplains realize they are protecting their own at the same time. I have seen more than a few dedicated and committed Christian chaplains who just could not adjust personally to this environment.

Many saw the requirement to accommodate the religious practices of other faiths as a direct affront to their own faith and over time departed chaplain ministry. I have also witnessed others see the correctional environment as a mission field where they seek to evangelize everyone in prison and do everything they can to suppress the religious practices of other faiths. Neither path is productive in the Federal Prison System. The mission of the Chaplaincy Department of the Federal Bureau of Prisons is

> to accommodate the free exercise of religion by providing pastoral care to all Federal inmates and facilitate the opportunity to pursue individual religious beliefs and practices in accordance with the law, Federal regulations, and Bureau of Prisons policies. Chaplains will provide religious worship, education, counseling, spiritual direction, support, and crisis intervention to accommodate the diverse religious needs of inmates. When appropriate, pastoral care may be extended to staff.[282]

In this mission statement, chaplains in the Federal Bureau of Prisons define their existence. They are truly frontline defenders of the free exercise of religion as defined in the First Amendment of the Constitution: "Congress shall make no law respecting an establishment of religion, or prohibiting the free

---

[282] "Ministry of BOP Chaplains," Bureau of Prisons, 18 November 2004, https://www.bop.gov/policy/technical/5360_02.pdf, accessed 28 September 2021.

exercise thereof. . . ."[283] The mission statement and the First Amendment provide the broad framework for the obligation of the Federal Prison Chaplain. However, several recommendations help ensure a successful and meaningful ministry in the Federal Bureau of Prisons.

## THE BOUNDARIES OF POLICY

Early in my first assignment at the Federal Correctional Institution in Tallahassee, Florida, my supervisor gave me good advice: not only to know policy, but if I always stayed within its boundaries, I would have a long career. I found this to be true time and time again. Every time a decision of mine was challenged, I could point to policy, and the matter would be resolved.

A "Religious Beliefs and Practices" policy guides chaplaincy in the Federal Bureau of Prisons. The policy purposefully has both bold and regular print. The bold type is "rules language" and is directly quoted from the Code of Federal Regulations. This code is a series of books that lay out clearly for agencies how laws are to be applied in their day-to-day operations. In "Religious Beliefs and Practices," the bold type emphasizes the direct interpretation of law. The Department of Justice receives petitions for changes or amendments of its verbiage and vets all proposed changes through public scrutiny and comment. I learned from experience this is a process that can take five years or longer. In other words, these words in policy are a serious guide for chaplains and their daily activities.

The regular font in the policy is "implementation language" and how the Federal Bureau of Prisons interprets the "rules language" at the agency level. With many different missions in the federal prison system, each facility produces a document called an Operations Memorandum that further defines the policy at the local level. Knowledge of and adherence to these policies are essential to a long and effective ministry in this arena.

## RELATIONSHIPS WITH INMATES

At the core of chaplaincy in the Federal Bureau of Prisons is the chaplain's rapport and communication with inmates. Ninety-five percent of the chaplain's

---

[283] See https://www.archives.gov/founding-docs/bill-of-rights/what-does-it-say, accessed 28 September 2021.

time will be spent in the presence of inmates from a variety of faith traditions, ethnicities, and racial and cultural backgrounds. The word *relationship* should never be used in describing how a chaplain and inmate interact. This is a slippery slope. I have seen chaplains who have lost their ministry, their families, and even spent time in prison themselves because they crossed the boundary into having a personal relationship with an inmate.

Yet, chaplains are called to be pastoral, compassionate, and caring in their ministry. This is a delicate balance to say the least, and not all ministers are well-suited to take on this role. Several rules apply that are timeless and effective. First, never take anything from or give anything to an inmate in your care. The simple act of mailing a letter for an inmate can spiral out of control and lead to more dangerous requests. Second, never share information about your personal life, including placing family photographs in your office. Some things are unavoidable.

For instance, at one prison where I served, the parking lot was just outside the fence from the recreation yard. An inmate approached me and had noticed I was driving a new car. She began asking questions about the car, if it would fit my family comfortably, how much it cost, and so on. My standard response was, "I'm sorry, but I don't discuss anything about my personal life." At first, as a compassionate minister, I worried this would hurt someone's feelings. It never did and always redirected the conversation.

Chaplains, however, are free to discuss and share their faith, as long as it doesn't denigrate or criticize other religions. I have an expression I have used dozens of times with inmates in my care: "I believe what I believe because I believe that what I believe is right. But so do you, so let's talk." This one silly phrase has led to hundreds of great conversations. The willingness to listen to someone else's beliefs without being judgmental or feeling threatened, had the remarkable effect of opening an opportunity for me to share my Christian faith.

Another effective way to build positive rapport with inmates in your care is to provide for their religious ceremonies to the extent appropriate. In the Federal Bureau of Prisons, every religious group has the opportunity to celebrate one "ceremonial or commemorative" meal each calendar year. These have been toned down a bit over the years, but they could be quite lavish in my early career. Some of the meals were ceremonial, like the Passover meal for the Jews, while some were more traditional, like the Eid Feast for Muslims, which officially ends the month-long fast of Ramadan.

Provision of these special meals is a clear and visible signal to the inmate population of how much the chaplains care about them and their faith. The invitation to join the meal, and I always waited for one, was the sign I had provided well, and that I, and my fellow chaplains, were welcome to share in their celebration.

A final way to establish positive rapport is to respond appropriately to a crisis. Beyond the expected emergencies of an illness or death in the family, unusual things always occur in the correctional environment. In 1995, I experienced a riot at the prison where I was serving. By the time I reported to the facility, my fellow chaplain was already there. Hundreds of inmates were being detained with plastic flexi-cuffs on their wrists and ankles in a long basement corridor. When I arrived, I witnessed a weary chaplain lifting inmates onto a rolling office chair, and wheeling them one by one to use the restroom. This personal, intimate, and caring response to meet a common human need earned this chaplain the respect of every inmate in the facility.

## MINISTRY TO STAFF

While the primary mission of chaplains is to provide for the equitable accommodation of religious practice and to offer a pastoral presence to inmates, when necessary, their ministry extends to staff as well. I have had the privilege of performing several weddings for fellow staff members. I have also responded to tragedies ranging from counseling couples in crisis, to performing a funeral service for a staff member murdered by his spouse. Day to day, I had numerous opportunities just to sit and speak with staff as they navigated the choppy waters of working in a prison.

The most crucial staff relationship the chaplain should cultivate is with the facility's warden. The warden carries a heavy load and has to appear unmoved by stress and crisis that are unceasing. Establishing this highly sensitive and confidential relationship will be invaluable to the warden who manages life and death situations every day.

## REWARDING BUT NOT FOR EVERYONE

Serving as a chaplain in the Federal Bureau of Prisons for twenty-one years was a rewarding and satisfying experience. This chapter does not begin to describe the vast number of opportunities to minister to people in one of the most desperate situations in life. Inmates are separated from family and friends, many have lost careers and reputations, and all will bear the stigma of "felon" for the rest of their lives. The loss of hope and sense of purpose in their lives is immense, and oftentimes it is through the chaplain that restoration takes place.

It is appropriate to close with an admonition that chaplains must take care of themselves and remember their priorities. Nurture your spiritual well-being by staying close to a community of faith; this will sustain you as you minister to others. Equally as important is placing your family ahead of your ministry in prison. I have seen many families fall by the wayside due to the neglect of a well-meaning, sacrificial chaplain. Take uncompromised time with your family. Finally, know when to walk away, even if for a short break. The burnout rate among chaplains is astounding and can lead to devastating results.

This ministry is not for everyone, but for those who feel called into this arena, may God bless you with the sensibilities and faith to sustain you.

# JAILS AND STATE PRISONS CHAPLAINCY

## Dr. Vance Drum

Distinctions exist between jails and state prisons. In the United States, jails are generally, but not always, facilities for holding arrested persons in pretrial detention. Prisons are nearly always used for incarcerating adults convicted of felonies. Opportunities for programmatic, rehabilitative treatment are frequently offered in juvenile facilities and prisons but seldom in pretrial detention jails.

## A BRIEF HISTORY

The first city jail with a penitential purpose was the Walnut Street Prison, a house for the penitent (hence, "penitentiary"), established in Philadelphia in 1773. The prison was closed in 1838 when officials discovered total solitary confinement in cells that eliminated all communication promoted insanity instead.[284] In 1870 in Cincinnati, Ohio, after witnessing starving prisoners of war straggling home at the end of the Civil War, concerned clergypersons, civic leaders, and prison wardens founded the National Prison Association, now the American Correctional Association. Their compassionate goal was to make prisons safer and more humane places to live and work. Ohio's reform governor, Rutherford B. Hayes, was elected the first president of the association; six years later, he was elected US president. Clergypersons had (and still have) an important role in corrections. For example, the Declaration of Principles adopted in 1870 by the association states: "Of all reformatory agencies, religion is first in importance, because [it is] most potent in its action upon the human heart and life."[285]

---

[284] Ashley Rubin and Keramet Reiter, "Continuity in the Face of Penal Innovation: Revisiting the History of American Solitary Confinement," *Law & Social Inquiry Journal of the American Bar Foundation* 43 (4) (Fall 2018), https://www.cambridge.org/core/journals/law-and-social-inquiry/article/abs/continuity-in-the-face-of-penal-innovation-revisiting-the-history-of-american-solitary-confinement/E3BE3440816D9608B8FDED536686B4C7, accessed 28 September 2021.

[285] "Declaration of Principles Adopted and Promulgated by the 1870 Congress of the National Prison Association," American Correctional Association, http://www.aca.org/ACA_PROD_IMIS/docs/1870Declaration_of_Principles.pdf, accessed 28 September 2021.

Chaplains are still a vital component of the correctional team. In the nation's more than eleven hundred state and federal prisons, the Pew Forum reported the presence of at least one paid chaplain or religious services coordinator resulting in the employment of about seventeen hundred professional chaplains.

## JAIL CHAPLAINCY

My feelings on first entering the massive, foreboding Dallas County Jail were a mixture of anticipation and apprehension. I had never been in a jail, juvenile detention facility, or prison for any reason—as a detainee or volunteer. The loud clanging finality of the gates closing and locking behind me, putting me in close proximity to thousands of inmates awaiting trial, was a bit unnerving. However, I went in as a volunteer with an experienced volunteer chaplain, and he assured me things would be OK. He was right.

The primary mission of city and county jails in the United States is to maintain secure custody of incarcerated persons within their walls. Most jail inmates are pre-trial detainees. A lesser number may be serving a short sentence, typically less than two years. The total adult jail population in the US in 2016 numbered approximately 810,000.[286]

A secondary mission of jails is to provide pastoral care for detained inmates. Spiritual care may include cell-side visitation by the chaplain, providing reading material including Bibles and other texts, authorizing emergency phone calls in the event of family member death or severe illness, and facilitating worship services.

When a person goes to jail, a number of emotions arise. For the person arrested for the first time, fear and dread of the unknown and of a court's judgment may be primary feelings. For others, who have been arrested and in court multiple times, there may be feelings of resignation and thoughts of "Here we go again." Some detainees see jail and even prison time as a normal part of the cost of doing business in the underworld. They may have no desire to change. Others, for whom doing time in jail or prison is getting old, may be open to doing their lives differently. Such persons may respond positively

---

[286] "Key Statistics: Total Correctional Population," Bureau of Justice Statistics, http://bjs.ojp.gov/data/key-statistics#citation--1, accessed 26 December 2020.

to a caring chaplain's pastoral initiatives. Some persons in jail learn a valuable life lesson through the experience and never return.

## STATE PRISON CHAPLAINCY

While some dynamics of jail experiences are also present in prisons, other factors are much different. Among jail and juvenile populations, internal bargaining with God often occurs. "God, if you get me out of this mess, I promise to change my ways and never come back." In prison, however, the die is cast, the judge and jury have spoken, and prisoners sit in a cell for two to fifty years, for life or life without parole. For the first-time inmate, the experience of taking a long ride on a chain bus from jail to prison, getting off, and walking behind the walls can be supremely sobering and disturbing.

However, all may not be lost when one goes to prison. It is not the end of the world, nor the end of one's life. It could be the beginning. Prison is a long-term arrest from a previous way of life. It is meditation time—lots of time to think. For those who believe in God, they may think: "God has stopped me. Thank God." Because of restrictions and supervision, opportunities for bad behavior are less abundant in prison than outside of prison. Of course, antisocial things still happen; but reaching the "bottom of the barrel" may mean giving up a dysfunctional and destructive life and being willing to consider alternatives.

It can be akin to Step One in the Alcoholics Anonymous program: "We admitted we were powerless over alcohol—that our lives had become unmanageable."[287] For many, if they were not in prison, they might be dead. Chaplains are aware of these intrapersonal dynamics, so they are interested in personally reaching out with pastoral care and faith-based programs to the inmate population, welcoming the help of trained community volunteers, and utilizing inmate volunteer assistance.

## PROGRAM MANAGEMENT

The days of the chaplain sitting in an office waiting to respond to the next emergency are over. Twenty-first century chaplaincy is robust and proactive.

---

[287] "The 12 Steps of Alcoholics Anonymous," American Addiction Centers, https://www.alcohol.org/alcoholics-anonymous, accessed 26 December 2020.

The facility administrator wants to know about your chaplaincy program, so stay in touch. But wardens do not want to know all the program details: they trust you to manage your program well. Stop at the front office with a friendly greeting to the administrators and staff daily when you arrive at the facility.

Part of chaplaincy management is providing worship services for the faith groups present, as much as possible, following the guidance of your state chaplaincy leaders and the institution's policies. It is important not to go beyond your written policies and procedures when arranging faith-group worship. Inmates may have requests you cannot honor. Respectfully let them know, without showing favoritism. For worship services of religions not your own, have your community or inmate volunteers, selected by you, conduct them.

Sometimes chaplains question whether they may conscientiously facilitate (not conduct) a worship service of a faith different than their own. Think of chaplains as First Amendment traffic officers, like those directing traffic on Christmas Eve outside a large city megachurch. The officer directs those who wish to worship into the parking lot, motioning others to go on down the road. His directing traffic does not make him an adherent of the faith of those going into the parking lot. It makes him an officer of the state honoring the First Amendment guarantee of freedom of worship. Chaplains are like that. They do not worship with practitioners of other faiths. Instead, they facilitate the "free exercise" right of others to do so.

Another aspect of inmate program management is vital: the supervision of programs. If inmates can carry on their conversations during a chapel program, the event will devolve into chaos. I posted and periodically explained a notice I placed on the chapel bulletin board: "The only chapel meeting which is authorized is the meeting I've called. S/ Chaplain Vance Drum." It was necessary, and I quietly and unobtrusively enforced the rule.

I always did some preaching and teaching in the Protestant services I conducted. Inmates needed to hear what I believed, and they needed to know my care for them by bringing Scripture to them. I preached both law and grace, with an emphasis on grace.[288]

---

[288] John 1:17 and Jas 2:13.

## PASTORAL CARE

Delivering emergency messages, consisting of family member death or illness, and providing a phone call, are priorities in the chaplain's day. I followed the institutional policy on emergencies. Otherwise, I would have become a "telephone chaplain" with a line a mile long outside my door. Do the delivery according to your agency's policy, always with gentleness, directness, and sensitivity.

Other chaplaincy duties in prisons include ministry to staff and administrative duties. I had to learn to love the staff. I began not having any love for them in 1985 when times were different. When I repented, things changed dramatically for the better. Be sure to greet all the staff you meet. God loves them too, and they have significant needs in a stressful work environment.

Finally, the word *administration* which we may think of as paperwork, is rooted in the word *ministration*. It is a ministry to create paperwork for volunteers to enter, programs to happen, and progress to be reported. Think of it as part of God's work, because it is.

# JUVENILE CHAPLAINCY

Chaplain R. Steve Lowe

## INTRODUCTION

Many in the church community resist working with teenagers, often seeing them as a hot mess of hormones, immaturity, instability, and a flux of identity changes. I am amazed at this attitude by older adults who can remember with clarity certain caring adults who willingly invested in them during their own "hot mess" teenage years. Combined with this troublesome resistance is the additional dynamic of teenagers in lockup, labeled as delinquents and losers who will never change. The result is a critical lack of juvenile chaplains and volunteers nationwide. With more than one thousand public juvenile facilities in America housing approximately fifty thousand youth on any given day, the field is ripe for harvest, but the workers are few.

One of the key obstacles in creating juvenile ministry is that most churches and community-based organizations choose the titles "Jail Ministry" or "Prison Ministry," which focus on adult-only ministry. As a result, juvenile ministry remains off the grid for anyone interested in pursuing it. Every time I have spoken at a church, people approach me with the same response, "I have had a burden for juveniles, but I did not know of any opportunities." Think of how many church members, both nationally and internationally, carry a God-given burden for youth in lockup but are entirely unaware of these ministry opportunities. Ministry to these troubled youth would be better recognized if every "jail or prison ministry" held the better title of "correctional ministry." However, this is rarely the case. Chaplains are in a vital position to help educate the faith communities about these concerns and the ministry needs of those in juvenile facilities.

## NEEDS OF JUSTICE-INVOLVED YOUTH

In my fifty-plus years of juvenile ministry, I have recognized several generalized and repetitive trends regarding these youths' beginnings in life. First, many of their conceptions may have been problematic, either unwanted or almost surely unexpected. During the pregnancy, the mother may have continued to drink, abuse drugs, smoke, or suffer severe anxiety. When born, the baby may have lacked proper perinatal care and essential bonding due to a lack of affection, holding, face-to-face contact, feeding lapses, keeping warm enough, and timely diaper changes. Add to this list the lack of words spoken during the formative years. It has been estimated that a youth born under these circumstances may hear as few as six hundred words spoken per hour, while a baby born to educated professional parents may hear up to two thousand words per hour.[289] These circumstances, especially the low number of words a baby or toddler hears, negatively affect school performance throughout childhood and adolescence. Such a youth will be perceived as a slow learner, always behind, easily distracted, and not favored by teachers. *Justice-involved youth are never the teacher's pet!*

When I meet an incarcerated youth for the first time, I ask three questions: What is your age, how many times have you been in juvenile hall, and where is your biological father? In most cases, the biological father has not been in the picture for years, if ever. So many youths do not know who their real dad is. Typically (and unfortunately), a caravan of men has come and gone, creating instability and chaos. When making a family chart with these youths, I am still amazed at the number of men in and out of their lives, the number of times they have moved, and the number of stepsiblings from different fathers (all representing broken relationships). None of this family dynamic is the youth's fault!

Every teenager needs bonding and proper modeling, especially entering puberty and the rapids of adolescence. Justice-involved youth forge life with a sense of "I am all that I have, and it is all up to me" and develop a street-smart coping style. However, while this approach may enable one to survive, it rarely allows one to thrive. And, since their basic human needs to connect, belong, and be accepted are not realized at home, these birds of a feather do flock together with others in similar states of being, resulting in early alcohol and drug use, early sexual activity, potential gang activity, and dangerous

---

[289] Betty Hart and Todd R. Risley, *Meaningful Differences in the Everyday Experience of Young American Children* (Baltimore: Paul H. Brookes, 1995).

exploits. I recall one youth who had allowed his fellow gang members to hold him upside down by the ankles over a busy freeway overpass while he tagged a freeway sign.

Of course, not every justice-related youth has had this background and upbringing. However, most of the youth I engage in ministry are in a state of adolescence on steroids, coping with an existential crisis of "Why was I born? Life has no meaning. Nothing matters. And this is not going to turn out well." When asked, "Where do you see yourself in ten years?" they often respond, "I will die of an overdose, I will die in a gang shooting, or I will be in lockup most of my life." These adolescents, primarily those aged fourteen to twenty-four and in lockup, are without hope. (A new corrections policy allows youth who commit their crime before the age of eighteen to serve their sentence in a county juvenile facility until the age of twenty-four). Here is precisely where the body of Christ can bring good news, news that to someone drowning in life itself is really good news. It is hope indeed!

## JUVENILE CHAPLAIN

Currently, the title *chaplain* is almost without any meaning. By default, unlicensed and/or unordained volunteers coming into a facility, even just one night a week, can receive the title *chaplain* from the host facility. If everyone can be a chaplain, the term has lost its meaning.

I understand the root problem. Federal/state/local law mandates every correctional facility in America provide for their population's spiritual/religious needs. But that is where the mandates end. They are mandated to do something but are given no real clarity as to what that something should be. So, each department scrambles to decide what religious programming they must provide to meet minimal legal demands. While federal prisons and most state-operated juvenile facilities pay for a full-time chaplain, counties do not. Since counties are where most of the justice-involved youth reside, these counties are most vulnerable in meeting legal mandates. The problem is counties are too quick to engage anyone wanting to be a chaplain or any local ministry wanting to provide religious programming.

Unless a chaplain is fully supported financially (for both personal living and ministry expenses), they will invariably be bi-vocational workers doing ministry part-time while balancing all the time and energy required to hold down a full-time job, meet family demands, and meet the demands of life itself.

Of course, a part-time chaplain is extremely valuable. Without their presence, the entire facility might be without much-needed spiritual provision. And any volunteer serving without the title of *chaplain* is equally as beneficial. The facility is fortunate to have them. But having said this, it would be optimal for each facility to have a full-time chaplain available to meet the needs of both facility staff and the youth, as both groups struggle under very stressful environmental pressures.

I would encourage anyone sensing a call on their lives to be a full-time correctional chaplain to cling to the reality of "Where God guides, He provides." One can begin their journey as a home missionary by joining a community-based juvenile ministry or petitioning their church to provide needed support. It is important to remember that with more than one thousand public juvenile facilities nationwide, their immediate need is for one thousand full-time chaplains. Again, the fields are ripe for harvest, but the workers are few.

## JUVENILE CHAPLAINCY MINISTRY

While Jesus' incarnational ministry exemplified and modeled the ministry principle that *needs do not constitute ministry* (Jesus did not attend to all the needs surrounding him during his three years of public ministry), I believe it is helpful to envision what a fully arched juvenile ministry might look like. So, let's brainstorm together.

1. **Bibles and Materials**—The word of God and age-related books, tracts, and other Christ-centered materials must be made available. All materials should be brand new and not tattered, as materials in a state of disrepair can send a message regarding the low value and dignity of the youthful recipients. Bibles used weekly in church services or studies can be used copies; however, a Bible or study material presented to a youth must be new.

2. **Church Service**—Church services should closely mimic those in the community so that there is a familiarity when youth are released and attend a local church. Church service should begin with a welcome and an opening describing how the period will unfold. Youth need structure and a heads-up overview to help alleviate anxiety and uncertainty, especially for first-time attendees. It is important to remember that for some youth, this will be the first church service they have ever attended. These youth need to hear the good news of the gospel.

3. **Bible Study**—As with church service, give a brief overview of how the period will unfold. Collect the names of those attending so you can pray for them during the week. Along with this list, ask the youth for prayer requests. Provide a short apologetic on why the Bible is worth studying, and then get into the word. As you conduct the Bible study, leave some room for questions and answers, but be careful not to allow anyone to hijack the study or get it off-topic. The news of forgiveness and redemption must be given.

4. **Pastoral Counseling**—The issue of confidentiality must be addressed. Can it be assumed that nonlicensed and/or nonordained volunteers automatically have confidentiality? Might the prosecutor in a trial be allowed to subpoena a volunteer who has talked with a youth about their case? I recommend that only licensed and/or ordained chaplains be allowed to conduct pastoral counseling. When volunteers conduct discipleship or mentoring, it is advisable to have the volunteer immediately tell the youth that they do not have confidentiality and will not discuss the youth's case. If a youth wants to talk about their case, please have them make a request to talk with the chaplain, who has confidentiality.

5. **Discipleship**—Youth who have made a redemptive decision to follow Christ and request discipleship should have access to a trained mentor who can take the youth through age-related discipleship curriculum. The key to discipleship is to move at the rate of the individual and progress only when the youth understands the material just covered. Because experiential learning is the goal, the mentor moves at the

adolescent's understanding and not at some predetermined goal like finishing a chapter or some other forced metric.

6. **Reentry and Reentry Mentoring**—Reentry must be done according to the policies of the department or facility. Some departments will not allow any contact with a released minor, even by the chaplain. I have lobbied hard for decades with my probation department to be able to have contact with youth upon release. Our current reentry mentoring is allowed by a juvenile's Professional Clergy Staff, Select Volunteers, or a youth's MatchPoint, leaders specifically trained to do reentry mentoring.

## CONCLUSION

A fully developed juvenile chaplaincy ministry takes time incrementally to build. The building of such a ministry depends on the ministry's demonstrated professionalism and submission to authority, thus earning the trust and credibility of the host agency. This time-intensive effort is well worth it. Young lives are hanging eternally in the balance.

# MEMORABLE MOMENT
## "THE LEAST OF THESE"

### Chaplain Joe Pryor

Throughout my twenty-one-year career as a chaplain for the Federal Bureau of Prisons, I have had countless memorable moments. Being present for staff, consoling inmates during a time of loss, and celebrating the variety of religious observances throughout the year are all moments burned into my memory.

One moment, however, stands out as not only memorable but poignant. From 2003 to 2006, I served as the Supervisory Chaplain at the Federal Medical Center (FMC) Carswell, located just outside Fort Worth, Texas, on Carswell Air Force Base. FMC Carswell is the only medical center for female inmates in the Bureau of Prisons (BOP). Along with the medical center, FMC Carswell housed female inmates in camp, general population, mental health, and high-security units. It was indeed a complex mission with many moving parts.

The medical center part of the facility looked precisely like any hospital you would walk into on a given day. The facility used to be a military hospital before the BOP took over the space and converted it into a prison. One of the staff had been born there during that time and then worked at the prison.

One sad but true reality of working at FMC Carswell was that there were a lot of inmate deaths. It was not uncommon for thirty to sixty deaths over any given year. The women housed at the prison were usually pretty sick by the time they got there. It was the practice of the facility and the chaplains' responsibility to offer a memorial service for every inmate that passed, and if the family did not or could not claim the body, perform a burial service at the gravesite contracted by the prison. Typically, the warden would attend the burial, and the executive staff of the prison would serve as pallbearers.

On this particular day, a woman in her early forties had passed away from an extended illness—in fact, several illnesses. The poor soul had lived a rough life, riddled with abuse and saturated with drug use. When I saw her body in the casket, I was shocked that this woman in her forties easily looked like she was well into her seventies. I recall only a smattering of inmates attended the memorial, but very few, if any, close friends. Sadly, no family member made contact, much less claimed her body for a family funeral.

Following the memorial service, I met the funeral director to ride out to the cemetery. The warden was out of the facility that day, but I fully anticipated meeting the executive staff at the gravesite. To my surprise and dismay, not a single person showed up. After waiting for thirty minutes or so, the funeral director told me to remain in the hearse, and he and his staff would bury this person who was as alone in death as she was in life.

At that moment, the Holy Spirit burdened my soul that she should not be buried with the same indignities she had suffered in life. I asked the funeral director to give me a moment before lowering her in the ground. As I stood at the head of the grave, I opened my Bible and conducted a brief graveside service, just she and I present. It's interesting that I still vividly recall the heat of the day, the dusty ground beneath my shoes, and the slight but hot breeze that circulated around me.

I learned in that moment just how much God loves even one whom the world would call "the least of these." I walked away a changed and humbled man.

## REFLECTION QUESTIONS

1. How is correctional chaplaincy similar and different at the federal, state, and juvenile levels? Which one would be more challenging to you? Why?
2. What are some of the challenges of providing spiritual or pastoral care in a potentially violent and restrictive environment?
3. Given the increasing religious diversity among the incarcerated population, how should chaplains approach their role in facilitating religious services for faiths different from their own?
4. How do you help incarcerated inmates find hope when their situation appears grim, dark, and hopeless? How would your approach change when engaging an adult or an adolescent?
5. Correctional chaplaincy is demanding and can lead to burnout. How can a chaplain maintain their spiritual and emotional health while still effectively serving the inmate population?

CHAPTER NINETEEN

# CORPORATE/WORKPLACE CHAPLAINCY

## Chaplain Karen Diefendorf

While laws and customs protect the free exercise of religion, a chaplain service is not required to ensure this essential freedom is safeguarded in the corporate world. Lawyers and human resource professionals are the front lines of ensuring employees' religious accommodation needs are addressed. Local houses of worship and clergy of all kinds are also readily available in communities.

So, what motivates a corporate entity to provide the unique service of chaplains to their team? Visionary leadership motivates a company to provide chaplain services to its workforce. Senior leaders, with the drive and authority to make things happen in the business environment, make corporate chaplaincy a reality. Visionary leaders, through experience, intuitively know chaplains in their workplaces will send a clear message that matters of faith and practice will be respected and supported.

## OVERVIEW

Like all types of chaplaincy, corporate or workplace chaplaincy is rooted in the First Amendment right to free exercise of religion without government establishing or giving preference to any one religion. The policies and regulations of the Equal Employment Opportunity Commission (EEOC) guide the workplace, which prohibit employers from discriminating against individuals because of their religion or lack of religious belief. Title VII of the

Civil Rights Act (1964) prohibits adverse employment decisions based on religion.

> An employer is prohibited from discriminating because of religion in hiring, promotion, discharge, compensation, or other "terms, conditions or privileges" of employment, and also cannot "limit, segregate, or classify" applicants or employees based on religion "in any way which would deprive or tend to deprive any individual of employment opportunities or otherwise adversely affect his status as an employee."[290]

The workplace must provide for religious accommodation. Title VII requires an employer reasonably to "accommodate an employee's religious beliefs or practices unless doing so would cause more than a minimal burden on the operations of the employer's business."[291] Examples of common religious accommodations include "flexible scheduling, voluntary shift substitutions or swaps, job reassignments, and modifications to workplace policies or practices."[292] For example, Tyson Foods has dealt with this issue by providing prayer rooms and time off for Muslim team members to be able to experience their religious traditions. The prevailing view is people should bring their "whole self" to work. Tyson validates this concept by establishing procedures such as these in order to accommodate religious expression. EEOC does have exceptions.

> An employer does not have to accommodate an employee's religious beliefs or practices if doing so would cause undue hardship to the employer. An accommodation may cause undue hardship if it is costly, compromises workplace safety, decreases workplace efficiency, infringes

---

[290] "Section 12: Religious Discrimination," *Compliance Manual on Religious Discrimination*, US Equal Employment Opportunity Commission, updated 15 January 2021, https://www.eeoc.gov/laws/guidance/section-12-religious-discrimination#h_8956232033161074856657, accessed 28 September 2021.

[291] "Employment Practices Toolkit: Religious Discrimination Federal Law Overview," Magmutual, 30 August 2019, https://www.magmutual.com/learning/toolkit/employment-practices-toolkit/religious-discrimination-federal-law-overview/, accessed 28 September 2021.

[292] "Section 12: Religious Discrimination," *Compliance Manual.*

on the rights of other employees, or requires other employees to do more than their share of potentially hazardous or burdensome work.[293]

It is not illegal to talk about one's faith in the workplace so long as it meets other criteria in which one prohibits religious harassment of employees and offensive remarks and does not create a hostile or offensive work environment. Unfortunately, a trend in America has been to lead by the "easiest" method. This approach assumes that religion and politics, as the old adage goes, should be avoided at all cost in the workplace.

However, that trend is changing rapidly in business. In February 2020, the Religious Freedom and Business Foundation created an index (Corporate Religious Equity, Diversity & Inclusion) that measured the faith-friendliness of the top Fortune 100 companies.[294] Much to many people's surprise, Google ranked number one. The reason was their highly proactive, faith-specific Employee Resource Groups. Other companies such as Tyson Foods, Intel, Target, American Airlines, Facebook, Apple, Dell, Goldman Sachs, and American Express also rank in the top ten because of such approaches.

When people's values and belief systems are respected, a greater understanding contributes to and does not detract from the workplace. Workplace chaplaincy is one way of proactively supporting religious, spiritual, and even nonreligious beliefs.

## GENERAL REQUIREMENTS AND QUALIFICATIONS

How does one prepare for such pluralistic service in the workplace? While various workplace chaplain programs have different hiring procedures based on experience and education, the trend is toward a more educated chaplaincy due to the complexities of the ministry. Preferred education includes a master of divinity degree or its equivalent and four units of Clinical Pastoral Education. Depending on the certifying body and the stringency of its requirements, if one is also board-certified, this can be a distinguishing

---

[293] "Section 12: Religious Discrimination," *Compliance Manual*.
[294] "Corporate Religious Equity, Diversity, and Inclusion (REDI Index 2021)," Religious Freedom and Business Foundation, 9 February 2021, https://religiousfreedomandbusiness.org/redi, accessed 28 September 2021.

factor. Credentialing bodies accredited through the Department of Education include groups such as the Association of Professional Chaplains (APC).

However, isolated rural areas may draw from indigenous clergy who may or may not have formal education but have cultural or linguistic skills. Some businesses seek out clergy who come from an immigrant population because of concern to meet their migrant workers' needs. While education will matter more and more in the future of chaplaincy, personality or "fit" for an organization still has a vote.

## TYPE OF MINISTRY: CONTRACT OR EMPLOYEE?

Corporate Chaplains of America and Marketplace Ministries are two of the largest contracting services for chaplains to workplaces. They are faith-based, Christian companies. They contract with various companies for the type of support desired, how often the chaplain will visit, and whether programs like Bible studies or memorial services will be included. Ministry in this context can be as varied or as limited as a business desires. The contract defines the services. The chaplain is the contractor's employee, not the company or companies for which they provide services.

Depending on the contract, chaplains may have limited access within a plant because of, for instance, industrial secrets. Contracted chaplains should not expect to be invited to company parties or company briefings. One reason is if a contractor is treated the same as an employee, the contractor could sue for employee benefits. However, chaplains are often viewed as part of the team and will be included. The point is that the contracted chaplain should not take offense if not included.

An example of the employee model of chaplaincy is Tyson Foods. It does not contract its chaplains. The chaplains are hourly employees supervised directly by the local human resources manager. Tyson Foods describes itself as a "Faith-friendly Company" and is free to hire chaplains from all religious traditions. Their emphasis of service is not on administering programs such as worship services or Bible studies and prayer groups. Tyson believes that is best left to religious institutions. Instead, Tyson's policy helps to avoid preferring one set of beliefs over another, which otherwise might be the practice of a local plant chaplain. However, that does not mean there are never any programs in plants or corporate locations. For instance, if a group of employees (known as team members) approaches a chaplain and asks for support to start a Bible study or prayer group, the chaplain will assist. Generally, programs are bottom-up, team-member-driven initiatives. Tyson focuses on direct care for people since programs can quickly consume the chaplain's time.

Whether contractor or employee, the setting dictates the "how." Just as context is important to verbal and written discourse, the setting dictates how chaplains disseminate or extend care. Needs within a company can change quickly, requiring the chaplain to be adaptable, flexible, creative, and responsive. Contracts should support the chaplain's adaptive response in a fluid environment.

The reverse can also be true. The chaplain may face the dilemma of not providing pastoral care to a contracted worker since it puts the company at risk. It is vital to clarify ahead of time how management views the relationship. Technically, contracted workers should be cared for by the employer unless the contract pays for borrowed services of a company chaplain, especially since the company and not the contractor is paying the chaplain. Boundaries are set by whoever is writing the check, not the caring heart of the chaplain.

## THE PLURALISTIC ENVIRONMENT

Chaplains must become comfortable with being uncomfortable. If chaplains are more focused on their comfort, they may miss out on opportunities to connect with employees. Experienced chaplains have learned to develop "poker faces" when what they wanted to do was smack their foreheads and say, "You did what?" Borrowing a term from anthropologist Margaret Mead, chaplains must be the "liminal persons."[295] They must learn to navigate between two worlds: between management and hourly employees. By nature of their call and gifting, chaplains are led to respond to a hurting world. Since employees seek out the chaplain to talk about life and their work concerns, it can be easy for the chaplain to be hooked by the employee's view. A seasoned chaplain knows that there are always two sides to a story. A workplace chaplain must develop open, trusting relationships with management to be able to hear both sides while also maintaining confidentiality. It takes maturity, self-discipline, and spiritual discernment.

---

[295] Margaret Mead, "Ritual and Social Crisis," in *The Roots of Ritual*, ed. James D. Shaughnessy (Grand Rapids: Eerdmans, 1973), 97.

Pluralism acknowledges multiple belief systems within a workplace. It does not mean chaplains do not have firmly held beliefs of their own. It does mean chaplains have chosen to constrain their own beliefs in order to hear the beliefs of others and to walk beside them as they process life.

Clinical Pastoral Education (CPE) strives to help chaplains deal with themselves so they can get out of their own way and be a steadying presence. Chaplains are not exempt from their own internal anxiety but must recognize it and manage it when it occurs. Wrestling with some issues before one has to experience them can be helpful; experiencing them, though, will challenge whatever one thought.

For instance, being asked to baptize a dying infant when your faith tradition does not do so, requires you to think through your soteriology, integrity, practical ministry, and grace at a moment's notice. Military chaplaincy uses the phrase "to perform or provide." In other words, a chaplain who cannot in good conscience personally provide a religious rite, sacrament, or requested need, should actively see to its provision. The conscious conflict occurs when one does not have any other assets or time to make a provision. Chaplains must deal with their own internal conflicts so they can be fully present to the needs in front of them. At times, this can feel very conflicting.

## THE GIFT OF LISTENING

One of the most important things chaplains do is give a listening ear: "swift to listen, slow to speak." Whatever one's training in pastoral counseling, it is not about giving advice. It is about listening, learning how to hear so the chaplain can help form intuitive questions. It is about empowering people to listen to themselves when they aren't sure why they are even talking to you. Employees usually see the chaplain as a nonthreatening person. Some find it difficult to open up to supervisors, so they speak with the chaplain, who seems a safe place for them to go.

Chaplains must be careful not to assume that they want you to fix it for them. Most just need to rehearse the issue and hear it out loud. And those who do want you to fix it for them need to be assisted in finding their own voices. It may feel great to have someone need you, or to think you fixed a problem, but creating dependency is not healthy for the chaplain or the employee.

The term "ministry of presence" should not be confused with just wandering around the workplace. A chaplain's ministry should be focused and purposeful, even when the appearance appears casual. "Ministry of presence" is akin to "management by walking around," developing relationships through others' knowledge you are there. In this way you become a trusted agent. Whether they are contracted or employees, chaplains must have permission to maintain confidence, or their work will be undermined.

Again, chaplains must develop relationships with management and leadership. Many leaders get anxious over the need for confidentiality. Chaplains can minimize their concern by building trust and by bringing issues without divulging the identity of the person involved to leadership. Chaplains provide great value as organizational and relational consultants who can process and give feedback. Identifying trends within an organization, based on multiple conversations, can assist leaders in solving issues, such as perceptions that policies are not being applied equitably, before they become problems. Much like military chaplains who serve as special staff to the commander and are valuable advisors, workplace chaplains bring soft skills to problem-solving that many managers often lack. Workplace chaplains may be asked to conduct training in relational skills, use personality inventories like the Birkman Method,[296] and mediate conflict among employees.

Being a liminal person, the chaplain determines when to advocate for the team member, being careful to hear reasons behind policy and procedure and cautious not to burn the bridge to the decision-maker. It may be difficult for chaplains who have been local pastors to remember they are not the decision-maker. Chaplains are under the authority of the employer. Asking reflective questions may assist the decision-maker in coming to a better decision, whereas pushing for one's own decision may create resistance. Chaplains must be careful not to assume "I already know" or "I know more." Being prideful, haughty, aloof, or elitist should be replaced with being vulnerable and transparent. When advising decision-makers, talk less and listen more. Don't become one more burden in their already stressed lives. If you identify

---

[296] Birkman International, "The Birkman Method," https://birkman.com/the-birkman-method/, and "Leadership Development," https://birkman.com/solutions/leadership-development/, accessed 28 September 2021.

a problem, offer a solution. They will appreciate that awareness and care for them. Keep them informed. No one likes surprises. Remember that "a broken and contrite spirit" will be noticed. The chaplain sets the example and can change the tone and climate in a meeting. We are all fellow strugglers on the journey of life.[297] Indeed, we too are wounded healers.[298]

Chaplains must be aware of what can put a company legally at risk. For instance, Tyson chaplains maintain confidentiality with two exceptions: (1) if a team member expresses the intention of self-harm or harm to others, or (2) if they divulge something that puts the company at risk (for instance, if a team member discusses with the chaplain that a supervisor or another team member has been making sexual advances).

The chaplain is a safe person to talk to, one who should assist the team member in identifying what to do about the situation—perhaps go with the team member to the HR office to report it and support the team member during the investigation. Sexual misconduct violates Tyson's policies, and as an employee, the chaplain must help team members have the courage to access the protection of those policies. Such violations require finesse by the chaplain when a team member does not want the issue reported. Fear of retaliation by the supervisor or peers is real. It is important to be clear and up front when someone asks, "Chaplain, can I talk to you?"

## WHAT DOES A WORKPLACE CHAPLAIN DO?

Settings in the workplace are so varied it is impossible to give a one-size-fits-all description, but we all deal with grief. Chaplains probably spend 70 percent of a workplace time navigating grief issues. These can be as varied as the death of a family member to the loss of a promotion, from the disappointment of a child squandering his potential to losing one's home. Loss adds stress to which there seems no solution. One way to describe much of what workplace chaplains do is to look at the types of work all chaplaincies

---

[297] John Claypool, *Tracks of a Fellow Struggler: Living and Growing through Grief* (Harrisburg, PA: Morehouse Publishing, 1974).
[298] Henri Nouwen, *The Wounded Healer: Ministry in Contemporary Society* (New York: Image Books Doubleday, 1979).

have in common. We all do hospital visits, funerals, and pastoral counseling. But what is unique about workplace chaplaincy?

One difference would be the settings. They vary from an industrial plant that can be loud with dangerous moving equipment to the quiet of a local pharmacy or bank. Industrial locations will need the chaplain for all shifts. Workplace chaplains become champions of the business culture, helping employees understand from the perspective of business management. Workplace chaplains often become liaisons with community agencies to find needed resources for employees' well-being, whether the local food bank, homeless shelter, or domestic violence shelter. In many ways, workplace chaplains provide a combination of pastoral care and social work. They work closely with Human Resources, often being supervised by HR, and with Occupational Health and Safety. Tyson chaplains serve on the Safety Committee and regularly collaborate with plant nurse(s) to assure coordinated care.

Workplaces normally have long-term, ongoing relationships. Hospital chaplains may experience that with staff, too, but much of their daily work is responding swiftly, creating trust in very brief moments with patients. Workplace longevity allows the chaplain to think about a conversation, return to it, and follow up on an employee's life event.

Workplace chaplains can expect predictable hours, like hospital chaplains, with on-call emergency responses when needed. Workplace chaplains may rotate shifts depending on the number of chaplains hired for that location.

Every institution has an ethos. Contracted chaplains who may provide care to two or three different types of companies must be able to adapt how they deliver care in each unique location. Ethos is created by values and mission statements. Understanding those helps clarify unspoken expectations and prevent integrity compromises. For instance, one ought not to assume that all hospitals have the same ethos. A faith-based, nonprofit hospital may have very different views on what is ethical and moral than a for-profit hospital. Military settings are different from prisons. Businesses are no different.

## SELF-CARE

Chaplains are involved in a people-caring profession that requires constant giving of oneself. Unless the chaplain takes time off regularly, the result will be burnout while trying to run on empty. This can negatively affect marital relationships, parenting needs, and physical health. We believe chaplains should "love others even as they love themselves." Properly loving yourself requires the admission that you are not a rescuer. You are not the only one who can help. It takes a team of friends, workers, counselors, professionals, medical staff, and spiritual leaders from the community to bring an employee to personal wholeness. When you take time for self-care, you are subscribing to that philosophy and enabling yourself to run a marathon of lifetime service, not a forty-yard dash to a quick exit.

# CONTRACTED SERVICE (MARKETPLACE) CHAPLAINCY

## Mr. Jason Brown

The convergence of today's mental health crisis, isolation, depression, and suicide, along with corporate America's Human Resources push for wellness, work-life balance, and employee well-being, have generated a tidal wave of companies implementing chaplain care services for their employees.

Many companies utilize chaplains for various reasons: spiritual or pastoral needs, human wellness, or effective business "return on investment" (ROI) constructs. By adding chaplain care services to their suite of benefits, many leaders view workplace chaplaincy as doing the right thing for those who may need extra help, regardless of the bottom-line impact. The results and positive benefits are quantitative. Company leaders typically comment: "It's the biggest no-brainer in business." "I cannot believe the utilization by our people." "During the last slow-down, our entire leadership team unanimously said we are not going to cut the chaplains." And "I can rest my head on the pillow every night knowing I have provided all I can to help our people."

Various options are available to implement this level of employee care. One method is for the company to set up an in-house chaplain, which appeals to many CEOs wanting to lead and have control. However, several challenges exist with this in-house model. Often leaders will hire their pastor, priest, or clergy as the chaplain. While logical and straightforward, several considerations need examination. What training will the person receive? Can they get out of their preacher role and transition into a chaplain role? What about gender-sensitive issues? Will the chaplain be knowledgeable about the bilingual and cultural issues of the employee population?

One chaplain alone may be ill-equipped to serve the entire needs of a company, especially if the company has multiple locations across the country. In addition, hiring a staff chaplain may raise several "red flags" in employees' eyes. Will employees open up to a chaplain who is a coworker? Will employees willingly share personal, sensitive, and confidential issues with a chaplain who is under Human Resources (HR) and a friend of the owner?

During crisis events, chaplains genuinely shine and are significantly utilized. But the real ministry of a workplace chaplain happens through developing relationships of trust and confidence. This trust facilitates people opening up about issues early on, giving the chaplain the ability to help them correct course, find resources, or get through challenging times. Given this proactive side of workplace chaplaincy, many companies realize the most important ROI results from chaplain services are averted crises and prevention of issues rising to a reportable level to leadership.

The second method companies utilize is contracted chaplain services through a third-party organization. The benefits of this model are numerous: lower cost, higher usage, and more flexibility. Helping people before their problems turn into crises (for example, bankruptcy, divorce, suicide, walking off the job, abuse, addictions) is to have a truly proactive service. The Chaplain Care Team provides the best model for high-level employee usage of chaplain services. This model excels when the team is neutral regarding company operations, is diverse, can converse in the employees' languages, understands cultural barriers, and is supported by a national team of chaplains.

A Chaplain Care Team ensures coverage of all shifts, multiple personalities, and several opportunities during weekly visits for employees to approach one of the care team members. A team also provides numerous touchpoints during a crisis. For example, during a workplace injury incident, the Chaplain Care Team can simultaneously dispatch its chaplains to the workplace, the employee's home, the family, the hospital, and even make the difficult injury notification to a relative in another state.

Marketplace Chaplains, the largest corporate chaplaincy organization, has over eighteen hundred trained, professional chaplains across the US and offers this type of coverage to public and private companies of any size. Marketplace hires and trains over three hundred workplace chaplains annually. Approximately twenty other chaplain contractor agencies exist across America.

Chaplains have long served in the military, hospitals, police and fire departments, sports teams, and hospice care groups. Today, the fastest-growing aspect of chaplaincy is in the world's largest mission field—the workplace.

## MEMORABLE MOMENT
## "LIFE SUPPORT"

### Chaplain Hector Perez

As I begin my day as a Marketplace Chaplain visiting worksites or making phone calls, the Holy Spirit reminds me that my mission is to share God's love with company leaders and employees. To do so effectively, I had to unlearn "sharing and talking about Jesus" before I "showed Jesus." Employees need to know this key message—I am here to listen and assist you with personal concerns or family issues. When employees have a crisis, it is critically important I be present to listen and assist. Unfortunately, company employees are not immune to tragedies.

One morning, the phone rang with a distressed company leader online. We knew each other, as I had the privilege of helping him in his personal life. He shared a tragic story about one of his employees and his son. As he spoke, I could hear someone in the background weeping loudly. The employee's twenty-six-year-old son was hit by a car as he crossed the street and experienced a traumatic brain injury, collapsed lung, and numerous bone fractures. The company executive asked if I could please speak directly with the employee and coordinate a time to meet with him and his family. The employee came on the phone. As I introduced myself, he began to break down in deep distress.

As the employee began to share his son's accident details, I was moved with compassion and offered to make a hospital visit that afternoon to see his son and meet his family. When arriving at the hospital, I met the spouse and ten family members. It was a sad and emotional gathering. Even though I have made numerous hospital visits as a chaplain serving different companies, this visit felt overwhelming.

As the spouse introduced me to the family members, I was fully aware of my inadequacy and weakness of not knowing what to say or do. I sat quietly, listened, and prayed for the Holy Spirit's guidance. Being invited to see their son, the father and mother escorted me to their son's ICU bed. He was on life support and bandaged from head to toe. Monitors and pumps hummed.

The doctors had sedated him to reduce the bleeding and swelling of his brain. With little brain activity, the medical team expressed concern. After first asking permission, we joined hands and prayed for the son, doctors, nurses, and staff caring for him.

Outside the ICU, the mother asked, "Hector, do you think God can heal my son who is on life support and suffered such a bad injury like this?"

I paused and shared the story in the Bible about Jairus, a religious leader who had a daughter near the point of death. Jairus was desperate, knelt before Jesus, and asked for His help. My reply was, "I believe our Lord Jesus honors crisis faith and can do the impossible. If it's His will, He can heal your son."

Being asked by the family, I returned to the hospital for the next five days and continued to pray for a miracle. Unfortunately, the son was not showing any signs of brain activity. After receiving a call from the father, I met with the entire family to discuss the neurosurgeon's recommendation to remove their son from life support. The doctor stated their son was considered brain-dead and would remain in a persistent vegetative state (PVS) for the rest of his life. I met with the family, heard their concerns, discussed their options, and developed a list of some very tough questions for the medical team. We continued to pray.

The family members met with their son's medical team on day seven. It was a very somber moment. The neurologist expressed her heartache as the son's medical condition had not improved. I shared with the team of doctors that the family had a list of questions. The team answered each question. The final question was, "If this were your son or daughter, would you take him or her off life support?"

Two of the five doctors began to weep. One of the doctors, the cardiologist, asked if she could answer the question. "I had a sixteen-year-old daughter who suffered an accident and was also on life support. Our family faced the same decision as you are facing today. It was the most heartbreaking and biggest decision of our lives. We knew taking her off life support was the right thing to do for our daughter, who would be in a vegetative state the rest of her life. A decision like this is overwhelmingly difficult, but it is the right thing to do for your son. The way he is now is the best he will be for the rest of his life."

After hearing the doctor's story and recommendation, the family and I wept for several minutes. As we gathered our composure, I asked the doctors to please give us some privacy. The doctors left, and I asked the difficult question, "What would you like to do?" The father and mother replied that taking their son off life support was not what they wanted to hear from the doctors but felt it was right action. The two siblings and an uncle were torn and needed more time.

When the phone rang, I remember it was a beautiful Saturday morning. With a broken voice, the father said to me, "Hector, our family has made the decision. We are taking our son off life support tomorrow morning. Would you please come to be with us and pray as we say our final goodbye to our son?" The pain of losing a child is unparalleled. I agreed to go and be with the family Sunday morning.

My heart was heavy. I felt a substantial weight in my soul as I began to pray for the family on the way to the hospital the following day. Thoughts flashed through my mind about the gravity of a father or mother taking their son off life support. I cried out, "O Lord, have mercy and come to our rescue." I arrived at the hospital and met with the family. We hugged, wept, and sat silent for a long moment. We made our way up to the ICU room, and the five of us surrounded the bed. We held hands and cried as I prayed. We committed his spirit, soul, mind, and body into our Savior's hands. Later that afternoon, he was taken off life support and passed into eternity.

As a Marketplace Chaplain, I realized again through this family crisis how vital the "ministry of presence" is and the importance of developing relationships of trust with company leaders and employees. Because of my previous care of the company leader who contacted me, he knew the father could trust me to walk with his family during this terrible time in their family's life. With the Holy Spirit's guidance and compassion, I had what I needed to be an empathetic chaplain, one who has a caring heart for broken and hurting people.

## REFLECTION QUESTIONS

1. Chaplain Diefendorf stated in her introduction, "While laws and customs protect the free exercise of religion, a chaplain service is not required to

ensure this essential freedom is safeguarded in the corporate world." With this perspective, what would you say to corporate leaders about the value of having a chaplain embedded in their companies?
2. Chaplains can serve companies either as an employee of the company, as in Tyson Foods, or as a contracted service, as in MarketPlace Chaplains. If you were a company executive wanting the support of a chaplain for your employees, which approach would you select and why?
3. What is the value of confidentiality for workplace chaplains, and what are the potential challenges it brings? How can a chaplain balance confidentiality with the responsibility to report serious issues, like workplace harassment or threats of harm?
4. What does "ministry of presence" mean to you in a corporate environment?
5. You are asked to perform a religious ritual, one that is not part of your tradition. You do not have someone who can immediately conduct the ritual. How do you handle the situation?

CHAPTER TWENTY

# PUBLIC SAFETY CHAPLAINCY

Chaplain Ken Schlenker

Chaplaincy within the public safety environment is both challenging and rewarding. Some refer to this category as "First Responder Chaplaincy." However, public safety is a broader term and is more inclusive in this category. Public Safety Chaplaincy includes ministry to various communities: police, correction, fire, EMS, dispatch, homeland security, border patrol, secret service, FBI, and district attorneys. Public safety chaplaincy maintains the integrity of an individual's belief system. In addition, this highly specialized ministry involves an approach that has a distinctive philosophy of ministry and is highly skilled based. In the past, seminaries did not train individuals for this environment or the unique issues such as domestic violence, suicide, homicide, line of duty death, line of duty injury, post-traumatic stress disorder, and many others. Organizations created specialized training, which is best delivered by those who have served in and understand the public safety community.[299]

## OVERVIEW

With their faith in action and specialized training, chaplains create and bridge the sacred and the secular. Public safety chaplains work as part of

---

[299] CAREForce is one example of a specialized training delivery system, providing crisis training, response, organizational development, and coaching for community and first-responder organizations. CAREForce's focus is within first responder, veteran, education, healthcare, faith-based, community at large, and business communities. See https://www.careforce.us/, accessed 14 August 2021.

an interdisciplinary team consisting of behavioral health, peer support, and chaplain professionals with a holistic focus (physical, emotional, cognitive, behavioral, and spiritual) of care for the wellness of all agency personnel and their families. A healthy program consists of three foci: (1) cradle to grave, (2) prevention, intervention, postvention programs, (3) tiered approach from command staff, supervisor, line officer, and family. Programs proactively address the issues faced to lessen the response's impact and prevent an escalation of symptoms.

Public safety chaplains provide ministry through a philosophy of purpose, presence, and peace.[300] A chaplain's ministry of **purpose** is a force multiplier to an individual or agency. A chaplain's actions are deliberate in their support of the primary mission of their agency and provide proactive and responsive support to every member. Therefore, decisions should be made on what ministry is appropriate while considering the unintended consequences and long-term effects, even while addressing immediate needs. Ministry, in any form, ought not to interfere with the mission of, or become a liability to, the agency.

A chaplain's ministry of **presence** entails being fully present to the person directly in front of you. It gives them your undivided attention (eyes, ears, nonverbal, and so on). To serve someone is to be present with them, pay attention to them, and not make judgments or comments about them or their situation but rather listen attentively and openly. Ministry of Presence encompasses being open, honest, direct, and transparent with others in verbal and nonverbal communication. It might sometimes imply a corollary ministry—the Ministry of Silence.

A chaplain's ministry of **peace** corresponds to the Hebrew concept of *shalom* (peace). It means that every aspect of an individual's life (physical, emotional, cognitive, behavioral, and spiritual) is in perfect harmony with God's desire for one's life. A chaplain's Ministry of Peace is to walk empathetically with people in their crises, to assist them holistically in restoring peace in their lives, and to do so in a sacrificially loving way. When someone is in

---

[300] CAREForce, *First Responder Chaplaincy Training Manual* (2021), 17, https://www.careforce.us/, accessed 14 August 2021.

crisis, their peace has been shattered and thrown into chaos. A chaplain's role is to assist in restoring control of the person's life and finding a new normal.

## AN EMBEDDED MINISTRY

Chaplains ministering within this environment join first responders as they react to the crisis of others. Chaplains are effective based on the level of their training, understanding of the issues, and ability to work within the scope of the agency's policies. They enter the life of this community. Representing their agency and remaining aligned with their faith, they come alongside others in physical, emotional, psychological, and spiritual pain. In doing so, chaplains walk alongside them to empower them to restore their *shalom*, or peace, so impacted by the crisis. Upon departing the scene, the chaplain's focus shifts to the responders' well-being and how they are processing the scene they just left. This environment demands specialized training for the chaplain and responders' safety and the trauma and crises they face daily.

The crisis itself is when a "bridge between the sacred and secular" occurs. Chaplains must "connect, assess, respond, and engage when responding to others in a crisis."[301] This model provides chaplains an effective ministry model of engaging individuals amid their crisis abyss. First, they **connect**. This is the ability interactively to build rapport and relationships in a consistently compassionate and credible manner. Rapport is established quickly through appropriate questions that employ an empathetic relational demeanor and active listening skills. Humility and a servant's heart are emphasized while meeting the practical needs of another, without imposing religious dogma or doctrine, and while respecting the diversity of individual beliefs.

Second, they **assess**. This is the ability to identify the various needs of other individuals correctly for the purpose of reducing the escalation of harm, allowing them to regain control of their situation and thereby restore peace to their lives. A chaplain assesses out of a genuine concern for the well-being of others and demonstrates this through their sacred core values. A chaplain also will properly employ effective crisis management techniques and active listening skills.

---

[301] CAREForce, *First Responder Chaplaincy Training Manual*, 28.

Third, they **respond**. This is the ability holistically to provide for the practical needs of an individual in crisis (physical, emotional, cognitive, behavioral, and spiritual). Chaplains utilize appropriate crisis intervention techniques, having appropriate allies, resources, and referrals preestablished to provide simple, brief, proximal, and immediate care that provides hope for restoration and recovery.

Fourth, they **engage**. This is the ability to deploy the right resources proactively and appropriately to restore the individual to normal functioning by meeting basic needs. The chaplain may engage through liaison, advocacy, cathartic ventilation, social support, information, stress management, problem-solving, conflict resolution, cognitive reframing, or spiritual care.

All of this falls within the purview of the chaplain as part of the responding team. With specialized training such as First Responder Chaplain Courses, Critical Incident Stress Management (CISM), Wellness and Resiliency, Suicide Prevention, Intervention and Postvention, Mental Health First Aid, Crisis Intervention Team (CIT), and Psychological First Aid, the chaplain can operate within this challenging and fulfilling environment.

A properly trained public safety chaplain can find a place to minister just about anywhere in the United States. With proper preparation and training, public safety chaplaincy opens the door to a wide range of ministry environments and provides abundant opportunities to develop relationships with our nation's heroes, our first responders.

# FIREFIGHTERS AND EMS PERSONNEL CHAPLAINCY

## Chaplain Brian Clingenpeel

In many localities throughout the country, firefighting and emergency medical services have been brought together under one umbrella. This means many employees and volunteers are cross trained in firefighting and in some level of pre-hospital care ranging from basic first aid to nationally registered paramedics or registered nurses. Many times, even in areas where two separate departments still exist, a symbiosis between the two disciplines has developed because they often show up at the same incidents and their basic goals are the same: to render aid, to rescue, and to save lives and property. While police departments are also first responders and are equally caring and compassionate, the fact that they enforce the law puts them in a different category, even when it comes to ministering to them as a chaplain.

Because of the inherent danger in what they do, first responders have their own culture and personality, and they are suspicious of outsiders. Because of this closed culture, providing ministry to them is more difficult but particularly important. This section focuses on ministry to firefighters and EMS providers.

Chaplains in the fire service have been around for about as long as the fire service itself. The shape of that ministry varies greatly from state to state and even from town to town. In some organizations, the chaplain is an elected position, like the treasurer; and their primary function is to pray at meetings and events or to send flowers to members who are sick, injured, or grieving. In large metropolitan departments, the chaplain may be a paid professional responsible for firefighter wellness or community services.

In the United States, few chaplains serve in full-time, paid positions due to budget constraints, limitations on how tax dollars or donations are spent, and "separation of church and state" concerns. Some denominations—Roman Catholics, for instance—might pay a priest to be a full-time chaplain for the local fire department. Many localities still have volunteer firefighters and emergency medical services, and their chaplains are usually volunteers.

Even in departments staffed by career firefighters and paramedics, many chaplains are volunteers.

As with any ministry opportunity, getting to know the culture and typical personalities of the personnel is crucial. Firefighters and EMS providers are special people. They face death and destruction daily. They depend on each other for their survival. While they are working, they often live together, which creates a closed, family atmosphere. This not only makes their culture unique among first responders, it also makes it difficult for a chaplain to penetrate. Firefighters spend a third of their lives with their firefighting family. They form a special bond by training together, sharing meals, sleeping in the same building, and doing daily duties like cleaning and cooking together.

The jobs of firefighting and emergency response and care attract a similar personality type: "people who choose a career with inherent powerful stressors have personalities that match them to the work, or they would find it intolerable."[302] The danger itself attracts a different kind of person than less risky professions do. Firefighters tend to be action-oriented people who like being in control but also do not mind taking risks, even in their recreational activities. They are highly dedicated to their jobs and need to be needed. They pay strong attention to detail, which is necessary for tasks such as making sure rescue ropes are tied correctly. Their nearly obsessive attention to detail can also set them up for failure when they do not meet their own high standards.

Fire/EMS chaplaincy programs differ greatly from one to another, depending on the system set by the local unit or chaplain. Some chaplain positions are ceremonial in nature and simply pray at graduations and other special events. Others focus primarily on the victims of disasters within the community. They do more in providing emergency shelter, clothing, and grief counseling. Some chaplains minister to victims of disaster on the scene and free responders to focus their specialized skills on rescue. Most firefighters are not trained to deal with the raw emotions of someone who is experiencing loss. As a result, they gladly hand this need to the chaplain, who performs emotional first aid. Chaplains to firefighters also typically make death notifications, both for the department and for the community. When

---

[302] Jeffery T. Mitchell and Gary Bray, *Emergency Services Stress* (Englewood Cliffs, NJ: Prentice-Hall, 1990), 19.

asked to officiate in major life events, like funerals and weddings, this may be a sign the chaplain is developing strong bonds with the firefighters.

With such a variety of Fire/EMS departments across the country, this means chaplain programs are also vastly different. Many of them depend on volunteers, especially local pastors to fill this ministry role. Some chaplains have their own nonprofit organizations and raise their support to be able to provide emergency pastoral care. Others, who are firefighters, double as chaplains. Some take other jobs in the department so they can be closer to firefighters and paramedics for the purpose of ministering to them.

The incarnational ministry model Jesus provided is a great place to start when seeking to develop relationships and ongoing ministry opportunities within this closed culture. Developing trust and relationships with firefighters requires a great deal of time. It means doing what they do. Run calls? Absolutely. Attend meetings and fundraisers? Absolutely. Visit stations and engage in kitchen table conversation? You bet. All of these are ways to be seen and be to be available. It is important also to be able to provide ministry and contact to all levels of the department, from the chief right down to the frontline firefighters and EMTs.

These firefighters are used to responding as soon as the bell sounds. They are committed to what they do. So, when the chaplain is requested on the scene of a call or for a member in need, it is important to show up as much and as soon as possible. Sometimes there is a short window of opportunity to be able to provide ministry. While availability and quick response is important, self-care for chaplains is also important. So, a team approach may work well for some departments. It takes time to earn the right to be heard by firefighters and to be given the privilege to listen to their heartaches and offer help.

Many stress factors affect how a chaplain ministers in this environment. The first one is adapting to shift work. Typically, firefighters work shifts that range from twelve to twenty-four hours. Some departments even work forty-eight hours at a time. Although most firefighters say they have adjusted to shift work, it is chronic stressor that impacts other areas of their lives, especially home life. Another source of stress is a lack of sleep. Working a twenty-four-hour shift means the potential of missing an entire night of sleep due to multiple EMS calls or a single, devastating fire call. Even when not running calls, most firefighters report not being able to sleep soundly for fear of missing a call, which could lead to a low job performance evaluation. Of course, interpersonal relations can also be a stressor for a firefighter. If you spend multiple hours with people, even those you consider family, eventually disagreements will occur. Downtime waiting on calls can cause boredom, which also adds to the stress on interpersonal relationships.

That is all day-to-day stress. Additionally, emergency personnel also experience critical incident stress, harmful stress caused by responding to critical calls. Although different for everyone, typically situations involving children, the death of a coworker, or a mass casualty incident creates this harmful stress. When left untreated, critical incident stress can lead to post-traumatic stress disorder (PTSD). The chaplain for a Fire/EMS agency should receive training in critical incident stress management (CISM).

Chaplains for a Fire/EMS agencies cannot be expected to be experts in every area of ministry. They should make connections with other professionals in order to make referrals for members of their department. Is professional mental health care needed for a member? Who are the providers around you to whom you could refer a firefighter? Does the department have an employee assistance program (EAP)? If so, how is it structured? Who runs it? This is good information for the chaplain to know and share with others. The Red Cross can also be an excellent resource for the chaplain, especially when it comes to victim assistance on the scene of a fire or other disaster. Keep in mind that not all firefighters are going to be from your faith background, and the policies of many local agencies state that the chaplain is to be nonsectarian in offering services. Do you know the local priest or rabbi or at least how to contact them if a member of your department or community should need their services?

Building a ministry to a fire department or EMS agency requires the chaplain to be available during times of crisis as well as during the day-to-day routines that occupy much of the members' time. Each department and chaplain program presents different ministry opportunities necessitating a slightly different approach. The challenge is for the chaplain to find those unique opportunities in their department and define a ministry that meets the situation.[303]

---

[303] William Lotz, *Fire Chaplain Institute Training Manual* (self-published, 2005), 41.

# LAW ENFORCEMENT, DISTRICT ATTORNEY, AND VICTIM ADVOCATES CHAPLAINCY

## Chaplain Ken Schlenker

Imagine riding with a deputy responding to multiple calls within a twelve-hour shift with different degrees of trauma (identity theft, robbery, child death, sexual assault, suicide). Each call has different levels of potential lethality and impact. Every call requires the deputy's head to be on a swivel. Welcome to law enforcement chaplaincy.

You are walking into a district attorney's office for special victims. You learn he is working on a case that involves physical, emotional, and sexual abuse of a mother and her four children. He explains he has been listening to details about the defendant dragging the mother to the front yard of their home and subjecting her to constant physical and sexual abuse. He would rather not have to hear this, but prosecuting is his job. Welcome to the district attorney chaplaincy.

You observe a victim advocate with her head in her hands. She indicates she is involved in a case involving sexually abused child victims. She tells you it has caused her to cry at night when she thinks about what these children have experienced. She has internalized this case and is experiencing some vicarious trauma. Welcome to victim advocate chaplaincy.

What do you do? How can you assist? How has seminary prepared you to face these issues? All the above specialized first responder chaplaincies require contextualized training to the environment. While needed skills and understanding of issues stretch across the spectrum, the culture, environment, and issues presentation are dynamically different. It is not a one-size-fits-all. Trained chaplains provide a supportive ministry to the organizations' responders, staff, and families. The chaplain's role is to provide a safe environment, building confidential and trusting relationships that allow individuals "verbally to throw up." Each context has a roller-coaster of physical, emotional, cognitive, behavioral, and spiritual impacts. The degree of influence depends on the individual's immunity, resiliency, and dosage of the event they process. These specialized environments require consistency and time to develop relationships to break down the walls so those you serve recognize you are a safe person who can keep confidence, be trusted, and comprehend their work environment.

Each type of chaplain must be adaptive, flexible, proactive, and reactive when required. Each incident has different degrees of stress and impact upon individuals. Eventually, if bottled up, the stress and trauma will ultimately explode like someone sitting on top of a volcano. The pressure escalates and needs to be released. In the same way, the chaplain provides catharsis through listening so the pain within may be expressed, thereby avoiding damage that can so easily occur to the individual, their roles, or their relationships. The chaplain empathetically walks alongside others and empowers them to regain control or express what is within them so they are not harmed. Chaplains must carefully listen, observe, and engage. By walking alongside others, chaplains assist in releasing squelched or hidden burdens.

Robust chaplain skill training should include topics like death notification, critical incident stress management, ceremonies and events, legal liability, confidentiality, ethics, responding to crises, substance abuse, suicide, officer injury or death, sensitivity and diversity, officer wellness, and resiliency, active listening, and critical incident desensitization protocols. Issue-based training should include depression, anxiety, post-traumatic stress, substance use, alcoholism, suicide, and many others. In addition, law enforcement chaplains should receive field training for typical types of calls needing chaplain assistance. Additionally, chaplains should not neglect agency policy and procedural training.

Providing specialized first responder chaplaincy is both challenging and rewarding. Training is a must. Once prepared and trained, the ministry door to law enforcement, district attorney, victim advocate personnel, and their families awaits.

# DISASTER RELIEF CHAPLAINCY

## Chaplain Steve Ballinger

Jesus tells us, "These things I have spoken to you, so that in Me you may have peace. In the world you have tribulation but take courage; I have overcome the world."[304]

People deal with tribulations and disasters. These calamities can be natural disasters (hurricanes, cyclones, tornadoes, floods, tsunamis, earthquakes, fires, drought). Or they can be man-caused disasters (terrorism, civil disturbance, homicide, suicide, domestic violence, child abuse, human trafficking, robbery, traffic collision, terminal illness, divorce, bankruptcy).

Disasters can impact a person in many different areas of life (physically, emotionally, cognitively, behaviorally, and spiritually). People in crisis can have thoughts they have never had before. People in crisis can act out in ways they have never acted before. They need assistance to deal with their issues. They require crisis intervention. They need grief counseling or disaster relief. Who helps them? The government? Yes. Private enterprise? Yes. The church? Yes. These organizations can provide disaster relief to the individual(s) in different ways, depending on their loss.

The government, through the Federal Emergency Management Agency (FEMA), can provide finances for rebuilding. Private agencies, such as the American Red Cross and Salvation Army, can provide shelter, food, and other supplies. Churches and other faith communities can assist by providing food, clothing, and spiritual care.

The disaster chaplain is another valuable resource for those affected by overwhelming circumstances. Disaster chaplaincy is a ministry of purpose, presence, and peace that provides sacred care.[305] I would add to this compassion and silence. A disaster chaplain provides both emotional and spiritual care and relief to men and women of all faith persuasions or no faith

---

[304] John 16:33
[305] Chaplain Ken Schlenker, CAREForce.US. Taken from California Peace Officer Standard and Training (POST) "Introduction to Law Enforcement Chaplaincy" student manual Version 5 cover page.

persuasion. Without allowing personal biases to interfere, a disaster chaplain ministers to everyone regardless of their race, ethnicity, sex, sexual orientation, or political affiliation.

Disaster chaplains can be a "bridge," encouraging those affected to find strength, support, and help through a faith community like a church, synagogue, or mosque. Disaster chaplains understand the importance of "Ministry on the Way,"[306] meaning one is constantly open to ministry opportunities by being sensitive to the leading of the Holy Spirit. Ministry can happen in the disaster field, a grocery store, a service station, or in a car while stopped at a stoplight. Ministry can be found anywhere and everywhere. The focus of care is on the individual.

Disaster chaplains should be competent and well trained. Many different organizations provide disaster training for chaplains. One should carefully choose training organizations that have an extensive training background, credentials, credibility, and certification.

Disaster chaplains have the heart of an Isaiah when the voice of the Lord said, "Whom shall I send, and who will go for Us?" Then I said, "Here am I. Send me."[307] When disaster strikes, these chaplains are ready and willing to respond immediately. They are ready to respond to wherever the disaster is (locally, nationally, internationally). They meet people in crisis where they are, and they minister to the person based on their need(s). They see themselves tangibly demonstrating God's love. They desire to help mitigate the distress in the person. They understand that in order to be heard, they must first be a good listener. The disaster chaplain realizes the person suffering does not care how much we know until they know how much we care.

---

[306] Trevor Freeze, "Ministry on the Way: Chaplains Go with the Flow," Billy Graham Evangelistic Association, March 2012, https://billygraham.org/story/ministry-on-the-way-chaplains-go-with-flow/, accessed 29 September 2021.

[307] Isa 6:8

# MEMORABLE MOMENT
## "IT'S ALL ABOUT RELATIONSHIPS"

### Chaplain Brian Clingenpeel

As I think back over my twenty-plus years in the fire service as a chaplain, I have had many memorable moments: weddings, funerals, debriefings, horrific calls, one-on-one talks with firefighters, baptisms, death notifications, hospital visits, and station visits. I come back to the very start of my fire chaplain ministry, my call and identity that make me who I am today.

While in seminary, I began the practice of doing police ride-alongs at the encouragement of my pastor. When I graduated from Southwestern Baptist Theological Seminary in 1995, I was in my first pastorate at Hillsboro Baptist Church in Crozet, Virginia. I continued the police ride-alongs in Crozet where I had developed friendships with police officers and listened to police and fire radio traffic on my scanner at home.

I was in an ecumenical pastors' meeting in Crozet when the pager of a Methodist minister in town went off. He explained he was the chaplain for the volunteer fire department. A few months later, a church member and another member of the department approached me to become their new chaplain because the previous chaplain was being moved to a new parish assignment. I did not have to think about it long. I readily accepted.

As I began my chaplain ministry, I met with him to find out what was involved. Little did I know that his words would be burned into my brain and my heart and become the foundation of my chaplain ministry for the next twenty years. His advice to me was: "The fire department is a very close-knit group, as they depend on each other for their survival. They are suspicious of outsiders. Your biggest job will be to build relationships with them. You do that by doing what they do. Run calls, go to business meetings, and participate in fundraisers."

I was pastoring a small country church that afforded me the time to do just those things. I also met early on with the fire chief who gave me a pager and a hard hat (not a firefighter's helmet) and told me he would like to have me present on bad car accidents and structure fires. And so, I just started showing up. I ran calls at night, I ran calls during the day. I ran the bad calls and the not-so bad calls. I went to business meetings and fundraisers.

After a few months of that, I was approached by the department and was told that I was among the top ten call-running members of the department. They wanted to know if I was interested in attending an upcoming class to get my state firefighter certification. They told me they wanted me to be safe while on-scene, and they could also use my help as a firefighter, especially during daylight hours. With the previous chaplain's advice to me ("do what they do") still ringing in my ears, I said, "Sure." Within another six months, I was a Virginia state-certified firefighter level 2.

Those were such formative years for me, and I didn't even realize it at the time. So much of what was advised has become the model of not only my chaplain ministry but also my pastoral ministry. Anybody close to me has heard me say more than once, "It's all about relationships." I am a firm believer in showing up. Maybe you don't feel like you can do a lot, but at least show up. As a chaplain, as a minister, regardless of how you are feeling that day, you represent the presence of God to a lot of people, and it's important to show up. The Federation of Fire Chaplains says, "It's a ministry of presence." Absolutely true. How do you build relationships? Do what they do. Especially in the fire service and elsewhere, people turn to those they know they can trust in times of trouble. If I want to be there for firefighters, EMTs, paramedics, and church members when they are suffering and asking questions, or celebrating life's joys, then they have to know me and trust me.

This became such a part of my calling as a chaplain that in 2007, I left the full-time pastorate to work for the fire department as their Community Outreach Coordinator, just so I can be present and do more of what firefighters do on a daily basis. Yes, I still pastor a small country church for now. But that decision to go to work for the fire department has been one of the best decisions I ever made. Why? Because of God's call on my life to minister to first responders. I am in the center of God's will for my life. God used the previous chaplain and fire chief to set me on this course. The words they spoke to me have become foundational for all I do. It's all about relationships, so show up, do what they do, and be ready to give account of your faith. Preach with your life, use words if necessary. You don't need to be their mother (correcting foul language, and so on) but live among them and seize those ministry opportunities.

## REFLECTION QUESTIONS

1. How does public safety chaplaincy compare and differ from other forms of chaplaincy? What are the unique challenges and opportunities for chaplains in this field?
2. Given the "closed culture" among personnel serving in public safety, what strategies might a chaplain use to develop trust and rapport with public safety personnel?
3. How can chaplains effectively integrate their personal beliefs into their work while respecting a public safety agency's secular and pluralistic nature?
4. As many in this culture suffer from cumulative levels of stress but are unwilling to seek help, how might you assist an individual who is increasingly becoming suicidal? How might you assist the leadership of the institution when one of its personnel commits suicide?
5. What self-care practices can chaplains adopt to avoid burnout and maintain their well-being?

CHAPTER TWENTY-ONE

# COMMUNITY/LIFESTYLE CHAPLAINCY

### Dr. Jim Browning

I have talked to many different types of chaplains and supporting organizations. I am amazed at the variety and, more importantly, the effective utilization of chaplaincy. Military, hospital, and correctional chaplains have long histories and are more familiar to most people. Heightened operations of emergency services and the growing influence of chaplains in the workplace have made the first responder and corporate chaplaincies increasingly visible. However, people are less familiar with community and lifestyle chaplaincy.

Chaplaincy is becoming increasingly accepted and influential wherever people congregate in secular venues beyond places of worship or whenever people share a similar lifestyle. The settings and purposes vary. Some chaplains serve formal institutions or well-organized service clubs, while others support informal affinity groups and hobbyists. Some minister to settled residents, while others support transient or leisure populations. Some work at transportation hubs, while still others minister at entertainment-related gatherings. Some of these ministries overlap with various types of workplace chaplaincy.

### OVERVIEW

This chapter offers various types of community and lifestyle chaplains. These are representative but not all-inclusive. Community and lifestyle chaplains serve in airports, retirement communities, residential treatment facilities, cruise ships, racetracks, legislatures, airports and seaports, civic clubs, private and nongovernmental organizations, labor unions, national parks, recreational theme parks—and the list continues to grow. Most of this growth is driven primarily not by institutional mandates and standards but by compelling needs, common interests, and strong support by grassroots organizational leaders.

While many of these organizations or communities utilize volunteers as chaplains, the qualifications to serve must be well beyond having a loving heart and an attitude of service. Regardless of the venue, chaplains should possess proper education, training, competencies, skills, cultural understanding, intimate knowledge of the organization, awareness of unique communal stresses and strains, and preferably endorsement and certification (as appropriate). Successful community and lifestyle chaplains are committed to lifelong learning and continuous refinement of their skills, regardless of whether they are bi-vocational or full-time, paid or volunteers. They devote themselves to serving everyone in their sphere of influence, regardless of religious preference. In all these ways, they are faithful to the chaplaincy's mission, ministry, and legacy.

# TRANSPORTATION INDUSTRY CHAPLAINCY

## Dr. Ron Fraser

Professional drivers are one of the unhealthiest professional populations. Truck drivers are at high risk for poor health outcomes due to low job control, chronic stress and fatigue, erratic schedules, disrupted sleep patterns, extreme time pressure, high levels of disrespect, excessive time away from support system(s), poor access to health care, and high cost of operation. The workload demands of trucking weigh heavily on a driver, developing burnout, anxiety, depression, sleep disorders, marital and family issues, sexual addictions, substance abuse, and diminished cognitive ability.[308] Stress and depression adversely affect health outcomes such as hypertension, myocardial infarction, stroke, wound healing, and cellular lifespan/aging. As a result, unhealthy drivers have a reduced quality of judgment and an increased risk of jeopardizing highway safety.[309]

Additionally, many uncontrollable factors also impact professional truck drivers. For example, long-haul drivers receive pay by the mile. Yet driving time and mileage are governed individually and in combination with government regulations, highway, traffic and weather conditions, equipment failures, loading and unloading issues, and more.

Thus, developing a driver's initiative that includes caring for our professional drivers' physical, psychological, and spiritual needs is essential. Christina Ross, a writer for the National Institutes of Health, states, "Unless and until medicine embraces the paradigm of the patient as a mental, physical and spiritual being, the medical industry is destined to be stuck in an infinite

---

[308] Mona Shattell et al., "Trucking organization and mental health disorders of truck drivers," *Issues in Mental Health Nursing* 33:7 (2012): 436–44, https://jhu.pure.elsevier.com/en/publications/trucking-organization-and-mental-health-disorders-of-truck-driver, accessed 28 September 2021.
[309] Yorghos Apostolopoulos et al., "Health survey of US long-haul truck drivers: work environment, physical health, and healthcare access," *Work (Reading, Mass.)* 46,1 (2013): 113–23, https://pubmed.ncbi.nlm.nih.gov/23324711/, accessed 28 September 2021.

quandary."[310] She concludes an individual's health care must include, at the very least, an awareness of the cultural and social issues individuals face and the implications for their health outcomes.[311]

The factors impacting the driver's mental, physical and spiritual dimensions are interlinked. TFC Global[312] is working collaboratively with industry stakeholders to provide the necessary integrated Professional Driver Care Model to predict better spiritual and physical outcomes and advance toward those outcomes. TFC Global is the largest transport chaplaincy organization, with chaplains across the United States, Canada, and five countries overseas. These chaplains seek to minister and provide spiritual care to professional drivers, families, and the trucking community at truck stops and trucking-related companies. On a day-to-day basis, they deal with addiction, pornography, depression, suicide, broken marriages, and human trafficking. It is unimaginable what goes on behind the scenes in this industry, affecting Christians and non-Christians alike.[313] TFC Global is about building relationships, sharing the gospel, and providing a place for drivers to regenerate physically, mentally, and spiritually. The TFC Global chaplaincy program provides an accessible and effective model that integrates physical, behavioral, and spiritual care as well as training programs designed specifically for the professional driver.

In the trucking community, chaplains play a vital role in encouraging those in the trucking industry to develop and strengthen their relationship with God. Healthy religious expression and involvement can help individuals cope with stress, depression, and anxiety and provide a greater sense of

---

[310] Christina L. Ross, "Integral Healthcare: The Benefits of Integrating Complementary and Alternative Medicine with a Conventional Healthcare Practice," *Integrative Medical Insights* 4 (19 October 2009): 13–20, https://www.ncbi.nlm.nih.gov/pmc/articles/PMC3093682/, accessed 15 July 2021.

[311] Ross, "Integral Healthcare."

[312] Transport for Christ, founded in 1951 by Canadian Reverend Jim Keys, now is headquartered in Pennsylvania and also partners with national ministries in Russia, Zambia, Brazil, Paraguay, and Tanzania. See https://tfcglobal.org/, accessed 28 September 2021.

[313] For more information, see Yorghos Apostolopoulos et al., "Sex work in trucking milieux: 'lot lizards,' truckers, and risk," *Nursing Forum* 47(3) (2012): 140–152, https://doi.org/10.1111/j.1744-6198.2012.00272.x, accessed 28 September 2021.

well-being, happiness, optimism, hope, meaning, and purpose. A chaplain's support of religious involvement can help individuals lower substance abuse, create healthier lifestyles, and encourage marital and family stability. This effort can also increase workplace reliability, job satisfaction, more productive employees, and less job turnover. For these reasons, many organizations, both trucking and non-trucking, Christian and non-Christian, invest in a chaplaincy program at their company locations.

# BIKER CHAPLAINCY

## Chaplain Jeffrey Claes

God's call to individual participation in a chaplaincy ministry is as varied as the assortment of people God calls. To some, the call to a community/lifestyle chaplaincy is a professional career role. For others, this call involves a bi-vocational responsibility. Some would ask, "Where can I go, and how can I serve?" The answer to this question may be right in front of them, next on their life's agenda. Author and pastor Henry Blackaby explained, "Knowing God comes through a relationship with a Person. This is an intimate love relationship with God. Through this relationship, God reveals Himself, His purposes, and His ways; and He invites you to join Him where He is already at work."[314]

Community or lifestyle chaplains provide ministry in a specialized setting that may include transient work locations like truck stops, parking lots, RV parks, national or state parks, boating marinas, golf courses, rodeo arenas, and sports facilities or activity locations for running, bicycling and in my case, motorcycling.

I have always ridden motorcycles. By the age of ten, I started a business refurbishing and selling bicycles. Within two years, I had motorized them and began riding. At age fifteen, I rode street-legal motorcycles. And by age eighteen, I made cross-country trips. Through my young adult years, well-meaning people cautioned me to stay away from the rough-looking fellas on heavy bikes who could cause pain and possibly rob or steal your machine. It was common practice to go out of your way to steer clear of such groups. I heeded that advice until the age of forty-eight, when I purchased my first Harley-Davidson motorcycle. At that point, I began to change my attitudes and practices. For twenty-seven years, I rode BMW motorcycles, generally alone. Culturally, a BMW rally is a coming together of two to three thousand individuals, whereas a Harley-Davidson rally is a coming together of fifty or

---

[314] Henry T. Blackaby and Claude V. King, *Experiencing God: Knowing and Doing the Will of God*, Workbook edition (Nashville: Lifeway Christian Resources, 1990).

so groups of twenty or more riders. The key point is individual identity versus group-affiliation identity.

One day, a Harley Owners Group (HOG) director at the local Harley-Davidson dealership called. He stated he knew I was a Sunday-school teacher and a deacon in a local church, and I had purchased a new Harley-Davidson out of state. He said he was a Christian and wanted an increased Christian influence in his group, and asked if I would join as a chaplain. God prepares you every day of your life and will present you with opportunities to serve Him and His good purpose. Sometimes that invitation is an extreme opportunity, and this was one such opportunity in my life. I knew Jesus and I knew bikes, but I had no vision or clue how to put the two together.

Through my affiliation with the Baptist General Convention of Texas (BGCT), I secured the chaplaincy training and endorsement that enabled me successfully and safely to operate in a cross-cultural chaplain ministry in motorcycle circles. A reasonably small number of groups delineate the motorcycle world and cultural activity. Many in these groups consider themselves to be outsiders, members of an alternative culture on the fringes of ordinary public life.

This being the case, access and interaction can be limited only to participants, and visibility may not be an objective. With developed and acquired cross-cultural knowledge, an understanding of respect, the confidence of the Holy Spirit and the integrity of Scripture, it is possible to share God's love in many diverse and limited-access settings. God will equip the called and use the equipped. If individuals commit to obtaining the knowledge required for the successful completion of the mission, a successful mission can be the result.

In my specialized chaplaincy setting of the highways and byways of North America, I have traveled more than three hundred thousand miles, riding my motorcycle across the continent for ministry participation over the past eighteen years. I have loved sharing Christ in all fifty of the United States and all ten Canadian provinces and three territories (including four trips to the arctic regions of Canada on motorcycle mission trips). My chaplaincy ministry has led to establishing an educational foundation dedicated to volunteer chaplain training, which I currently direct, and forming the "Rushing Wind Biker Fellowship" mission church in a motorcycle dealership. I am presently their pastor. I am also a Regional Director for the patched Motorcycle Ministry Bikers for Christ and do church planting and mission consulting.

God's call to individual participation in a chaplaincy ministry is rich with opportunity and variety in whatever setting it may be. The key question is our response to God's call.

# SPORTS CHAPLAINCY

## Dr. Mark Louis Johnson Sr.

The Cleveland Indians baseball team's twenty-two-game win streak caused mass hysteria, revealing the insanity of sports rarely experienced by players, coaches, owners, or fans. The atmosphere was electric, maybe even intoxicating, as thousands of supporters flocked to get a glimpse of anything remotely connected to Major League Baseball's (MLB) Cleveland Indians Organization, a team poised to break the 1916 New York Yankees' twenty-six-game consecutive win record. Although advancements in technology, nutrition, and athletic performance enhanced the game, not many teams had threatened this historical record in over one hundred seasons. However, the 2017 Cleveland Indians put together a regular season winning streak that sped the heartbeats of millions of Yankee fans wanting to keep the record in New York.

Media outlets converged in Cleveland, Ohio, with their top sports reporters seeking a story to lead the evening news or headline the morning newspaper. Impassioned baseball fans surrounded the secured player parking lot in hopes of catching a glimpse of their favorite athlete entering the ballpark. As the team chaplain, I had player clearance and could move freely throughout the stadium. Entering the player parking lot meant I, too, received cheers from adoring fans who waved wildly in my direction. And yes, I waved back. Walking down restricted corridors next to multimillion-dollar athletes offered an exhilarating sense of pride and belonging as people watched "us" in awe. However, if being in the limelight, enjoying access to players, or craving fan adoration became stimulating in a negative way, I could compromise the gospel and fall prey to the "privilege of access."

Over the years, I have received emails, phone calls, and conversed with individuals expressing a call to sports chaplaincy. I quickly communicate that Jesus did not send His disciples to sports chaplaincy but to people. I share this reality for two reasons: first, to shatter any glorified perception of sports chaplaincy, and second, to broaden the mindset of sports chaplaincy. I define a sports chaplain as "a disciple of Jesus ministering to people in a sports context."

While ministering to the athletes is primary, the sports context includes families, season ticket holders, ushers, beer vendors, and security guards, all with ministry needs. Ministry opportunities are at every turn, and the sports chaplain must focus on God and avoid becoming enamored of the "privilege of access." Athletes are influencers in high school, college, or professional ranks, and ministering to them requires three foundational characteristics: humility, personal discipline, and patience.

First, humility is a core Christian value. The apostle Paul urged believers in Philippi to "Do nothing from selfishness or empty conceit, but with humility of mind regard one another as more important than yourselves."[315] In an ego-driven profession, humility is critical for reaching athletes. Chaplains with arrogant or know-it-all personas will lose credibility with athletes. For example, with access to the players' clubhouse, I could enter at any time. However, I decided never to enter unless invited by a player, and even then, there were times when I greeted them from the hallway, reminding them of our designated time for chapel. I humbly walked, not taking advantage of the "privilege of access."

Second, personal discipline is essential for personal growth and modeling. If sports chaplains expect players to grow, spiritual growth must continue to occur within the sports chaplain. In 1 Corinthians 11:1, the apostle Paul tells believers at Corinth, "Be imitators of me, just as I also am of Christ." As team chaplain, questions about my walk with Christ led to discussions on prayer, devotions, and discipleship as players sought to grow spiritually. Think about it; athletes receive instruction from coaches, many of whom are former players and can model a throwing, catching, or hitting motion. When athletes desire to grow in the faith, the sports chaplain is the "coach" and is expected to explain and model how to follow Christ. So, lead by example.

Third, patience is needed to defeat the negative thoughts a sports chaplain may encounter when serving. Despite the many chapel services, Bible studies, coffee meetings, and corridor conversations, it is easy for chaplains to drift into a period of doubt. Patience is needed to overcome internal struggles, giving chaplains the strength to fight feelings of inadequacy. With 162

---

[315] Phil 2:3.

games, most days are not exhilarating. Staying patient leads to a faithfulness that becomes routine over time. Athletes live in routines, so stay patient.

Lastly, with family, friends, coaches, media, sports agents, and fans vying for athletes' attention, the sports chaplain must be capable of making the gospel message relevant and applicable. The opportunity to lead athletes is nothing to take for granted. Athletes at all levels are influencers and ministering to influencers can impact those influenced by the athletes.

Do you still want to be a sports chaplain? Start with your local recreation center, neighborhood softball league, middle school football program, or local bowling association. If a person is serious about being a sports chaplain, it does not matter the team. For example, I ministered to a high school basketball team while serving as the chaplain of the Cleveland Indians. It is the laborers that are few, not the harvest.

On Friday, 15 September 2017, the Cleveland Indians' winning streak ended with a one-run loss to the Kansas City Royals. Following the loss, the media frenzy subsided, the number of fans surrounding the players' parking lot returned to normal, and the heightened security diminished. However, what remained consistent was the Sunday chapel service. Jesus was the topic of conversation, not the win streak, not the loss, just Jesus. After the chapel time, each player and coach in attendance received my traditional sports embrace accompanied by the words, "Have a good day at work."

As the players left, one turned back and said, "Thanks for not treating us like celebrities."

# INDEPENDENT SCHOOL EDUCATION CHAPLAINCY

## Dr. Will Whitmore

I grew up in Minnesota and attended public school. As a result, I was never exposed to a boarding school and assumed one attended such an institution for only three reasons. First, you were an athletic phenom who needed to be in a specific environment (like Sydney Crosby, who attended the hockey powerhouse Shattuck St Mary's in Faribault, MN). Second, you were a juvenile delinquent who was one more problem away from prison (like a boy in my sixth-grade class who got sent to military school). Finally, your parents were wealthy and sent you away to an institution to raise you (uncommon in the greater Twin Cities metro area). My only frame of reference was the 1989 movie *The Dead Poet's Society*, which did not paint a positive picture of daily life at one of these institutions. So, it was with much amazement and surprise that I felt God leading me to pursue ministry in a boarding school or independent day school. I discovered not a world of spoiled or undisciplined children, but a unique educational environment that can be highly conducive to chaplaincy.

While chaplaincy at the preuniversity level has been around for a long time, there is minimal writing or research on the subject. When literature addresses education chaplaincy, it is often from the perspective of those serving in institutions of higher learning. As a result, chaplains who serve in other educational settings, such as elementary/primary and secondary schools, are often omitted from this discourse. Furthermore, some may assume a transference between the various levels of education, which is not entirely accurate.

Serving primary or secondary schools as a chaplain occurs within independent schools, often at an institution with some religious history.[316] As religious identity continues to decline numerically within the Western world, many schools continue to honor their religious roots by employing a

---

[316] At the time of writing, some states are considering the introduction of chaplains in public schools in various states. This essay intentionally avoids discussing the current debate on this issue.

chaplain. Still, they may not require worship, affirm religious pluralism, and see the chaplain as a person who serves all regardless of one's faith perspective (or none). As a result, chaplains serving in independent schools need to be mindful of their school's history, viewpoints toward religion both historically and contemporarily, and expectations regarding support for students, regardless of belief. Roles within this ministry are varied. If a school is religiously affiliated, the chaplain will likely lead worship and attend to the duties of a minister, including pastoral care to the entire community (including alumni and parents). They are also often asked to provide religious support for individuals of other faiths and help educate faculty and students regarding various religious traditions. Chaplains also fulfill other tasks within the institution, including teaching, coaching athletics, supervising dormitories (if a boarding school), advising students, and sitting on various administrative councils. Many chaplains who serve boarding schools live on or near campus, intertwining their lives with the lives of students and colleagues.

The breadth of roles and skills used in this ministry is often more expansive than other forms of ministry. For example, I currently serve at a secondary boarding and day school where I lead Christian worship on Sunday (not required attendance for students) while ensuring my non-Christian students' diverse faith needs are met. I also teach nonsectarian courses on spirituality, focusing on the individual's spirit and its development. Additionally, I teach multiple classes, perform various administrative duties, advise a group of seven students, and provide pastoral care to a community of more than five hundred faculty and students. My family and I live a block off campus, welcome students to our home, and spend time on campus regularly going to sporting events or eating in the dining hall. Ministry is constant, engaging, rewarding, and full of blessings.

While a unique ministry in many forms, two elements are more pronounced. First, chaplains can affect the growth of individuals at a crucial time in their lives. Education chaplains need to be literate in childhood and adolescent development, understand how the brain functions at various age levels, and remain mindful of the societal pressures young people face. Chaplains can help teenagers discover who they are and who they can be. Chaplains can challenge them to see their value outside grades and college acceptance and help each student develop personally. Second, chaplains who serve in independent schools get to work with students for a prolonged period. At the secondary school level, I will work with the same students for four years, keep in contact with many after graduation, and serve faculty who may stay for decades. This engagement is even more pronounced when chaplains serve schools that offer primary and secondary education. Juxtaposed with places such as a hospital or airport, where interaction with individuals is short, chaplains in independent schools can provide a sustained ministry of care and support. These elements allow us to dive deeply into individual's lives and care for them during a formative period.

While this ministry was unexpected, I feel fortunate to serve an intentional community where the chaplain's care for students has the potential to impact the rest of their lives.

# HIGHER EDUCATION CHAPLAINCY

Rev. Dr. Janet Fuller and Rev. Dr. Joanne Sanders

When I was eleven, I (Jan) threw myself—weeping—on my bed. It was clear to me then that as a girl in my Baptist upbringing, I would have to choose between being smart and being faithful. Some in my church considered my questions as "doubting" and no one would entertain my wanting to know "why" we believed or practiced aspects of our faith. I consider that day my first call to higher education chaplaincy.

Through a campus minister, I learned that faith and intellect serve each other and create wholeness in college. And I was not the only one struggling, parking faith at the gates of our colleges. In my undergraduate years, it was clear that ministry in higher education was where I wanted to serve, to help students hold their hearts and minds together. Since then, I have served for forty meaningful and wonderful years as chaplain to three academies of higher education: Yale, Hollins, and Elon. University students are developmentally primed to ask the big questions that guide them in life, to name but a few: What kind of person do I want to be? Do I need a religion? What will my family look like? What is my part in systems of injustice and the work of creating justice?

Midway in my career, the attacks of 11 September 2001 challenged many other chaplains and me to attend to our non-Christian, religiously fluid, and secular students. Building a multifaith and interreligious community became a second focus as ministry became intentionally more diverse. I have found, over the years, that when students (and professionals) have a real engagement with religious diversity, especially with a friend or peer, they grow in their spiritual self-understanding as well. Interfaith relationships and experiences act like mirrors in our lives, inviting us to deepen our understanding and commitments, inviting us to more worthy questions.

As a first-generation college student and student athlete, I (Joanne) was deeply inspired and impacted by teachers and coaches. They changed and transformed my life. I wanted to be a part of doing the same for others. It was no surprise that following a twenty-year career combined in teaching and intercollegiate coaching, most of which involved higher education, I found a newfound vocation and call as an Episcopal priest, which opened a pathway to twenty more years in higher education at Stanford University.

This time I served as a different kind of coach. Every day, as I made my way to campus, an ever-present prayer and aspiration remained: How may I be a priest in this place today? It was there I discovered that I, along with others, held a crucial permission-granting practice to invite and accompany students, faculty, and staff to be their wholly human, best selves, often a countercultural act in the academic enterprise.

When we are hired as chaplains by universities and colleges, we tend to the needs of the whole campus community—students, faculty, and staff. Some universities and colleges also welcome and recognize campus ministers employed by and commissioned to represent their denominations, organizations, or parachurch groups on campus.

Higher education chaplains function as mentors to young adults, as they individuate from family and home, find a home in residential education, make friends, search for meaning in spiritual or secular contexts, engage the diversity of the campus, entertain the big questions of their rich developmental moment, and experience a fundamental transformation of body, soul, and mind. Chaplains are also available to faculty and staff; develop, design, and preside at campus rituals; take central leadership roles in moments of crisis or death; and act as the face of public prayerfulness and appropriate ritual. Many chaplains are also responsible for multifaith engagement and programming on campus, collaborating with colleagues across the university, and offering a discerning voice and presence among institutional committees and focus groups.

On any given morning, the chaplain may discuss the morale of the division with Student Life leaders, counsel students questioning their sexual identity, meet Afghan students to plan a vigil for their country, field a report of bias from a student unable to join a required field trip or take an exam because of a holy day observance, and write and publish a reflection for those struggling with anxiety.

During lunch, one may join a discussion of an antiracism book, walk across campus to check in with the president and staff, chat with anxious faculty colleagues about fall plans, or invite a new student sitting alone outside to have coffee later in the week. Afternoons may offer a meeting with a task force to improve the Latinx experience on campus and the possibility of adding a Spanish Mass to the campus religious offerings. In the evening, the chaplain might pick up food for and attend an interfaith dialogue group. Later, the chaplain might answer an email application for the chaplain's discretionary fund from a struggling student. Before bed, the chaplain might prepare for a developmental supervision conversation with a chaplain colleague, write a note to and offer a listening ear to a staff member whose spouse has died, and compose a prayer for a campus gathering.

Higher education chaplaincy takes place primarily in private secular institutions committed to the wholeness of their members and to their communities. University chaplains represent and resource all faiths. They often function as a moral compass or conscience in times of decision or conflict. They sometimes have a faculty or lecturer appointment, teaching in their fields. They participate in searches, bridge silos, advocate for those in need, and remain intentionally present in many settings. Many universities are navigating their secular identities built on religious roots and can seem ambivalent about religion. And while young adults are increasingly anxious and struggling with mental health concerns, academic communities are healthy, vibrant, and diverse. The work of chaplaincy is as varied and unpredictable, strenuous and joyous, as spiritual life can be.

The Association of Chaplaincy and Spiritual Life in Higher Education (ACSLHE, pronounced "axle") is a robust organization supporting chaplains and spiritual life professionals in higher education. Seminarians interested in this exciting and engaging chaplaincy work might consider becoming associate members at www.acslhe.org.[317]

---

[317] Sharon Daloz Parks, *Big Questions, Worthy Dreams: Mentoring Emerging Adults in Their Search for Meaning, Purpose, and Faith*, 2nd ed. (San Francisco: Jossey-Bass, 2011).

# NEIGHBORHOOD CHAPLAINCY

## Chaplain Mary Flin

Urban neighborhoods are among the most challenged spaces in the United States. In urban neighborhoods, many who are poor, sick, addicted, and mentally ill congregate for survival. The currency, ethics, practices, and systems are unique to each neighborhood community. Fear, fate, and fatigue to the point of total exhaustion rule and lead to inertia. Neighborhoods are "tribal" in that people sort themselves into groups and form alliances for survival.

The urban poor are found in jails, prisons, hospitals, hospices, and mental health facilities. Sometimes, people think of the urban poor and the related challenges of poverty as the world's biggest problem. Furthermore, urban churches serving this population may be isolated and may quickly become overwhelmed by the needs of those around them.

But something seems to be unfolding that gives us new hope, and it comes from asking a curious question: "What do urban neighborhoods and other community spaces have in common?" One answer is chaplains! When people are incarcerated, they encounter jail or prison chaplains. Additionally, people interact with chaplains in healthcare settings. The idea of chaplaincy is familiar to urban individuals.

Our vision is to train and deploy chaplains who will work alongside urban churches in our most challenged neighborhoods. These men and women in secular spaces can practice chaplaincy in ways that extend the reach of busy, often overwhelmed urban faith communities as they become a place of peace in the middle of neighborhood storms.

In Topeka, Kansas, we are developing the Neighborhood Chaplaincy model, a form of community chaplaincy that focuses on the spaces around the chaplain's church. As with each form of chaplaincy, neighborhoods require careful consideration regarding theology, ethics, and practice.

The oft-quoted Message Bible version of John 1:14 is an excellent basis for practicing God's presence in these difficult and challenged areas: "The Word became flesh and blood, and moved into the neighborhood." Historically, St. Martin of Tours, with nothing else to give, cut his own cloak and wrapped it around a cold, destitute man. He would dream that night that Jesus wore that shared half of his cloak. Today, with only a little imagination, we can envision chaplains practicing the Presence of the Holy by covering the poor around our abandoned neighborhoods with a cape of love as unto Christ himself.

The theology and historical roots of this urban neighborhood ministry lead to several common ethical considerations for chaplains, such as beneficence, nonmaleficence, justice, autonomy, and restored relationships. To these ethics, we add incarnational ministry, cultural humility, and sacrifice (living among those we serve and sharing in their struggles and victories).

Chaplains ministering in urban spaces should practice at the same level of competence as should be expected of chaplains in any other space. Therefore, we require a year of sound theological training and are collaborating with other seminaries, institutions, and organizations to identify, train, and deploy chaplains into neighborhoods. We train our chaplains in a broad range of necessary skills and build relationships with key individuals in neighborhood churches, police departments, correctional facilities, hospitals, hospice centers, and mental health organizations, any of whom might be a part of the neighborhood chaplain's interdisciplinary team.

These interdisciplinary teams may also include multiple chaplains in the same neighborhood. While many think of high-poverty spaces as one-dimensional, a variety of missional communities may exist in each community. A chaplain might be interested in homeless individuals or formerly incarcerated people. They might love working with children, single and working parents, or older adults—many of whom rarely see the outside of their urban neighborhoods. Perhaps the chaplain has a heart for serving women, men, or teens. Each of these missional communities comes together to make up urban neighborhoods, and each can experience the space created by having their "own chaplain."

It is this created space that allows chaplaincy to have a significant impact. The chaplain has a reason to be present in communities that are suspicious of outsiders. The chaplain is "one of us," especially as they demonstrate incarnational ministry, cultural humility, and sacrifice.

I had been "neighboring on purpose" in my high-poverty neighborhood for a decade before I became a chaplain. We seldom use the term *missionary*, but I consider myself an urban missionary and moved to the neighborhood where I attended church, a once-beautiful center of our state capital, now boasting the highest infant mortality rate in our state and one of the highest rates of violence in our city. During that decade, I made friends, led neighborhood Bible camps, and hosted home groups. Four years ago, I was moved literally around the corner where I would become friends with people who are primarily homeless, suffering from active addictions and mental-health challenges, and caught in the inertia of a housing crisis. Even in this short-distance move, I was now in a new missional community. Each group taught me a great deal. Yet, I have discovered that I have much more to learn in both the practical aspects of chaplaincy and in cultural humility.

The ethic of "cultural humility" came into focus for me while studying Clinical Pastoral Education (CPE). I realized that while I need to continue to strive for *competence* in understanding those who live in my diverse community, a higher aspiration is cultural *humility*. I am the "sojourner" and, as such, the learner in my community; and no matter how much I learn, I will never actually "know."

In reflection, I remember that my first lessons in chaplaincy and cultural humility came at the feet of women in our local homeless shelter several years ago. The shelter graciously allowed my daughter and me to set up a "spa day" each year for several years. We brought in soft lights, rugs, hot cocoa and chocolates and set up foot baths and paraffin waxes for hands. Women and little girls whose feet bore the evidence of the struggles of homelessness and poverty came in, and I had the opportunity to sit at their feet while they soaked in warm, bubbly, scented water and humbly allowed me to massage their feet. I didn't counsel, give advice, or even talk much. I just massaged their feet and listened. Each year, these women visited with one another, and I heard their perspectives on that season's community problems, personal heartaches, and latent dreams. They showed me how to be a learner through listening and conversations, and I commit to remaining a learner, humbly growing in understanding but acknowledging that I will always stop short of fully knowing the cultures around me.

We have built our missional community around the table, which we have found to be a powerful space. We share a community meal each Sunday night attended by an average of sixty people, many of whom live in garages, campers, sheds, houses without utilities, or on the streets. We call our community meal "Neighbor Night."

One night, early in our neighborhood chaplaincy initiative, we had just finished Neighbor Night and one of several shootings over a few months occurred. I experienced the sirens, helped calm a frantic victim, tried to navigate the 911 call, and was the only one who could stay and wait for police and ambulance due to the complex relationship between my neighborhood and the police. I went to the hospital, where I would typically have to wait in my car, but because I am a chaplain, they immediately gave me access, a place to wait, and later escorted me to my neighbor to pray with him before his surgery. I spent a long night with the victim's friend in a nearly empty waiting room. This friend turned out to be someone with an untold story, which had caused her pain for several years. I listened to her story through the night and greeted my neighbor's family, who arrived later in the morning.

When I visited my neighbor in his room, we talked about God, life, and death—topics we had never discussed in the neighborhood. As I listened, I learned he had thought quite a bit about God. He appreciated our praying together, even though we each had different spiritual perspectives. As I left, I said, "I'll be back soon, friend." He replied, "Thank you, (short pause) friend." My neighbor taught me how many practical things I need to learn to be effective at neighborhood chaplaincy. He allowed me into all the spaces he had to navigate during his crisis. He shared his story, thoughts, and questions. And, most important, he allowed this chaplain to move from neighbor to friend.

Many times since then I have heard "Thank you for being my friend." At 11 p.m. when gardening with a headlamp or during a jail visit or on the steps or at dinner or porch sitting, neighbors have let me into the complications of their lives through the doorways of conversations and stories that would never be heard in a structured practice. As a result, our neighborhood is eating together, praying together, solving problems together, and slowly healing together. Our experience encourages us to continue to chase the question, What if every neighborhood had a chaplain of its own?

# MEMORABLE MOMENT
# "HALLELUJAH"

### Chaplain Maytal Saltiel

University chaplains are blessed with many memorable moments—times of heartbreak, self-discovery, and dark nights of the soul. I have had the privilege of watching generations of students find their voices and discover meaning and purpose in their lives. I have walked with them through grief and heartrending pain and helped them celebrate life's splendor. However, I want to share a moment that has stuck with me throughout the years and illustrates the sacred, surprising, and joyful nature of a university chaplain's work.

Every year the Yale Chaplain's Office takes a group of sophomores down to Washington, DC, for a week during spring break. We train these students to be our Chaplaincy Fellows—to experience radical hospitality from diverse religious communities and learn how to facilitate conversations rooted in life's big questions around meaning, purpose, success, and growth when they are back on campus. We look for students who are interested in working with people from a broad spectrum of backgrounds and beliefs. They are curious, humble listeners looking to expand their horizons.

In our week-long trip to DC, we visit religious communities, learn from activists, and participate in community service projects. In 2014 when I took students on this remarkable trip, we started our week at a worship service at a Sikh Gurdwara. We sat on the basement floor with our hosts to share in *langar* (the community meal) together during the visit. As the week went on, we learned from a Cambodian Buddhist monk, met with a housing equity organizer, experienced a *maariv* (evening) service at an Orthodox synagogue, put in flooring for an afterschool center, spoke with missionaries at the Mormon Temple visitors' center, and visited an Islamic community center. We traveled from community to community, experiencing the warmth and welcome while our hosts patiently answered questions and shared a sacred glimpse into their worlds. It is a memorable experience for our students; they enter spaces and meet with communities they often knew nothing about before.

One of our evenings, about halfway through our week, we went to a Bible study at an African Methodist Episcopal (AME) megachurch. The

AME congregation was in their typical weekday worship service, complete with a praise band and sermon. Our hosts were warm and welcoming, with hugs free-flowing in this pre-pandemic moment. Though we were tired at the night's end, we came back together for "circle-up" time.

Every evening after the day's adventures, we had time to process and share. Some were touched by the welcome they experienced at the church. Others reflected on the vital role the afterschool center played in the community. A sweet Hindu pre-med student shyly asked a question.

"I was wondering if you could tell me what *hallelujah* means."

In my excitement, I launched into an explanation of the root of the Hebrew word.

"Oh," he responded, "I had only ever heard it in 'It's Raining Men'" (a popular cover song by The Weather Girls).

We all burst into laughter. Our divinity student intern laughed so hard he nearly peed his pants. It took a good five minutes for us all to calm down, remembering yet again how the things we sometimes take for granted are novel and confusing to others. Living in a diverse community is a joyful blessing full of surprise and delight.

## REFLECTION QUESTIONS

1. Reflect on the various settings where community and lifestyle chaplains serve. How might the specific environment, such as a truck stop, a sports arena, or a university, shape the approach and priorities of a chaplain's ministry?
2. Each community has its own culture, rituals, and language. Why is it essential for a chaplain to understand their community along with its uniqueness and culture? What is the risk of ignoring a community's heritage and culture?
3. When listening or offering spiritual care, at what point do you refer a counselee, such as a student, faculty, or staff member, to a counseling center? How would you do this?
4. How can chaplains establish trust and build meaningful connections in transient or leisure communities where individuals may reside temporarily?
5. Reflect on the challenges in specific communities, such as truck drivers dealing with isolation and stress. How can chaplains address these issues and provide holistic care that includes emotional and spiritual support?

APPENDIX ONE

# A MENTORING TOOL—
# TOWARD COMPETENCY
# AS A PROFESSIONAL CHAPLAIN

Chaplain Dick Millspaugh

Following a modified version of Martin Broadwell's construct in chapter 3, I highlighted a learning process—a journey in awareness, managing anxiety, and reflective practice that results in competency growth. This learning moves from Unconscious Incompetence to Conscious Incompetence to Conscious Competence and finally to Unconscious Competence. Before proceeding, I suggest the reader review chapter 3, "Professional Competencies."

Five certifying chaplaincy organizations have published a common set of competencies needed to be a proficient professional chaplain, and others have established their own.[318] Commonly accepted chaplain competencies provide a foundation for educating and examining potential chaplains.

---

[318] In 2016–2017 five board certifying organizations agreed on and published the "Common Qualifications and Competencies for Professional Chaplains." See https://www.professionalchaplains.org/files/2017%20Common%20Qualifications%20and%20Competencies%20for%20Professional%20Chaplains.pdf, accessed 21 July 2020. Established by the Association for Clinical Pastoral Education, the Association of Professional Chaplains, the Canadian Association for Spiritual Care, the National Association of Catholic Chaplains, and Neshama: Association of Jewish Chaplains. Anyone pursuing professional chaplaincy is encouraged to join one of these organizations as soon as possible to learn what they have to offer, as well as to learn about their certifying track. The Spiritual Care Association (SCA) established its own standards and examination process for certification, while accepting qualifying certified chaplains from many other organizations. The

As it relates to functioning as a chaplain, each competency is defined in four arenas on the following pages. I call these arenas because each involves a dynamic struggle within a person's awareness. Essentially, this struggle is a search to find oneself as distinct from and in relationship to others. The arenas on the left side of each competency below illustrate a person who lacks understanding of what has shaped the person's sense of self and has little empathic connection with others. As a person grows in empathy, as a person comes to understand that the reality of others is different, as a person is able to have compassion for others, then the person moves to arenas on the right side of each grid.

As this growth occurs, this person will have less need to defend the person's self-image, will gain a desire to gain a deeper insight into how the person's personality and spirit has been formed, and will experience a willingness to explore differences and similarities with others. This maturation often results in a passion to serve others.

What follows is derived from what I have learned in my journey, a partial, illustrative list of competencies for those who seek to become chaplains. While you will likely discover a multitude of ways to use this list, let me suggest several possible uses.

**For those considering chaplaincy.** Review the list of competencies. Can you see yourself in such a list? If so, notice in what areas you feel you are well on your way. Notice what areas you would be excited to learn more. Pick one or two competencies to work on developing. Find someone to help you in that arena. Keep track of and celebrate your progress.

**For students in formal chaplaincy education.** Review the list and rate yourself. In which areas do you consider yourself to be strong and in which areas can you use your supervisor, your peers, other disciplines to help you in your journey toward fuller competency? Ask them to rate you. How close are their assessments to each other? How close are their assessments to yours? Have you identified any blind spots for you that merit more attention? In

---

SCA is an affiliate of HealthCare Chaplaincy Network TM (HCCN), which established evidence-based scope of practice and evidence-based quality indicators prior to establishing SCA in 2016. See https://www.spiritualcareassociation.org/certification.html.

addition, if a specialized field appeals to you, check the required standards and competencies of those organizations.

**For faculty or supervisors of Clinical Pastoral Education.** Consider sharing this tool with students as one way to focus on competencies and growth. After establishing meaningful relationships, ask students to rate themselves and each other. After reflecting on peer group input, ask each student to select one or two competencies to analyze and to develop a plan to engage a learning process, which can be assessed at a given time by the student, peers, and supervisor.

Several words of encouragement:

1. Don't be overwhelmed by the following list of competencies. No one person is fully competent, comfortable, or confident in all these areas. Choose to work on one or two areas that will enhance your particular interest in chaplaincy and your personal life. Once you feel growth in those areas, choose one or two additional competencies to develop.
2. The purpose of this grid is to help students and educators choose areas of competency for intentional growth and celebration. This grid should not be used as a scientifically researched, peer-reviewed tool to determine job performance.
3. This grid does not contain an all-inclusive or prioritized list of competencies for any specialized ministry but rather is a living, amendable document.
4. Note that various specialized settings will have different competencies.
5. These competencies would benefit from a more thorough set of definitions.
6. I encourage research directed to the relationship of a particular competency to outcomes.

Each competency below moves from 1. Unconscious Incompetence, to 2. Conscious Incompetence, to 3. Conscious Competence, to 4. Unconscious Competence. Each competency moves from self-absorption to service of the patient or client, the institution, the community, and the world. Welcome to an exciting and humbling journey.

## 1. EMPATHY/COMPASSION—Empathy is the ability to experience another person's feelings and thoughts. Compassion is the desire to help another person for whom one has empathy.

| Stays emotionally distant from, feels sorry for, or pities the patient. | | Seeks empathic connection with patient, but often fails to do so. | | A. Makes solid empathic connection with patient, resulting in deepening relationship.<br><br>B. Moves from empathy to help patient understand self on a motivational level resulting in patient developing a more compassionate relationship with self. | | Models empathic response with staff, and peers, thus teaching by example. Helps staff empathize with difficult patient/family resulting in creation of a healthy environment in conflicted situations. Helps the institution empathize with the needs of employees and community and take steps toward healing. | |
|---|---|---|---|---|---|---|---|
| 1 | 2 | 3 | 4 | 5 | 6 | 7 | 8 |

## 2. CONTAINMENT—Containment is the capacity internally to manage thoughts, feelings, and behaviors such that the power of the professional position is not used to the advantage of the chaplain, or personal issues are not projected into the chaplain-other relationship.

| Takes personally patient's anger, sadness, withdrawal, etc. and reacts defensively. | | Seeks to contain and objectively interpret the patient's emotional content but often becomes defensive, or still sees self as responsible for patient's reality. | | A. Often contains responses to patient's emotional content, avoids taking it personally, and empathically helps patient feel understood.<br><br>B. Nearly always contains responses to patient's emotional content, understands and appropriately helps patient understand the real sources of emotions, resulting in patient's expressed sense of understanding and relief and gratitude. | | Models containment with staff and peers. Is able to teach containment by example and didactics. | |
|---|---|---|---|---|---|---|---|
| 1 | 2 | 3 | 4 | 5 | 6 | 7 | 8 |

**3. PERSONAL IDENTITY**—Personal identity is how one views the self as one interacts with the world, outside of a professional role. Personal identity consists of all the aspects of one's history and experience in a "gestalt" by which one understands and represents oneself.

| Lacks awareness of personal history, gender, sexual identity, race and any disabilities and their influence on self-understanding and functioning. | | Grows in awareness of personal history but finds difficulty in owning or discussing basic themes. | | Clearly understands and is able to articulate personal history as it applies to and is differentiated from professional and pastoral identity and is often able to use personal history in patient assessment and treatment resulting in:<br><br>A. patient spiritual healing and<br><br>B. patient being able to integrate the pastoral care experience resulting in ongoing healing outside the pastoral relationship. | | Is able to help staff and institution understand the impact of personal and institutional history on current self-understanding and functioning and challenge each to make healthy choices. | |
|---|---|---|---|---|---|---|---|
| 1 | 2 | 3 | 4 | 5 | 6 | 7 | 8 |

**4. AUTHORITY**—Authority is the power that comes with the professional role of being a recognized chaplain, as well as a person's ability to claim one's own rights and value as a human being equal to all others.

| Is threatened by or avoids authority, uses authority abusively, or takes a subservient or antagonistic role. | | Is able to discuss issues of conflict with present and historic authority figures, but rarely able to claim their own authority. | | Understands, owns and articulates their authority issues, and is able to use one's authority with patients and staff in a way that results in spiritual healing. Advocates on behalf of patients and staff and institution for just and ethical interventions. | | Uses authority to build systems which provide ethical, compassionate care to patients, staff, physicians, that challenges misuse of institutional or personal authority and encourages institutional community building and service. | |
|---|---|---|---|---|---|---|---|
| 1 | 2 | 3 | 4 | 5 | 6 | 7 | 8 |

## 5. PASTORAL IDENTITY

Pastoral identity is the assumption and execution of pastoral roles such as counselor, teacher, intercessor, preacher, evangel, shepherd, and much more, but often summarized as pastor, priest, and prophet.

| Confuses role of chaplain with personal identity. | Is able to discuss role/function of chaplain but has difficulty discussing how pastoral identity relates to and differs from personal identity. | A. Has integrated and is able to discuss how personal identity informs pastoral and professional identity. Is able to function within identified roles/functions and use personal identity as a resource in patient care.<br><br>B. Is remarkably skillful in using pastoral skills well integrated with personal and professional identity resulting in patients often experiencing spiritual healing. | Is able to help staff differentiate and integrate personal and professional identities. |
|---|---|---|---|
| 1   2 | 3   4 | 5   6 | 7   8 |

## 6. SELF-CARE

Self-care is the regular practice of behaviors that maintain and promote physical, mental, and spiritual health.

| Is unaware and does not practice self-care of body, mind, and spirit. | Is able to define basic practices in self-care of body, mind, and spirit as they relate to self, has created a plan for the same. | Has started regular actions toward an established self-care plan, has markers for goals, has recruited one or more persons as an accountability agent. | Is able to articulate the stages leading to behavioral change and teach them. Models healthy self-care. May teach one area of body, mind, or spiritual self-care. |
|---|---|---|---|
| 1   2 | 3   4 | 5   6 | 7   8 |

**7. PROFESSIONAL IDENTITY**—Professional identity is the self-concept one assumes when acting as a member of a given profession that has established norms, practices, ethical responsibilities, beliefs, and values. Professional identity results in the assumption and execution of the authorities and responsibilities granted and dictated by the profession as its members relate to those they serve, to other team members, to the institution and certifying bodies to which they relate.

| Does not understand professional function/role or its relationship to practice of patient spiritual care. | | Has minimal awareness of relationship between personal, pastoral, and professional identity and is somewhat able to discuss how that relates to other professions in a way to provide positive patient care. | | Has a well-integrated and articulated professional identity which one effectively uses in relating with patients and other professions. Is able to describe how one's functioning complements the treatment team in providing integrated care for the patient resulting in team member's awareness of the chaplain's contribution, and seeking the same. | | So effectively practices chaplaincy that team members seek chaplain's collaboration that they may contribute to the patient's spiritual well-being from within their disciplines, resulting in earlier discharge of a more spiritually healthy patient, connected with community resources and or a patient more able to face death or disability with spiritual resources and spiritual comfort. | |
|---|---|---|---|---|---|---|---|
| 1 | 2 | 3 | 4 | 5 | 6 | 7 | 8 |

## 8. USE OF SOCIAL AND BEHAVIORAL SCIENCE

Use of social and behavioral science refers to the integration of these disciplines of knowledge into the practice of chaplaincy care.

| Is unable to describe or use social or behavioral science in relationship to the practice of patient care. | | Is able to describe social or behavioral science in relationship to practice of patient spiritual care, but rarely demonstrates ability to use this knowledge to the advantage of the patient. | | Has a well-integrated knowledge and use of social and behavioral science within a theological framework and demonstrates ability to use this knowledge consistently for the patient's advantage as often acknowledged by the patient and/or other staff. | | Has thoroughly integrated a specialized social or behavioral science into theological framework, is consistently able to use it to the patient's advantage and teaches peers its use. | |
|---|---|---|---|---|---|---|---|
| 1 | 2 | 3 | 4 | 5 | 6 | 7 | 8 |

## 9. COMMUNICATION

Communication refers to the knowledge and practice of means to receive and send information from and to others in such a way as to establish a mutual understanding of meaning.

| Is unable to engage communication that builds trust and deepens relationships. Lacks the competence to summarize and document pastoral care. | | Is able to communicate in ways that form trusting relationships which make disclosure safe. Has the ability to document pastoral care in a way that communicates with other care providers in a clear, concise, and coherent way. | | Uses communication skills in multidisciplinary settings in ways that contribute to the tasks at hand. Chaplain's service is requested by staff and patients. | | Is recruited by the institution to serve its mission in arenas other than chaplaincy because of communication competence. | |
|---|---|---|---|---|---|---|---|
| 1 | 2 | 3 | 4 | 5 | 6 | 7 | 8 |

**10. THEOLOGICAL EXPERTISE**—Theological expertise in professional chaplaincy is the capacity to understand the hopes, needs, and resources of those served, the team, and the institution in theologically meaningful terms and to interpret from theology to the "language" of those served in ways that provide insight, encouragement, and healing.

| Is unable to articulate an internally consistent theology or is unable to allow any theology other than their own. | Is able to articulate an internally consistent theology but is only rarely able to use one's theology to inform patient assessment/treatment in a way that results in the patient experiencing spiritual healing. | Is able to articulate an internally consistent theology to inform patient assessment / treatment in a way that results in the patient experiencing spiritual healing. Is clearly able to work within patient's theology, even if different from the chaplain's theology. | Is able to help staff understand patient's situation from a theological perspective consistent with the language of one's disciplines, which enhances one's ability to care for the patient. Is able to help staff integrate their religious/spiritual history and their discipline. |
|---|---|---|---|
| 1    2 | 3    4 | 5    6 | 7    8 |

**11. ABILITY TO LEARN**—Ability to learn refers to the capacity: to receive and retain information, to receive and integrate constructive feedback, appropriately to apply new information to specific situations, and to manage the inherent anxiety that often comes with learning.

| Is threatened by learning situation and remains defensive and inflexible when challenged or invited to consider another viewpoint. | Is able to state one feels threatened in learning situation and is able to take beginning steps toward new learning. | A. Readily uses learning opportunities<br><br>B. Is able to learn and apply learning to patient's benefit. Seeks constructive feedback and takes it nondefensively. | Understands dynamics of learning and is able to use support and confrontation to enhance the learning of staff and the institution. |
|---|---|---|---|
| 1    2 | 3    4 | 5    6 | 7    8 |

## 12. AGE LEVEL COMPETENCE—Age level competence is the behavior that tailors pastoral assessments and care to the unique abilities, needs, capacities at specific age level development.

| Is unable to articulate how age levels impact identity, perception, and function. | Articulates a basic understanding of age level development but often fails to incorporate this into pastoral assessment or practice. | Is often able to integrate age level development understanding into pastoral assessment and practice in a respectful manner leading to appropriate targeted interventions resulting in healing and growth for the patient. | Is able to teach others regarding the connection between age level development and pastoral practice. |
|---|---|---|---|
| 1  2 | 3  4 | 5  6 | 7  8 |

## 13. MULTICULTURAL MULTIFAITH COMPETENCE—Multicultural, multifaith competence is behavior that tailors pastoral assessments and care to the unique beliefs, values, and customs of the persons being served.

| Is unable to articulate the impact of one's own culture and faith upon one's identity and professional or pastoral functioning. | Is able to utilize one's faith and culture to inform, assess, and intervene in care for others of like faith and culture. Is able to articulate common themes that most faiths and cultures share. Finds it difficult to provide healing pastoral care to those outside the chaplain's own faith tradition, culture, gender orientation, or ethnicity. | Is able to articulate approaches to persons of other faiths and cultures that demonstrates sensitivity, respect, and awareness of vital issues, in such a way as a trusting relationship is formed, is able to refer to professionals outside one's faith or cultural experience. | Is able to teach others regarding the need for sensitivity when dealing with persons of differing faiths or cultures. Helps others identify approaches, issues, resources in dealing with persons of different faiths or cultures. Challenges and facilitates the institution to grow in sensitivity, respect, and responsiveness as regards the needs of persons from differing faiths and cultures. |
|---|---|---|---|
| 1  2 | 3  4 | 5  6 | 7  8 |

**14. ETHICAL COMPETENCE**—Ethical competence is the application of relevant ethical knowledge to the specifics of a given situation in a way to clarify issues and provide ethical guidance for decision-making.

| Is unable to describe ethical principles, or articulate ethical issues abstractly or as related to a particular case. | | Describes ethical principles, issues of ethics often found in practice and to some degree ethical implications or issues of a particular case. Is aware of and able to describe the basics of the Common Code of Ethics for Chaplains, Pastoral Counselors, Clinical Pastoral Educators, and Students. | | Uses ethics to assess patient care and intervene in a manner that clarifies values and empowers others effectively to cope with presenting dilemmas. Upholds and practices the principles of the Common Code. | | Teaches application of ethics. Is able to invite and challenge organized systems to create and utilize structures to provide ethical consultation, education, and policy formation. | |
|---|---|---|---|---|---|---|---|
| 1 | 2 | 3 | 4 | 5 | 6 | 7 | 8 |

**15. GROUP DYNAMICS COMPETENCE**—Group dynamics is the variety of functions group members and leaders may perform to advance the tasks and cohesion of a group.

| Lacks awareness of the dynamics of how groups function and tends to complicate group processes due to personal agenda. Does not seem to be able to stay on the task of the group or contribute to the maintenance of group needs. | | Is able to describe the dynamics of how groups function and is able to contain personal needs from disrupting group functioning. Is able to contribute to the task of the group and support the maintenance needs of the group. | | Demonstrates an ability to comprise groups of peers and trans-disciplinary groups successfully to advance agendas germane to the mission of the organization. Exerts leadership in groups to keep the group on task and contributes to the well-being of the group. Helps to deal with conflictual issues in groups that lead to resolution. | | Is asked to lead groups to advance the mission of the organization. Facilitates or leads community clergy continuing education and introduction to ministry within that institution. | |
|---|---|---|---|---|---|---|---|
| 1 | 2 | 3 | 4 | 5 | 6 | 7 | 8 |

## 16. ABILITY TO ENGENDER A SENSE OF SAFETY AND COMFORT—Ability to engender a sense of safety and comfort is the capacity to assess and respond to the needs, hopes, and resources of those being served in such a way as to build trust and confidence in the chaplain-other relationship.

| Chaplain's own anxiety, lack of skills or uncertainty creates more anxiety or defensiveness in the patient. | Is able to maintain self-comforting and manage their own anxiety so that the patient does not react with anxiety or defensiveness. | A. Chaplain's own sense of peace, self-assurance, awareness of boundaries and self-comforting, engenders a sense of safety to allow the patient to discuss issues relevant to spiritual hopes, needs and resources, promoting healing.<br><br>B. Chaplain's self-acceptance and self-comforting creates a felt sense of healing, non-anxious presence which the patient is able to internalize. | Chaplain's non-anxious presence helps staff and institution maintain or regain a sense of calm. Chaplain is sought out by staff and institution to help bring a sense of hope and reassurance in the midst of unique challenges. |
|---|---|---|---|
| 1    2 | 3    4 | 5        6 | 7    8 |

## 17. FAITH DEVELOPMENT COMPETENCE—Faith development competence is the applied knowledge of theories of faith development to specific situations resulting in a deeper understanding of faith formation and growth for those being served.

| Is unable to articulate faith development theory as it relates to providing spiritual care. | Is able to articulate faith development theory as a means appropriately to assess and intervene in spiritual care needs of the other, but often fails to practice these skills. | Is regularly able to make relational connection with persons of all ages, sensitive to and respectful of faith development issues, leading to healing, integration, and growth for the patient. | Is able to teach others regarding faith development and its relevance to healing and growth, and is able to demonstrate practical intervention skills. |
|---|---|---|---|
| 1    2 | 3    4 | 5    6 | 7    8 |

## 18. ATTENDANCE COMPETENCE

**18. ATTENDANCE COMPETENCE**—Attendance competence is the ability to set aside the chaplain's personal issues in order to be fully present to the person being served.

| Interrupts patient with personal agenda, distracting comments, or inappropriate use of humor; leaves the conversation abruptly. | | Seeks to attend to patient's verbal and nonverbal communication but often misses overt and covert messaging. | | A. Attends to patient's verbal and nonverbal communication resulting in patient-focused conversation.  B. Attends so well to patient's verbal and nonverbal communication that the patient experiences healing and expresses relief or gratitude. | | Is able to teach others skills in attendance by example and didactics. Is able to confront those whose inability to attend to the needs of others does harm. | |
|---|---|---|---|---|---|---|---|
| 1 | 2 | 3 | 4 | 5 | 6 | 7 | 8 |

**19. OFFICIATES AT PUBLIC & PRIVATE RITES, RITUALS & WORSHIP COMPETENCE**—The chaplain is able to perform rites, rituals, and worship within the context and needs of those being served.

| Leads without consideration of the needs of those in attendance. Conveys a sense of anxiety to the degree that those in attendance are distracted or uncomfortable. Or avoids leadership in these areas. | | Gives minimal attention to making the services consistent with the culture of the institution and needs of those in attendance. | | A. Gathers information regarding the needs of those to be in attendance prior to the event. Creates events that speak directly to those needs.  B. Speaks with confidence in ways that bring insight and solace for issues being addressed.  C. Draws participants into being active agents in services. | | Is able to mentor others in the role of facilitating such services. Is available for such services in a larger community or institutional setting. Is sought by the institution to create services and rituals that address unique traumas or celebrations impacting the institution and its staff. | |
|---|---|---|---|---|---|---|---|
| 1 | 2 | 3 | 4 | 5 | 6 | 7 | 8 |

# APPENDIX TWO

# CASE STUDIES[319]

## HEALTHCARE CHAPLAINCY

1. You are a hospital chaplain who sits as a consultant and voting member of the ethics committee of the regional hospital where you are employed. Your input is vital to decisions the committee makes concerning medical-ethical issues. The committee meets routinely from 9 to 11 a.m. on the third Wednesday of every month or as an emergency requires. You are also the hospital's CPE (Clinical Pastoral Education) supervisor, and you conduct a class with your four CPE students from 2 to 4 p.m. every Tuesday and Thursday. This Thursday, you are scheduled to conduct an oral mid-term examination for the students. You are the only person qualified to give the exam; you must be present. The students have been preparing for eight weeks for the exam, and it will take two hours to administer. It is now just a few minutes before 2 p.m., the scheduled time for the exam, and an emergency meeting of the ethics committee has been called. The committee must decide how to advise the hospital staff concerning a life-or-death situation that must be resolved within the next two hours. The problem is very complicated, and it will probably take the entire two hours to resolve. What will you do and why?[320]

---

[319] While these case studies are US-centric, students and instructors should adapt them to fit their region or locale. Thanks to the chaplains who submitted some of these case studies. Note that some case studies are footnoted to "real-life" examples.

[320] Elizabeth Lanphier and Jake Earl, "Abortion Restrictions Put Hospital Ethics Committees in the Spotlight—But What Do They Do?," Ohio Capital Journal, June 26, 2023, https://ohiocapitaljournal.com/2023/06/26/abortion-restrictions-put-hospital-ethics-committees-in-the-spotlight-but-what-do-they-do/, accessed 30 October 2024.

2. The hospital's floor nurse supervisor asks you, as their hospital chaplain, to see Sara because staff are concerned that she is depressed. When you visit her, she expresses profound anger at her family and God for putting her in the facility. With tears, she speaks of feeling not simply deserted but persecuted. She finishes with the question, "Why does God hate me?" How should you respond?

3. As a hospital chaplain, you serve on a community engagement committee. The group gathers after a terrible week of activity and grief within your hospital. In the local high school, a shooting incident left several students dead and many others wounded. The community, school administrators, and student body are traumatized, with many feeling unsafe. Even the hospital staff is affected. It is a small town and hospital, so you are the only chaplain in the community. You know you must do something, but what? Your hospital administrator calls and asks about your plans to assist the hospital and the community. How do you approach such an overwhelming need? What are your priorities and your plans?[321]

4. A staff member calls out to you as the institution's hospice chaplain. You turn to the staff member who asks you to see Yasmin. She is dying. You have not spoken to Yasmin previously, so you knock on her door and enter when she says, "Come in." You introduce yourself. Yasmin smiles and says, "Hello, how can I be right with God?" (no lead-up or small talk). Your window to engage is under three minutes before she falls asleep. (In the real-life situation, she never regains consciousness and dies the next day.) What would you say?

5. The hospice chaplain encountered a terminally ill mother who prided herself in homeschooling her two teenage daughters. But as her health declined and she became bedbound, the patient's spouse and older daughter dutifully took over responsibility for educating the younger daughter. Engaging the patient in conversation, the chaplain immediately uncovered strong feelings of anger related to the fact that her homeschooling responsibilities had been

---

[321] Ericka Anderson, "Uvalde Pastors Mourn Losses Close to Home," *Christianity Today*, May 26, 2022, https://www.christianitytoday.com/2022/05/texas-school-shooting-uvalde-pastor-mourn-chaplain-pray/; accessed 30 October 2024.

taken away from her. These feelings of rage were mixed with depression (loss of meaning and purpose in life) and attempts to micromanage the household. How might the chaplain respond to both the terminally ill mother and family?

6. Betty is a ninety-three-year-old lady whom you have known for nine months. She moved into the long-term care facility due to falls, so she uses a walker and is in the early stages of dementia. Another staff member asks you to visit Betty as she seems "down." When you introduce yourself to Betty, she is initially reserved. She begins to respond to you as you use reflective listening, silence, and presence. Betty tells you she has always felt ashamed that her father sexually abused her for many years as a child. She also discloses that she has struggled with suicidal thoughts throughout her adult life, and given her physical restrictions, the impulse is getting worse. She is considering suicide by jumping off the balcony opposite her room. How do you respond, and what should you do? Are you bound to confidentiality? Why or why not?

7. Martha is visually upset and walks throughout the facility. Each time she sees a staff person, she begs them to help her get home as her young children need her to cook lunch for them. Her panic heightens each afternoon. For this reason, Martha's adult children admitted her to a secure dementia unit. Everyone around her finds her distress painful. The staff asks you, as their chaplain, to visit her. Martha made the same complaint and asked for your assistance. You want to relieve her anxiety, so you consider using therapeutic lying by telling her that her "young children" are well-fed and they will be up to see her later. Is this a good approach? Why or why not?

## MILITARY CHAPLAINCY

8. You are the senior Navy chaplain on an aircraft carrier in the home port for six months. It is scheduled to set sail for a four-month combat tour and has passed a series of routine inspections to prepare for deployment. You are responsible for all aspects of spiritual care on the ship, and you also advise the captain and the MWR (morale, welfare, and recreation) officer concerning matters of health, welfare, and morale that are crucial in helping to determine the fitness of the crew for deployment. You are also a leading minister

in a denominational group that is hosting a regional, five-state conference that began yesterday with about one thousand ministers in attendance. An ordination service to induct a dozen new ministers is scheduled for 7 p.m. this evening. You are to preach the ordination sermon. The worship service and your commitment to preach the sermon have been on the calendar for a year. Just moments ago, you were alerted that a surprise inspection aboard the ship was announced for this evening. The captain's all-staff meeting will begin at 6 p.m. The inspection will last at least three hours. Typically, you might ask a subordinate chaplain to stand in for you, but you have discovered that some alarming problems concerning health and welfare have recently surfaced, which is one of the main reasons for the inspection. What will you do, and why?

9. As a military chaplain, one of your roles is to advise your commander. The commander calls you in and asks, "What do we call the Christmas Tree Lighting? Is it proper to call it a 'Christmas' Tree when people of other faiths attend? Should it be called Holiday Tree Lighting?" How do you advise your leadership about this issue?

10. Your commander's language is offensive and vulgar. Not long after you arrive, people within the unit come to you and ask you to "say something" to the unit commander. They ask if you can get the commander to clean up his language because it's affecting the morale. What do you tell the people within the unit? What do you say to the commander?

11. A family asks you, their daughter's military chaplain, to conduct their loved one's funeral and tells you that they "are not religious." You are not obligated to do the funeral. Do you accept the request? How do you conduct that funeral? What text or emphasis would you take? When leading a funeral or memorial service, would you open the floor for anyone else to speak? Why or why not? At the funeral, one of the family members asks, "Chaplain, do you think she is in heaven?" What do you say?

12. You are meeting with the family of a young Marine pilot, Jack, who was killed in a training accident. Jack's parents and his fiancée have traveled to your base to meet with leaders and receive condolences before memorial services. Lindsey, Jack's fiancée in her mid-twenties, asks to speak with you.

She tells you that she and Jack were to be married after his deployment. Their wedding was to take place three months from now. Lindsey shares her dreams of marrying Jack and raising a family. Now, she says her dreams have died with him, and she declares she will never fall in love again. Lindsey questions whether it is worth continuing to live now that she has lost Jack. "How can I go on?" she asks. As a military chaplain, how might you respond to Lindsey?

13. You get a call to a workplace where Chuck, a military veteran, has had an explosive outburst with his coworkers. Not knowing what had set him off or how to respond, a supervisor called for a chaplain. As you sit with him, Chuck begins to share some traumatic experiences he had during his time in uniform, particularly on one deployment. Chuck recounts his deep regrets over taking lives during the war. He shares that, on this deployment, he looked men in the eyes while taking their lives. Chuck feels tremendous guilt over those experiences, but there's something more. He has a darker secret that he eventually confides. During his deployment, Chuck was also sexually assaulted by another man. He feels ashamed and emasculated by the experience. These things have combined in his heart and mind to create an overwhelming sense of guilt and regret. He's ashamed of what was done to him and guilty about the killing he did. Over and over, he declares: "I know I'm going to hell for what I did." How might you connect with him, and what could you say to Chuck?

14. You and your unit are deployed in a combat area. You are visiting your soldiers at the forward operating base (FOB), knowing this unit has been recently under fire and their patrols attacked with improvised explosive devices (IEDs). While there, you learn of an incident that happened two nights ago. While on guard duty, Private First Class (PFC) Smith watched the road leading into the location. About 150 yards out, he and his battle buddy saw a person digging alongside the road. PFC Smith called leadership and received permission to fire. He missed. The other soldier with him at the observation post identified the person as a child. The team was then sent out to see what was happening. They found a young girl burying her cat at 2 a.m. in the place where it had died. PFC Smith is upset, knowing he almost killed a child. His battle buddy asks you to speak to PFC Smith as he no longer wants to touch a weapon. When you approach him, he says, "Sir, can

I talk to you? I'm having trouble sleeping." As you assess his situation, what are the critical issues? What would you say to him? What would you say to the commander?

15. Your unit has been mobilized for a disaster response. The Guard members have eaten Meals Ready to Eat (MREs) for over a week. The Support Platoon Leader purchased pizzas for the outposts where guard members are on guard duty to keep looters from entering the areas where the Mississippi River was likely to overflow its banks and the levees. When he reached the end of his work area, he came to a site that had a Muslim soldier. The Muslim soldier wants to speak with the chaplain. After all, he could not eat any pizza because all that was left was pork sausage or bacon toppings. What is the issue, and how would you engage the Muslim soldier and back brief leadership?

16. As their chaplain, you know your soldiers have been pressed hard by back-to-back deployments. With recruiting new soldiers down, those who remain have seen a higher "operational tempo." They barely had time back home with their families before getting another tasking order to deploy. What used to feel like a sprint now feels like a marathon but at the same pace. Everyone is exhausted. You get a frantic call from your base back home in the middle of the night. Evidently, a soldier texted his father, "Dad, I love you. I have no one to blame but me. Goodbye." After a frantic search, the young soldier is found, almost dead from his suicide attempt. He is medivaced to a hospital but dies a day later. Word quickly finds its way back to the commander. The commander refuses to support a memorial service at the forward operating base due to how he died. You know his fellow soldiers would benefit from honoring his life, not memorializing how he died. You ask to speak to the commander. What do you say?[322]

## CORRECTIONAL CHAPLAINCY

17. You are the only correctional chaplain in a local unit of the state prison system. The governor and some of her staff are visiting the prison this afternoon,

---

[322] Janet Reitman, "A Disaster of the U.S. Military's Own Making," *New York Times*, June 19, 2024, https://www.nytimes.com/2024/06/19/magazine/suicide-military-austin-valley.html.

and the warden is hosting a reception for them, followed by lunch. You are to say the blessing at lunch. The reception has just concluded. As you prepare to go to lunch, you receive word that an inmate has been rushed to the infirmary in critical condition and death is imminent. What will you do and why?

18. As a correctional chaplain, you are faced with many challenges. One such challenge is helping people who have lost all hope. You are approached by a young man who appears lean and haggard. He informs you he contracted AIDS because of a homosexual relationship with an infected person in prison. He was sick, dying, without family, and had been ostracized by other prisoners because of his illness. He was alone and had lost all hope. How do you assess his situation? How might you approach the young man? How do you engage the warden and guards without violating confidentiality?

19. You have been recently hired as a juvenile corrections chaplain. You notice several young men who always appear angry, which leads to frequent conflicts with one another and the staff. Just yesterday, many of them got into a fistfight, resulting in bruises and a couple of broken noses. The warden calls you in and asks for your help. How do you approach this situation with the young men? What actions or programs might you establish for them both in the facility and knowing they will eventually be released back into society?[323]

## CORPORATE/WORKPLACE CHAPLAINCY

20. You are the chaplain for a local manufacturing company. You get an "I got to see you today" message on the company's app from one of the employees. Upon arriving, you seek out the employee. She is upset. The two of you find a quiet place. You barely sit down when she begins to cry uncontrollably and tells you how angry she is. You practice good listening skills. She tells you she learned last night that her fifth-grade son was required by his teacher to

---

[323] Brad M. Griffin, "Turning the Corner on Youth Violence," Fuller Youth Institute, May 2, 2007, https://fulleryouthinstitute.org/blog/turning-the-corner-on-youth-violence; Patricia Rice, "Chaplains: Juveniles Need Support Outside to Maintain Changes Learned in Detention," St. Louis Public Radio, November 2, 2014, https://www.stlpr.org/arts/2014-11-02/chaplains-juveniles-need-support-outside-to-maintain-changes-learned-in-detention.

read a book titled My Shadow Is Pink. The book illustrates a boy who sees his shadow as pink, representing "your inner-most you." The boy then wears a dress to school and convinces his dad to put on a dress too. Last night, your son talked to you about his own gender identity. You also learn that your son was told to share this book with his kindergarten brother. She finally calms down and asks you, "What am I to think about all of this? What should I do?"[324]

21. You are a supervisory chaplain for a business operating at forty sites in four states: Texas, Oklahoma, Arkansas, and Louisiana. You oversee the work and ministry of thirty chaplains. Your employer requires that you make personal (face-to-face, physical presence) contact with each chaplain at least twice annually. You visit each chaplain on-site once a year and require them to attend an annual training conference that you conduct in their states. You hold four of these conferences every year—one in each state. The chaplain ministry is funded by two sources: half of the money comes from a line item in the budget, and private donors fund the other half. The annual training session for Arkansas is scheduled for next Tuesday evening in Little Rock. Three donors plan to attend the evening banquet. They have been giving modest but regular amounts for the past five years. Meanwhile, the corporate development officer has been trying to schedule a meeting with a "significant" prospective donor in Houston. He just called. The meeting is finally on, and the prospective donor wants to meet with you personally. But he can only meet with you and the development officer next Tuesday evening—at the same time as your training conference and more than four hundred miles from Little Rock. What will you do, and why?

## PUBLIC SAFETY / FIRST RESPONDER CHAPLAINCY

22. For two decades, you have worked two jobs. During the week, you work for a major city fire department. You are also a pastor of a local church. The

---

[324] "California School District Won't Let Parents Opt Children Out of Books That Promote Gender Ideology," First Liberty, September 24, 2024, https://firstliberty.org/media/encinas/, accessed 30 October 2024; Stuart Shepard, "School Forces Transgender Book on Kids," First Liberty Live, September 24, 2024, https://youtu.be/0AwfGfvBoKA, accessed 30 October 2024.

fire chief has supported you as the unofficial public safety chaplain to the firefighters and support staff. The department has welcomed your chaplaincy support, especially following challenging situations typically involving loss of life in a fire. The fire chief pulls you aside to talk to you privately. He says his city manager asked him to attend leadership training. He chose a faith-based leadership summit. He invited three other staff members to join him. All paid their own expenses. The fire chief returned and reported to his city manager, "It was the best leadership training I've ever attended and highly beneficial for my career." The city manager responded, "Your choice of leadership training is unacceptable because you chose a faith-based seminar." Three days later, the fire chief received a letter of termination with ten charges of improper behavior by the fire chief. The first five were all related to his religious faith and activities. The city manager even admitted his termination was for attending the "religious event" and allowing others to attend. The fire chief believes the city manager is persecuting him personally with extreme anti-religious bias. He asks for your help understanding the issues and what he should do next.[325]

23. Sam is a fellow chaplain on staff with you. The past month has been filled with crisis after crisis, and Sam has been the primary responder for each of these. He has provided counseling and grief care to three families after accidents where their sons were killed. In addition, he has been continuing his regular workload, but you notice he appears more tired each week. You are concerned that he may not be practicing good self-care, but he insists he is fine and continues leading memorial services, counseling sessions, and regular ministry assignments. One day, during a meeting, it becomes clear that Sam has missed a deadline on a project, and the supervisor asks him about it. Uncharacteristically, Sam snaps back, raising his voice and complaining that nobody understands his stress. He storms out of the room. Later, you stop by his office to check on him. He engages you privately, explaining that he has not felt like himself lately. He hasn't been sleeping well the past several nights.

---

[325] Jorge Gomez, "Fired California Fire Chief Appeals to U.S. Supreme Court," First Liberty, October 18, 2024, https://firstliberty.org/news/fire-chief-appeals-to-u-s-supreme-court/, accessed 30 October 2024; "Faith Under Fire: Ron Hittle's Story," First Liberty Live, March 9, 2023, https://youtu.be/iyIeCJu1exg?list=TLGGJ0HrpCyuh7AzMDEwMjAyNA, accessed 30 October 2024.

He apologizes for his outburst in the meeting and says he can't understand what came over him. How do you assess Sam's condition? How might you respond to Sam? What short- and long-term support could you give Sam?

24. At a police chaplains' gathering sponsored by FIRST H.E.L.P.,[326] you meet Beth. She and her children are attending a special memorial honoring the public safety / first responder personnel who have died by suicide. Her husband had committed suicide less than six months before. Like all his fellow officers, he never complained or sought help, even though the grind of his work weighed heavy on him. Beth explained to you that one week before his suicide, two of his colleagues were returning to the police station when a drunk driver ran headlong into their vehicle and killed them both. Even then, Beth indicated that her police husband did not show any indicators of the stress and trauma of the job. Upon returning from the store with sodas for himself, his wife, and his teenage daughter, he sat in their vehicle for a few minutes and used his service revolver to kill himself. Beth expressed anger and deep disappointment because the police chief refused to give him formal, full honors[327] and meet with her separately. Beth asks you what she should do. She is struggling with it all. As a chaplain, how would you engage Beth? If you had an opportunity, what would you say to the police chief? How would you advise the department to support its officers?

25. You have volunteered to serve on your area's disaster relief team. You are called to respond after a significant storm rips through an adjoining area. You know from early news reports that the storm's destruction is severe. You arrive early to find people without electricity, drinking water, and habitable homes. The storm also pulverized roads, destroyed businesses, toppled trees, and strewed debris everywhere. Officials, knowing deaths occurred, have not released any information. They quietly tell you that they expect the numbers to increase as searches of the area are made. The injured are being moved to a triage area, and the dead to a makeshift mortuary. Officials tell the gathering news media, "The damage done has been historic. We've never seen a flood

---

[326] "Honoring the Service of First Responders Who Died by Suicide," https://1sthelp.org/.
[327] "Law Enforcement (Police) Funeral Service Rituals," Funeral Wise, https://www.funeralwise.com/funeral-customs/police/, accessed 30 October 2024.

event like this. We've never seen a storm surge of this magnitude." At the moment, you are the only identified chaplain. What should you do immediately? How do you prioritize your actions? You know you have additional chaplains coming and have been asked to lead the chaplaincy response. How do you coordinate their activities? What guidance would you give them? Prepare a short brief for the city mayor, who has asked you for an update.[328]

26. The death count rises to at least ninety-five people after a flooding disaster in Spain. The national government has declared three days of mourning for those killed in the flash flooding disaster. You are asked to coordinate a memorial event in one of the major cities impacted by the flooding. What elements would you have for the event?[329]

27. You are serving as a disaster chaplain for a major faith-based organization. You respond to an area that was recently affected by severe wildfires. Hundreds of families have evacuated, many of whom have completely lost their homes and personal belongings. The children and elderly individuals are in a daze with severe anxiety and emotional trauma. You are assigned to work with individuals and families, providing a calming presence, helping them cope with their loss, and guiding them to resources for mental health support. You see a lone figure standing amid the rubble. In her search, she just found her wedding ring and a single framed picture of her wedding. You walk up to her, and she tells you her husband and young son died in the fire. It came over the ridge so fast that they could not escape. How would you handle her situation and grief? Later that evening, you know you must

---

[328] Patricia Mazzei, Nicholas Bogel-Burroughs, Frances Robles, and Jack Healy, "Hurricane Ian's Staggering Scale of Wreckage Becomes Clearer in Florida," *New York Times*, September 29, 2022, https://www.nytimes.com/2022/09/29/us/hurricane-ian-florida-damage.html, accessed 30 October 2024; Jayme Gershen, Orlando Castro, and Christina Kelso, "Florida Business Owner Assesses Damage Left by Hurricane Ian," *New York Times*, September 30, 2022, https://nyti.ms/3C45D8C, accessed 30 October 2024.

[329] Luke Cooper, "Spanish Government Declares Three Days of Mourning After Dozens Killed in Flash Flooding Disaster," ABC News (Australia), October 30, 2024, https://www.abc.net.au/news/2024-10-30/over-95-dead-in-spain-flash-flooding-emergency/104539978.

debrief with your team's supervisor. What do you plan to share?[330] What would you need from your supervisor?

28. You notice one of the felony prosecutors sitting behind her desk staring into space. As the chaplain, you stop to check in, and she tells you about her day. She came from a tough court docket in which an angry defense attorney accused her of hiding exculpatory evidence before the judge and other attorneys. She knows nobody believed this, but being accused of doing something wrong always makes her anxious because her entire job is about her reputation for honesty and integrity. To make matters worse, the prosecutor gave in to the pressure and made a plea bargain agreement to avoid a conflict with the defense. The plea bargain did not include adequate terms for restitution, which she knows the victim in the case wanted. She is dreading calling the victim to tell her what happened and hearing the victim's reaction. How would you respond? What support could you give her?

## COMMUNITY/LIFESTYLE CHAPLAINCY

29. You are the sports chaplain for a state football team. The lead coach has openly displayed his faith, regularly shares faith-based messages on social media, engages in team prayers, and has an open-door invitation to the chaplain to lead a morning devotional in the team's locker room. A secular activist group sent a letter to the university complaining that the coach's use of team prayers and chaplains following games was unconstitutional. According to the activist group, having a chaplain lead prayer with the team at a public institution amounts to religious coercion, violating the rights of players and staff members who may not share the same beliefs. This isn't the first time the coach has faced criticism for his religious practices. When he first arrived at the school, the same group also raised concerns about his open display of faith with his team, prompting the university to give him additional training on the boundaries of religious expression in public institutions. The university's

---

[330] "Chaplains Ministering to California Wildfire Victims," Billy Graham Evangelistic Association, October 12, 2017, https://billygraham.org/story/chaplains-ministering-to-california-wildfire-victims/, accessed 30 October 2024.

director of athletics wants the chaplain to provide a brief on the issues from both sides of the debate, reference any legal precedent, and recommend how to resolve the issue. Ultimately, should the coach and the chaplain be restricted from the team? Is being offended the same as being coerced?[331]

30. A driver in Melbourne, Australia, performs a U-turn in the middle of the afternoon but crashes into a primary school fence. The driver's car plows into a table where five children are seated. Four of the students, ages ten and eleven, are rushed to the hospital and remain in stable condition. Unfortunately, one of the eleven-year-old boys dies of his injuries. You are the school chaplain and have been asked to set up a space for the community to grieve and receive pastoral and spiritual support. Members of the community pay tribute to the victims of the crash by laying flowers against a wall. What coordination is needed for you to do your job? Who do you ask to assist you? How do you support the family, students, teachers, and grieving community members? Later, the driver's spouse arrives at the crash site and is immediately recognized. The grieving crowd begins to express anger toward the spouse. You know the situation can quickly get out of control. What do you do?[332]

31. You are a new neighborhood chaplain responding to your first scene of violence. You have been unable to introduce yourself to everyone you will encounter at the scene and during follow-up. What will you do first? How can you prepare for the "firsts" you will encounter in such a diverse environment?

32. Describe your feelings as a neighborhood chaplain about diverse, high-poverty communities. What does it mean to operate on "their turf"? Do you feel you have ingrained biases and embedded theologies that will be

---

[331] Kenny Lee, "Deion Sanders' Use of Team Chaplain Caught Up in Argument Over Constitutionally," *Sports Illustrated*, October 16, 2024, https://www.si.com/college/colorado/buffs-social/deion-sanders-use-of-team-chaplain-caught-up-in-argument-over-constitutionally, accessed 30 October 2024.

[332] "Support Hub to Be Established as Community Grieves 11yo Student Jack Davey Killed in Melbourne School Crash," ABC News (Australia), October 30, 2024, https://www.abc.net.au/news/2024-10-31/auburb-south-primary-school-community-hub-crash/104540232.

challenged as you live and serve the urban poor? How will you grow in self-awareness and competency for this work?

33. You serve as a neighborhood chaplain in a challenged, high-poverty neighborhood. You want to increase your empathy with those in your diverse environment. Yet, you struggle to remain open to serve everyone involved. You want to take sides in conflict between neighbors, authorities, and systems. You can listen to police, emergency responders, community leaders, and neighbors. How do you stay in your spiritual lane and practice the Presence of the Holy for all you encounter? What are the boundaries for advocacy as you sojourn with others?

34. On October 7, 2023, Hamas and other Palestinian militants led a raid into Israel. Israeli civilians were killed, and several hundred were taken hostage in Gaza. The attackers cited, as they claimed responsibility, the need for attention to justice for the occupied Palestinian people in Gaza and the West Bank. Israel's immediate response was a deep and sustained military invasion of the Palestinian territory called Gaza, with the automatic support of the United States. Campuses all over the nation are thrown into chaos. You are the lead chaplain at a major university with a diverse student population. The campus and dorms are erupting with tension, especially between different ethnic groups. You immediately reach out to the leadership of various groups. As the campus chaplain, the leader of spiritual and religious life for the community, you share the responsibility for safety, communication, and support for all perspectives on the campus. Both groups refuse to meet, at least in the first weeks.

You want to put out a statement to the campus expressing grief and alarm on behalf of all, claiming to represent the Holy One of peace. What does it say and why? What do you have to think about before sending it? Immediately, opposing campus groups invite you to participate in protests. Do you agree? What do you say or do? What might you plan? In consultation with students, you decide to plan a vigil or prayer service for those affected, for peace, and for justice. Is such a gathering possible? If so, how do you proceed? What do you hope to accomplish? Who in the university leadership do you need to speak with? What will be the shape of such a gathering? When and where will it be held and why? Who will you enlist to participate, and what will they do? What other issues must you consider as political tensions blow over campus constituents? If you decide that a prayer vigil is impossible, why? What might you choose to do instead? Can you think of events you might plan and host? What students need your care? What communities need your attention? What is your obligation to the whole university as well as your academic integrity and freedom of speech? What do those who are not religious need to hear from the chaplain at a time like this? And then how do you care for yourself, your heart and mind, in the fray as it becomes hotter and thorny?

# RESOURCES

## PROFESSIONAL ORGANIZATIONS[333]

### A sample list of professional chaplain organizations outside the United States:

Association of Certified Chaplains in South Africa (CCinSA, https://ccinsa.co.za/)
Australian and New Zealand Association for Clinical Pastoral Education (ANZACPE, https://www.anzacpe.org.au/)
Canadian Association for Spiritual Care (CASC/ACSS, https://www.spiritualcare.ca/)
College of Health Care Chaplains (CHCC – UK, https://www.healthcarechaplains.org)
Deutsche Gesellschaft für Pastoralpsychologie e.V. [German Society for Pastoral Psychology] (DGfP, https://www.pastoralpsychologie.de/)
European Network of Health Care Chaplaincy (ENHCC, https://enhcc.eu)
Global Sports Chaplaincy Association (GSCA, https://sportschaplaincy.com)
International Association of Chaplains in Higher Education (IACHE, http://www.iache.org/)
International Military Chiefs of Chaplains Conference (IMCCC, https://www.eucom.mil/topic/imccc)
New Zealand Healthcare Chaplains' Association (NZHCA, https://sites.google.com/view/nzhca/home)
Spiritual Care Australia (SCA – Australia, https://www.spiritualcareaustralia.org.au)
UK Board of Healthcare Chaplaincy (UKBHC, https://www.ukbhc.org.uk/)

---

[333] This listing is not exhaustive and represents primarily national or regional organizations supporting chaplains and their ministries. The list is intended to give readers a starting point as they are encouraged to do searches for their region or country as chaplain resources continually change. We verified each URL in our research; however, we are aware that any listing of URLs can be problematic as these change without notice. Additionally, resources may exist for other countries and a particular locale or region. Also, the reader should research denominational and endorser websites for information about their chaplaincy services and support. A listing in this resource does not represent any endorsement by the editors.

# A sample list of professional chaplain organizations within the United States:

## General

ACPE Psychotherapy Commission – acpe.edu
American Association of Christian Counselors – aacc.net
Association for Clinical Pastoral Education – acpe.edu
Association of Certified Christian Chaplains – certifiedchaplains.org
Association of Muslim Chaplains – associationofmuslimchaplains.org
Association of Professional Chaplains – professionalchaplains.org
Billy Graham Rapid Response Team – rrt.billygraham.org/become-a-chaplain
Buddhist Chaplain Registry & Library – buddhistchaplains.org
Canadian Association for Spiritual Care – spiritualcare.ca
Chaplaincy Innovation Lab: Home – chaplaincyinnovation.org
Dewey Center for Chaplaincy – charlestonsouthern.edu/academics/center-for-chaplaincy
International Association of Christian Chaplains – christianchaplains.net
Marsh Institute for Chaplains – marshinstituteforchaplains.org
Muslim Chaplains Association – muslimchaplains.org
National Association of Catholic Chaplains – nacc.org
National Chaplains Association – nationalchaplains.us
Neshama: Association of Jewish Chaplains (NAJC) – najc.org
North American Hindu Chaplains Association (NAHCA) – hinduchaplains.com

## Healthcare Chaplaincy

Clinical Pastoral Care International – cpe-international.org
College of Pastoral Supervision and Psychotherapy – cpsp.org
HealthCare Chaplaincy Network – healthcarechaplaincy.org
Healthcare Chaplains Ministry Association – hcmachaplains.org
Institute for Clinical Pastoral Training – icpt.edu
National Association of Veterans Affairs Chaplains – navac.net
Spiritual Care Association Community of Chaplains – spiritualcareassociation.org/community-of-chaplains.html

## Military Chaplaincy

Archdiocese for the Military Services – milarch.org
Military Chaplains Association – mca-usa.org/
National Commission Ministry to the Armed Forces – ncmaf.net/
US Air Force – airforce.com/careers/specialty-careers/chaplain

US Army – m.goarmy.com/chaplain.m.html
US Navy – navy.com/careers/navy-chaplain
Warrior's Journey, The – thewarriorsjourney.org

## Correctional Chaplaincy

American Correctional Association – aca.org
American Correctional Chaplains Association – correctionalchaplains.org
Center for Church and Prison – churchandprison.org
Chaplains Association – correctionalchaplains.org
Community Chaplaincy Association – communitychaplaincy.org.uk
Correctional Ministries and Chaplains Association – cmcainternational.org
Correctional Ministries Institute – correctionalministries.org
Prison Seminaries Foundation – prisonseminaries.org
Restorative Justice Ministries Network of Texas – rjmntexas.com

## Workplace Chaplaincy[334]

Chaplains Associates, Inc. – chaplainsassociates.com
Corporate Chaplains of America – chaplain.org
Employee Care of America – employeecareofamerica.com
Marketplace Chaplains – mchapusa.com
Missional Chaplains – missionalchaplains.org
National Institute of Business and Industrial Chaplains – nibic.com
Occupational Chaplains of America – ocachaplains.com
Religious Freedom & Business Foundation – religiousfreedomandbusiness.org
TFC Global – tfcglobal.org
Workplace Chaplain Services – workplacechaplainservices.com
Workplace Chaplains – workplacechaplains.us

## First Responders / Public Safety Chaplaincy

CAREForce (Resilient Communities Through Collaborative Action) – careforce.us
Chaplains International – chaplainsinternationalinc.com
Federation of Fire Chaplains – firechaplains.org
International Association of Chiefs of Police Chaplain Section – theiacp.org/working-group/section/police-chaplain-section
International Conference of Police Chaplains – icpc4cops.org

---

[334] In addition to companies hiring contract chaplains, some companies hire chaplains as employees. One example is Tyson Foods (tysonfoods.com/).

International Critical Incident Stress Foundation – icisf.org
International Fellowship of Chaplains (I.F.O.C.) – ifoc.org
International Police & Fire Chaplains Association – ipfca.org
Law Enforcement Chaplaincy Foundation: LECF – lecf.org
United Nations Chaplains Association – uncpa.us

## Community/Lifestyle Chaplaincy

Association for Chaplaincy and Spiritual Life in Higher Education (ACSLHE) – acslhe.org
Bikers for Christ – bfctx.org
Global Sports Chaplaincy Association – sportschaplaincy.com
International Association of Chaplains in Higher Education – iache.org/
International Association of Civil Aviation Chaplains: IACAC – iacac.aero/
Race Track Chaplaincy of America – https://www.rtcanational.org/
Rural Chaplains Association – rcahome.org

# ENDORSING ORGANIZATIONS

The Armed Forces Chaplains Board (AFCB) maintains a current list of Endorsing Agencies and Endorsers. For names of endorsers, refer to prhome.defense.gov/M-RA/MPP/AFCB/Endorsements/.

Advent Christian General Conference
African Methodist Episcopal Church
African Methodist Episcopal Zion Church
Aleph Institute, The
Alliance of Baptists, Incorporated
American Association of Lutheran Churches, The
American Baptist Association
American Baptist Churches in the U.S.A.
American Muslim Armed Forces and Veterans Affairs Council
Anglican Catholic Church, Inc., The
Anglican Church in America, The
Anglican Church of the Americas, The
Anglican Mission in the Americas, The
Antiochian Orthodox Christian Archdiocese of North America
Apostolic Catholic Orthodox Church
Assembly of Canonical Orthodox Bishops of the U.S.A. (ACOBUSA)
Assemblies of God, General Council of
Assemblies of God, International Fellowship (CFGC)

Associate Reformed Presbyterian Church (PRCC)
Association of Evangelical Gospel Assemblies (AEGA—Int., Inc.)
Association of Independent Methodists, The
Association of International Gospel Assemblies, Inc. (CFGC)
Association of Reformed Baptist Churches of America (ARBCA)
Association of Unity Churches DBA Unity Worldwide Ministries
Augsburg Lutheran Churches
Baptist Bible Fellowship International
Baptist General Conference (CONVERGE)
Baptist General Convention of Texas (BGCT)
Baptist Missionary Association of America
Bethel Ministerial Association, Inc.
Bible Churches Chaplaincy
Bible Fellowship Church
Bible Presbyterian Church (General Synod)
Brethren Church, Inc., The (Ashland, OH) (NAE)
Buddhist Churches of America
Calvary Baptist Church (All Points Baptist Mission)
Calvary Chapel of Costa Mesa
Catholic Apostolic National Church
Central Conference of American Rabbis (Reformed) (JWB)
Charismatic Episcopal Church of North America
Christian and Missionary Alliance, The
Christian Church (Disciples of Christ)
Christian Churches and Churches of Christ
Christian Evangelical Churches of America, Inc. (NAE)
Christian Methodist Episcopal Church
Christian Reformed Church in North America
Christian Renewal Church (CFGC)
Christ-Immanuel Ministerial Association (CFGC)
Church of Christ
Church of God (Cleveland, TN)
Church of God (Holiness) (NAE)
Church of God in Christ, Inc.
Church of God Ministries
Church of God of Prophecy
Church of Jesus Christ of Latter-day Saints, The (LDS)
Church of the Lutheran Brethren
Church of the Nazarene

Church of the United Brethren in Christ (NAE)
Church on the Rock, International (CFGC)
Churches of Christ in Christian Union
Churches of God, General Conference
Community of Christ
Congregational Christian Church in American Samoa (CCCAS)
Congregational Methodist Church, The
Conservative Congregational Christian Conference
Conservative Lutheran Association (NAE)
Cooperative Baptist Fellowship, Inc.
Coral Ridge Christian Fellowship
Cumberland Presbyterian Church, The (PCCMP)
Cumberland Presbyterian Church in America (PCCMP)
Elim Fellowship, Inc. (NAE)
Episcopal Church, The
Episcopal Missionary Church, The
Evangel Fellowship International (CFGC)
Evangelical Church Alliance
Evangelical Community Church (NAE)
Evangelical Congregational Church
Evangelical Covenant Church, The
Evangelical Episcopal Churches, The Communion of
Evangelical Free Church of America
Evangelical Friends Church International (NAE)
Evangelical Gospel Assemblies Ministries International, Inc.
Evangelical Lutheran Church in America
Evangelical Lutheran Conference and Ministerium
Evangelical Methodist Church, The
Evangelical Presbyterian Church
Faith Christian Fellowship Int'l Church, Inc. (CFGC)
Fellowship of Churches and Ministers International (CFGC)
Fellowship of Grace Brethren Churches, The
First Church of Christ, Scientist, The
Foundation Baptist Fellowship Int'l
Free Lutheran Congregation, Association of (NAE)
Free Methodist Church of North America
Full Gospel Baptist Church Fellowship, International
Full Gospel Fellowship of Churches and Ministers International
Full Gospel Pentecostal Church

General Association of General Baptists
General Church of the New Jerusalem, The
Grace Churches International
Grace Gospel Fellowship (NAE)
Grace Place
Harvest Network International (CFGC)
Holy Spirit Association for the Unification of World Christianity
Horizon Christian Fellowship (CFGC)
Independence Branch, The
Independent Assemblies (CFGC)
Independent Assemblies of God International (CFGC)
Infaith
International Christian Church
International Church of the Foursquare Gospel
International Convention of Faith Ministries, Inc. (CFGC)
International Council of Community Churches
International Ministerial Fellowship
Islamic Society of North America
Kingsway Fellowship International (CFGC)
Korean-American Presbyterian Church (PRCC)
Korean Evangelical Church of America
Korean Presbyterian Church of America (PRCC)
Liberty Baptist Fellowship for Church Planting, Inc.
Liberty Fellowship of Churches and Ministers, Inc. (CFGC)
Living Word Christian Center (CFGC)
Lutheran Church—Missouri Synod, The
Lutheran Congregations in Mission for Christ
Messianic Jewish Congregations, Union of
Missionary Church, Inc. (NAE)
Moravian Church in America
National Association of Congregational Christian Churches
National Association of Free Will Baptists
National Baptist Convention, USA, Inc.
National Baptist Convention of America, Inc.
New Testament Association of Independent Baptist Churches
North American Baptist Conference
Old Holy Catholic Church, The, Archdiocese of Christ the King
Open Bible Standard Churches
Original Free Will Baptists Convention

Orthodox Anglican Church
Orthodox Catholic Archdiocese, North America, The (OCANA)
Orthodox Church in America, The
Orthodox Presbyterian Church
Pentecostal Assemblies of the World, Inc.
Pentecostal Church of God, Inc.
Pentecostal Churches of the Apostolic Faith Assn.
Pentecostal Holiness Church, International
Philadelphia Church (CFGC)
Pirchei Shoshanim
Plymouth Brethren
Polish National Catholic Church of America
Presbyterian Church (U.S.A.), The (PCCMP)
Presbyterian Church in America, The
Progressive National Baptist Convention, Inc.
Rabbinical Assembly (Conservative), The (JWB)
Rabbinical Council of America (Orthodox) (JWB)
Reformed Church in America
Reformed Episcopal Church
Reformed Presbyterian Church in America
Regular Baptist Churches, General Association of
Rhema Bible Church (CFGC)
Rock Church (CFGC)
Roman Catholic Church, The
Russian Orthodox Church Outside of Russia (ROCOR)
Salvation Army, The
Seventh-day Adventists—United States, General Conference of
Seventh Day Baptist General Conference U.S.A. and Canada
Southern Baptist Convention
Southern Methodist Church, The
Sovereign Grace Baptist Association of Churches
Trinity Full Gospel Fellowship (CFGC)
Ukrainian Orthodox Church of the U.S.A.
Unaffiliated Baptist Churches of America
Union of Messianic Jewish Congregations
Unitarian Universalist Association, The
United Catholic Church of America
United Church of Christ
United Episcopal Church of North America, The
United Evangelical Churches (CFGC)

United Full Gospel Church (CFGC)
United Methodist Church, The
United Pentecostal Church International
Unity Worldwide Ministries
Victory Christian Center (CFGC)
Wesleyan Church, The
Western Orthodox Christian Church
Westside Christian Family Chapel (NAE)
World Baptist Fellowship, Inc.
World Council of Independent Christian Churches, The

## ADMINISTRATIVE ORGANIZATIONS

American Council of Christian Churches (ACCC)
Assembly of Canonical Orthodox Bishops of the U.S.A. (ACOBUSA)
Associated Gospel Churches (AGC)
Chaplaincy Full Gospel Churches (CFGC)
Coalition of Spirit-Filled Churches Inc. (CSC)
National Association of Evangelicals (NAE)
National Jewish Welfare Board (JWB)
Presbyterian and Reformed Commission on Chaplains and Military Personnel (PRCC)
Presbyterian Council for Chaplains and Military Personnel, The (PCCMP)

# WORKS CITED

Abarim Publications' Free Online Dictionary of Biblical New Testament Greek, s.v. "καιρος." 2017. Accessed 22 August 2021. https://www.abarim-publications.com/DictionaryG/k/k-a-i-r-o-sfin.html.

Abrams, A. "Hospital Chaplains Stick to the Heart of the Job Amid Health Care Industry Changes." Religion News Service (31 May 2019). Accessed 21 September 2021. https://religionnews.com/2019/05/28/hospital-chaplains-stick-to-the-heart-of-the-job-amid-health-care-industry-changes.

Act 4 Juvenile Justice [Overview of the Juvenile Justice Reform Act of 2018]. "Core Requirements." Accessed 26 December 2020. https://www.act4jj.org/what-jjdpa/core-requirements.

Administration for Community Living. "What Is Long Term Care and Who Needs It?" Accessed 5 April 2021. https://acl.gov/ltc.

Air Force Reserve Command. "Chaplain Candidate Program." Accessed 12 May 2021. https://www.afrc.af.mil/About-Us/Chaplain/Chaplain Candidate/.

American Addiction Centers. "The 12 Steps of Alcoholics Anonymous (AA)." Accessed 26 December 2020. https://www.alcohol.org/alcoholics-anonymous.

American Correctional Association. "Declaration of Principles Adopted and Promulgated by the 1870 Congress of the National Prison Association." Accessed 28 September 2021. http://www.aca.org/ACA_PROD_IMIS/docs/1870Declaration_of_Principles.pdf.

American Correctional Association, Department of Performance-Based Standards and Accreditation. "Performance-Based Expected Practices for Adult Correctional Institutions," 5th edition, 2018.

Apostolopoulos, Yorghos, Sevil Sönmez, Mona M. Shattell, Clifford Gonzales, and Caitlin Fehernbacher. "Health Survey of US Long-Haul Truck Drivers: Work Environment, Physical Health, and Healthcare Access." *Work* 46, no. 1 (2013): 113–23. Accessed 28 September 2021. https://pubmed.ncbi.nlm.nih.gov/23324711/.

Apostolopoulos, Yorghos, Sevil Sönmez, Mona Shattell, and Jennie Kronenfeld. "Sex Work in Trucking Milieux: 'Lot Lizards,' Truckers, and Risk." *Nursing Forum* 47, no. 3 (2012): 140–52. Accessed 28 September 2021. https://doi.org/10.1111/j.1744-6198.2012.00272.x.

Appelquist, A. Ray. *Church, State and Chaplaincy.* Washington, DC: General Commission on Chaplains and Armed Forces Personnel, 1969.

Ariens, Michael S., and Robert A. Destro. *Religious Liberty in a Pluralistic Society*, 2nd ed. Durham, NC: Carolina Academic Press, 2002.

Association of Professional Chaplains, *A Brief History of the Association of Professional Chaplains* (n.d.). Accessed 21 September 2021. https://www.professionalchaplains.org/content.asp?pl=24&sl=31&contentid=31.

———. "Common Code of Ethics for Chaplains, Pastoral Counselors, Pastoral Educators and Students." Accessed 4 October 2021. https://www.professionalchaplains.org/files/professional_standards/common_standards/common_code_ethics.pdf.

———. "Common Qualifications and Competencies for Professional Chaplains." Accessed 21 July 2020. https://www.professionalchaplains.org/files/2017%20Common%20Qualifications%20and%20Competencies%20for%20Professional%20Chaplains.pdf.

———. "Common Standards for Professional Chaplains." 2004. Accessed 21 September 2021. https://www.professionalchaplains.org/Files/professional_standards/common_standards/common_standards_professional_chaplaincy.pdf.

Beasley-Murray, Paul. *Dynamic Leadership.* Oxford: Monarch Books, 1990.

Beauchamp, Tom L., and James F. Childress. *Principles of Biomedical Ethics*. 4th ed. New York: Oxford University Press, 1994.

Beckner, Thomas. *Correctional Chaplains: Keepers of the Cloak*. Orlando, FL: Cappella Press, 2012.

Beiner, Ronald. "Machiavelli, Hobbes, and Rousseau on Civil Religion." *The Review of Politics* 55, no. 4 (Autumn 1993): 617–38. Accessed 18 April 2021. http://www.jstor.org/stable/1407609.

Birkman International. "The Birkman Method." Accessed 28 September 2021. https://birkman.com/the-birkman-method/.

———. "Leadership Development." Accessed 28 September 2021. https://birkman.com/solutions/leadership-development/.

Blackaby, Henry T., and Claude V. King, *Experiencing God: Knowing and Doing the Will of God*. Nashville: Lifeway Christian Resources, 1990.

Board of Chaplaincy Certification, Inc., "About Certification and the Application Process." Accessed 21 September 2021. https://bcci.professionalchaplains.org/content.asp?pl=25&sl=26&contentid=26.

Boulder Community Health. "Nurturing Caregivers with 'Tea for the Soul.'" June 2017. Accessed 23 August 2021. https://www.bch.org/latest-news/2017/june/nurturing-caregivers-with-tea-for-the-soul.

Broadwell, Martin M. "Teaching for Learning (XVI)." *The Gospel Guardian*, 20 February 1969. Accessed 21 July 2020. http://wordsfitlyspoken.org/gospel_guardian/v20/v20n41p1-3a.html.

Buber, Martin. *I and Thou*. Translated by Ronald Gregor Smith. New York: Scribner, 1958.

Bureau of Justice Statistics. "Key Statistics: Total Correctional Population." Accessed 26 December 2020. http://bjs.ojp.gov/data/key-statistics#citation--1.

Cadge, Wendy. "The Rise of the Chaplains." *The Atlantic*, 24 September 2020. Accessed 24 August 2021. https://www.theatlantic.com/ideas/archive/2020/05/why-americans-are-turning-chaplains-during-pandemic/611767/.

Cadge, Wendy, Irene Elizabeth Stroud, Patricia K Palmer, George Fitchett, Trace Haythorn, and Casey Clevenger. "Training Chaplains and Spiritual Caregivers: The Emergence and Growth of Chaplaincy Programs in Theological Education." *Pastoral Psychology* 69 (2020): 187–208. Accessed 30 August 2021. https://doi.org/10.1007/s11089-020-00906-5.

CAREforce. "Resilient Communities through Collaborative Action." Accessed 14 August 2021. https://www.careforce.us/.

*Carter v. Broadlawns Medical Center*. 857 F2d 448 (8th Cir. 1988). Accessed 20 July 2021. https://casetext.com/case/carter-v-broadlawns-medical-center-3/?PHONE_NUMBER_GROUP=C.

Celebrate Recovery: A Christ-Centered 12-Step Program. "What Is Celebrate Recovery?" Accessed 28 September 2021. www.celebraterecovery.com.

Chief of Naval Operations Instruction 1730.1E. "Religious Ministry in the Navy." 25 April 2012. Accessed 5 October 2021. https://www.secnav.navy.mil/doni/Directives/01000%20Military%20Personnel%20Support/01-700%20Morale,%20Community%20and%20Religious%20Services/1730.1E.pdf.

Claypool, John. *Tracks of a Fellow Struggler: Living and Growing through Grief*. Harrisburg, PA: Morehouse Publishing, 1974.

*Code of Canon Law.* "Canon 959: The Sacrament of Penance." Accessed 3 April 2021. https://www.vatican.va/archive/cod-iuris-canonici/eng/documents/cic_lib4-cann959-997_en.html#TITLE_IV.

Commandant of the Coast Guard Instruction 1730.4C. "Religious Ministry within the Coast Guard." 9 March 2012. Accessed 27 September 2021. https://media.defense.gov/2017/Mar/06/2001707724/-1/-1/0/CI_1730_4C.PDF.

Commandant of the Marine Corps Order 1730.6F with Administrative Change. "Religious Ministry in the Marine Corps." 16 August 2018. Accessed 27 September 2021. https://www.marines.mil/Portals/1/Publications/MCO%201730.6F%20Admin%20Change.pdf?ver=2018-08-24-065538-480.

Cox, Harvey, ed. *Military Chaplains: From a Religious Military to a Military Religion.* New York: American Report Press, 1972.

Crossley, K. "Professional Satisfaction among US Healthcare Chaplains." *Journal of Pastoral Care & Counseling* 56, no. 1 (March 2002): 21–27. Accessed 21 September 2021. https://doi.org/10.1177/154230500205600104.

*Cutter v. Wilkinson.* 2005. Accessed 28 September 2021. https://www.law.cornell.edu/supct/html/03-9877.ZS.html.

Davidson, J. E., P. Graham, L. Montross-Thomas, W. Norcross, and G. Zerbi. "Code Lavender: Cultivating Intentional Acts of Kindness in Response to Stressful Work Situations." *EXPLORE* 13, no. 3 (2017): 181–85. Accessed 23 August 2021. DOI: 10.1016/j.explore.2017.02.005.

Department of Defense Instruction 1300.17. "Religious Liberty in the Military Services." 1 September 2020. Accessed 8 August 2021. https://www.esd.whs.mil/Portals/54/Documents/DD/issuances/dodi/130017p.pdf.

Department of Defense Instruction 1304.28. "The Appointment and Services of Chaplains." 11 June 2004. Accessed 5 October 2021. https://www.esd.whs.mil/Portals/54/Documents/DD/issuances/dodi/130428p.pdf?ver=scWFipz2YzfxGxhj5mdYwg%3D%3D.

Douhet, Giulio. *The Command of the Air.* Translated by Dino Ferrari. Air Force History and Museums Program, 1998. Accessed 5 October 2021. https://media.defense.gov/2010/Sep/24/2001329765/-1/-1/0/AFD-100924-017.pdf.

Drazin, Israel, and Cecil Curry. *For God and Country: The History of a Constitutional Challenge to the Army Chaplaincy.* Hoboken, NJ: KTAV Publishing House, 1995.

Drum, Vance. "Professional Correctional Chaplains: Fact and Fiction." Workshop, American Correctional Association Congress of Correction. Kansas City, MO. 13 August 2007. Accessed 28 September 2021. http://www.correctionalchaplains.org/.

Eisenberg, Seth. *PAIRS ESSENTIALS, A PAIRS Curriculum for Successful Relationships.* Hollywood, FL: PAIRS Foundation, 2010–2012.

Fairchild Air Force Base. "Base Chapel: Chaplain Corps Mission." Accessed 22 May 2021. https://www.fairchild.af.mil/Information/Fact-Sheets/Indextitle/B/.

*Federal Rules of Evidence.* "Rule 501: Privilege in General." Accessed 3 April 2021. www.uscourts.gov/sites/default/files/Rules%20of%20Evidence.

Fedrigo, John A., and LTG Brian T. Kelly. "SAF/MR and HAF/A1 SASC Personnel Oversight." *Department of the Air Force Presentation to the Subcommittee on Personnel, Committee on Armed Services, United States Senate.* 11 March 2020. Accessed 20 October 2020. https://www.armed-services.senate.gov/imo/media/doc/Fedrigo--Kelly_03-11-20.pdf.

Frank, A. W. *The Wounded Storyteller: Body, Illness, and Ethics.* Chicago: University of Chicago Press, 2013.

Franklin, Dan. *Disaster Spiritual Care: A Training Manual for Spiritual Care Providers.* Self-published, 2017.

———. *Chaplaincy: Hands-on Ministry: Ministering Beyond the Walls of the Church.* Self-published, 2020.

Freeze, Trevor. "Ministry on the Way: Chaplains Go with the Flow." Billy Graham Evangelistic Association, 2012. Accessed 29 September 2021. https://billygraham.org/story/ministry-on-the-way-chaplains-go-with-flow/.

"Geneva Convention Relative to the Treatment of Prisoners of War." The Geneva Conventions of January 1949. Accessed 4 October 2021. https://www.icrc.org/en/doc/assets/files/publications/icrc-002-0173.pdf.

Gennep, Arnold van. *The Rites of Passage.* Translated by Monika B. Vizedom and Gabrielle L. Caffee. Chicago: University of Chicago Press, 1960.

Hallett, Michael, Joshua Hayes, Byron Johnson, Sung Joon Jang, and Grant Duwe, *The Angola Prison Seminary: Effects of Faith-Based Ministry on Identity Transformation, Desistance, and Rehabilitation.* New York: Routledge, 2017.

Harris, Susan. "Chaplains' Roles as Mediators in Critical Clinical Decisions." *AMA Journal of Ethics* 20, no. 7 (July 2018): 670–74. Accessed 24 August 2021. https://journalofethics.ama-assn.org/article/chaplains-roles-mediators-critical-clinical-decisions/2018-07.

Hutcheson, Richard G., Jr., *The Churches and the Chaplaincy*. Rev. ed. US Government Printing Office, 1998.

Joint Guide 1-05 Religious Affairs in Joint Operations. 2018. Accessed 28 August 2021. https://www.jcs.mil/Portals/36/Documents/Doctrine/jdn_jg/jg1_05.pdf.

*Katcoff v. Marsh*. 1985. Accessed 5 October 2021. https://law.justia.com/cases/federal/district-courts/FSupp/582/463/1759882/.

Kraft, Emile S. "Chaplains." The First Amendment Encyclopedia. Middle Tennessee State University, 2009. Accessed 8 February 2021. http://www.mtsu.edu/rst-amendment/article/909/chaplains.

*Lemon v. Kurtzman*. 1971. Accessed 12 March 2021. https://www.law.cornell.edu/supremecourt/text/403/602.

Libby, B. W. "The Chaplain's Allegiance to His Church." *Military Chaplains' Review* 12, no. 3 (Fall 1983): 32–36.

Lotz, William. *Fire Chaplain Institute Training Manual*. Self-published, 2005.

Lyons, Chaplain (Major) Robert C. "A Chaplain's Guide to Privileged Communication." Master's thesis, Duke University, 10 April 2001.

MacDonald, Gordon. *Ordering Your Private World*. Nashville: Thomas Nelson, 2012.

Magmutual. "Employment Practices Toolkit: Religious Discrimination Federal Law Overview." Accessed 28 September 2021. https://www.magmutual.com/learning/toolkit/employment-practices-toolkit/religious-discrimination-federal-law-overview/.

Masci, David, and Michael Lipka, "Americans May Be Getting Less Religious, But Feelings of Spirituality Are On the Rise." Washington, DC: Pew Research Center, 2016. Accessed 30 August 2021. https://www.pewresearch.org/fact-tank/2016/01/21/americans-spirituality/.

Mead, Margaret. "Ritual and Social Crisis." In *The Roots of Ritual*. Edited by James D. Shaughnessy. Grand Rapids: Eerdmans, 1973.

*Medical Dictionary for the Health Professions and Nursing*, s.v. "Clinical Judgment." 2012. Accessed 22 August 2021. https://medical-dictionary.thefreedictionary.com/clinical+judgment.

*Military Rules of Evidence*. "Part III, Rule 503: Communications to Clergy." Accessed 3 April 2021. https://jsc.defense.gov/Portals/99/Documents/MREsRemoved412e.pdf.

Miller, David. *God at Work: The History and Promise of the Faith at Work Movement*. Oxford: Oxford University Press, 2007.

Mitchell, Jeffery T., and Gary Bray. *Emergency Services Stress.* Englewood Cliffs, NJ: Prentice-Hall, 1990.

National Archives. "America's Founding Documents. The Bill of Rights: What Does It Say?" Accessed 28 September 2021. https://www.archives.gov/founding-docs/bill-of-rights/what-does-it-say.

Niebuhr, Reinhold. *Leaves from the Notebook of a Tamed Cynic.* San Francisco: Harper and Row, 1980.

North American Nursing Diagnosis Association, *Nursing Diagnosis: Definitions and Classification 2009–2011.* Oxford: Wiley-Blackwell, 2011.

Nouwen, Henri. *The Wounded Healer: Ministry in Contemporary Society.* New York: Image Books Doubleday, 1979.

Pacific Youth Correctional Ministries. "Reaching Youthful Offenders and Children in Protective Custody with the Gospel of Jesus Christ." Accessed 26 December 2020. www.PacificYouth.org.

Paget, Naomi K., and Janet R. McCormack. *The Work of the Chaplain.* Valley Forge, PA: Judson Press, 2006.

Palmer, Stuart. *Role Stress.* Englewood Cliffs, NJ: Prentice-Hall, 1981.

Parker, Andrew, Nick J. Watson, and John B. White. *Sports Chaplaincy: Trends, Issues and Debates.* London: Routledge, 2016.

Pattison, Stephen. "Situating Chaplaincy in the United Kingdom: The Acceptable Face of 'Religion'?." In *A Handbook of Chaplaincy Studies: Understanding Spiritual Care in Public Places*, edited by Christopher Swift, Mark Cobb, and Andrew Todd. Burlington: Ashgate Publishing, 2015.

Pedersen, Pederson, Daniel Shapiro, and Ann McDaniel, "Inside America's Toughest Prison." *Newsweek* (6 October 1986): 46–61.

Pescosolido, Bernice, and Sharon Georgianna. "Durkheim, Suicide, and Religion: Toward a Network Theory of Suicide." *American Sociological Review* 54, no. 1 (February 1989): 33–48. Accessed 18 April 2021. https://www.jstor.org/stable/2095660.

Pew Research Center. "America's Changing Religious Landscape: Christians Decline Sharply as Share of Population; Unaffiliated and Other Faiths Continue to Grow." Washington, DC: Pew Research Center, 2015. Accessed 30 August 2021. https://www.pewforum.org/2015/05/12/americas-changing-religious-landscape/.

Prior, Karen Swallow. *On Reading Well: Finding the Good Life through Great Books.* Grand Rapids: Brazos Press, 2018.

Prison Seminaries Foundation. "Leading the Way to Moral Rehabilitation in Prison Systems of the World." Accessed 5 October 2021. www.prisonseminaries.org.

Rable, George. *God's Almost Chosen Peoples: A Religious History of the American Civil War.* Chapel Hill: UNC Press, 2010.

Radel, F. Robert, II, and Andrew A. Labbe. "The Clergy-Penitent Privilege: An Overview." Accessed 19 May 2021. https://cdn.ymaws.com/thefederation.site-ym.com/resource/resmgr/docs/Quarterly/Archive/V64N4_Radel.pdf.

Rae, Scott B. *Moral Choices: An Introduction to Ethics.* Grand Rapids: Zondervan, 2018.

"Religious Discrimination." US Equal Employment Opportunity Commission, 2021. Accessed 8 August 2021. https://www.eeoc.gov/religious-discrimination.

Religious Freedom and Business Foundation. "Corporate Religious Equity, Diversity, and Inclusion (REDI Index 2021)." Accessed 28 September 2021. https://religiousfreedomandbusiness.org/redi.

Religious Land Use and Institutionalized Persons Act of 2000 (RLUIPA). Accessed 28 September 2021. https://www.justice.gov/crt/religious-land-use-and-institutionalized-persons-act-0.

Rosenfeld, Jordan. "The 11 Qualities of a Good Death According to Research," *Quartz,* July 2016. Accessed 8 December 2020. https://qz.com/727042/the-11-qualities-of-a-good-death-according-to-research.

Ross, Christina L. "Integral Healthcare: The Benefits of Integrating Complementary and Alternative Medicine with a Conventional Healthcare Practice." *Integrative Medical Insights* 4 (19 October 2009): 13–20. Accessed 15 July 2021. https://www.ncbi.nlm.nih.gov/pmc/articles/PMC3093682.

Rubin, Ashley, and Keramet Reiter, "Continuity in the Face of Penal Innovation: Revisiting the History of American Solitary Confinement." *Law & Social Inquiry Journal of the American Bar Foundation* 43, no. 4 (Fall 2018). Accessed 28 September 2021. https://www.cambridge.org/core/journals/law-and-social-inquiry/article/abs/continuity-in-the-face-of-penal-innovation-revisiting-the-history-of-american-solitary-confinement/E3BE3440816D9608B8FDED536686B4C7.

Schuhmann, Carmen, and Annelieke Damen. "Representing the Good: Pastoral Care in a Secular Age." *Pastoral Psychology* 67, no. 4 (2018): 405–417. Accessed 8 September 2024. https://doi.org/10.1007/s11089-018-0826-0.

Secretary of the Navy. Instruction 1730.7E. "Religious Ministry within the Department of the Navy." 11 March 2019. Accessed 5 October 2021. https://www.secnav.navy

.mil/doni/Directives/01000%20Military%20Personnel%20Support/01-700%20 Morale,%20Community%20and%20Religious%20Services/1730.7E.pdf.

———. Instruction 5351.1, Change Transmittal 1. "Professional Naval Chaplaincy." 2 July 2015. Accessed 5 October 2021. https://www.secnav.navy.mil/doni/Directives/05000%20General%20Management%20Security%20and%20Safety%20 Services/05-300%20Manpower%20Personnel%20Support/SECNAV%20 5351.1%20CH-1.pdf.

Shattell, Mona, Yorghos Apostolopoulos, Chad Collins, Sevil Sönmez, and Caitlin Fehrenbacher. "Trucking Organization and Mental Health Disorders of Truck Drivers." *Issues in Mental Health Nursing* 33, no. 7 (2012): 436–44. Accessed 28 September 2021. https://jhu.pure.elsevier.com/en/publications/trucking-organization-and-mental-health-disorders-of-truck-driver.

Spiritual Care Association. "About Board Certification." Accessed 21 September 2021. https://www.spiritualcareassociation.org/requirements-for-board-certification.html.

———. "Become a Board Certified (BCC) or Credentialed Chaplain (CC)." Accessed 5 October 2021. https://www.spiritualcareassociation.org/certification.html.

Statista. "Active and Reserve US Military Force Personnel Numbers in 2020 by Service Branch and Reserve Component." Accessed 1 March 2021. https://www.statista.com/statistics/232330/us-military-force-numbers-by-service-branch-and-reserve-component/.

Swinton, John. "A Question of Identity: What Does It Mean for Chaplains to Become Healthcare Professionals?" *Scottish Journal of Healthcare Chaplaincy* 6, no. 2 (2003): 2.

Texas Department of Criminal Justice. "Annual Review of Fiscal Year 2017." Accessed 4 January 2021. https://www.tdcj.texas.gov/documents/Annual_Review_2017.pdf.

———. "Mission Statement." Accessed 28 September 2021. www.tdcj.texas.gov.

Texas Department of Criminal Justice, Office of Executive Services. "Publications." Accessed 4 January 2021. https://www.tdcj.texas.gov/publications/index.html#Executive.

*Texas Health and Safety Code.* "Title 4, Subtitle F, Chapter 313: Consent to Medical Treatment Act." Accessed 9 June 2021. https://statutes.capitol.texas.gov/Docs/HS/htm/HS.313.htm.

*Texas Rules of Evidence.* "Rule 505: Privilege for Communications to a Clergy Member." Accessed 3 April 2021. https://www.txcourts.gov/media/921665/tx-rules-of-evidence.pdf.

Timmins, Fiona, Sílvia Caldeira, Maryanne Murphy, Nicolas Pujol, Greg Sheaf, Elizabeth Weathers, Jacqueline Whelan, and Bernadette Flanagan. "The Role of the Healthcare Chaplain: A Literature Review." *Journal of Health Care Chaplaincy* 24, no. 3 (July–September 2018): 87–106. Accessed 7 September 2021. DOI: 10.1080/08854726.2017.1338048.

Toner, James H. *Morals Under the Gun: the Cardinal Virtues, Military Ethics, and American Society.* Lexington: University Press of Kentucky, 2000.

Transport for Christ. "TFC Global." Accessed 28 September 2021. https://tfcglobal.org/.

Turner, Victor. *The Ritual Process: Structure and Anti-Structure.* New York: Aldine de Gruyter, 1995.

United States Air Force. "Chaplain Officer: Providing Spiritual Care." Accessed 12 May 2021. www.airforce.com/careers/specialty-careers/chaplain.

United States Army. "Soldiers." Accessed 5 October 2021. https://www.army.mil/soldiers.

———. "Who We Are: The Army's Vision and Strategy." Accessed 5 October 2021. https://www.army.mil/about/.

United States Army Chaplain Corps. "Chaplain Candidate Program." Accessed 5 October 2021. https://www.goarmy.com/chaplain/become-an-army-chaplain/candidate-program.html.

———. "The Army Chaplain Corps: A Sacred Calling to Serve God and Country." Accessed 5 October 2021. https://www.goarmy.com/chaplain.html.

United States Department of Justice, Federal Bureau of Prisons. "Ministry of BOP Chaplains." Accessed 28 September 2021. https://www.bop.gov/policy/technical/5360_02.pdf.

United States Department of Veteran Affairs, Patient Care Services. "VA Chaplains: Comfort, Support, Lead, Advocate, Counsel, Mediate and Educate." Accessed 5 October 2021. https://www.patientcare.va.gov/chaplain/What_Do_Chaplains_Do.asp.

United States Coast Guard. "Missions." Accessed 5 October 2021. www.mycg.uscg.mil/Missions/.

United States Equal Employment Opportunity Commission. *Compliance Manual on Religious Discrimination.* "Section 12: Religious Discrimination." 15 January 2021. Accessed 28 September 2021. https://www.eeoc.gov/laws/guidance/section-12-religious-discrimination#h_89562320331610748566057.

VandeCreek, L., and L. Burton, eds., "Professional Chaplaincy: Its Role and Importance in Healthcare." *Journal of Pastoral Care* 55, no. 1 (Spring 2001): 81–97. Accessed 21 September 2021. https://pubmed.ncbi.nlm.nih.gov/11303456/.

Vandenhoeck, Anne. "The Impact of the First Wave of the Covid-19 Pandemic on Chaplaincy in Health Care: Introduction to an International Survey." *Journal of Pastoral Care & Counseling* 75, no. 1 (March 2021). Accessed 21 September 2021. https://journals.sagepub.com/doi/full/10.1177/1542305021992044.

Vickers, Robert C. "The Military Chaplaincy: A Study in Role Conflict." DMin diss., Vanderbilt University, 1984.

Visser, Anja, Hetty Zock, and Hanneke Muthert. "Positioning Chaplaincy in the Pluralistic and Multidisciplinary Dutch Care Context." *Religions* 14, no. 9:1173 (2023). Accessed 7 September 2024. https://www.mdpi.com/2077-1444/14/9/1173.

Vlasblom, J. P., J. T. van der Steen, D. L. Knol, and H. Jochemsen. "Effects of a Spiritual Care Training for Nurses." *Nurse Education Today* 31, no. 8 (November 2011): 790–96. Accessed 21 September 2021. https://pubmed.ncbi.nlm.nih.gov/21146259/.

Wallace, Ruth. "Durkheim and the Civil Religion Concept." *Review of Religious Research* 18, no. 3 (Spring 1977): 287–90. Accessed 6 September 2021. https://www.jstor.org/stable/3510218.

Westbury, Joe, ed. *Going Where Others Cannot Go*. Atlanta: Home Mission Board, 1995.

Wicks, Robert. *Bounce*. Oxford: Oxford University Press, 2010.

Williams, George H. "The Chaplaincy in the Armed Forces of the United States of America in Historical and Ecclesiastical Perspective." In *Military Chaplains: From Religious Military to a Military Religion*, edited by Harvey Cox. New York: American Report Press, 1973.

World Health Organization. "Palliative Care." 5 August 2020. https://www.who.int/news-room/fact-sheets/detail/palliative-care.

Zehr, H. "Justice for Children Whose Parents Are in Prison." Eastern Mennonite University, Zehr Institute for Restorative Justice Blog. 10 December 2010. Accessed 5 October 2021. https://emu.edu/now/restorative-justice/2010/12/10/justice-for-children-whose-parents-are-in-prison/.

# BIBLIOGRAPHY

## GENERAL

Appelquist, A. Ray, ed. *Church, State, and Chaplaincy: Essays and Statements on the American Chaplaincy System.* Washington, DC: General Commission on Chaplains and Armed Forces Personnel, 1969.

Baker, Alan. *Foundations of Chaplaincy: A Practical Guide.* Grand Rapids, MI: Eerdmans, 2021.

Beauchamp, Tom L., and James F. Childress. *Principles of Biomedical Ethics.* 4th ed. New York: Oxford University Press, 1994.

Burton, Arthur Laurel. *Making Chaplaincy Work: Practical Approaches.* Binghamton: Haworth Press, 1988.

Cadge, Wendy, and Shelly Rambo, eds. *Chaplaincy and Spiritual Care in the Twenty-First Century: An Introduction.* Chapel Hill: University of North Carolina Press, 2022.

Caperon, John, Andrew Todd, and James Walters. *A Christian Theology of Chaplaincy.* Philadelphia: Jessica Kingsley Publishers, 2018.

Chander, Vineet, and Lucinda Mosher. *Hindu Approaches to Spiritual Care: Chaplaincy in Theory and Practice.* Philadelphia: Jessica Kingsley Publishers, 2019.

Chemerinsky, Erwin, and Howard Gillman. *The Religion Clauses: The Case for Separating Church and State.* New York: Oxford University Press, 2020.

Cook, E. Dean. *Chaplaincy: Being God's Presence in Closed Communities, a Free Methodist History, 1935–2010.* Bloomington, IN: AuthorHouse, 2010.

Corbitt, Otis. *An Introduction to Chaplaincy Ministry: An Evangelical Christian Perspective.* Independently published, 2020.

Crick, Robert. *Outside the Gates: The Need for Theology, History, and Practice of Chaplaincy Ministries.* Oviedo, FL: HigherLife Development Services, 2012.

Drakeman, Donald L. *Church, State, and Original Intent.* Cambridge; New York: Cambridge University Press, 2009.

Ernstmeyer, M.S., ed. *They Shall Not March Alone: Glimpses into the Life and History of the Chaplaincy of the Lutheran Church, Missouri Synod.* St. Louis, MO: Concordia Publishing, 1990.

Franklin, Dan. *Chaplaincy: Hands-on Ministry: Ministering Beyond the Walls of the Church.* Self-published, 2020.

Fuller, Janet. *Blessings for Your Students: Prayers for Interfaith Communities in Higher Education.* New York: Church Publishing, 2024.

Gennep, Arnold van. *The Rites of Passage.* Translated by Monika B. Vizedom and Gabrielle L. Caffee. Chicago: University of Chicago Press, 1960.

Giles, Cheryl A., and Willa B. Miller. *Arts of Contemplative Care: Pioneering Voices in Buddhist Chaplaincy and Pastoral Work.* Boston: Wisdom Publications, 2012.

Gilliat-Ray, Sophie, Muhammad Mansur Ali, and Stephen Pattison. *Understanding Muslim Chaplaincy.* Burlington, VT: Ashgate Publishing, 2013.

Graves, Joel Curtis. *Leadership Paradigms in Chaplaincy.* Boca Raton, FL: Dissertation.com, 2007.

Hiser, Bethany Dearborn. *From Burned Out to Beloved: Soul Care for the Wounded Healer.* Downers Grove, IL: InterVarsity Press, 2020.

Holst, Lawrence E., and Harold P. Kurtz. *Toward a Creative Chaplaincy.* Springfield: Charles C Thomas Publisher, 1973.

Hutcheson, Richard G., Jr. *The Churches and the Chaplaincy.* Atlanta: John Knox Press, 1975. Rev. ed. Government Printing Office, 1997.

Irons, Peter. *God on Trial: Landmark Cases from America's Religious Battlefields.* Penguin Books, 2007.

Jumper, Mark A., Steven E. Keith, and Michael W. Langston. *Chaplaincy: A Comprehensive Introduction.* Grand Rapids, Michigan: Baker Academic, 2024.

Keefe, Rachael A. *The Lifesaving Church: Faith Communities and Suicide Prevention.* Chalice Press, 2018.

Langston, Michael W., and Kathy J. Langston. *A Journey to Hope: Healing the Traumatized Spirit.* Lampion Press, 2016

Malone, Kobutsu. *Prison Chaplaincy Guidelines for Zen Buddhism: A Sourcebook for Prison Chaplains, Administrators, and Security Personnel.* Sedgwick, ME: Engaged Zen Foundation, 2006.

Military Chaplains Association. *Voices of Chaplaincy: Ministry Roles and Functions.* Arlington, VA: MCA, 2012.

Osmer, Richard R. *Practical Theology: An Introduction*. Grand Rapids, Michigan: Eerdmans, 2008.

Paget, Naomi, and Janet McCormack. *The Work of the Chaplain*. Valley Forge, PA: Judson Press, 2006.

Pattison, Stephen. "Situating Chaplaincy in the United Kingdom: The Acceptable Face of 'Religion'?" In *A Handbook of Chaplaincy Studies: Understanding Spiritual Care in Public Places*, edited by Christopher Swift, Mark Cobb, and Andrew Todd. Burlington: Ashgate Publishing, 2015.

Platt, David. *Counter Culture: Following Christ in an Anti-Christian Age*. Revised edition. Tyndale Elevate, 2017.

Plummer, David B. "Chaplaincy: The Greatest Story Never Told." *The Journal of Pastoral Care* 50 (1996): 1–12.

Possamai, Adam. *Sociology of Religion for Generations X and Y*. Routledge, 2016.

Purves, Andrew. *Reconstructing Pastoral Theology: A Christological Foundation*. Louisville: Westminster John Knox Press, 2004.

Sanders, Matt. *Chaplaincy: A Ministry of Presence*. Lulu.com, 2016.

Skanse, John. *A Chaplain's Experience: A New Paradigm*. Ocala, FL: Atlantic Publishing, 2018.

Staudacher, Rosemarian V. *Chaplains in Action*. New York: Vision Books, 1962.

Sullivan, Winnifred. *A Ministry of Presence: Chaplaincy, Spiritual Care, and the Law*. Chicago: The University of Chicago Press, 2019.

Swift, Christopher, Mark Cobb, and Andrew Todd, eds. *A Handbook of Chaplaincy Studies: Understanding Spiritual Care in Public Places*. Abingdon, UK: Routledge, 2015.

Swinton, John. *Practical Theology and Qualitative Research*. 2nd edition. London: SCM Press, 2016.

Tharp, Lt Col David F., and Capt Katherine A. Tharp. *The Combat PTS(D) Resilience and Reintegration Workbook: Resiliency Formation Training Series for Combat-Related Post-Traumatic Stress*. Independently published, 2019.

Turner, Victor. *The Ritual Process: Structure and Anti-Structure*. New York: Aldine de Gruyter, 1995.

Toner, James H. *Morals Under the Gun: The Cardinal Virtues, Military Ethics, and American Society*. 1st edition. Lexington: University Press of Kentucky, 2000.

Trelfall-Holmes, Miranda, and Mark Newitt. *Being a Chaplain*. London: SPCK, 2011.

United Church of Christ Task Force on Ministries to Military Personnel. *Ministries to Military Personnel: Report of a United Church Task Force to the Ninth General Synod, St. Louis, Missouri, June 22–26, 1973*. Philadelphia: United Church Press, 1973.

Visser, Anja, Hetty Zock, and Hanneke Muthert. "Positioning Chaplaincy in the Pluralistic and Multidisciplinary Dutch Care Context." *Religions* 14, no. 9:1173 (2023). https://www.mdpi.com/2077-1444/14/9/1173.

West, Steve. *The Bronze Scar: Understanding How PTSD Feels to Help Victims and Those Who Support Them*. C&S Publishing, 2021.

Wicks, Robert J. *Bounce: Living the Resilient Life*. New York: Oxford University Press, 2009.

Wilkes, C. Gene, and Calvin Miller. *Jesus on Leadership: Timeless Wisdom on Servant Leadership*. Wheaton, Ill: Tyndale Elevate, 1998.

Woodward, Whit. *Ministry of Presence: Biblical Insight on Christian Chaplaincy*. North Fort Myers, FL: FaithLife Publishers, 2011.

## HEALTH CARE

Albers, Robert H., William H. Meller, and Steven D. Thurber, eds. *Ministry with Persons with Mental Illness and Their Families*. 2nd edition. Minneapolis: Fortress Press, 2019.

Anderson, Robert, and Mary Fukuyama. *Ministry in the Spiritual and Cultural Diversity of Healthcare: Increasing the Competency of Chaplains*. New York: Routledge, 2004.

Bueckert, Leah Dawn, and Daniel S. Schipani, eds. *You Welcomed Me: Interfaith Spiritual Care in the Hospital*. Kitchener, Ontario: Pandora Press, 2010.

Burck, J. Russell. "The Chaplain amid Dilemmas of Health-Care Ethics." *American Protestant Hospital Association Bulletin* 47(3) (1983): 69–76.

Burton, Laurel Arthur, ed. *Health Care Chaplaincy in Oncology*. New York: Haworth Pastoral Press, 1992.

———, ed. *Chaplaincy Services in Contemporary Health Care*. Schaumburg, IL: College of Chaplains, 1992.

———, ed. *Making Chaplaincy Work: Practical Approaches*. New York: Haworth Press, 1988.

Cadge, Wendy. *Paging God: Religion in the Halls of Medicine.* Chicago: The University of Chicago Press, 2012.

Carder, Kenneth L., and Kenneth H. Carter Jr. *Ministry with the Forgotten: Dementia through a Spiritual Lens.* Nashville: Abingdon Press, 2019.

Drumm, William Martin. *Hospital Chaplains: An Historical Synopsis and Commentary.* Washington DC: Catholic University Press of America, 1943.

Faith, Gerald. *Health Care Ministries: Organization, Management, Evaluation.* St. Louis: Catholic Health Association of the United States, 1980.

Fitchett, George, Kelsey B. White, and Kathryn Lindes, eds. *Evidence-Based Healthcare Chaplaincy: A Research Reader.* Philadelphia: Jessica Kingsley Publishers, 2018.

Fitchett, George, and Steve Nolan, eds. *Spiritual Care in Practice: Case Studies in Healthcare Chaplaincy.* Philadelphia: Jessica Kingsley Publishers, 2015.

Fletcher, Jean, ed. *Chaplaincy and Spiritual Care in Mental Health Settings.* London and Philadelphia: Jessica Kingsley Publishers, 2019.

Gemmell, Alexander. *Hospital Chaplain.* Edinburgh: St. Andrew Press, 1970.

Grainger, Roger. *Watching for Wings: Theology and Mental Illness in a Pastoral Setting.* London: Darton, Longman and Todd, 1979.

Grosch-Miller, Carla. *Trauma and Pastoral Care: A Practical Handbook.* Norwich: Canterbury Press, 2021.

Hayes, Helen, Cornelius J. Van der Poel, and National Association of Catholic Chaplains. *Health-Care Ministry: A Handbook for Chaplains.* New York: Paulist Press, 1990.

Hesch, John B. *Clinical Pastoral Care for Hospitalized Children and Their Families.* New York: Paulist Press, 1987.

Holst, Lawrence, ed. *Hospital Ministry: The Role of the Chaplain Today.* Eugene, OR: Wipf & Stock Publishers, 2018.

Ihewulezi, Cajetan N. *Hospital Preaching as Informed by Bedside Listening: A Homiletical Guide for Preachers, Pastors, and Chaplains in Hospitals, Hospice, Prison, and Nursing Home Ministries.* Lanham, MD: University Press of America, 2011.

Kelly, Ewan, and John Swinton. *Chaplaincy and the Soul of Health and Social Care: Fostering Spiritual Wellbeing in Emerging Paradigms of Care.* London and Philadelphia: Jessica Kingsley Publishers, 2019.

Kilgore, James E. *Pastoral Care of the Hospitalized Child.* New York: Exposition Press, 1968.

Kerr, Audrey Elisa. *Normal: A Chaplain, a Community with HIV/AIDS, and the Eternal Life of Stories.* Eugene, OR: Cascade Books, 2018.

Levin, Jeff. *Religion and Medicine: A History of the Encounter between Humanity's Two Greatest Institutions.* New York: Oxford University Press, 2020.

Matthews, Pia. *Ethical Questions in Healthcare Chaplaincy: Learning to Make Informed Decisions.* Philadelphia: Jessica Kingsley Publishers, 2018.

McCall, Junietta Baker. *Practical Guide to Hospital Chaplaincy: Healing Ways.* New York: Haworth Pastoral Press, 2002.

McClelland, Kate. *Call the Chaplain.* Norwich, UK: Hymns Ancient & Modern, 2014.

Mitchell, Kenneth R. *Hospital Chaplain.* Philadelphia: Westminster Press, 1972.

Nash, Paul. *Paediatric Chaplaincy: Principles, Practices and Skills.* London and Philadelphia: Jessica Kingsley Publishers, 2015.

Naughton, Margaret. *Healthcare Chaplaincy: An Unfolding Narrative: "Standing in the Gap."* Peter Lang Ltd, International Academic Publishers, 2022.

Oman, Doug, ed. *Why Religion and Spirituality Matter for Public Health: Evidence, Implications, and Resources.* Cham, Switzerland: Springer International Publishing, 2018.

Orchard, Helen, ed. *Spirituality in Health Care Contexts.* Philadelphia: Jessica Kingsley Publishers, 2001.

Roberts, Stephen, ed. *Professional and Spiritual Care: A Practical Clergy and Chaplain's Handbook.* Woodstock, VT: SkyLight Paths Publishing, 2012.

Smeets, Wim. *Spiritual Care in a Hospital Setting: An Empirical-theological Exploration.* Translated by M. Manley. Leiden: Brill, 2006.

Swift, Christopher. *Hospital Chaplaincy in the 21st Century,* 2nd ed. Farnham, UK: Ashgate, 2014.

Swinton, John. "A Question of Identity: What Does It Mean for Chaplains to Become Healthcare Professionals?" *Scottish Journal of Healthcare Chaplaincy* 6, no. 2 (2003): 2.

VandeCreek, Larry, ed. *Contract Pastoral Care and Education: The Trend of the Future?* New York: Haworth Pastoral Press, 1999.

———, ed. *Professional Chaplaincy: What Is Happening to It During Health Care Reform?* New York: Haworth Pastoral Press, 2000.

VandeCreek, Larry, and Laurel Arthur Burton, eds. *Chaplain-Physician Relationship.* New York: Haworth Press, 1991.

VandeCreek, Larry, and Marjorie A. Lyon. *Ministry of Hospital Chaplains: Patient Satisfaction.* New York: Haworth Pastoral Press, 1997.

VandeCreek, Larry, and Sue Mooney, eds. *Parish Nurses, Health Care Chaplains, and Community Clergy: Navigating the Maze of Professional Relationships.* New York: Haworth Press, 2002.

Wilson, Michael. *The Hospital—A Place of Truth: A Study of the Role of the Hospital Chaplain.* Birmingham, England: Institute for the Study of Worship and Religious Architecture, 1971.

Wirpsa, M. Jeanne, and Karen Pugliese, eds. *Chaplains as Partners in Medical Decision-Making: Case Studies in Healthcare Chaplaincy.* Philadelphia: Jessica Kingsley Publishers, 2020.

Wong, Agnes M.F. *The Art and Science of Compassion, A Primer: Reflections of a Physician-Chaplain.* New York: Oxford University Press, 2021.

# HOSPICE

Behers, Richard. *Spiritual Care for People Living with Dementia Using Multisensory Interventions.* London; Philadelphia: Jessica Kingsley Publishers, 2018.

Binkewicz, Matthew P. *Peaceful Journey: A Hospice Chaplain's Guide to the End of Life.* Ithaca, NY: Paramount Market Publishing, 2005.

Casto, John. *The Basics of Hospice Chaplain Ministry: Practical Help for the New Chaplain.* Hisway Prayer Publications, 2019.

Labinski, Catherine. *The Exchange of Gifts in Hospice: Memories of a Hospice Chaplain.* Waukesha, WI: Orange Hat Publishing, 2018.

Murphy, Karen, and Bob Whorton, eds. *Chaplaincy in Hospice and Palliative Care.* London and Philadelphia: Jessica Kingsley Publishers, 2017.

Nolan, Steve. *Spiritual Care at the End of Life: The Chaplain as a Hopeful Presence.* London and Philadelphia: Jessica Kingsley Publishers, 2011.

O'Connor, Brian, Daniel J. Cherico, Austin H. Kutscher, eds. *The Role of the Minister in Caring for the Dying Patient and the Bereaved.* New York: Arno Press, 1978.

Sullivan, Douglas. *The World of Hospice Spiritual Care: A Practical Guide for Palliative Care Chaplain.* Meadville, PA: Christian Faith Publishing, 2017.

Woods, Deborah. *Death Angel: The Journey of a Hospice Chaplain.* Bloomington, IN: AuthorHouse, 2007.

## CLINICAL PASTORAL EDUCATION

Hilsman, Gordon J. *How To Get the Most out of Clinical Pastoral Education: A CPE Primer.* Philadelphia: Jessica Kingsley Publishers, 2018.

Karaban, Roslyn. *Body and Soul: The Continuing Story of the Clinical Pastoral Education Movement, 1992–2017.* Morrisville, NC: Lulu Publishing Services, 2019.

Lawrence, Raymond. *Recovery of the Soul: A History and Memoir of the Clinical Pastoral Movement.* New York: CPSP Press, 2017.

LeBat, Sean J. *Anton Boisen: Madness, Mysticism, and the Origins of Clinical Pastoral Education.* Lanham, MD: Fortress Academic, 2021.

Powell, Robert Charles. *Anton T. Boisen, 1876–1965: Breaking an Opening in the Wall between Religion and Medicine.* Buffalo, NY: Association of Mental Health Clergy, 1976.

Thornton, Edward E. *Professional Education for Ministry: A History of Clinical Pastoral Education.* Nashville: Abingdon Press, 1970.

## MILITARY

Abercrombie, Clarence L. *The Military Chaplain.* Beverly Hills, CA: Sage Publications, 1977.

Barish, Louis. *Rabbis in Uniform: The Story of the American Jewish Military Chaplain.* New York: J. David, 1962.

Bergen, Doris, ed. *Sword of the Lord: Military Chaplains from the First to the Twenty-first Century.* Notre Dame, IN: University of Notre Dame Press, 2004.

Bergsma, H. L. *Pioneers: A Monograph on the First Two Black Chaplains in the Chaplain Corps of the United States Navy.* Washington: Chaplain Corps, US Navy, 1981.

Bershon, Richard Y. *With the Cross of Jesus: A History of the Church of God Chaplaincy and Ministry to the Military.* Cleveland, TN: Pathway Press, 1991.

Bock, Martin. *Religion within the Armed Forces: Military Chaplaincy in an International Comparison.* Strausberg, Germany: Sozialwissenschaftliches Institut der Bundeswehr, 1998.

Bohlman, Brian. *For God and Country: Considering the Call to Military Chaplaincy*, 2nd ed. West Columbia, SC: Chaplain Resource Center, 2011.

Brekke, Torkel, and Vladimir Tikhonov, eds. *Military Chaplaincy in an Era of Religious Pluralism: Military-religious Nexus in Asia, Europe, and USA*. New Delhi: Oxford University Press, 2017.

Budd, Richard M. *Serving Two Masters: The Development of Military Chaplaincy 1860–1920*. Lincoln, NE: University of Nebraska Press, 2020.

Corbitt, Otis. *An Introduction to Chaplaincy Ministry: An Evangelical Christian Perspective*. Self-published, 2020.

Cox, Harvey, ed. *Military Chaplains: From a Religious Military to a Military Religion*. New York: American Report Press, 1972.

Craughwell, Thomas. *Heroic Catholic Chaplains: Stories of the Brave and Holy Men Who Dodged Bullets While Saving Souls*. Charlotte, NC: TAN Books, 2018.

Cross, Christopher. *Soldiers of God: True Story of the US Army Chaplains*. New York: E.P. Dutton, 1945.

Drazin, Israel, and Cecil Curry. *For God and Country: The History of a Constitutional Challenge to the Army Chaplaincy*. Hoboken, NJ: KTAV Publishing House, 1995.

Fowler, Albert G. *Peacetime Padres: Canadian Protestant Military Chaplains, 1945–1995*. St. Catharines, Ontario: Vanwell Publishing, 1996.

Germain, Aidan Henry. *Catholic Military Chaplains, 1776–1917*. Washington, DC, 1929.

Grant, Dorothy Fremont. *War Is My Parish*. Milwaukee, WI: Bruce Publishing, 1944.

Hadley, Michael L., and Leslie A. Kenny, eds. *Chaplains in War and Peace: Ethical Dilemmas of Conscience and Conflicting Professional Roles in Military Chaplaincy in Canada*. Victoria, BC: Center for Studies in Religion and Society, University of Victoria, 2006.

Hansen, Kim. *Military Chaplains and Religious Diversity*. New York: Palgrave Macmillan Publishers, 2012.

Hassner, Ron E. *Religion in the Military Worldwide*. Cambridge: Cambridge University Press, 2014.

Jacques, Michael. *A Chaplain's Battle: Transcending Powerlessness in an Explosive World*. Self-published, 2020.

Jensen, Wollom A. *Moral Warriors, Moral Wounds: The Ministry of the Christian Ethic.* Eugene, OR: Cascade Books, 2016.

Keith, Bill. *Days of Anguish, Days of Hope.* StoneGate Publishing Company, Inc., 2010.

Kramer, Philip A. *The Proximity Principle: Army Chaplains on the Fighting Line in Doctrine and History.* Fort Leavenworth, KS: Combat Studies Institute Press, 2015.

Kurzman, Dan. *No Greater Glory: The Four Immortal Chaplains and the Sinking of the Dorchester in World War II.* New York: Random House, 2004.

Laing, John. *In Jesus' Name: Evangelicals and Military Chaplaincy.* Eugene, OR: Wipf & Stock, 2015.

Larson, Duane H., and Jeff Zust. *Care for the Sorrowing Soul: Healing Moral Injuries from Military Service and Implications for the Rest of Us.* Eugene, OR: Cascade Books, 2017.

Linzey, Paul E., B. Keith Travis, and Jeff Iorg. *Military Ministry: Chaplains in the Twenty-First Century.* Wipf and Stock, 2022.

Loveland, Anne C. *Change and Conflict in the US Army Chaplain Corps Since 1945.* Legacies of War. Knoxville: University of Tennessee Press, 2014.

Mansfield, Stephen. *Faith of the American Soldier.* Lake Mary, FL: Charisma House, 2005.

Mole, Robert L. *God Also Loves Military People: A Brief Story of the Seventh-Day Adventist Church and the American Military Chaplaincy, 1860–1976.* Washington, DC: General Conference of Seventh-Day Adventists, 1977.

Moore, S. K. *Military Chaplains as Agents of Peace: Religious Leader Engagement in Conflict and Post-Conflict Environments.* Lanham, MD: Lexington Books, 2013.

Oliver, Kenneth. *Chaplain at War.* Chichester, England: Angel Press, 1986.

Patterson, Eric, ed. *Military Chaplains in Afghanistan, Iraq, and Beyond: Advisement and Leader Engagement in Highly Religious Environments.* Lanham, MD: Rowman & Littlefield, 2014.

Powell, Anthony. *Black Chaplains in the United States Army, 1863–1946.* Self-published, 1994.

Rennick, Joanne, and Dallaire Romeo. *Religion in the Ranks: Belief and Religious Experience in the Canadian Forces.* Toronto, Canada: University of Toronto Press, 2011.

Schuette, Kim M. *Christian Science Military Ministry 1917–2004.* Indianapolis, IN: Brockton Publishing, 2008.

Stahl, Ronit. *Enlisting Faith: How the Military Chaplaincy Shaped Religion and State in Modern America.* Cambridge, MA: Harvard University Press, 2017.

Takken, Hanneke. *Churches, Chaplains and the First World War.* New York: Routledge/Taylor & Francis Group, 2018.

Todd, Andrew, ed. *Military Chaplaincy in Contention: Chaplains, Churches, and the Morality of Conflict.* Explorations in Practical, Pastoral, and Empirical Theology. Burlington, VT: Ashgate, 2013.

Toole, Mary M. *Handbook for Chaplains.* New York: Paulist Press, 2006.

Tretera, Jiri Rajmund, and Zaboj Horak. *Spiritual Care in Public Institutions in Europe.* Berlin: Berliner Wissenschafts-Verlag, 2019.

Van Dress, Valeria R. *For Man and Country: Atheist Chaplains in the US Army?* Fort Leavenworth, KS: Army Press, 2016.

Waggoner, Edward. *Religion in Uniform: A Critique of US Military Chaplaincy.* Lanham, MD: Lexington Books, 2019.

Walden, Kenny J. *Challenges Faced by Iraq War Reservists and Their Families: A Soul Care Program for Chaplains and Pastors.* Eugene, OR: Pickwick Publications, 2012.

Yee, James. *For God and Country: Faith and Patriotism under Fire.* New York: Public Affairs, 2005.

Zahn, Gordon C. *Military Chaplaincy: A Study of Role Tension in the Royal Air Force.* Toronto, Canada: University of Toronto Press, 1969.

# HISTORY OF MILITARY CHAPLAINS (IN CHRONOLOGICAL ORDER)

Crowder, Jack. *Chaplains of the Revolutionary War: Black Robed American Warriors.* Jefferson, NC: McFarland and Company, 2017.

Headley, Joel. *The Chaplains and Clergy of the Revolution,* 2016 reprint. New York: C. Scribner, 1864.

McLane, C. Rogers. *American Chaplains of the Revolution.* Louisville: National Society Sons of the Revolution, 1991.

Armstrong, Warren. *For Courageous Fighting and Confident Dying: Union Chaplains in the Civil War.* Lawrence, KS: University Press of Kansas, 1998.

Brinsfield, John. *The Spirit Divided: Memoirs of Civil War Chaplains.* Macon, GA: Mercer University Press, 2006.

Brinsfield, John, and William Davis. *Faith in the Fight: Civil War Chaplains*. Mechanicsburg, PA: Stackpole Books, 2003.

Budd, Richard. *Serving Two Masters: The Development of American Military Chaplaincy, 1860–1920*. Lincoln: University of Nebraska Press, 2020.

Crerar, Duff. *Padres in No Man's Land: Canadian Chaplains in the Great War*. Montreal: McGill-Queen's Press, 1995.

Dorsett, Lyle. *Serving God and Country: United States Military Chaplains in World War II*. New York: Penguin Group, 2012.

Robinson, Alan C. *Chaplains at War: The Role of Clergymen During World War II*. London: Tauris Academic Studies, 2008.

Brown, Jack E. *Another Side of Combat: A Chaplain Remembers Vietnam*. Nashville: Cold Tree Press, 2006.

Whitt, Jacqueline. *Bringing God to Men: American Military Chaplains and the Vietnam War*. Chapel Hill: University of North Carolina Press, 2014.

# HISTORY OF US ARMY CHAPLAINS (IN CHRONOLOGICAL ORDER)

Thompson, Parker. *The United States Army Chaplaincy: From Its European Antecedents to 1791*, vol. 1. Washington, DC: Office of the Chief of Chaplains, 1978.

Lawson, Kenneth E. *Reliable and Religious: US Army Chaplains and the War of 1812*. Washington, DC: Department of the Army, Office of the Chief of Chaplains, 2012.

Miller, Benjamin L. *In God's Presence: Chaplains, Missionaries, and Religious Space during the American Civil War*. Lawrence: University Press of Kansas, 2019.

Norton, Herman Albert. *The United States Army Chaplaincy, 1791–1865: Struggling for Recognition*, vol. 2. Washington, DC: Office of the Chief of Chaplains, 1977.

———. *Rebel Religion: The Story of Confederate Chaplains*. St. Louis: Bethany Press, 1961.

Pitts, Charles Frank. *Chaplains in Gray: The Confederate Chaplains' Story*. Nashville: Broadman Press, 1957.

Stover, Earl. *The United States Army Chaplaincy, 1865–1920: Up from Handymen*, vol. 3. Washington, DC: Office of the Chief of Chaplains, 1977.

Shay, Michael. *Sky Pilots: The Yankee Division Chaplains of World War I.* Columbia: University of Missouri Press, 2014.

Gushwa, Robert. *The United State Army Chaplaincy, 1920–1945: The Best and Worst of Times,* vol. 4. Washington, DC: Office of the Chief of Chaplains, 1977.

Linde, Richard. *We Also Fought: A World War II Navy Chaplain Remembers.* Enumclaw, WA: Pleasant Word, 2008.

Venzke, Rodger. *The United States Army Chaplaincy, 1945–1975: Confidence in Battle, Inspiration in Peace,* vol. 5. Washington, DC: Office of the Chief of Chaplains, 1977.

Brinsfield, John. *The United States Army Chaplaincy, 1975–1995: Encouraging Faith, Serving Soldiers.* Washington, DC: Office of the Chief of Chaplains, 1997.

Lawson, Kenneth E. *Faith and Hope in a War-torn Land: The US Chaplaincy in the Balkans, 1995–2005.* Fort Leavenworth, KS: Combat Studies Institute Press, USACAC, 2015.

Brinsfield, John, Douglas McCullough, Kenneth Lawson, and Gaylord T. Gunhus. *Courageous in Spirit, Compassionate in Service; The Gunhus Years, 1999-2003.* Washington, DC: Office of the Chief of Chaplains, 2003.

Brinsfield, John, and Kenneth Lawson. *A History of the United States Army Chaplaincy: The Hicks Years, 2003–2007.* Washington, DC: Office of the Chief of Chaplains, 2007.

Patterson, Eric, ed. *Military Chaplains in Afghanistan, Iraq, and Beyond: Advisement and Leader Engagement in Highly Religious Environments.* Lanham, MD: Rowman & Littlefield, 2014.

Tyger, George. *War Zone Faith: An Army Chaplain's Reflections from Afghanistan.* Boston: Skinner House Books, 2013.

# HISTORY OF US NAVY CHAPLAINS

*The History of the Chaplain Corps, United States Navy* (Washington, DC: US Bureau of Naval Personnel), in eleven volumes.

    Volume 1, 1778–1939, comp. Clifford Drury, 1949.

    Volume 2, 1939–1949, comp. Clifford Drury, 1950.

    Volume 3, 1778–1945, biographical sketches, comp. by Clifford Drury, 1948.

    Volume 4, 1946–1952, comp. Clifford Drury, 1953.

Volume 5, 1953–1957, comp. Clifford Drury, 1957.

Volume 6, 1950–1954, comp. Bureau of Naval Personnel, 1960.

Volume 7, 1957–1972, ed. Joseph Tubbs, 1974.

Volume 8, 1972–1981, ed. H. Lawrence Martin, 1981.

Volume 9, 1954–1975, ed. H. Lawrence Martin, 1985.

Volume 10, 1982–1991, ed. Michael Halley, 1993.

Volume 12, 1949–1958, ed. H. Lawrence Martin, 1958.

Moore, Withers. *Navy Chaplains in Vietnam, 1954–1964*. Washington, DC: Chief of Chaplains, Bureau of Naval Personnel, 1968.

Bergsma, H. L. *Chaplains with Marines in Vietnam, 1962–1971*. History of Museums Division, Headquarters, USMC, 1985.

Kroll, Douglas. *A History of Navy Chaplains Serving with the U. S. Coast Guard*, 2nd ed. Washington, DC: US Navy Chaplain Corps, 1993.

## HISTORY OF AIR FORCE CHAPLAINS

Jorgensen, Daniel. *The Service of Chaplains to Army Air Units 1917–1946*, vol. 1 of USAF Chaplain Service. Washington, DC: Office, Chief of Air Force Chaplains, 1961.

———. *Air Force Chaplains, 1947-1960*, vol. 2 of USAF Chaplain Service. Washington, DC: Office, Chief of Air Force Chaplains, 1963.

Scharlemann, Martin. *Air Force Chaplains, 1961-1970*, vol. 3 of USAF Chaplain Service. Washington, DC: Office, Chief of Air Force Chaplains, 1972.

Groh, John Elliot. *Air Force Chaplains, 1971-1980*, vol. 4 of USAF Chaplain Service. Washington, DC: Office, Chief of Air Force Chaplains, 1986.

———. *Facilitators of Free Exercise of Religion, 1981-1990*, vol. 5 of USAF Chaplain Service. Washington, DC: Office, Chief of Air Force Chaplains, 1991.

## CORRECTIONAL

Adams, Tom. *Jail: Mission Field for Churches*. Nashville: Broadman Press, 1985.

Atherton, Richard. *Summons to Serve: The Christian Call to Prison Ministry*. London: G. Chapman, 1987.

Atkins, Charles E. *The Word Confined: Bible Study in an American Prison*. Hauppauge, NY: Nova Science Publishers, 2020.

Baker, John. *Celebrate Recovery: A Recovery Program Based on Eight Principles from the Beatitudes.* Grand Rapids, MI: Zondervan, 2012.

Baker, Mark W. *You Can Change: Stories from Angola Prison and the Psychology of Personal Transformation.* Minneapolis: Fortress Press, 2020.

Beckford, James A., and Sophie Gilliat. *Religion in Prison: Equal Rites in a Multi-Faith Society.* Cambridge: Cambridge University Press, 1998.

Beckner, W. Thomas. *Correctional Chaplains: Keepers of the Cloak.* Orlando, FL: Cappella Press, 2012.

Beckner, W. Thomas, and Jeff Park, eds. *Effective Jail & Prison Ministry for the 21st Century.* Charlotte, NC: Coalition of Prison Evangelists, 1998.

Blevins, Johnny, Jason Karch, and Terry Solley. *Exiles: A Prisoner's Daily Devotional.* Bellville, TX: The Heart of Texas Foundation Press, 2015.

Bowe, Michael B. *Getting Out: A Restorative Approach to Prison Ministry.* Resource Publications, 2020.

Brandner, Tobias. *Beyond the Walls of Separation: Christian Faith and Ministry in Prison.* Eugene, OR: Cascade Books, 2014.

Brown, Mary. *Confessions of a Prison Chaplain.* Hook, UK: Waterside Press, 2014.

Cain, Burl, and Vance L. Drum. "The Warden-Chaplain Relationship: An Interdependent Team." *Corrections Today* (May/June 2018): 12–14.

Drum, Vance L. "Covid-19 Era Corrections: What to Know and How to Respond." *Corrections Today* (January/February 2021).

———. "The Faith Factor: Prison Culture Transformation through Religious Efforts." *Corrections Today* (November/December 2017).

———. "Professional Correctional Chaplains: Fact and Fiction." Workshop, American Correctional Association Congress of Correction. Kansas City, MO, 13 August 2007, accessed at www.correctionalchaplains.org.

———. "Restorative Justice: New Paradigm for Ministry." *Chaplaincy & Specialized Ministries,* Office of Chaplaincy Services, Center for Leadership and Ministry, Christian Church (Disciples of Christ), (Summer 1999).

———. "Transforming a Texas Prison: A Brief History." *Corrections Today* (September/October 2022).

———. *Pastoral Care at Eastham Prison: A Program for Training Inmates to Help as Peer Counselors.* (Doctoral thesis) Abilene, TX: Abilene Christian University, 1991.

Drum, Vance L., and Kristi B. Miller. "Inmate Peer Ministry: The Chaplain's Role." *Corrections Today* (March/April 2019).

Hallett, Michael, Joshua Hays, Byron Johnson, Sung Joon Jang, and Grant Duwe. "Inmate Ministry as Contextual Missiology: Best Practices for America's Emerging Prison Seminary Movement." *Perspectives in Religious Studies* (45) 2018, 69–79.

———. "Prisoners Helping Prisoners Change: A Study of Inmate Field Ministers Within Texas Prisons." *International Journal of Offender Therapy and Comparative Criminology* (2019, 1–28, Original Manuscript).

———. *The Angola Prison Seminary: Effects of Faith-Based Ministry on Identity Transformation, Desistance, and Rehabilitation.* New York: Routledge, Taylor & Francis Group, 2017.

Hoke, Chris. *Wanted: A Spiritual Pursuit through Jail, among Outlaws, and across Borders.* New York: HarperOne, 2015.

James, J. T. L. *A Living Tradition: Penitentiary Chaplaincy.* Chaplaincy Division, Correctional Services of Canada, 1990.

Johnson, Byron R. *More God, Less Crime.* West Conshohocken, PA: Templeton Press, 2011.

Kadosh, Reuben Ben. *Training Manual for the Jail and Prison Chaplain.* Scotts Valley, CA: CreateSpace Independent Publishing, 2016.

Kerley, Kent. *Religious Faith in Correctional Contexts.* First Forum Press, 2013.

———, ed. *Finding Freedom in Confinement: The Role of Religion in Prison Life.* Santa Barbara, CA: Praeger, 2018.

Lyons, Adam J. *Karma and Punishment: Prison Chaplaincy in Japan.* Cambridge, MA: Harvard University Asia Center, 2021.

O'Connor, Thomas P., ed. *Religion, the Community, and the Rehabilitation of Criminal Offenders.* New York: Haworth Press, 2002.

Opata, Josiah N. *Spiritual and Religious Diversity in Prisons.* Springfield, IL: Charles C Thomas, 2001.

Press, Aric. Reported by Daniel Pedersen, Daniel Shapiro, and Ann McDaniel. "Inside America's Toughest Prison." *Newsweek* (6 October 1986), 46–53, 56, 58, 61.

Quinby, Hosea. *The Prison Chaplaincy and Its Experiences.* Concord, NH: D.L. Guernsey, 1873.

Recinella, Dale S. *When We Visit Jesus in Prison: A Guide for Catholic Ministry.* Chicago: ACTA Publications, 2016.

Sainz-Hall, Phillip Anthony. *From the Bullet to the Bible: A Gangster's Tale.* Columbus, OH: Gatekeeper Press, 2018.

Schilder, David M. *Inside the Fence: A Handbook for Those in Prison Ministry.* Staten Island, NY: Alba House, 1999.

Sehested, Nancy Hastings. *Marked for Life: A Prison Chaplain's Story.* Maryknoll, NY: Orbis Books, 2019.

Shaw, Richard. *Chaplains to the Imprisoned: Sharing Life with the Incarcerated.* New York: Haworth Press, 1995.

Shere, Dennis. *Cain's Redemption: A Story of Hope and Transformation in America's Bloodiest Prison.* Chicago: Northfield Publishing, 2005.

Shropshire, James M., Mark C. Hicks, and Richmond Stoglin, eds. *I Was in Prison: United Methodist Perspectives on Prison Ministry.* Nashville: General Board of Higher Education and Ministry, 2008.

Smith, Earl, and Mark Schlabach. *Death Row Chaplain: Unbelievable True Stories from America's Most Notorious Prison.* (Brookwood, TN: Howard Books, 2015.

Stoesz, Donald. *A Prison Chaplaincy Manual: The Canadian Context.* Victoria, BC: Friesen Press, 2020.

Sullivan, Winnifred. *A Ministry of Presence: Chaplaincy, Spiritual Care and the Law.* Chicago: University of Chicago Press, 2019.

———. *Prison Religion: Faith-Based Reform and the Constitution.* Princeton, NJ: Princeton University Press, 2011.

Swanson, Karen. *Answering the Call.* Wheaton, IL: Institute for Prison Ministries, Billy Graham Center, Wheaton College, 2018.

van Eijk, Ryan, Gerard Loman, Theo W. A. de Wit, eds. *For Justice and Mercy: International Reflection on Prison Chaplaincy.* Amsterdam: Deel, 2016.

# CORPORATE / WORKPLACE

Cleal, C. H. *The Chaplain in the Factory.* London: S.C.M. Press, 1945.

Lizardy-Hajbi, Kristina, and Matthew Floding, eds. *Explore: Vocational Discovery in Ministry*. Rowman & Littlefield Publishers, 2022.

Miller, David. *God at Work: The History and Promise of the Faith at Work Movement*. Oxford: Oxford University Press, 2007.

Miller, David W., Faith Wambura Ngunjiri, and James D. LoRusso, "Human Resources Perceptions of Corporate Chaplains: Enhancing Positive Organizational Culture," *Journal of Management, Spirituality & Religion* 14:3 (2017), 196–215, DOI: 10.1080/14766086.2016.1260044.

Mullis, David. *Business and Industrial Chaplaincy: The Chaplain's Ministry Plan*. DMin diss., Regent University, School of Divinity, 1999.

Seales, Chad E. "Corporate Chaplaincy and the American Workplace." *Religion Compass* 6/3 (2012): 195–203.

Stevens, Paul R. "The Marketplace: Mission Field or Mission," *CRUX* XXXVII, No. 3 (2001): 7–16.

Stewart-Darling, Fiona. *Multi-Faith Chaplaincy in the Workplace*. London and Philadelphia: Jessica Kingsley Publishers, 2017.

Stricklin, Gil A. *Chaplain*. Plano: RBC Print Services, 2014.

Thompson, Yancy Samuel. *Industrial Chaplaincy: The Concept of Industrial Evangelism in Light of the General Thinking of the Evangelical Movement*. Boston: Christopher Publishing House, 1956.

Torry, Malcolm. *Bridgebuilders: Workplace Chaplaincy—A History*. Norwich, UK: Canterbury Press, 2010.

Wright, Chris. "Following Jesus in the Globalized Marketplace." *ERT* 31:4 (2007): 320–30.

## PUBLIC SAFETY

Ashley, Willard, and Steven Roberts. *Disaster Spiritual Care: Practical Clergy Responses to Community, Regional and National Tragedy*, 2nd ed. Nashville: SkyLight Paths Publishing, 2017.

Bennett, Larry. *First Responder Chaplains: Spiritual Caregivers*. Scotts Valley, CA: CreateSpace Independent Publishing, 2016.

DeRevere, David, Wilbert Cunningham, Tommy Mobley, and John Price. *Chaplaincy in Law Enforcement: What It Is and How to Do It,* 2nd ed. Springfield, IL: Charles C Thomas Publishing, 2005.

Franklin, Dan, ed. *Chaplaincy: Hands on Ministry—Ministering Beyond the Walls of the Church*. Independently published, 2020.

———. *Disaster Spiritual Care: A Training Manual for Spiritual Care Providers*. Self-published, 2017.

Harrington, Thomas J. *A Call to Save: The Memoirs of a Fire Chaplain*. Edited by Marsha L. McCabe. New Bedford, MA: Spinner Publications, 2006.

Lawson, Lowell. *International Conference of Police Chaplains: Serving All Law Enforcement Chaplains*. Paducah, KY: Turner Publishing, 2001.

McLaughlin, Paul Francis. *The Chaplain's Evolving Role in Peace and Humanitarian Relief Operations*. Washington, DC: United States Institute of Peace, 2002.

Middlebrooks, Mike. *The Police Chaplain: An Effective Strategy for Police Chaplain Ministry*. Independently published, 2020.

Morgan, Terry. *The Chaplain's Role: How Clergy Can Work with Law Enforcement*. Scotts Valley, CA: CreateSpace Independent Publishing, 2012.

Perkins, Robert. *The Practical Guide to Police Chaplaincy*. Niagara Falls, Ontario: Aristotle Media Publishing, 2018.

Robertson, Mark Alan. *EMERGENCY ROOM CHAPLAIN: Crisis Response and Clinical Care for First Responders And Combat Veterans*. Independently published, 2022.

Shane, Thomas W. *Crisis Pastoral Care: A Police Chaplain's Perspective*. Prescott, AZ: Hohm Press, 2012.

Wagner, Walter. *God Squad*. [Detroit Police Chaplaincy] Garden City, NY: Doubleday, 1979.

Weber, Martin. *God Was There: True Stories of a Police Chaplain*. Nampa, ID: Pacific Press Publishing Association, 2009.

# COMMUNITY/LIFESTYLE

## Educational

Brummett, Barbara. *Spirited Campus: The Chaplain and the College Community*. New York: Pilgrim Press, 1990.

Consultation of the Future of the Campus Ministry, *The Professional Identity of the Campus Minister*. Cambridge, MA: Church Society for College Work, 1970.

Forster-Smith, Lucy, ed. *College and University Chaplaincy in the 21st Century: A Multifaith Look at the Practice of Ministry on Campuses across America*. Woodstock, VT: SkyLight Paths Publishing, 2013.

Forster-Smith, Lucy A. *Crossing Thresholds: The Making and Remaking of a 21st Century College Chaplain.* Eugene, OR: Cascade Books, 2015.

Goodliffe, J. B. *School Chaplain.* New York: St. Martin's Press, 1961.

Hammond, Phillip E. *Campus Clergyman.* New York: Basic Books, 1966.

Smith, Seymour A. *American College Chaplaincy.* New York: Association Press, 1954.

White, Stephen. *College Chaplain: A Practical Guide to Campus Ministry.* Cleveland, OH: Pilgrim Press, 2005.

Younger, Steve. *Time for Reflection: A Guide to School Chaplaincy and Spiritual Development.* Saint Andrew Press, 2018.

## Sports

Adogame, Afe, Nick J. Watson, and Andrew Parker, eds. *Global Perspectives on Sports and Christianity.* Routledge, 2017.

Guy, Richard. *With God You're Always a Winner: The Chaplain of Stock Car Racing.* Xulon Press, 2012.

Mims, Madeline. *Chaplaincy in the History of the Olympics: US Sport Chaplaincy at the Olympic Level.* Tulsa, OK: Insight International, 2018.

Parker, Andrew, Nick Watson, and John White, eds. *Sports Chaplaincy: Trends, Issues, and Debates.* Abingdon, UK: Routledge, 2016.

## Other

Hillhouse, John. *Horses, Hoofbeats and Halos: The History of Race Track Chaplaincy of America, Inc. 1969–1999.* Graceville, FL: Hargrave Press, 1999.

MacNair, John Van. *Chaplain on the Waterfront: The Story of Father Saunders.* New York: Seabury Press, 1963.

The National Conference of Catholic Airport Chaplains. *Airport Chaplaincy: A Catholic Handbook.* Scotts Valley, CA: CreateSpace Independent Publishing, 2011.

Seveska, Richard. *The Truck Stop: The Chaplain's Stories.* Independently published, 2021.

www.ingramcontent.com/pod-product-compliance
Lightning Source LLC
Chambersburg PA
CBHW051622230426
43669CB00013B/2152